WE ARE
GOING IN

WE ARE GOING IN

The Story of the 1956 Grand Canyon Midair Collision

SECOND EDITION

MIKE NELSON

RIO NUEVO
PUBLISHERS

Rio Nuevo Publishers®
P. O. Box 5250
Tucson, AZ 85703-0250
(520) 623-9558, www.rionuevo.com

Text © 2017, 2012 by Mike Nelson.
Illustrations © 2017, 2012 by Mike Nelson.

Cover design: David Jenney Design
Cover photo (below): Mike Buchheit

Library of Congress Control Number: 2017934294

Printed in the United States of America.

10   9   8   7   6   5   4   3   2

ACKNOWLEDGEMENTS

THE WORK OF a great many authors was invaluable in the preparation of this book, and each of them could appropriately be thanked in this section, but I have left that as implied in the Table of Resources, which cites many of them and their work.

In this list of acknowledgements I wanted to mention only those persons with whom I was actually involved, whether by correspondence, by telephone, or face-to-face. People were generally far more helpful than the work left in an archive or a library by someone I never met or spoke to, or even wrote to. I learned a lot more by communicating with people than by reading their inanimate work, which can neither listen nor respond, and can never offer anything of its own accord. The people themselves were creative, spontaneous and insightful, and in interacting with them I learned by collaboration; nearly always, the topics turned in directions I could never have anticipated, and I honestly have to credit at least half of this book's content to that serendipity.

More than anyone else I want to thank Captain Robert C. Sherman, who was a captain with TWA at the time of the accident, and worked in several capacities for TWA's retired pilots' association, TARPA, for many years after his retirement as an airline pilot. He had a tremendous fund of knowledge, based in a lifetime of paying attention and learning; he also had a terrific memory. Captain Sherman stuck with me for years, from nearly the beginning of this project, and he was always enthused and glad to be of help, no matter how frequently I spoke with him and no matter how rudimentary or repetitious my questions may sometimes have been. He also never balked at the difficult questions

I asked him, and he took them on as exciting challenges to ponder or research. The captain's explanations were lucid, his wit was sharp, and he had a knack for cutting through confusion or complexity to the heart or the essence of an issue, often helping me to clarify my *questions* as much as to answer them. The debt I owe him I have no idea how to measure, and my gratitude is equally difficult to try delineating. Maybe this will suffice to address both of those: it has been a privilege to know him.

Second to no one but Captain Sherman, I want to thank L. David Lewis, who contended personally with the aftermath of the disaster, and who was the first man to reach the practically inaccessible United crash site, after many experts had for many days been convinced it was impossible. Mr. Lewis is responsible for most of my understanding of what was done to retrieve the victims' remains, a phenomenal feat by any standard. As a mountaineer and life-long physicist, his insights and incisive intellect gave me an exceedingly clear picture of the problems and dangers entailed in that great humanitarian effort. And like Captain Sherman, Mr. Lewis' memory was excellent.

The third-most helpful person was Captain Jasper Solomon, a TWA pilot who worked at the TWA crash site. He gave me countless hours of his time, in numerous phone calls, and welcomed me into his summer home in Minnesota. Captain Solomon taught me as much about how airplanes work as anyone, especially the Lockheed Constellations. I also credit Captain Solomon with getting me started. He was there in the early days of my work on this book, bolstering my confidence that I could grasp the complexities of flight and of air traffic control rules, when I might well have come to the opinion that it was too much for a lay person to truly absorb. He always seemed to be sure that I could understand him, at least ultimately, and never tired of my questions; I am grateful to him for his support.

Quite a few younger people, who were children at the time of the accident or had yet to be born, were also instrumental in the creation of this book. Some of them provided extremely valuable records, which

I could scarcely believe still existed. Also, a great many other people from the generation that dealt with the accident helped with insights or information, or references to others who helped in turn. Often what they gave me and modestly regarded as minor, turned out to be of major importance or value, but the overriding things that tied nearly all of them together were their friendliness, their willingness or enthusiasm to help, and their readiness to trust me, a complete stranger with nothing but the name of a friend to introduce himself to them, and in many cases not even that one name. They were a pleasure to work with and I wish I could have known them better. The following is a list of most of them, with their credentials given as they stood at the time of the accident, where applicable, unless specifically stated to be more current.

Ralph Anglea, air traffic controller at Oakland, involved in CAB rule making, and later, FAA rule making.

Milo Bacon, United Air Lines captain, knew Captain Shirley, flew with Harms and Fiore.

Ken Barmore, United Air Lines crew scheduler at Los Angeles International Airport.

Louis Barr, TWA flight engineer.

Edward G. Betts, TWA captain and later, unofficial historian for TARPA.

P.K. Bonde, United Air Lines captain, flew with Captain Shirley.

Ralph Breyfogle, United Air Lines copilot and later captain, brother of Forrest Breyfogle.

Hal Bryan, United Air Lines captain.

James Casteel, United Air Lines crew scheduler at Los Angeles International Airport.

George Cearley, Jr., airline historian and author some years after the tragedy.

William Cordell, TWA captain, attended flight training school with James Ritner.

Dick Cosgrave, United Air Lines captain, helped Mrs. Harms to face the reality.

Larry De Celles, TWA captain, accident investigator, later ALPA National Safety Chairman.

Ed Delaney, Chief of Dispatch with United Air Lines at Los Angeles International Airport.

Adrian Delfino, United Air Lines' Corporate Historian.

Marge Dixon, United Air Lines stewardess.

William E. Dunkle, United Air Lines captain, author, knew Harms and Shirley.

Maggie Eiseman, river rafting guide, was at the scene at Chuar Butte a few days after the accident.

Clem Ellington, United Air Lines captain, knew Girardo Fiore well.

Stephan Fusco, United Air Lines captain, good friend of Robert Harms.

Harry Gann, Douglas Aircraft Company Historian.

Marge (Harms) Gibson, widow of Robert Harms, provided very moving descriptions of what she went through at the time.

Bud Gimple, United Air Lines copilot, later captain.

Morel Guyot, United Air Lines captain, flew DC-3 transport missions for canyon operations.

Tom Haggerty, FAA Library, years after the tragedy.

Lorraine (Nelson) Hallberg, my mom, and the sister of Jack Groshans, provided her memories of that terrible time.

Stuart Halsey, CAA Watch Commander on duty at Salt Lake City ARTC when the planes crashed, coordinated the initial search, and released responsibility to the U.S. Air Force.

Gordon Hargis, TWA captain, flew with Captain Gandy.

Mel Heflinger, United Air Lines captain, ALPA accident investigator, worked at United site.

Lynn Hink, Air Traffic Controller, knew some of the contollers involved with TWA 2 and United 718.

Ginny Husak, TWA radio and Teletype operator.

Paul Husak, TWA dispatcher at Los Angeles International Airport.

Mike Ideran, friend, advisor, and uniquely insightful, genuine human being, bolstered my sense that the book was important far beyond its biographical and documentary faces.

Bob Justice, TWA mechanic at Los Angeles International Airport, towed the *Star of the Seine* to the gate on the day of the accident.

Jim Kennedy, manager of the Denver Pulicity Office with United Air Lines, attended the United interment and memorial services.

George Kidera, United Air Lines' Corporate M.D., worked on identifications of victims, in Flagstaff.

Linda (Harms) Kiracibasi, Robert Harms' daughter, provided photos of her dad.

Joyce (Groshans) Klug, Jack Groshans' widow, provided documents and very moving memories.

Ed Krieger, United Air Lines mechanic at Los Angeles International Airport, friend of Girardo Fiore, listened to tape of Harms' mayday message.

George Legere, United Air Lines captain, worked at Medicine Bow Peak accident.

Joe L'Episcopo, TWA dispatcher from Idlewild and later, an NTSB Accident Investigator.

Jim Loosen, TWA Manager of Crew Scheduling at Kanasas City, knew the crew of Flight 2.

Roland MacDonald, ARTC controller at Albuquerque ARTC.

Gwen Mahler, TWA hostess, knew the hostesses aboard Flight 2, later author of cabin attendants' history books, one time president of TWA's Clipped Wings group for retired hostesses.

Peter J. Marson, authority on Lockheed Constellations, author years after the accident, provided opinions about the type designation of the *Star of the Seine*.

Merle Nichols, ATC controller at Los Angeles tower, contended with reporters at the time of the tragedy, accident expert.

Virgil Nolte, United Air Lines' Manager of Crew Scheduling at Los Angeles International Airport.

Nancy Palmer, librarian at Flagstaff Public Library, many years after the tragedy.

Ethel Pattison, Los Angeles International Airport Historian, since just before the accident.

Joe Pepito, American Airlines mechanic, worked on DC-7s.

Jim Peters, owner of Crawford-Peters Aeronautica long after the accident, provided nearly 100 out-of-print books on pertinent aviation subjects.

Andy Pitas, Air Traffic Control Association.

Ned Preston, FAA Historian's Office long after the accident.

Jon Proctor, *Airliners* Magazine well after accident, provided lots of information and encouragement.

Charles Quarles, expert on and collector of antique cabin attendants' uniforms.

David Richwine, TWA captain, knew Captain Gandy well, went to flight training school with him.

Matt Rodina, Jr., self-appointed keeper of voluminous, esoteric United Air Lines records that were slated to be discarded.

Fred Romanski, National Archives, Civil Records Division, well after the accident.

Robert Rummel, TWA's head engineer, later author of *Howard Hughes and TWA*.

Dick Russell, United Air Lines captain, later accident investigator.

Francis Shamrell, Manager of Flagstaff Municipal Airport.

Gaylord Stavely, river rafting expert, was at United crash area shortly after the accident.

Sara Stebbins, librarian at Grand Canyon National Park, well after the accident.

Lionel Stephan, American Airlines captain, flew through the crash area just minutes after the accident.

Gene Tritt, United Air Lines captain, later president of United's retired pilots' association, RUPA.

Gail Walter, TWA Teletype operator at Los Angeles International Airport.

Richard Wegner, TWA pilot, friend of James Ritner, hired same day as Ritner.

Connie White, United Air Lines stewardess.

John Whittle, aircraft historian, later author of *The Douglas DC-6 and DC-7 Series*.

Bill Wolf, TWA captain, tour guide at Airline History Museum in later years, enabled me to sit in both pilots' seats in the museum's restored Constellation and take numerous photos, showing the instruments and cockpit visibility.

Vicy Morris Young, United Air Lines stewardess, historian, past president of United's retired stewardesses' association, Clipped Wings.

I would also like to thank the following organizations.

Airline History Museum
Air Traffic Control Association
ALPA Accident Investigation Department
ALPA Engineering and Air Safety Department
Civil Aeronautics Administration
Civil Aeronautics Board
FAA Accident Investigation School
FAA Historian's Office
FAA Library
Fort Huachuka, Historian's Office
Grand Canyon National Park Library
Luke Air Force Base, Historian's Office
National Archives

National Climatological Reporting Center
National Transportation Safety Board
Northern Arizona University Library
Save-A-Connie, Inc.
U.S. Coast and Geodetic Survey
U.S. Congress
U.S. Geological Survey
Western Climatological Data Center

There is one more person I want to thank, whose help honestly surpassed even that of Captain Sherman, although in an almost wholly different vein: namely, my wife, Barbara. Year after year she sacrificed the nice things she could have had in order to enable me to spend much of our very modest extra cash on my research; even more, she agreed to my earning money less than full time for several years, so that I could devote myself first and foremost to the incredibly involved project I had taken on. She was also my sounding board countless times when I was having trouble clarifying what I wanted to say or how to say it, and those talks were priceless. I can't begin to estimate how many times it all came to me through talking to her about it. Barbara believed in me and in what I was doing, and as if all of this were not enough, near the end of the endeavor she typed nearly the entire manuscript, over and over through several major revisions.

Now that I have noted what she did, I still feel something missing—my actually thanking her. So here it is: Thanks, Barbie.

CONTENTS

e. Misleading stories that the planes had been on "collision courses"

f. False stories that Flight 2's ascent to 21,000 feet caused the accident

g. Public misconception that ARTC should not have approved flight plans with courses that crisscrossed each other

h. The actual great safety of the system

i. Limits of ARTC's authority and responsibility

j. Outrage at the U.S. Government and its instrument ARTC for the apparent deadly loophole: the one thousand on top clearance

k. The erroneous story that TWA 2 changed to a VFR clearance en route

l. TWA 2's relinquishment of ARTC's protection, in taking the one thousand on top clearance

m. The complete irrelevancy of TWA 2's relinquishment of ARTC's protection in the accident

n. The false view that Captain Gandy was irresponsible in ascending to 21,000 feet even under the provisions of the one thousand on top clearance, after ARTC declined to approve that altitude

o. The way things really were, against all the false ideas and stories

p. The subtle, sole criticism that could have been made of Gandy and never publicly was

q. ARTC's true view that both flights would be exceedingly safe, even with no supervision

r. The libeling, by newspapers, of the Salt Lake City ARTC controller who handled both flights, for errors he never made and attitudes he never had

s. The damage done to the controller's family

t. The parallel damage done to Captain Gandy's family

u. The reality outside the wrangling over who or what to blame: the unspeakable awfulness of the tragedy

10. The United crash promontory
11. The TWA memorial plaque
12. The United memorial stone

FOREWORD

THE SUBSTANCE OF this book is the heartfelt sentiment that people matter. On June 30, 1956, two airliners collided in midair over the Grand Canyon. Both were so seriously damaged that they fell from the sky and were destroyed. 128 persons lost their lives in that terrible accident. Because they mattered to me, I wanted to honor the people whose lives were crushed by that disaster, both the victims and their loved ones, through caringly, passionately, incisively writing an account of what happened to them. In keeping with this, all of the people in this book are real, and I have portrayed them as they actually were. Some of their names I didn't use, nor did I fabricate substitutes. All of the names that I explicitly give are the real ones.

We Are Going In is the story of that disaster. It is a dramatic portrayal, a factual history, and an analysis of it, and considers it to be a human event, a physical event, and more. The book's analytic thrust gives clarity and meaning to the drama, and its dramatic thrust gives value and life to the analysis. In short, it is a heartfelt documentary.

The basic format of the book amounts to telling a very involved, cohesive, true story, and to that end I have given quite a lot of circumstantial description, creating an evolving setting and a factual backdrop and foreground, analogous to profusely illustrating the book with photographs. Photographs are clear, but by themselves they are lifeless images; they have to be given meaning by whoever views them or describes them. The same is true of the factual underpinnings of this book: it is the humanity in them that vivifies them with meaning and worth. It is the people who were there at the time, and it is the people who are here, investing themselves now, whether by writing this or by reading it. I have included many dramatic depictions of the events and of what I feel intuitively sure the people involved in them experienced, starting well before the accident, when it was nothing but a stirring of things to come. In the case of surviving loved ones, many of the depictions are as certain as they could be—in that the people themselves told me.

One thing I have *not* included is footnotes. All of the facts that I have presented that seemed important enough to give some accreditation, I either identified as to their sources right in the text where I introduced them, or cited in the Table of Resources in the order I introduced them, chapter by chapter. Even though the foundation of this book is significantly scholarly, the book is not a treatise; I had no intention of attempting to make it so, and instead wanted to write it as a story, a very detailed story but a story nonetheless. It simply seemed contrary to this more friendly spirit to complicate many of the pages with footnote or endnote numbers or symbols, and especially with fine print in the footers. There is also no index. For this reason I made the Contents table extremely detailed, so that it could serve as an index, albeit one that would be of use primarily to people who have already read part or all of the book, and have at least a rough idea of which chapter contained the information they want to look up.

Along with the dramatic portrayals and the factual descriptions of the circumstances, I offer a substantial amount of background in aviation, to support an articulate understanding of the material facts of what occurred. This will please some readers and displease others. Some readers may find the volume and detail of this information burdensome or tedious, presumably because they would rather stay more purely or directly with the human side of the story; for them, making the effort to digest the technical explanations would probably be like struggling through a road construction detour. I suggest that these readers skip over the more technical subjects. Most of them are consolidated into four principal sections, all of which can be omitted without disrupting the continuity of the human drama or even losing the basic nature or facts of the tragedy. By taking that streamlined route through the book, however, the reader will inescapably forfeit much of *understanding* what happened. The parts that can be skipped while maintaining the primary substance of the story are: chapters 2 and 3 entirely; all of chapter 6, except for its last three paragraphs; and chapter 9, except for its last six paragraphs.

Whichever path the reader takes through the pages, the most important parts are preserved: the parts that pertain directly to the people involved. Whether the book is treated as a drama or as an investigative study of the facts and circumstances of the accident, the victims and their families constitute its framework. I have largely rejected proffering the accident as the context in which many persons' lives were ended or ruined, and I have instead written the book from the converse point of view that the people involved in the accident were the context in which the accident happened.

The introduction sets this tone for the whole book and is as much one of its chapters as any of the numbered ones. I was always one of those people who skipped prefaces, forewords, and introductions to get right to the story, and I have to wonder how much I have lost in that way. I strongly recommend reading the introduction; in this instance, at least, doing that *is* getting right to the story, because it begins there. It opens with a man's name, a name that mattered because he mattered. In that spirit I want to say a simple word concerning his surname. It was an unusual one that nearly everyone who had not previously heard it would mispronounce upon reading. With an "o" like that in "show," and an "a" like that in "father," it is pronounced "gross´-hanse," though it is spelled Groshans.

Mike Nelson, 2011

Introduction

Guy Groshans was a gentleman. He believed in things that mattered, and he stood with dignity for the things he believed.

Guy was an optimist. He had made a success of himself, and his confidence showed. He was a man content with his life. His wit was sharp, and his satisfaction with how he lived gave him the capacity for heartfelt humor.

Guy was an accountant for the Armour Meat Packing Company in Chicago and was approaching retirement. After thirty-six years of marriage, he was still devoted to his wife, Mildred, who had been his teenage sweetheart. He had provided a comfortable home for her, and he did chores and handyman projects around the house. Guy and Mildred had made a family and had raised their children with values, character, and dignity.

His daughter, Lorraine, had become a grade school teacher and then a housewife, and she had brought Guy's first grandson and third granddaughter into the world. His son was the elder and had made Guy a grandfather. Jack Groshans had become a mechanical engineer and then a purchaser in outside manufacturing for Lockheed Aircraft Corporation; he had established a home for himself, his wife, and their two daughters. Like his father, he was a gentleman, a decent man who believed in things that mattered and stood for the things he believed. He also had his father's sense of humor.

At just thirty-three years of age, an accident took this wonderful young man's life, broke his home, and broke his father's heart. Guy Groshans was never again an optimist.

Guy was alone grieving at his house one day after the accident, filled with thoughts of his son. He went to his basement workshop, the place that was his own; it was his refuge, where he could feel comforted, and his sanctuary, where he could find clarity. At least, it always had been, and needing these things, he was drawn there.

More than twenty years before, he had worked repeatedly into the night in that room, creating a beautifully detailed model train station for Jack's Lionel train set. Guy designed it and built it from wood and other raw materials, fashioning all of the pieces by hand. It was a model of a brick building that had arched windows and doors, framed with heavy limestone blocks. He simulated the framing stones in relief through notches he carved in the wood where the mortared cracks between them would be. The doors were hinged and could be opened. Inside was a wooden ticket counter reminiscent of a judge's bench, stained dark and varnished, with working miniature lamps standing on both ends. On the roof was a skylight made of real safety glass embedded with wire. He painted the station inside and outside, in all the right colors. All of this Guy remembered, sitting on the stool at his workbench, and in an unremitting series of images, other investments he had made in his son's life came to him. He remembered fixing Jack's bicycle, helping him learn how to ride it, showing him how to make things of wood, advising him about right friends and wrong ones, and talking about girls. He thought about how much he had loved his son, and his adoration swelled in his chest more fully, more tenderly, and more powerfully than it ever had before. Tears filled his eyes, and he saw that all he had given had been destroyed.

For a moment he took shelter in denying that any of it was real, but his pain spoke the truth. Jack was gone, and Guy would never again be able to give him his love. He shook his head in despair and cried out. For the first time in his life, Guy could not stand up for what he held most dear. His aimless love and his grief surged and rose and amplified each other, until he could no longer bear it and feared he was losing his mind. In a last act of defiance, his will to survive arose to overthrow what was killing him, and his agony became rage. Soft-spoken, genteel Guy Groshans became a wild man, grabbing and throwing every tool, every piece of lumber, every can of paint that he could assault, screaming, "God dammit! God dammit! God dammit!" over and over and over until he lost his voice and was too weak to throw anything else.

He collapsed on the cement floor and wept.

Guy Groshans was my grandfather. Grandpa is gone now, and with him went his suffering. All that tangibly remains of it are the drops and runs of paint that rendered it so clearly and persuasively over half a century ago. Can after can of paint was crushed by the impact of hitting the basement wall or the workbench or the floor, and burst open, spraying its contents in impassioned mayhem in all directions. A chaos of pigments portrayed his spiritual disintegration, his death as a person, all over the walls and everything else in the room. I have many of his tools. They are all splattered with ten or twelve colors of paint, from a single palette. The artist is gone, but his tortured artwork has survived him.

Uncle Jack died in an airplane crash. On June 30, 1956, a United Air Lines DC-7 and a TWA L-1049 Constellation collided in midair over the Grand Canyon. Uncle Jack was on the DC-7. All 128 persons aboard the two planes lost their lives.

This book tells their story. My attempt is to present a purely factual account. I have reported the truth as I found it, without altering it for convenience, fluidity, cohesiveness, or dramatic effect. The story in this book is true and is more than dramatic enough and involved enough to be in no need of fictionalizing.

Much of what I found was purely a matter of discovery and commensurately entailed no risk of my inadvertently concocting it—after establishing it, I simply passed it along. Many things, however, were not so straightforward. History is largely a matter of interpretation and deduction, and it becomes increasingly so as the event it concerns recedes into the past. The facts are often not clearly spelled out and have to be reconstructed, which requires a good deal of reasoning and, in many cases, a feel for what the truth must have been. Whether it is called intuition or hunches or heartfelt concordance, it is akin to the feelings of familiarity and realism and validity that we acquire in actually being wherever we live, living our lives. The more a historian studies a historical event, the more he comes to empathize with the people who were involved in it, to feel a certain kinship with them, almost as if he were there. Correspondingly, he gains a dual sense of propriety about their world and impropriety about things that are incongruous with it. It becomes instinctive to feel what belongs and what does not, just as it is for each of us in our actual lives.

I have kept the story factual by looking for both intellectual soundness and heartfelt authenticity in all of its more important aspects. The best way to identify the truth is to call upon the testimony of both the intellect and the heart. Whether the truth is concrete or abstract, reason describes it and explains its form, and feeling intuits its substance. Everything has both form and substance, and so everything can be recognized in both ways; and the surest evidence of having found the truth occurs when reason and feeling *agree* about it.

Because the accident mattered as much as it did to me, I needed to take it a lot farther than identifying the truth. That merely amounted to knowing what the facts were. What I needed was to understand the facts. I needed to *grasp* the truth, which is what it really means to *know* it.

Honestly grasping a thing comprises both comprehending its meaning and feeling its value. I can't grasp tragedy without feeling sad, any more than I can grasp a beautiful day without feeling joyful. No matter how much my intellect may be going on in detail about the various noteworthy aspects of the beautiful day—its rarity, the unique shade of blue in the sky, the perfect temperature and humidity, pertinent explanations of meteorology, and so on—if I don't also feel joy in it, then I don't get it at all. And the more beautiful the day, the deeper my emotion will correspondingly be if I truly get it. There's a big difference between a beautiful day and a glorious day.

Likewise, along with intellectually comprehending it, grasping tragedy is feeling sad and frustrated and appalled and compassionate and many other things, and at times feeling these ways profoundly. I wrote this book from a collaborative interplay of both perspectives, which was not only richly satisfying but also vital. Any portrayal can be accurate, meaningful, or inspiring only to the extent that the person who creates it grasps its object. This applies whether the object is an element of material reality or is something in the intangible realm of perceptions, ideas, and emotions. Whether physical or spiritual, I can't very well portray it if I don't get it.

Through a lack of perspective, whether that of the heart or the intellect, the truth is always left wanting, and this applies whether the side lacking is literally absent or is absent in the sense of being understated. Emphasizing the meaning of a thing over its value, or emphasizing its value over its meaning, distorts it. Either way, the truth is always misrepresented. As part of finding and grasping the truth, I was dedicated to illustrating it in true proportion, and so I needed to pay attention to my intellect and my heart equally and embrace whatever they told me with equal openness.

Naturally this simple outline is idealized—I couldn't help but have some bias, because irrespective of how sincerely I tried to be open, I still had values and beliefs, and commitments to both, that I couldn't honestly relinquish or even suspend, not even in the name of discovering the truth. I see no way around this. Everyone's view is relative, meaning that it's the partial view that can be had from his unique standpoint. I can't possibly avoid having a predisposition, because what that really means is having knowledge, and I can't return to being a newborn, in that pure state of utter receptivity that exists before knowledge. What I can do is make a sincere effort to *learn*.

That is where real openness lies; it is the foundation of learning. It is not disavowing or setting aside who I am. It is meeting what's in front of me, fully as who I am, and letting my whole self be impressed and moved. It is the sincere willingness and interest to grow, to evolve; it is the balance point between hesitancy and zealousness, between passiveness and aggressiveness. It is a kind of readiness. That was the attitude I kept seeking while writing this book, and from that inner balance I found what I believe to be a balanced view of its subject.

Despite all of my efforts to ensure that the whole story I tell is true, there may still be some errors, which would amount to unintended fictions, but I am sure that the overwhelming preponderance of purported truths, whether empirical facts or reasoned conclusions, is just that: the truth. Similarly, despite my efforts to make sure that I didn't exaggerate or underestimate or distort what I wrote about, I may still have inflected a few things with some partiality. To be completely frank about it (again), I am sure that this is impossible to avoid. As I see it, personality is itself a form of partiality, and of course throughout the research and the writing, I remained a person. I have no idea how I might dispense with my personality because it defines me, but even if I could, it would not be desirable. Without my own personality I would be unable to imbue my work with any. It would then be flat and lifeless, and no one would want to read it. Besides that, it wouldn't be honest. Part of telling a true story is telling it truthfully, and along with everything else, this means saying it in my own voice, not someone else's, and certainly not no one's. Rather, an authentic book is one in which the author does a good job of keeping his work free of pretentiousness, egoism, timidity, ambivalence, and ambiguity, while maintaining its fidelity. To put a different slant on it, the author keeps it genuine, humble, resolute, and truthful, even if it is sometimes partial. This is what I have tried to do.

As I went along in the research for this book, from one person to another who had been involved in the situation as it developed on the day of the accident or in the aftermath, and from one archive to another, I discovered that there were many crucially important unanswered questions, and also many unsatisfactorily answered questions, some of them answered only sketchily and others in highly suspect ways or even clearly incorrectly. I began to tackle these. I had all the time I chose because this was a totally freelance project. As a matter of fact, at first I was not even intent upon writing a book, but only upon learning all I could about what had happened to my uncle.

Part of my effort included educating myself in aeronautics and aviation. This involved me with numerous aviators and took me through numerous books. As I grew in sophistication, I returned to one question after another, reassessing it and attempting anew to answer it, often several times. It was much like walking up a mountain on a road that spiraled upward around it. On every circuit I ascended a little more and also came back to the side on which I had started, so that I could see the same panorama again, from a higher vantage point. The results are in the book. Concomitantly, I have included a great amount of technical background information—enough, hopefully, to enable the reader to amply understand the answers proposed in the book. Whether or not it will also be enough for the reader to come to his own conclusions depends on what questions he asks and from what perspectives he asks them. If the questions are about the same as mine were, and the perspectives are similar, then there's a good chance that the technical information I have included will be adequate—but there's simply no way for me to anticipate that. One pertinent principle of inquiry is that usually the more creative a person's questions are, the less he can depend on others for the answers or even for help in finding them, and the more he will have to discover new knowledge and devise new methods in order to arrive at the answers himself.

What happened on that terrible midsummer day in 1956 has never been fully determined and probably never will be. This book tells as much as possible of what was previously known, all compiled in one place, and it also presents a number of previously unknown facts and probabilities. I offer a number of new conclusions, and I attempt to undo some of the long-standing ones that I strongly mistrust or feel sure are incorrect.

The tragedy at the Grand Canyon is the literal, ostensible subject of this book, and the corresponding purpose of this book is to document it for posterity. People who care will then have one more way to find out what happened. Underlying the literal history, however, there is a theme, which in its simplest form can be stated in just two words: loss matters. In each of its ramifications, how people respond to loss is a fundamental and timeless human issue. The will to contend with loss, to find its meaning and to come to terms with it, is innately human, and the struggle is part of what renews and furthers our humanity. This is true whether the loss with which we grapple is our own or someone else's.

When we suffer a great loss, we are confronted with ourselves as much as with our bereavement. Issues like our powerlessness and our ignorance, and the grief and fear that these instill, are suddenly and overwhelmingly emphasized, and we must find a way to survive the trauma, a way to survive the reality of being human. Likewise, when we absorb a great loss suffered by others, our values and perceptions of ourselves are challenged. The experience is emotionally powerful, and we have to find a way to reconcile our new insights and feelings with our old beliefs. In each case the process is a struggle with our humanity, and when we struggle with our humanity, even in loss, we always gain.

For the people who lose a loved one to tragedy, there is no choice. The tragedy has happened to someone who was part of them and in that sense has happened to them also. They are in a fight for their emotional, mental, and spiritual lives. For them the tragedy is inescapable, and they must struggle with it or lose their humanity or their minds.

For the rest of us there is a choice. We can care about what has happened and try to absorb it, or we can turn away. Humane means having the good qualities of human beings, as distinguished from the middling and bad qualities, and so to become humane is to become a good person rather than a mediocre one—or, most pitifully, a wretched one. Struggling with loss when it's not our own requires compassion and empathy, and in drawing on these virtues we nurture them and strengthen them. The choice to care arises from compassion and empathy and also in turn evokes both of them. It makes us more humane. It is in choosing to care when we don't have to that our values are most affirmed and honored and incorporated into our beings. It is here that we create ourselves, rather than simply existing or passively proceeding, and in freely choosing to be humane, the self created is truer and better.

The affirmation that loss matters is a choice to care, and in that spirit I have written this book. I offer it to the reader who chooses to care, and it is my hope that the book will affirm the reader in return.

Chapter 1

To approach Los Angeles International Airport from the air was like coming upon a large aquarium with many small fish gliding slowly in it, coasting lazily around at various depths. There were many aircraft in the area, at many altitudes and moving in many directions. Seen from aloft and from a distance, all of the planes in the sky near the airport seemed to be floating on air, moving too slowly to be held up by their own wings, peacefully drifting in the invisible currents in the atmosphere.

For a fanciful moment of daydreaming, it seemed as though mankind had finally freed itself of haste and aggression, as if it were a view of a utopian future where people were neither driven by fear and ambition nor burdened with disrespecting and resenting one another. It was a scene that was at once busy and calm, as though mankind were conducting its ventures purely because they mattered or felt good, not because of insecurity or vanity or want.

From nearer in, the flyer would see two long runways close together and parallel to each other, extending a great distance westward toward the Pacific Ocean on a huge plain. They were like futuristic concrete highways left curiously unfinished, going nowhere, so advanced that they had nearly rendered themselves unnecessary. There was no need of more pavement, because what was there launched the vehicles that traversed it into the open air.

In the summer of 1956 these pathways to the sky were about 8,000 feet long, set on grounds covering several square miles and spreading to the seashore. A string of small buildings ran parallel to the runways, removed to the north by a distance of about 2,000 feet. There was a TWA maintenance hangar in line with the thresholds of the runways at their eastern ends, followed westward by the control tower, the Los Angeles Department of Airports Administration building, several airline terminal buildings and an included restaurant, and then more hangars arranged in a quarter-circle pattern that curved away northward. A wide band of concrete bordered the buildings on the airfield side and was parceled off into parking aprons for airliners, immediately to the south of their respective company terminal buildings. Separating this pavement from the runways, and likewise separating the runways from each other, were fairways of grass crisscrossed by paved taxiways.

The control tower was an austere, purely functional setup, hardly more than a box on stilts. It consisted of a small roofed enclosure encircled with windows and sided with corrugated steel, which sat high atop an open structure of steel girders, built along much the same design as a high-tension electrical line tower. To reach the room on top, called the cab, controllers had to walk up several flights of fire escape-like stairs, open to the elements. From this humble facility, controllers performed the remarkable job of safely coordinating and guiding the departures and arrivals of about seven hundred fifty commercial, business, private, and military flights daily. This was an average of one every two minutes, only half of that handled by Chicago's Midway, the world's busiest airport at the time, but that was like saying, "Only half a deluge," which is still a torrent. There was always activity at Los Angeles International, like a city that never sleeps, and at peak times the rate at which planes came and went became hectic.

United Air Lines and TWA shared the terminal building nearest the runway thresholds. It was divided inside by a wall that made it a duplex. Like all of the terminal buildings, it was a two-story structure facing northward toward the parking lot, with passenger facilities on the ground floor and offices on the second floor. As viewed from the parking lot, the United half was on the left and the TWA half was on the right. Each side featured a brick façade with a large glass picture window, and a pair of double glass doors that greeted approaching visitors. On the roof of the building each airline had its own weather station, for the use of its dispatch department in advising flight crews.

The ground floor lobbies where passengers waited gave the overall impression of a stylized bus terminal. In each there was a concession stand with a magazine rack and candy, chrome-bar chairs with leather upholstery worn shiny, and a bank of rental lockers going for ten cents apiece. From the ceiling hung numerous fluorescent lighting fixtures and fire-extinguishing water sprinklers. The floors were of asphalt tile aged with countless scuff marks and scratches, strewn with cigarette butts during the busier times and almost all of the time in the areas that could not be readily swept, like far under the seats. People not only smoked freely in public buildings then, but they also dropped the still-lit butts to the floor and crushed them out with the soles of their shoes. The check-in and ticketing counters were appealingly designed and well kept, and the employees were generally friendly even though they were frequently rushed.

When it was time for a flight to board, passengers would walk out the back of the building, the south side, across a shared observation patio, and out onto the airfield along the ramp. This was a partly covered, fenced-in, ground-level walkway analogous to a marine pier. The ramps extended from near the observation patios of all the terminal buildings southward, toward the runways, and could accommodate several aircraft on each side. United Air Lines and TWA shared the ramp nearest the runway thresholds. Five airliners could be parked on each side, and each airline had five passenger gates on its own side, all of which were enclosed in shelters for the comfort of the passengers while they waited their turn for their tickets to be checked. Here they were protected not only from the weather but also from blasting, gritty air blown by nearby airliners' propellers, and from the noise. They could hear the gate agent, whereas outside the shelter with a plane departing nearby, no one could have heard anything.

To get from the observation patio to the ramp, the passengers had to walk down a flight of stairs to a short tunnel that sloped upward to it, passing under a causeway for vehicles such as baggage tractors. Vehicles frequently crossed the narrow area between the ramp and the patio, and the idea was to have the passengers walk underneath rather than across the causeway, for the sake of safety.

To the west of the joint United Air Lines and TWA ramp were two others, serving American Airlines, Pan Am, and others. The terminal building just west of the United and TWA one was larger and housed Mike Lyman's Flight Deck Restaurant on the second floor. The most obvious attraction of the dining room was a bank of picture windows that looked out directly on American's aircraft, and afforded excellent views of takeoffs and landings on the runways beyond. Waiters dressed in tuxedos served elegant meals, and patrons could enjoy the food and the sights in air-conditioned comfort, which was still something special in 1956.

TWA Flight 2 and United Air Lines Flight 718 had occurred hundreds of times without the least hint that there might be something unusually dangerous about them, and in fact there was not. They both always left Los Angeles at around the same time and traveled separate routes to the area of the Grand Canyon, where sightseeing was a customary bonus for the passengers. And every time since their inception, they had both made it to their destinations. But on Saturday, the thirtieth of June, in that fateful year, all of that was to change. Never had they nearly collided over the Grand Canyon, but on this most tragic of days that impossible event happened. Like a storm building invisibly beyond the horizon, the coming disaster gave no sign of itself. Everything seemed normal that Saturday morning, as normal as it normally was.

The flight crewmembers for TWA 2 that day were Captain Jack Silvetus Gandy, First Officer James Henry Ritner, and Flight Engineer Forrest Dean Breyfogle. They arrived a little before 8:30, and their first stop at the airport was the ramp office (plainly enough, the office near the ramp, also called the dispatch office), where either Captain Gandy or First Officer Ritner signed all three of them in. Here they received the latest weather reports and forecasts for their route and a dispatch release, a document that formally authorized a captain to operate the particular airplane that would be used for his flight. The dispatch release specified the terms under which the plane would be released to the captain.

The dispatcher filled out this form prior to the crew's arrival, in consideration of the current local weather, the anticipated weather down the line, and any special circumstances in the condition of facilities along the route, such as construction at the destination airport, a radio station along the way being out of order, and so on. He took into account anything that might affect the flight and from that determined any necessary deviations in the route. Based on that, and allowing for the crew to use the engines in the least fuel-efficient way, he calculated the maximum fuel required to reach the destination. To this he added enough fuel for the flight to be diverted to an alternate airport near the intended destination, in case some unforeseen problem were to prevent the flight from landing where it had planned. Finally he added more fuel for the plane to circle at the alternate airport for an hour, which included the forty-five minutes' worth required by law and another fifteen minutes' worth stipulated by TWA's company policy, in order to exceed rather than just meet the federal safety requirements.

All of this was represented in the dispatch release and was presented to the captain as an educated proposal. The dispatcher and the captain were a team, although the captain had the greater authority, commensurate with the greater responsibility he would take in having the lives of all on board his plane directly in his care. The captain could dispute the dispatcher's selection of an alternate airport and other matters, and he could insist on even more fuel being loaded, but never less fuel than the dispatcher recommended. This policy made doubly sure that a flight would have at least as much fuel as it needed, by always using the greater of the dispatcher's and the captain's fuel estimates whenever they did not agree.

While Captain Gandy considered the release and read the weather reports and forecasts, First Officer Ritner began to fill out the company flight plan. This was a record of the trip that would be completed en route and turned in at the destination, for the use of the company's dispatch department. On this he wrote in the crewmembers' names, the fleet number of the plane, and the date, to which he would add the specifics of the fuel load and the alternate airport, and other details, once the captain made his decision and signed the release. During flight, Ritner would add estimated times of arrival at certain points along the way and actual arrival times for comparison, along with ground speeds he would calculate between points.

Ritner also filled out the Air Route Traffic Control Flight Plan (ARTC Flight Plan), which notified the cross-country air traffic control network of Flight 2's intentions in specific terms and served as a request for approval. On it he wrote the airline name and flight number, the type of plane, their proposed departure time and estimated time en route, their proposed cruising speed and altitude, the airfields of origin and destination, and the particular route desired, detailed in all of its segments, including a specific series of locations from which the flight would check in with someone on the ground. Once the captain okayed it or altered it, Ritner filed this flight plan. The crew would receive confirmation of the plan later while they were under way, whether ARTC approved it as filed or with changes.

At about the same time as the crew of TWA 2 arrived at Los Angeles International Airport, Mrs. Lorraine Nelson happened to glance at her clock and noted that it was almost 10:30. She was in her kitchen in the Chicago suburb of Evergreen Park, 1,700 miles and two time zones away, and she was thinking about her brother, Jack Groshans, who was to be flying that day from Los Angeles to Chicago. The unsettling realization occurred to her, "If anything happened to Jack, I would be an only child." She said a prayer for his safety and then returned to her day: cleaning the house and taking care of her two children, my sister and me. Just over an hour later, Jack Groshans boarded United Flight 718.

While she was saying her prayer, only one of the persons who would board United 718 was at the airport: First Officer Robert Harms, the copilot. United 718 was not scheduled to depart until 9:45 a.m. PDT, and he was early. He had been scheduled for Flight 732 to Chicago, departing at 8:30, but the DC-7 on which Harms was to have flown had developed a mechanical problem and had to be replaced with another plane. This ostensibly unimportant circumstance was in reality the one on which the man's entire life and fate turned. There was no DC-7 available for the substitution, so a DC-6 had to be used instead. A minor consequence of this was that the trip would take about half an hour longer, since the DC-6 was not quite as fast.

The legal limit on flying time for pilots of commercial passenger airliners was eighty-five hours per month, a limit imposed to ensure for its part that they would never be exhausted while they were flying. (Pilots actually worked quite a few hours more than this per month, the remainder consisting of making flight plans, performing ground checks of their airplanes, taking on-going training classes to keep in step with the continual improvements in equipment and safety, and so on.) It was the end of the month, the last day of June, and Harms had accumulated over seventy-nine hours of flying time. He had just enough time left for a five-and-a-half-hour DC-7 flight to Chicago, but he could not legally be scheduled for a six-hour DC-6 flight to Chicago. As a result, the crew scheduler on duty had to pull Harms off of Flight 732 and try to find another flight for him. That flight was 718.

The crew scheduler telephoned the copilot who was scheduled for Flight 718 at his home in the northern Los Angeles suburbs, and he asked him if he would take the earlier Flight 732 in Harms' place. This other copilot was a man of less than amiable temperament, who detested last-minute changes and customarily would have made quite a stink over the phone or even refused, but that day he responded with equanimity and agreed to the change without objecting or even questioning it. Years later he and the crew scheduler would meet by chance and share what had been their mutual puzzlement and awe at his out-of-character response.

A little before 8:00, Harms said goodbye to his captain and flight engineer. They left him and became absorbed in the world of the living, the world that had been Harms' world, while he remained at the ramp office and became enveloped in a separate world—one that would forever part him from them. And there he waited, probably drinking coffee, already gone from this life. The choices had been made, and his fate was decided.

At about 8:30 Harms was joined by his new fellow crewmembers, Captain Robert F. Shirley and Flight Engineer Girardo Xavier Fiore. The first passengers for either flight walked through TWA's doors just about then, and not long after, Flight 732 departed—late, because the substitute copilot had had to drive too far for the time available when he was contacted. He had gotten there in a hurry but was late nonetheless. Harms may have seen or even greeted the man that chance or destiny had chosen to live in his place, as he quickly passed through the ramp office on his way out to the waiting DC-6.

Soon, passengers were beginning to arrive for United Flight 718, and many for TWA Flight 2 had already congregated in TWA's terminal. Some drove themselves and left their cars in the parking lot, intending to return and retrieve them in a few days or a week; some were brought by friends or relatives, or a chauffer; some came by taxicab, some by rental car, some by bus. Far more diverse were their personalities, their lifestyles, their occupations, their social and financial statuses, and the circumstances that had brought them to the airport for these particular flights. Some of these differences were superficial or extraneous, but even the most important of them were secondary to what made everyone alike: in the act of checking in, they had committed themselves to an uncertain venture in which their lives were at stake. Each one who was old enough to make his own decision had placed his trust in the airline, and all of them were about to take the same risk.

For many of those who recognized it and faced it, this engendered a humble feeling of kinship with the others, and they gratefully felt a friendly familiarity with these strangers. The remainder who were aware of the risk they were facing disregarded or resisted knowing, denying the fact of it or suppressing their anxiety, and they were left with less desirable sentiments like feeling isolated or aloof or tense, or falsely calm. And then there were probably a few persons who simply did not see. Whichever of these was their approach to life on that day, the overriding reality shared by everyone was their sameness, and the only relevant differences between them in that pivotal circumstance lay in the extent to which they knew this.

The waiting areas in each terminal became congested. All of the seats had been taken, and many people were standing or ambling around, fumbling with change in their pockets, fixing their makeup, picking through magazines for sale, buying candy bars, puffing distractedly or contemplatively on cigarettes, or walking outside to the observation patio to pass the time by watching the airplanes. Inside, bluish-white tobacco smoke billowed and hung in the air, swirling around itself until it lost its form and blended with the atmosphere. It annoyed some of the adults and made the children's eyes burn, but the adults tolerated it because it was customary to smoke, and the children had no choice.

Outside on the observation patio were the smells of gasoline and oil, and the smoke of their combustion. Fuel was frequently spilled in small amounts, oil leaked from most engines and was splotched all over the aircraft parking aprons, and most engines burned a little oil, especially when they were started. With its propeller initially rotating so slowly that the individual blades could be counted, an engine would fire, belching clouds of oily exhaust fumes from its stacks as it caught hold of itself and quickly accelerated to a running speed. All of these smells suffused the air and were blown gently across the patio.

And then there were the sounds. The noise made at the ramp by a four-engine piston airliner was tremendous. The thunderous roar of the engines was like a god beating on the roof with a great hammer, in strokes of superhumanly rapid succession whose individual beats lay beyond the threshold of perception yet could be subliminally apprehended and concretely felt. One could feel the resounding thrumming of the engines but hear only the steady roar. This sound was blended with the wondrous, high-pitched, staccato of the huge propeller blades slapping the air, like the ultimate realization of a boy's imagining that his bicycle was an airplane, with the sound of the playing card slapping the spokes.

As Captain Shirley and Flight Engineer Fiore found out about the copilot exchange and greeted First Officer Harms in United's ramp office, Flight Engineer Forrest Breyfogle informed Captain Gandy that the *Star of the Seine*, the Lockheed Constellation to be used for Flight 2, was held up in the hangar by work that hadn't quite been finished. Breyfogle had gone to the maintenance office to check the maintenance log for the plane while Ritner was working on the flight plans. It was part of Breyfogle's job to ensure that any problems or abnormalities reported by previous crews had been addressed if they affected the plane's airworthiness. What he found may be lost to history, but whether it was a repair or simple maintenance, the work had to be finished before the plane could be released, and TWA 2 was going to be late getting off that day.

While the crew of TWA 2 waited, the crew of United 718 received its own dispatch release and the weather reports and forecasts for the route. Harms went to work filling out the flight plan while Captain Shirley considered the conditions and conferred with the dispatcher. United Flight 708, a nonstop, first class DC-7 flight to New York City, was just then finishing boarding and cargo loading. The call for boarding of TWA Flight 24, a tourist class flight (an economy flight) to Kansas City on an older model Constellation, came right about then, too. Flight 732 got airborne, having finished their final engine checks at high power out on the airfield. The substitute DC-6 took off and carried Harms' life away with it.

At about nine o'clock, United Flight 465, a coach flight to San Francisco on a DC-4, departed from the ramp and began taxiing out toward the airfield. TWA ground crewmembers rolled a transportable stairway called a boarding ramp up to another Constellation, the plane to be used for TWA Flight 18, a tourist class flight to Oklahoma City. United ground crewmembers rolled their own boarding ramp into place at the main entry door of the *City of Vancouver*, the DC-7 that would be used for Flight 718, which was already parked at its gate along the ramp. There were many similar activities among personnel of other airlines nearby. In all, Los Angeles International was a very busy place that Saturday morning.

Nancy Lou Kemnitz and Margaret Ann Shoudt, the stewardesses for United 718 that day, ascended the twelve steps of their boarding ramp and walked onto the DC-7, and despite their familiarity with it they were at once taken by how quiet it was, insulated from the noise outside. Venturing into the plane was audibly like the experience one has on an elevator when the doors shut—the immediate quiet feels very close and tangible, nearly always a surprise.

In a way, a first-class flight was like a restaurant in the sky. The stewardesses checked the silverware, the dishes, the cups, and the glasses; they made sure that the beverages were stocked and that the magazine racks displayed a good selection of popular periodicals; they checked that the lavatories were stocked with toiletries, and that the entire cabin was clean. When the food was brought on board from the commissary, the girls checked it, to make sure that there was enough and that it was what the menu promised. They even created a welcoming atmosphere similar to that of an elegant restaurant, by turning on a custom, flight-worthy reel-to-reel tape recorder that played background music throughout the cabin.

Not long after Nancy Kemnitz and Margaret Shoudt went to work on the *City of Vancouver*, the *Star of the Seine* was towed into position at its gate on the opposite side of the ramp. Using a wide, low-profile tractor called a tug, a mechanic wheeled the plane around so that its nose faced away from the ramp, like the *City of Vancouver* and every other airliner parked at one of the other gates. This made it easy for the flight crew to taxi away toward the airfield, because they would not have to turn about-face on the apron.

Sitting placidly docked so close together, without a trace of conflict or even competition between them, who could have guessed that these two beautiful, magnificent machines would again come together in a little over two hours in the most terrible, violent of meetings, destroying each other and all of the human beings riding in them? Looking at the two airliners, clean and nearly flawless, who could have credited the suggestion that they might soon both be annihilated as anything more than an absurd and morbid fantasy? Even after the tragedy happened, many people, including some of those who saw the irrefutable proof in the outcome, the wreckage itself, could not believe it. Far from the mere expressions of surprise or indignation that they normally were, statements like "I can't believe it" or "It's beyond belief" became literal revelations of the speaker's inability to simply confirm the thing without also denying it. It was commonplace to believe a thing without knowing it, like believing that glaciers once sculpted the land or that the sun would one day exhaust itself and die out, but for many, the tragedy that was nearly at hand would become a bizarre instance of knowing a thing without believing it.

The *Star of the Seine* was quickly outfitted with a boarding ramp, and one of the mechanics opened the main passenger cabin entry door to admit the cabin crew, whom TWA called hostesses. The hostesses for Flight 2 that day were Tracine Elizabeth Armbruster and Beth Ellis Davis; they had been waiting and promptly got onboard, whereupon they began the same preparatory routine as United 718's stewardesses. Before long, TWA 2 caught up and was ready to accommodate passengers.

While these four young women prepared for the flights, something terrible was mounting in the ground beneath them and the air around them. Even with the wrenching clash between their innocence and vulnerability, and the awful gravity of their impending doom, they apparently felt no tremors of premonition. There was nothing but discordance between their soft laughter over things like new jokes about how to contend with a drunken passenger, and the terror that would soon signify their ends, and yet they carried on like little girls humming a tune in an air raid. In the most crucial moment of their lives—their last chance to save themselves—they were oblivious.

Or maybe they did begin to have premonitions, subtle and vague twinges of something noticeable but indefinable, odd sensations of being ill at ease, which they kept to themselves in the rational but fatally incorrect belief that it was only some quirk within them, like runaway anxiety left over from some other circumstance in their lives. Maybe they feared that giving in to fear, even to the extent of pausing to take it seriously and examine it, or to confide their strange wariness to anyone, was the beginning of being controlled by it. Maybe they refused it in alarmed self-defense, misconstruing it to be the onset of the dreaded panic that mysteriously struck many fliers well into their careers, well after they had become accustomed to flying and comfortable with its risks. And maybe to some extent they actually did believe their intuitions but were ashamed to act on them without proof, thinking that they would be making fools of themselves. If they felt anything at all, then it was their last chance to recognize the peril they were in, and they discarded it—and with it, unbeknownst to them, they discarded their lives.

The girls continued using the few remaining minutes of their lives for things as small as counting the dinner napkins on board, as if those things were priceless, without realizing that because these *were* their last minutes, even the smallest elements of their lives right then and there actually were priceless.

Meanwhile, the flight engineers were portraying correspondingly fatuous, extravagant roles outside the planes, conducting tragically purposeless business of their own. What else could any of them do? If crazy means believing in an alternate reality, they would have to have been crazy to save themselves. Not having that aberrant insight, they ended their lives as they had lived them. The stewardesses and hostesses prepared the cabins, the flight engineers checked the airplanes, the first officers filed the flight plans, and the captains evaluated and supervised and finally took control of the airplanes.

*   *   *

It was the flight engineer's duty to preliminarily ensure in detail that the airplane was airworthy; he would hand over the plane to its pilots with the guarantee for his part that it was fit to fly, and they depended on him. Forrest Breyfogle and Girardo Fiore walked around the exteriors of their respective aircraft and examined the numerous features. Their inspections were incredibly thorough for the time available, covering over two hundred points. They checked door latches, propeller blades, aileron hinges, tires, radio antennae, oil leakage, exhaust stacks, and so on. After they finished checking the outsides of the planes, the flight engineers moved inside and began extensive interior inspections, checking yet another multitude of items.

The four pilots finished their flight plans and came aboard to begin their own regimen of preflight checks. Captain Shirley and First Officer Harms boarded the DC-7 via the main passenger entrance, not the crew entrance up front; likewise Captain Gandy and First Officer Ritner ascended the boarding ramp and entered the Constellation through the main cabin door. The private crew entrance, which opened directly onto the flight deck from outdoors, was uncomfortably small on the Constellation, more a hatch than a door, and the rolling crew stairs for both planes were steep and were usually oily and dirty from having been used by mechanics. To preserve the immaculate appearance of their uniforms, flight crewmembers usually boarded the same way everyone else did.

The pilots greeted the cabin attendants and walked up the aisle to the flight deck, to join or be joined by their flight engineers. The assembled flight crews ran through standard checklists on each plane, with one person reading off items sequentially to another, who would check them and respond. This involved all three of the flight crewmembers, and served as an extra precaution that nothing would be overlooked. Any experienced crew could have run down the items from memory, but on the principle that sometimes thorough familiarity and the confidence that goes with it lead to complacency and carelessness, the procedure was a rule. The formal checklists had saved many a flight from disaster.

Around 9:30 the call for boarding resounded in both airlines' terminals. Suddenly there was a lot of excitement in both lobbies, a flurry of new talk overlaid on many of the preexisting conversations, and people began moving from their seats or their standing positions toward the rear doors that opened onto the airfield. Many people felt the excitement viscerally, as a deep-seated, nervous stimulation—the prospect of flying, now made entirely real by the boarding call, was not just thrilling but also a little scary.

The observation patio behind the building was separated from the huge ramp area, with its parking aprons and aircraft, by a chain-link fence. Visitors could go this far, but no farther. Here many people lovingly and jovially said good-bye. They hugged each other, or shook hands or kissed. The visitors wished the travelers good fortune or smooth and safe flying, or fun. Some asked to be telephoned from the other end, so that they could be sure their loved one arrived there safely; some promised to meet at the airport at a prescribed time, days or weeks from then; some visitors expressed last-minute thoughtfulness, like giving the traveler some pocket money or a package of gum, or straightening a man's tie or hat. Reluctantly or with resolve or with happy faith, each passenger left the friend or the loved one who was seeing him off and departed.

As the people who had come to see them off waved and called good-bye from behind the fence, the boarders merged with the throng, receding along the ramp. They had been absorbed into another world, another life, set apart from the stationary, narrow, terrestrial existence of the ones who stood on the other side of the fence. Theirs was a world of movement, of space and distance. The travelers had entered a realm of adventure, while those who stayed behind kept the ordinary. But this time the sky would not give up its adventurers, despite countless safe returns in the past. This time the faith that each one had chosen to invest would be betrayed. This time only their fear or apprehensiveness or nervousness would be confirmed. What was already being drawn together, already being assembled from its elements, was complete and total disaster.

Side by side, many of the passengers for both flights mingled and walked out the ramp to their respective gates. On the ramp many of the people that would fatally collide with each other in two hours were near enough together to touch each other. Surely some did, if only accidentally, exchanging apologies. Others greeted the people walking beside them and made friendly inquiries about each other's travel plans. Someone among them must have felt something, a rustling of fear or of recognition, almost as though in remembrance of something long forgotten. Someone knew, gazing into the face of another, that the stranger was actually a person of great importance, and that the chance meeting was a very significant incident, disguised as the ostensibly trivial act of speaking for no apparent reason other than proximity or accidentally bumping together. Someone must have felt at least the vaguest stirrings of realizing that he and the other person had an intimate bond in something outside of this life.

The mix divided at the two gates, and the passengers for each flight congregated in their own small shelters, where the gate agent checked their tickets and let them pass onto the apron itself. People naturally had feelings of familiarity and congeniality toward those who were boarding their own plane with them, instinctive feelings of kinship with their traveling companions based in common plans or in their taking the same chance on the same plane. Despite the reassuring comforts of comradeship, some people must also have perceived their shipmates in curiously unsettling ways, yet almost no one could have clearly apprehended the import of the queer sensation, and known it to mean that he was in danger and should go no farther.

*　*　*

At the foot of United's boarding ramp, a company representative called a passenger agent greeted and welcomed the passengers. It was his job to make sure that the flight got off smoothly, and with that purpose he had already done a number of things, such as issuing tickets and checking baggage and helping load cargo. His routine duties included compiling a weight tally of everything loaded onto the plane for the crew, so that they would know what they were carrying, and supervising the various final activities outside the plane to prepare it for its trip. The passenger agent usually wore a uniform similar to a pilot's, though lacking stripes of rank on the cuffs of the coat; sometimes he appeared in a business suit.

At the landing atop the boarding ramp, one of the stewardesses met the passengers and welcomed them aboard. The other stewardess inside took jackets and hung them in the coat closet near the door, and she also ushered passengers to their seats. All seating on United's DC-7 flights was specifically reserved by location, which not only afforded the customers the privilege of choosing their own seats in advance, but also politely spared them the subtly undignified and embarrassing scramble for seats, however discreet, that would otherwise take place on board. On most flights at the time, reservations entitled the passengers only to space, not a particular location, like general admission in a theater.

The ticket holder had the right to claim a seat on the plane, but it was not specified which one.

Likewise, TWA's passengers boarded Flight 2. One or a few at a time, they were let past the gate agent and filed out to the boarding ramp, where the passenger agent, whom TWA called a transportation agent, greeted them. At the head of the stairs and just inside the plane, each hostess welcomed them, and the one inside relieved passengers of their wraps, tagging them and hanging them in the coat closet. For those who needed help, she also stowed light luggage and gentlemen's hats in the overhead hat rack (the term that airline personnel used in reference to the carry-on baggage rack). These two women represented the flight itself—the airplane and the trip it would make—and in their manner and their appearance they gave the passengers their first impressions of the real thing. From an interpersonal or social standpoint, they set the tone for the whole experience.

Miss Armbruster and Miss Davis wore TWA's sea green summer uniform. Their blouses were white and had large triangular lapels, and their shoes were brown and white high heels of a style called spectators. The suit consisted of a tapered, long-sleeved jacket with four buttons and no lapels, complemented by a long, belted skirt that was hemmed several inches below the knees. The matching hat was styled after a sailor's cap. In fact, the whole uniform gave the impression of military influences in its design, as though it were a peacetime, civilian rendition of the armed forces themes. Rather than imbuing a hostess' appearance with an aura similar to that of a soldier fighting for a noble cause, it made her seem to be an ambassador of virtue. The ensemble was very tastefully designed and colored, and had it had a little more flourish and slightly less professional formality, the only word to describe it would have been "beautiful."

The uniform worn by United's stewardesses was nearly identical in this aesthetic, as were the uniforms worn by the stewardesses of nearly every airline. Cabin attendants were part of the crew, essential personnel for conducting a flight safely. Someone had to ensure that the passengers had all fastened their seatbelts correctly before takeoffs and descents; someone had to supervise the passengers, to encourage and maintain order in the cabin; someone had to be in the cabin at all times to calm and to instruct the passengers in the event of an emergency, and so on. The flight crew obviously couldn't do this—they had to spend most of their time on the flight deck, flying the airplane—so additional crewmembers were hired expressly to be in charge of the cabin. Because their services were indispensable, they were given the authority with which to carry them out, and to facilitate that, their uniforms were designed to reflect their status.

The look was developed partly in a commensurate effort to coordinate stewardesses' uniforms with those of pilots and flight engineers, which had been deliberately patterned after military forms to denote their authority over the aircraft and everyone on board. An airline captain had much the same powers as a commercial ship captain, such as the authority to refuse to return to port to let off a passenger who changed his mind about the voyage, and the authority to expel an unruly passenger at any port. Captains of commercial sailing vessels had always been vested with an abridged version of the powers held by naval captains, probably out of a tradition originating in the times when there was little distinction between naval and trade vessels, when armed self-defense was a necessity on the pirate-infested seas. Correspondingly, captains of commercial ships had always worn uniforms similar to those of captains of naval ships, and the parallel extended down the hierarchy of command. When airliners came along, they were regarded as ships of the air, and many of the maritime customs were simply carried over. Pilots and flight engineers wore military-like uniforms, and with an added aspect of attractiveness in the design, so did stewardesses and hostesses.

To complete the sharp picture, the hostess' uniform was embellished with the TWA logo, embroidered in red on the jacket just below the right shoulder, and with a red, white, and blue cockade attached to the left forward area of her cap. The cockade was in turn decorated with pinned-on, silver hat wings, as they were called, even though this was one item with one wing on it. Undoubtedly the reference was plural because when a hostess qualified herself, she "earned her wings," not just her wing; this would hardly be an honor if it suggested the image of a bird attempting to fly with only one wing, a ludicrous enterprise that at best would send it off on a corkscrew path, if it could fly at all. This ornament was intricately detailed to represent a bird's wing and held the TWA logo in raised relief, and like the wings of most airlines at the time, it was a piece of jewelry as much as it was a badge.

The hostesses themselves fit a hiring profile that stipulated they be young and of medium female height and trim appearance. In addition to this a dress code required them to wear their hair short, refrain from using colorings, and use a red lipstick. Part of the idea was that in their uniform appearance they fostered a reassuring feeling of familiarity in their repeat passengers. No matter who was attending in the cabin, she seemed familiar because she looked and acted much like any other. Whether it was a passenger's first flight with the airline or his hundredth, she conveyed an impression of femininity and beauty. Hostesses were simply lovely, and were a pleasure to behold. One could hardly become so accustomed to them as to not notice them.

United's stewardesses were equally appealing and observed essentially the same code of dress. Miss Kemnitz and Miss Shoudt wore United's light blue summer uniform. They had on blue and white spectators and white blouses with very large notched lapels. The suit was a form-fitted, long-sleeved jacket and a long skirt that was hemmed below the knees. The jacket had four buttons, V-shaped pockets, and no lapels, and the skirt had one large pleat down the centers of the front and the back. On their heads were brimless caps suggestive again of naval styling, colored light blue to match the jacket and skirt. The finishing touch was supplied by the silver hat and jacket wings, sculpted much like TWA's wings and bearing the United Air Lines logo in red and blue enamel. (The jacket wings really were wings, plural; there was a left wing and a right wing, joined by the logo.)

Whether in the dress of United Air Lines or TWA, the cabin attendants exemplified the contemporary image of beauty as it was conceived and praised in this country. Moreover, most stewardesses and hostesses were women of virtuous character and had amiable, friendly dispositions. They were for the most part simply decent people. These of course were qualities that could not be mandated or regulated; they had to come from honest, free choice. The average hostess or stewardess was a good person in the best sense—namely, because she wanted to be one. The role that her company had in this was primarily subtractive rather than contributory, even though each company promoted character in its employees. Supervisors did endeavor to ensure that the cabin crewmembers were nice, but they accomplished this mainly by weeding out the ones that weren't.

One by one, the passengers of United 718 and TWA 2 were welcomed aboard by these appealing, friendly representatives of American idealism, and they could not help but be cheered. By all appearances, it was going to be a good flight.

CHAPTER 2

TWA FLIGHT 2 was a purely first-class luxury operation. It ran eastward daily from Los Angeles to Washington, D.C., using a large, four-engine, propeller-driven airplane called a Lockheed L-1049 Constellation. The route was divided into three segments by intermediate stops at Kansas City and St. Louis.

A fourth segment ran under the same flight name from Washington, D.C., to Baltimore and was performed at the end of the night using a twin-engine airplane called a Martin 404. Insofar as the foremost distinguishing characteristic of Flight 2 was that it was a transcontinental flight, this thirty-mile jaunt was more extraneous than intrinsic, as though it were appended as an afterthought. In the 1950s, transcontinental flights like Flight 2 were still something remarkable, and that qualification was satisfied each day by the Constellation's landing at Washington, D.C., on the coast opposite from where it started. The fourth, brief excursion up the coastline added nothing to that achievement; if anything it was anticlimactic. Besides this, the plane that flew across the entire country was done at Washington and went no farther. For these reasons the fourth leg seemed artificial, and this book disregards it, treating Flight 2 as an exclusively transcontinental venture.

Including stopovers, Flight 2 took about nine and three-quarters hours. In the summer months it began at 9:30 a.m. PDT at Los Angeles International Airport and ended at 10:15 p.m. EDT at Washington National Airport. In airline parlance arrivals and departures were in reference to boarding gates; a flight departed whenever it left the gate, but it might not leave the airport (i.e., take off) for another five or ten minutes, or longer. Similarly, a flight always landed before it arrived. Flight 2 routinely involved a crew change halfway across the country at Kansas City Municipal Airport, where it was scheduled to arrive (at the gate) at 3:25 p.m. CST, four hours and fifty-five minutes after departing at Los Angeles International Airport. (The arrival time for Kansas City is given in standard reckoning because in 1956 Kansas City was one of the many towns that still did not use the Daylight Saving Time system.)

United Air Lines Flight 718 was also a transcontinental luxury flight, having only first-class seating. It was a daily operation that ran from Los Angeles to Newark in the summer months and from Los Angeles to New York City the rest of the year. In the same abstract sense that TWA 2 extended to Baltimore even though the primary airplane that flew the breadth of the country wasn't the one used on that last leg, United 718 began each day at San Diego rather than Los Angeles. The segment from San Diego to Los Angeles was completed with a different type of plane, performing under the name Flight 659, which continued up the coastline from Los Angeles to San Francisco, Seattle, and Vancouver, British Columbia. Passengers for Flight 718 would get off at Los Angeles and transfer to the plane that was heading eastward from there, and so they were considered to have been on Flight 718 from the outset. United's timetable description of Flight 718 promoted this detail. This book, however, downplays it in the view that it is artificial. Throughout the year most of the people who got on Flight 659 at San Diego did not transfer to the eastbound plane at Los Angeles, so the coastal route from San Diego northward to Vancouver would have continued in existence even if the transcontinental route from Los Angeles eastward had been abandoned. On the other hand, had the coastal route been abandoned, the transcontinental plane used for Flight 718 would not have been re-routed to start its flying for the day at San Diego, nor would the coastal plane formerly used for Flight 659 have been kept on duty just to ferry the occasional passengers for

Flight 718 from San Diego to Los Angeles. The leg from San Diego to Los Angeles would surely have been discontinued, vanishing with Flight 659. In the best senses the two routes and flights were independent of each other, and for that reason this book regards Flight 718 as having originated at Los Angeles.

Considered as a trip from Los Angeles to Newark, Flight 718 consisted of four segments, divided from each other by intermediate stops at Chicago, Detroit, and Philadelphia. The flight employed a large, four-engine airplane called a Douglas DC-7, a craft slightly more advanced and capable than TWA's L-1049 Constellation, for the whole trip. Like the Constellation, the DC-7 was propeller-driven, as were all airliners in the United States at the time.

In the summer the complete flight from Los Angeles, including stopovers, took an average of ten hours and twenty-five minutes. Flight 718 was scheduled to depart at Los Angeles International Airport at 9:45 a.m. PDT and to arrive at Newark Airport at 11:10 p.m. EDT. (The rest of the year the times were 10:00 a.m. PST at Los Angeles International Airport, and 11:05 p.m. EST at New York International Airport.) A fresh crew always took over at Chicago's Midway Airport, where arrival was scheduled for 5:25 p.m. CDT, five hours and forty minutes after departing at Los Angeles International.

In the official accident investigation report, the definitions of the two flights were abridgements based upon flight plans. Captain Gandy filed a flight plan for the trip from Los Angeles to Kansas City. He took command of his plane at Los Angeles and would have relinquished it at Kansas City and been finished flying for the day. Captain Shirley filed a flight plan for the trip from Los Angeles to Chicago. He took command of his plane at Los Angeles and would have turned it over to someone else and been done flying for the day at Chicago. Correspondingly, the official report described Flight 2 as running from Los Angeles to Kansas City, and Flight 718 as running from Los Angeles to Chicago, and that's all. At least on the day of the accident, they were no more than that.

How each flight might most accurately be defined is probably not a meaningful question, because there are several senses in which to regard it, all of them legitimate and worthwhile. It could be thought of as a route with one or more intermediate stops, or as a single jump between two airports even if the route extended farther, or as a trip on a single airplane exclusive of connecting flights, and so on.

How each flight is *best* defined is a better question. In the most important vein the answer is personal: it depends upon the values and perceptions and needs of the person doing the defining. Someone who was awaiting a loved one at Washington National Airport, for example, would not agree that TWA Flight 2 was a trip from Los Angeles to Kansas City, but would rightly insist that it was a trip from Los Angeles to Washington, D.C.

In this book several definitions, each hopefully appropriate and clear contextually, will be used. Additionally, any terms that denote the flights will sometimes refer simply and concretely to the airplanes themselves and the people aboard them, wherever they happened to be at a particular moment. They then represent the people and things *making* the trips more so than the trips they were making.

Two final points on the flights' names: first, the acronym TWA is used to represent Trans World Airlines, but UAL is not used to stand for United Air Lines, because they didn't call themselves UAL at the time; and second, the common noun part in the names of most airlines was of course a common allusion to the trails or "lines" that their vessels followed and to the fact that they traveled across the air, but each company decided as a matter of its own aesthetics whether to describe itself as "Airlines" or "Air Lines," one word or two.

Lockheed Aircraft Corporation designed and produced many models of their legendary Constellation series, most notably the L-049, L-749, and L-1049. Each model was ultimately produced in two or more fundamental variations, significantly differing from each other mechanically, with all but the first denoted further by alphabetic suffixes. (And of course there were innumerable differences in interior design from one airline to the next, but these did not define aircraft types anymore than furniture defined a building.)

At the time of the accident, TWA owned many of each of the types L-049, L-749, L-749A, L-1049, and L-1049G. In all, only twenty-four of the original L-1049 aircraft, as distinguished from subsequent variants like the L-1049G, were ever built. Ten of them were owned by TWA and the other fourteen by Eastern Air Lines. The usual plane for TWA Flight 2 was one of the company's ten original L-1049s, and it was one of these airplanes that was used for the trip on June 30, 1956.

The name "Constellation" has magic in it, unlike most numbers, and so it is used repeatedly throughout the book in referring to the plane, but because there were many Constellation models, it is often used together with the type designation. The "L" stands for Lockheed, and because the company was famous for its Constellations, the "L" is in a sense superfluous. Besides this, a name like "L-1049 Constellation" borders on cumbersome and, if used repeatedly, becomes tedious. For these reasons this book omits the "L-" in referring to the plane that was involved in the tragedy. It is variously called a "Constellation," a "1049 Constellation," and a "1049."

An obscure oddity associated with the tragedy was that the documentary record contradicted itself regarding the type designation of the TWA Constellation that was lost in the Grand Canyon disaster. The official accident investigation report finally issued by the Civil Aeronautics Board (CAB), the agency responsible at the time for investigating airline disasters, called the plane a 1049A, not just a 1049. However, an equally authoritative agency called the Civil Aeronautics Administration (CAA), which among other things certificated aircraft, did not recognize any such thing as a 1049A. The CAA issued a multi-page document called the Type Specification Sheet, in which they listed and described in great detail every Constellation variant, with no mention of a 1049A. By default they asserted that they had never certificated a 1049A, and therefore that none existed.

To further the confusion the TWA hostess' manual at the time, called the TWA Flight Service Manual, referred to the plane again as a 1049A. The manual was very specific as to which planes it referred, denoting them additionally as the group with "900 series" TWA fleet numbers. Airlines used their own numbers to designate the planes in their fleets, and TWA's ten basic 1049 Constellations were numbered in the block from 901 to 910, taken from the block of their federal, CAA registration numbers, which ran from N6901C to N6910C. The plane in the disaster had fleet number 902 and registration N6902C. No other TWA aircraft had 900-series fleet numbers or registrations ending in 900-something, so the hostess' manual could only have referred to the ten original-type 1049s, "A" or not.

But among the TWA pilots and flight engineers who flew them, these planes were never called anything but a 1049. The 1049G, on the other hand, was always called a 1049G or a "Super-G," never just a 1049. Also, in their own manual, called the TWA Constellation Flight Crew Operating Manual, a great deal of information appeared for the 1049 and the 1049G, but there was no mention at all of any 1049A.

Maybe the CAB spuriously appended the "A" in order to make it explicitly clear that the plane in the tragedy was not a later refinement, but was of the first sort of 1049. Similarly, the hostess' manual may have incorporated an illegitimate "A" in order to help the hostesses keep it straight which plane they were talking about, an original 1049 or a revised edition 1049G. Their concern was appropriately for the people in their care, not the machines on which they cared for them. For lack of interest, most hostesses didn't pay much attention to the particulars of design or equipment that subtly differentiated one model in a series from another, and so they were often less than crystal clear about which was which.

Many documents extended the controversy, but most referred to the plane as a simple 1049, not a 1049A. Maybe to cut through it all, it is sufficient to note that pilots and flight engineers were undoubtedly the best authorities on what they were flying. Accordingly, this book will call the plane a simple 1049.

The particular 1049 of which Captain Gandy took charge on the day of the tragedy had been christened with the name *Star of the Seine*, which was painted on the side of the fuselage just below the cockpit windows. Immediately below this was the French equivalent, *Etoile de la Seine*. Like all of TWA's 1049 Constellations, the *Star of the Seine* was beautiful to look at, a graceful, streamlined creation in white and silver and accented in red. Poised as it was atop unusually tall, spindly landing gear, the plane seemed somehow filled with the urge to simply ascend straight up away from the earth. It was as though the plane were unwilling to come any nearer to the ground than the stilts on which it postured would allow.

The belly of the fuselage was bare metal, to about the extent that would have been submerged if the plane had been a yacht floating in the water. Except for the insignia and narrow walkways of friction paint, the wings, too, were unpainted. Above the "waterline" the fuselage was painted white from nose to tail. Sixteen square cabin windows ran its length on the port side, and eighteen were on the starboard. Overlaying the white paint, two parallel red stripes underlined the windows from end to end on each side, and in large capital letters Trans World Airlines was spelled out above the windows. The words were slanted to suggest speed, and just ahead of them on each side was a large, forty-eight-star American flag. Finishing the fuselage, the three-letter TWA logo was painted at both ends on both sides, in line with the red stripes and matching their color.

The wing insignia were simply large red numerals and capital letters spelling out the TWA logo on the top left and bottom right surfaces, and the federal registration number, N6902C, on the top right and bottom left surfaces, just the opposite of the logo. On the tail the overall paint scheme was carried through: the vertical surfaces were painted white with paired red horizontal stripes, and the horizontal surfaces, analogous to the wings, were bare metal.

In its appearance the airplane had an uncomplicated beauty that felt clean, and it seemed to be saying that it was proud to be clean. Its sharply conceived and executed paint job was an outstanding work of paint, but was more noble and uplifting than artistic. Rather, it was in its physical structure that the plane became real art. Its shape was truly inspired and truly inspiring.

The most striking feature was the futuristic triple tail. Unlike most airplanes, the Constellation had *three* vertical tail fins, not just one. There was one in the center as usual, projecting upward from the rear-most area of the fuselage, but this one was flanked left and right by two others, positioned at the far ends of the horizontal tail structures. When the plane turned, the three vertical fins worked together, with the hinged rudders at their rear edges veering toward one side in a single movement. Having three tail fins made the plane seem scientifically advanced, not only physically developed and expanded along the basic theme of having a tail, but representative of entirely new knowledge, a breakthrough in the science of aerodynamics. To look at the plane, a person could not help but be thrilled with the impression that it must fly better and more capably, that it must be the next stage in the evolution of flying machines.

After the marvel of the tail there was the futuristic shape of the fuselage. In its graceful curvature it was contoured like the body of a dolphin, with all the primary features: the smooth, elongated beak, the pronounced forehead, the well-proportioned arching of the back and the upturned thrust of the rear just ahead of the tail fluke. Where other planes had straight, uniform fuselages as though they were meant to pierce the sky like arrows, the Constellation looked as though it were meant to *ride* the sky. It seemed as though the plane had been designed to glide up and down over the rolling surfaces of great fantastic waves in the upper atmosphere, hitherto unknown to man.

United's DC-7 was also one of a series of planes. Douglas Aircraft Company produced many models in their Douglas Commercial series with variations in most. The culmination of many years' refinements was the DC-7, which at the time of the accident was Douglas' most technically advanced airplane, although most pilots and airline executives would have argued that Douglas' DC-6 was actually their best. The DC-7 was also in a major sense the last of the line: the DC-8, which was to enter airline service in 1959, was a jet.

United owned many of the types DC-3, DC-4, DC-6, DC-6B, and DC-7. In all, Douglas built 106 basic DC-7 aircraft, as distinguished from later variants like the DC-7C. United bought a total of fifty-seven of the original DC-7s, which were delivered beginning in 1954 and ending in 1958. At the time of the accident the airline possessed twenty-seven, one of which was the *City of Vancouver*, and it was that particular plane that Captain Shirley commanded on that day.

Like all DC-7s, the *City of Vancouver* could have been better described as handsomely shaped than beautifully shaped. It had solid proportions and contours, and like most aircraft, the fuselage was predominantly a simple, uniform cylinder tapered at the ends, like a cigar. Also in keeping with convention, it had only the usual, single vertical tail fin, but the plane's decoration more than compensated for what it lacked in physical grace. As all of United's DC-7s, the *City of Vancouver* had one of the most strikingly beautiful paint jobs ever to grace an airplane.

The total effect of the plane was like that of looking at a stupendous American flag. It was a huge white and blue machine with red accents, and in having the colors of our flag in beautifully proportioned combination, it thrillingly symbolized our ideals and our identity as a people. It even had the word "United" boldly spelled-out in several places on it, which could not help but bring to mind the United States.

A wide stripe of navy blue paint ran the length of the fuselage on each side, encompassing the long rows of passenger cabin windows and the elevated cockpit windows, and spreading fully over the nose of the plane. In the cockpit area, the upper and lower edges of the stripe curved backward and inboard to meet their mirror-image counterparts from the other side. Below this stripe the fuselage was unpainted. The horizontal tail planes were unpainted, too, and except for their insignia and large patches of corrosion preventative coating, so were the wings. Above the blue stripe the fuselage was painted white. The vertical tail fin and rudder were also painted white, and they were encircled horizontally with red and navy blue stripes near their bases, above which appeared the name "United" in large, navy blue slanted capitals. Above that, high on the tail, was painted "DC-7," with the "DC-" in gray and the "7" in red. At the other end of the airplane the cockpit windows were outlined in sky blue, making a beautiful, tonally harmonious contrast with the dark blue background. Several short, sky blue stripes extended rearward from the back edges of the rear-most cockpit windows on each side, suggesting speed and motion through the air stream. Just behind these was "United" in very large, slanted white capitals outlined in red, strikingly again set on the field of navy blue. In huge lettering, "United" was also done in navy blue outlined in white on the top surface of the left wing, and white outlined in red on the bottom surface of the right wing. The equally huge federal registration numbers, N6324C, on the bottom left and top right wing surfaces, were black outlined in white. Under the cockpit windows appeared the title "DC-7 Mainliner," and under that the name *City of Vancouver*. Red and navy blue stripes were painted at the tips of all sixteen propeller blades, completely encircling them, and red, white, and navy blue chevrons adorned the trailing edges of the wings. As if this were not enough, the United Air Lines shield logo decorated the sides of the nose and the beautiful world globe Douglas Aircraft Company logo embellished the area just to the rear of the main cabin entry door, in view of passengers as they boarded.

Beneath the paint the plane portrayed the character of its makers as explicitly as its decoration, despite its unremarkable shape. In its science and its mastery of flight, the plane represented our dreams and achievements; in its seemingly unfettered capacity to wander the open sky, it affirmed our values of freedom and individualism; and in its strength without extravagance, it revealed our honor, our dignity, and our humility. As a creation of man, almost any airplane might have suggested the best in human character, but one that also emblazoned the traditional colors of American patriotism made all of the other impressions feel stirringly, personally American.

The 1049 and the DC-7 were big and prestigious. Along with just a couple other models, they were the premier American airliners of their time, being the largest, most modern and most capable. If the two planes had been parked side by side or nose to tail on a football field, they would have filled it, leaving only small margins around and between them of twenty to twenty-five feet. To the nearest foot the 1049's measurements in length, wingspan, and tail height from the ground were 113, 123, and 25 feet respectively. To the nearest foot the DC-7's corresponding measurements were 109, 118, and 29 feet. In simple proportions the DC-7 had 96 percent the length and breadth of the 1049, and 115 percent its tail height.

The 1049 weighed 69,000 pounds empty and 120,000 pounds loaded to capacity; the DC-7 weighed 65,000 pounds empty and 122,000 pounds fully loaded. In general the planes were not operated at their limits, and of course never at their empty weights, which were without fuel and people aboard. More meaningfully, the *Star of the Seine* and the *City of Vancouver* weighed 108,000 pounds and 106,000 pounds respectively when they left Los Angeles on the day of the tragedy. Individually these weights were about the same as the total weight of seven or eight hundred average adults, and combined they equaled the weight of a full-grown blue whale, the largest animal that has ever lived.

Both planes were also faster than most other large transports of their day. Typical cruising speeds relative to the moving air mass, not the stationary ground, were roughly 330 mph for the DC-7 and 310 mph for the 1049 (in fact, on the day of the accident the two crews filed flight plans proposing 288 knots and 270 knots, respectively, or 331 mph and 311 mph); the DC-7 was normally operated 6 or 7 percent faster than the 1049, due primarily to its having more powerful engines. The 1049's engines could develop 2,800 horsepower apiece for takeoff and could comfortably sustain over half of that for cruising, while the DC-7's engines, being a slightly more advanced model in the same series, could produce well over 3,000 horsepower for takeoff and could maintain nearly 2,000 for cruising. Both types were actually rated at higher cruising performances by the CAA, which certificated not only whole airplanes but also individual engine types, but the airlines imposed their own more conservative restrictions, and it was these that gave a measure of the engines in practice.

Each plane had four Wright Aeronautical eighteen-cylinder piston engines of a configuration called twin row radial. The cylinders were arranged like the spokes of a wagon wheel and were divided into two circular banks of nine, sandwiched together in tandem. Both models were massive engines, weighing over one and a half tons and having displacements of 3,350 cubic inches, the latter equivalent to about ten V-8 pickup truck engines. (Each plane had the incredible power of about forty heavy-duty pickup trucks.) Both models were supercharged with intake blowers that forced fresh air into them under pressure for combustion and served the primary purpose of enabling the planes to fly in the thin air at high altitudes, by helping them "breathe." In addition, the DC-7's engines were outfitted with devices called power recovery turbines, which captured some of the waste energy in the blasting exhaust gasses and transferred it to the crankshaft, increasing the power output at the propeller shaft. All of these features lay hidden under engine cowlings, but there was an obvious difference in propulsion between the two planes: the 1049 had three-bladed propellers, and the DC-7's propellers had four blades. This could be spotted immediately and from a distance when the engines weren't running.

TWA's 1049 Constellation was configured for strictly first-class operation. In this vein it had only sixty-four passenger seats, a modest number considering that Eastern Air Lines had configured theirs for eighty-eight passengers. Modesty of course was hardly the point, which was to make the plane lavishly roomy and comfortable. (See Appendix 1 for a floor plan.)

The passenger cabin was divided into forward and aft sections, by an intervening galley that was partitioned off and straddled the aisle. The forward compartment accommodated sixteen passengers in five rows of seats and featured a coat closet, an auxiliary entry door, and a shared restroom for men and women. From the rear of the galley all the way back to the last row of seats, the arrangement was consistent four-abreast seating, divided by the central aisle into port and starboard pairs. The rear passenger compartment contained twelve rows, capable of seating forty-eight passengers.

The seventeen rows of seats on the plane were numbered from one through *eighteen*; the number thirteen was skipped in obeisance to the superstitious belief that it cursed all those associated with it. TWA was far from alone in observing this quaint tradition—many skyscrapers, for instance, had no thirteenth floor, not by number. The prevalence of the belief, however, makes a person wonder if perhaps there was something to it after all. It would not be the first piece of folklore that turned out to be true after long being ridiculed by sophisticated, enlightened society.

The main entryway was located on the port side, right behind the last row of seats. Standing in the doorway and looking in, a passenger could see two diminutive hostesses' jump seats attached to a partition to the right, and the entrance and wall of the men's restroom across the aisle. On the backside of the partition were a drinking fountain and a coat closet, both accessible from the aisle, and rear of the men's restroom was a restroom for women. The aft walls of the women's restroom and the coat closet formed the forward walls of the lounge.

The lounge was the rear-most space in the cabin and seated seven people. For an airplane, that was spacious. It was a place like a comfortable hotel lobby in conception, where passengers could get away and relax, escaping the confines of their seats like hotel guests escaping their rooms. The lounge had a window on each side and was outfitted during flight with a card table that was stowed by the coat closet for takeoffs and landings. Passengers could go there to read or to talk, or to play cards or use the table for business paperwork.

A delightfully surprising feature of the plane's interior was that the forward passenger compartment was like a sunken living room. Passengers boarded the plane through the main entryway near the rear whether they were going to sit in the rear compartment or the forward compartment, and those of them that were going to sit forward had to walk through the galley to get there. The walk was all on one level until they reached the doorway at the forward end of the galley, where they took a step downward into the forward compartment, giving them a magical feeling of being in a special place sequestered from the rest of the plane.

Beyond the next doorway forward was the flight deck. This was the place from which the plane was flown, hence its name, and it was divided conceptually into two areas, the forward being the cockpit, where the two pilots sat, and the rearward being the flight engineer's station. Here there was another surprise, which few passengers ever saw: the flight engineer's station was sunken in turn, on a level another step down from the forward passenger compartment. The cockpit was one step back up from the flight engineer's station, but that by itself would have been normal; it was the two steps down that were unusual. They conformed to the unusual shape of the fuselage, which curved downward from the wing area toward the nose.

The cabin décor was uncomplicated and luxurious. From the top edges of the windows upward, the walls were a light tan color, and this scheme was carried through by the lengthwise overhead shelving for carry-on baggage on each side of the aisle, and the arched ceiling in between. From the top line of the windows downward to the floor, the walls were sea green, as was the carpeting that covered the floor from wall to wall. The fixed outside panels of the aisle seats, along with all of the armrests, were upholstered in the same green, and the seat cushions were upholstered in a tan fabric. Cream-colored curtains with horizontal brown stripes hung alongside all of the cabin windows and could be drawn by the passengers.

The seats were luxuriously wide, and their backs were tall enough so that no separate headrest was needed. Plain white cloths covered the upper back of each seat where passengers' heads would rest. Overhead, on the undersides of the carry-on baggage racks, were individual fresh air vents and miniature, recessed spotlights for reading. The doorways between sections were framed in chrome molding, which was duplicated along the top, aisle-side edges of the baggage racks, down the whole length of the passenger cabin. Chrome plated ashtrays and seat adjustment levers outfitted the forward ends of the aisle-side and widow-side armrests; the shared middle armrests were plain. A bank of lighting panels ran the whole length of the cabin along the center line of the ceiling, providing bright illumination for nighttime boarding and disembarking; alternatively, they provided soft illumination for lighting the walkway at night during flight, without interfering with passengers' sleeping.

The restrooms, which were called lavatories by airline personnel, were outfitted with stainless steel fixtures and supplied with toiletries. There were cloth towels hanging on towel rods, and in the men's restroom, there were also shavers and a bottle of astringent, all furnished for communal use. The galley equipment likewise was made of stainless steel, kept very clean and polished. In the galley were stored eating utensils and serving ware, beverages, cooked foods, and dry goods such as crackers and cookies. Meals were arranged in the galley rather than cooked there, using pre-prepared dishes that had been placed aboard at the airport. These were heated or kept warm in special defrosting and warming ovens during flight.

The galley on United Air Lines' DC-7 was only about half the size of its counterpart on TWA's 1049, yet it supported essentially the same quality of service to nearly as many passengers. United Air Lines called this facility a buffet rather than a galley, to reflect the fact that food was merely served from there rather than cooked there. Like TWA's larger station, the buffet contained counters and storage compartments, along with a warming oven and heated urns for coffee, and for water from which to make tea by the cup.

The buffet was near the rear of the plane and was confined to the port side of the cabin. It straddled the very short entry walkway at the main cabin entry door rather than the aisle, extending inward only as far as the aisle, about four feet. As a passenger entered the airplane, he stepped through the buffet on either side of him and then turned left or right to walk lengthwise down the aisle. Utilitarian as this facility was, it was a subtly welcoming touch to have passengers walk through it, reminiscent of entering a friend's home by the back door through the kitchen.

The passenger cabin was divided into forward and aft compartments by the buffet and a partition opposite its rear, with the forward compartment being much longer than the aft. This was the reverse of TWA's arrangement, but on both planes the food service facility divided the compartments from each other.

Like TWA's 1049, United's DC-7 was configured for purely first-class operation even though one of its compartments could have been set up for the cheaper tourist service. The plane was outfitted with fifty-eight passenger seats arranged in sixteen rows, twelve in the forward compartment and four in the rearward. (See Appendix 1 for a floor plan.) In the forward section the first ten rows were four-abreast, two seats on each side of the aisle. The eleventh and twelfth rows had only two seats apiece, on the starboard side, opposite the buffet and the main entry door. In all, the forward section seated forty-four passengers, and the rear compartment seated fourteen.

In the rear section the thirteenth row contained a small coat closet on the port side attached to the aft wall of the buffet, and two seats on the starboard side. United Air Lines rejected the popular apprehensiveness connected with the number thirteen and designated these seats 13C and 13D. However, they were often among the last ones sold; no one wanted to sit there. Apparently United's faith in modern, scientific thinking and the enlightenment of the average patron was somewhat misplaced.

The last three rows were four-abreast seating again, divided by the aisle. Behind the sixteenth row was a heavy-gauge, clear Plexiglas partition, open at the aisle, separating the lounge from the rest of the cabin. Cigar and pipe smoking were permitted in the lounge, unlike the rest of the plane, where only cigarettes were allowed. There were five very comfortable oversized seats, three small end tables, and a central drop-leaf card table. Encircling the card table, the other furnishings wrapped around the lounge in a crescent-shaped pattern, conforming to the dome-shaped curvature of the rear end of the cabin. (The rear wall was called the pressure dome and had been designed with that shape to be stronger than a flat wall would have been, so that it could better resist the stresses of high-altitude pressurization.) At the front of the lounge on the port side there was an end table, followed by two seats, another end table, two seats at the rear, a third end table, and one seat on the starboard side. All eight of these pieces were bolted to each other and to the walls and the floor. Where a sixth seat might have been by symmetry, near the front of the lounge on the starboard side, there was instead an emergency door. It measured only two feet wide by four and a third feet tall and opened inward. Besides being peculiarly small, the door was an odd contrivance in that it was not hinged; rather, it simply came free of the jamb when it was unlatched, and would have to be tossed aside out of the way in an emergency. In this hatch and right next to it were windows, and there was a matching pair of windows facing these from the port side.

United's DC-7 had two lavatories, not three like TWA's 1049. These were immediately ahead of the forward passenger compartment, in line with the engines, and because of that and their lack of carpeting they were about the noisiest places on the airplane. The men's was on the port side, and the women's was opposite it on the starboard. In the aisle, which separated them from each other, was a stewardess' fold-down jump seat attached to the wall of the men's lavatory. One stewardess used this special seat, facing the women's lavatory, for takeoffs and landings; she sat sideways. This was more than a thrifty innovation. Passengers were typically the most anxious during takeoffs and landings, and because there was no door at the front of the compartment, the stewardess was in view seated in her jump seat, to reassure them simply by her presence.

The washrooms were constructed predominantly of stainless steel, which made them aesthetically austere. At first glance the equipment seemed almost rustic. There was simply a lone faucet with a single valve at the washbasin, so the water temperature could not be adjusted. Behind this somber appearance, however, was a delightful surprise: the water was enjoyably hot and ideal for washing, or even for softening a man's beard so that he could shave. A special heater held the water tank at 120°F. The purpose behind this convenience was doubtless to conserve water, by eliminating the waste unavoidably involved in finding the right balance of hot and cold by trial and error—a good idea on an airplane, with a necessarily modest reservoir. The DC-7 had a single, shared wash water tank in the ceiling between the two lavatories; it held twenty-six gallons, slightly over one and a half quarts per person when the plane was full, making thrift essential. In this instance, however, economy felt more like luxury. Having the water prepared by the airline was another way to be pampered.

Luxury or not, there were some features that were amenities by design. For example, the restrooms were outfitted with 110-volt AC outlets, enabling the men to plug in their electric razors to refresh their appearances on the longer flights. Outside in the hallway were small, lighted signs that read, "Vacant" and, "Occupied," gratifyingly modern in their era, where electrical automation and gadgetry was fast coming to symbolize man's scientific and cultural advancements. Inside, another lighted sign that could be switched on remotely by the crew announced that it was time to, "Return to cabin," meaning that it was time for passengers to return to their seats.

Ahead of the lavatories were twin port and starboard coat closets, and ahead of these in turn was an unusual feature: an on-deck baggage room. This special facility was sandwiched between the flight deck and the two forward coat closets, and it supplemented the traditional cargo hold in the belly of the plane. Luggage was stowed on deck, with shipping crates below. This expedited unloading luggage and returning it to its owners at the destination airport. The main aisle divided the room into port and starboard mirror-image halves, consisting of racks with netting and straps for securing the baggage stowed on them. At each end the room was outfitted with doors that swung open outward from it, one opening onto the flight deck, and the other opening into the hallway between the coat closets.

United's interior colors were blues and grays. (Was this consciously or unconsciously intended to symbolize the harmonious "United"-ness of the Union and the Confederacy, melded as the United States?) The ceiling and walls were light gray, and the wall-to-wall carpeting was dark blue. At the top edges of the windows was a compact valance that ran the length of the cabin. Seat number placards were attached to the valance over every window, and curtains hung from behind it alongside every window, held open by straps fastened to the walls. Over the window seats, upholstered utility panels extended the length of the cabin, sloping upward away from the walls. Joined to them from above were cabin length shelves that held blankets and pillows and served as carry-on baggage racks. The sloped utility panels concealed fresh air ducting and contained adjustable fresh air vents and reading spotlights.

As with TWA's 1049, United's DC-7 had wide, comfortable seats. Their backs were tall enough that no accessory headrest was needed. The seats were slightly different from TWA's in that they were drawn in along a line near the top to sculpt a sort of head pad in the cushioning. White cloths imprinted with the United shield logo were tucked into the creases and pinned on the rear side of the seat. The fixed side panels and the armrests were upholstered in dark blue, and the adjustable seat and back cushions were covered in medium gray fabric with a coarse weave. There were chrome seat adjustment controls and ashtrays at the ends of the window-side and aisle-side armrests, as well as small circular receptacles in all three armrests of every seat pair, for accommodating the ends of food tray support bars. Just the same as on TWA's 1049, the trays were plugged into the armrests at mealtime. This was a sturdy, stable arrangement and had the added advantage of being more genteel than the system of using a fold down tray built into the back of the next seat ahead, which could not help but transmit a diner's movements and occasionally distract or disturb the person sitting there.

Like the 1049, the DC-7 was outfitted with a cabin-length trough of ceiling light fixtures containing numerous incandescent bulbs. These lights could be dimmed to twenty percent of their full brightness to provide a safe yet soothing, unobtrusive level of light in the aisle during the night, enabling passengers to sleep comfortably. Ultimately, what tied the whole environment together was the lighting: natural sunlight streamed through the windows in the daytime, and artificial light was used at night. Light, modulated by curtains or by circuits, developed the mood of the cabin, setting its emotional tone and color.

These were the settings in which the passengers of Flights 2 and 718 were to spend the last two hours of their lives. Like the theater, the accommodations felt opulent, though without being lavish. Seated in their comfortable chairs, it was as if the passengers were there to see a show, to be entertained, to be taken on a journey that was not only literal but also, and more importantly, an inner experience, an adventure and an evolvement like that to be had in the best of the theater. The whole atmosphere offered a curious and welcome sense of well-being, of being deep inside, as though reposed in an inner sanctum, enfolded and protected. It was a stimulating, gratifying feeling of security that prevailed even in the face of natural apprehensiveness—and in a way, because of it. A peripheral awareness of the risks of flying accentuated for what purpose the planes had been built like strongholds, clarifying how capable they were.

These impressions were real, though the realities they reflected were inadequate for the assault that was to come. The planes were able to withstand the fury inside the black heart of a raging thunderstorm, full of hail and lightening and violent updrafts; they were strong and yielding and secure, and more soundproof than a sound studio, and yet the feeling of safety that they elicited was fatally misleading, like mistaking the lethargy of a caged lion for tameness.

CHAPTER 3

AFTER EVERYONE HAD boarded, the passenger agent or transportation agent came on board to give the flight crew the final tally weight slip, accounting for all cargo and for all passengers on board. As he left the plane, he stopped on the boarding ramp landing, where he closed and secured the main cabin door using a special recessed, outside door handle. A stewardess or hostess on the inside had only to verify that he had properly latched the door shut, so that it could not possibly come open in flight of its own accord. There were seventy persons aboard TWA's *Star of the Seine* and fifty-eight persons aboard United's *City of Vancouver*.

As the passengers settled in or stowed their carry-on baggage in the overhead racks or used the lavatories, the passenger agent or transportation agent advised the ground crewmembers that the flight was ready, and he stood by. While the ground crew removed the cargo tractor and cart, the crew stairs, and the boarding ramp from the area, the flight crewmembers were just finishing their pre-starting checks.

A ground crew mechanic removed the locking pins from each of the three landing gear; wrapped them in their red, attention-getting streamers; and tossed them up to the flight engineer, through the open crew entry door. The flight engineer then closed and latched the crew door, and showed the pins to both pilots, saying aloud, "Three pins." The purpose of the pins was to prevent all possibility of the landing gear collapsing before the plane departed, a serious mishap that was very dangerous and would seriously damage the airplane. This was dramatized in the 1951 film *No Highway in the Sky*, starring James

Stewart and Marlene Dietrich, in which Stewart's character, Theodore Honey, wrecks an airplane by deliberately raising its landing gear on the ground. The pins were left in place until they absolutely had to be removed. Crews would physically verify the removal of the pins by having all three actual pins aboard, rather than taking anyone's word for it that they had been removed, lest they should have to return to the airport after discovering in flight that the landing gear could not be retracted. Besides, the pins would be needed to lock the gear at the destination, and the best bet was for the crew to carry their own.

The ground crew mechanic ensured that no people or objects were near the engines, and that the ground crewmember serving as fireman was on hand with his equipment in case an engine caught fire during starting. He then called the flight engineer on a special interphone that he had plugged into a jack on the nose gear strut, saying to him, "Clear to start engines. Wing flaps clear." The flight engineer relayed this to the captain, who in return ordered the flight engineer to start the engines, by which he meant to begin the *process* of starting the engines. Before actually running them, each engine was turned through four full revolutions of its crankshaft with the ignition off, to clear the lower cylinders of any oil that might have accumulated in them overnight. The propellers were geared down in a 16:7 ratio from the crankshafts, so that the engines themselves had to complete slightly over two revolutions to turn the propellers around just once. Taking advantage of this fact, the ground crew mechanic would watch a propeller slowly being rotated until it had revolved at least twice, and would then signal the flight engineer that the safety cycling had been completed. To do this, he simply counted the propeller blades as they passed a given point in succession, until he had counted eight passages. With its four-bladed propellers, this amounted to just two rotations of the propeller on the DC-7, and with its three-bladed propellers, eight blades meant two and two thirds rotations on the Constellation. The standard was eight blades because even though six would have sufficed for the Constellation, it prevented the error of absent-mindedly counting only six for planes with four-bladed props, where the count should have been eight.

The idea of clearing the cylinders of oil before starting an engine was that any appreciable pool of oil could cause a hydraulic lock, and if this were to occur under power, the engine could be damaged. The impulsive movement would be quicker than the speed at which the piston in the flooded cylinder could expel the oil through the exhaust valve if the valve were open, and it might be too forceful for the oil to safely stop the engine if the valve were shut. The piston would slam into the oil and attempt to compress it, but fluids being practically incompressible, the result would at least be that the engine would immediately, jarringly seize, leaving its propeller blades quivering like tuning forks. Usually this did no harm, but it was certainly embarrassing.

The ground crew mechanic called out the blade count, "One blade . . . two blades . . . three blades," and so on to the flight engineer over the interphone until he reached the eighth blade, whereupon the engineer ceased turning the engine starter motor.

The flight engineer finally informed the captain, "Eight blades," and the captain ordered him to start the engine. The engines were numbered from port to starboard, left to right in the order 1-2-3-4, but the starting sequence used by both airlines was 3-4-2-1, right inboard first and left outboard last. For the very first engine to be started, the captain said to the flight engineer, "Start three," or, "Contact three." The reason behind this odd sequence being used, rather than something more obvious like simply starting the engines in order from left to right, was partly logical and partly an obsolete custom carried over from earlier times when it had served a real purpose. It was useful to start one of the inboard engines first because they drove the hydraulic pumps. The hydraulic system could then be brought up to full pressure sooner, and the mechanisms that were operated hydraulically could be checked sooner. Either inboard engine could accomplish this, because the pumps they drove were redundant; only one pump was needed to fully pressurize the system. In this regard the choice of number three over number two was arbitrary, though it had once served a purpose. Passengers boarded on the port side, and in the days where engines were started before everyone had boarded, starting the engine or engines on this side last often spared stragglers from being blasted by prop wash and exhaust fumes, as well as droplets of oil if the engines leaked—and most did. By the fifties, the convention of starting no engines until everyone was aboard had been firmly established, and the custom of starboard first had become obsolete.

One by one the mammoth engines on both planes burst to life, coughing up thick clouds of bluish-white smoke to announce their awakenings. On the United DC-7, Captain Shirley picked up his microphone and switched it over to the public address system. He greeted the passengers with a simple message, something like this: "Good morning, ladies and gentlemen. May I have your attention, please? This is your captain, Robert Shirley, speaking. On behalf of United Air Lines, my crew, and myself, I would like to welcome you aboard Flight 718, nonstop to Chicago. We will be departing in about ten minutes. After passing through a local overcast, we expect clear skies for the remainder of the trip. Our cruising altitude will be 21,000 feet, and our cruising speed will be 288 knots, about 330 miles per hour. We estimate arrival on time in Chicago at 5:25 p.m., Central Daylight Saving Time. Please fasten your seatbelts now and have a pleasant trip."

At about the same time, Captain Gandy made a very similar announcement to his passengers aboard the TWA Constellation. The lighted signs in the main cabins of each plane, which instructed passengers to fasten their seat belts and informed them that there was to be no smoking for the time being, had been switched on, and in the lavatories corresponding messages to return to the cabin had lit up. It was time to go.

As the passengers settled into their seats and strapped on their safety belts, the stewardesses and hostesses walked up the aisles of their respective airplanes and checked to make sure that everyone's belt was properly fastened and tightened, and helped the passengers who did not know how to use them. Once they had completed this task, one of the cabin crewmembers on each plane entered the flight deck and informed the captain that everyone in the main cabin was ready.

On the United DC-7, one of the stewardesses walked to the vacant lounge at the rear, chose a seat, and buckled herself in. The other stewardess folded down the small jump seat in the aisle just forward of the first row of passenger seats and fastened the attached safety belt. On the TWA Constellation the hostesses sat side by side in their jump seats in the main entryway at the rear. Like United, TWA did not sell the lounge seats and did not allow passengers to occupy them for takeoffs or landings, except in rare and extreme circumstances, even though the lounge seats were equipped with safety belts. One stewardess sat alone in the *City of Vancouver's* lounge, and the *Star of the Seine's* seven-place lounge remained entirely empty. The hostesses buckled in by the doorway and prepared to go.

Before departing, each crew needed to contact Los Angeles Ground Control for permission to taxi away from the gate and out toward the runways. Ground control was not so much a facility as a person, an air traffic controller who worked in the control tower. With the exception of the runways themselves, which were handled by another type of controller, it was the ground controller's responsibility to oversee and facilitate, and in some cases literally control the movements of all aircraft on the ground at the airport, as the title implies. It was neither his job nor the job of any other sort of air traffic controller to command a crew, except in emergencies, and so he did not normally control them per se. Rather, controllers diplomatically facilitated and influenced the operating of aircraft that were, strictly speaking, under the sole control of their crews. They did this by advising crews of whether or not there was room physically and legally for them to do what they wanted to do. Usually this would be a response to a pilot's requesting permission for a specific movement or a particular status, like taxiing through a given area, rather than a communication initiated by the controller. A pilot would ask for this permission in the form of asking for a clearance to do or to have whatever it was he wanted, meaning that he was asking the controller to vouch that the way was clear of conflicting aircraft and of regulatory prohibitions. If it were, the controller would inform the pilot that he was clear to do or have the action or status in question. By law, most movements and statuses were allowed only if they had been cleared, so in a passive, indirect sense the controller was in fact in control, but not with any latitude for arbitrariness. He was required to give the requested clearance if the way was clear, just as pilots were required by the same laws to obtain it as their authorization to proceed. The balance of authority and limitations between the two groups was delicate, and both groups were diplomatic in their mutual interactions. Besides diplomacy being gentlemanly and keeping it straight who was in charge of what, it also preserved the mutual faith shared by the two groups so that they could work well together as a team. It was conducive to getting flights into the air and to their destinations safely and efficiently.

At 9:54 TWA 2 got on the radio and called Los Angeles Ground Control to ask for clearance to taxi from the gate to the runways, and the ground controller cleared them routinely. Over the interphone Flight Engineer Breyfogle then asked the ground crew mechanic to remove the wheel chocks. The mechanic complied and in turn informed Breyfogle that he was disconnecting ground power, the generator that had run the plane's electrical systems while its own generators were inoperative. The mechanic then said, "Watch the signal man on your left," unplugged his two-way phone set from the nose gear jack, and moved away. The signaler was ahead and to the left, in plain view of Captain Gandy, and he motioned him to come forward. The captain looked over at the transportation agent, who had been standing by, and the two exchanged salutes. Captain Gandy released the parking brakes, and the *Star of the Seine* began to move. It was 9:55 a.m. PDT, twenty-five minutes behind their scheduled time of departure. Ponderously, the great airplane rolled forward away from the ramp and, guided by the signaler, turned leftward to head toward the airfield. (See Appendix 2 for a diagram of the airport.)

As they passed the far end of the ramp toward the south, TWA 2 turned left again onto the taxiway that led eastward to the thresholds of the two main runways. These were designated 25L and 25R. The numeric part stood for the compass direction of the runway, considered as a multiple of ten degrees. Thus "25" meant, "250 degrees to the nearest ten degrees," nearly west. "L" and "R" meant left and right, as defined looking in the same direction. Straight lines of course extend in two directions, not just one, and to eliminate this ambiguity, runways were named according to the sense in which an incoming or outbound flight would use them. Except in rare cases, takeoffs and landings at Los Angeles were always performed from inland toward the ocean, not the other way around, so the runways were named in the westward sense. Normally, a flight coming in over the ocean would overfly the airport and circle around to head back toward it to land in the preferred direction. In the rare cases where a landing was made from directly over the ocean, however, the runways were called "7L" and "7R," meaning, "Seventy degrees, left hand," and, "Seventy degrees, right hand." (Seventy degrees is of course the direction 180 degrees removed from 250, i.e., the opposite direction.) Therefore 7L was one and the same strip of pavement as 25R, and 7R was 25L. The idea behind this nomenclature was that a pilot coming in to land could determine if a runway was the one on which he had been cleared to land simply by aligning himself with it and noting his compass reading, even if he were totally unfamiliar with the airport. This was a great benefit in safety, especially in conditions of poor visibility where the runway might be seen, but not the number painted on it, no matter how huge or bold.

The preparations for United 718's departure involved essentially the same routine as those for TWA 2. At 9:58 the *City of Vancouver* began to move, thirteen minutes behind their scheduled departure time. They then called the control tower for their taxi clearance, backwards in order since they were already taxiing. The reversal was no great infraction but was bad form in etiquette because it seemed presumptuous and usurped what little control the ground controller actually had. Whether it annoyed him or not, he cleared them to the runways without an objection or a hitch.

Like Captain Gandy, Captain Shirley wheeled his aircraft out toward the airfield himself rather than having his copilot do the steering. It was company policy at both TWA and United for the captain and the first officer not to trade seats on the bigger planes, and for the captain to operate the nose gear steering wheel. This was located on the left side of the cockpit by the captain's seat, and it was one of the few controls not duplicated on the right by the copilot's seat. The captain did the driving.

A minute or two before the *City of Vancouver* began rolling, the *Star of the Seine* reached the area between the thresholds of the two runways and parked there temporarily, out of the way. Controllers called the area the holding pad, because in their frame of reference the area was designed to accommodate aircraft that were standing by or being held, awaiting a clearance to enter one of the runways. Flyers called the area the run-up pad, corresponding with their intention that it be used as a place in which to run the engines up to full power to test them—here there were never any people or planes behind them. The dichotomy was the same in principle as that in which one and the same machine is called a tape player and a tape recorder, depending upon which is intended to be done with it.

TWA 2 had taxied only up to the runways and had stopped there to separately request a clearance to cross the one they had come upon: 25R. They were granted the second clearance and crossed 25R, swinging around into the run-up pad between and behind the runway thresholds, to face westward toward the runways. Captain Gandy reset the parking brakes and called for the run-up, and by 9:57 Breyfogle was performing the tests.

The idea behind separate clearances to taxi up to the runways and to cross either of them was one of safety. Crossing a runway was like crossing an intersection, and it was essential to be sure that no one was coming before entering it. The tower provided the ensuring and notified a crew that it was safe, meaning that nobody was coming in to land, by telling them that they were clear to cross. Similarly, flights were separately cleared to enter a runway, meaning to park on it, parallel with it, and to take off from it. Each movement was individually regulated for the sake of maximum safety. They took one step at a time, and only if someone who could see the whole picture advised them that it was safe.

In pairs, Breyfogle gave his engines nearly full power and examined their performances on his panel of gauges, as well as by their vibrational feel and their sound. He also checked the mechanisms that adjusted the pitch of the propeller blades—basically how big a bite they would take out of the air—and ensured that the engines could be safely shut down if need be. One of the pilots checked the magnetos, of which there were two per engine. Redundancy was a prevalent theme in aircraft design because engine failures in flight were obviously more serious than engine failures in trains or boats, which would slow to a stop rather than crash for lack of power. The engines could run perfectly well with either magneto supplying the energy to the spark plugs, of which there were two per cylinder, and it was a simple matter to check the magnetos one at a time by switching out their partners.

Captain Gandy and First Officer Ritner checked the flight controls—elevators, ailerons and rudders—through their full ranges, and finally Captain Gandy called for the "before takeoff" checklist. They ran through this point by point and were finishing just as the *City of Vancouver* was approaching them. One of the pilots, probably Ritner, called the tower to inform them that TWA 2 was ready for takeoff. It was now a second controller, called the local controller, who handled TWA 2. He was responsible for the active runway and for the airspace in the immediate vicinity of the airport. Airspace was of course a "space in the air," and being a *space,* it was 3-dimensional. An airspace could be localized or stretched out across a hundred miles. Airspaces were located and defined in reference to coordinates or landmarks or radio beacons. In the case of the airspace in the immediate vicinity of the airport, it was probably all three.

Like the ground controller, the local controller worked in the tower cab. He had a good view of the whole airport and of the sky in the surrounding areas in clear weather. He also had a radarscope with which to pinpoint where a plane was, even in bad weather and at night. The time was between 9:59 and 10:00 when the local controller said, "TWA Two, as soon as the United Seven clears, taxi well into position two-five-right. Have a clearance for you in about forty seconds."

The United Seven was the *City of Vancouver*. United 718 had been cleared to cross 25R and was about to pass right in front of the *Star of the Seine* from right to left, taking up a holding position next to them on the run-up pad. As United 718 rolled across in front of TWA 2, Captain Shirley took a quick look at the Constellation on his left and probably saw both Gandy and Ritner in the cockpit. The captains may have saluted each other, but Captain Shirley would have been brief in diverting his attention from driving. In their momentary repose, Gandy and Ritner had a much better chance to look. Perhaps they unconsciously began to assess the man who, in a removed sense, would be their undoing. In that lingering moment after he turned back to look ahead, and while they idly continued to watch him, they might have slipped into the enchanted realm of absent-mindedness and found the intuition for which it makes room. In that fleeting suspension of their wills, they might have felt something mystical about the prior instant in which they and Shirley had looked at each other eye to eye, like a sublime meeting of opposing commanders on the field before a battle, appraising each other and in their countenances defying each other, though these were allies and would destroy each other by accident.

They were not the only ones who briefly made contact with each other. As the DC-7 taxied across in front of the Constellation, many passengers on each of the planes watched the other. Several of them must have seen their counterparts through the cabin windows, and surely some exchanged glances. The morning sun was high enough in the sky at 10:00 a.m. that no one looking toward the east was blinded by it, even without sunglasses. As the *City of Vancouver* passed in front of the *Star of the Seine*, everyone who looked at the Constellation to the left had a clear view of it, and looking westward, away from the sun, it is a foregone conclusion that anyone on the *Star of the Seine* who looked at the DC-7 had a clear view of it, too. Reflective glare may have interfered from just the right angle, but because the DC-7 was in motion, this perfect alignment was only momentary. With the planes so close together, probably not over a hundred feet apart, the passengers could see each other in enough detail to recognize each other from the ramp. A few may even have waved to each other across the space between them.

Undergirding this happy circumstance of each group watching the other embarking upon their journey, there was an ultimate reality that a few of them must have glimpsed but none understood: it was the final moment in which to choose. Their destinies stood in perfect balance, poised on a razor's edge. The entirety of what life had been to all of them and of what it might become in the future was concentrated, focused in that one spot for all to see. They could preserve it or lose it, depending upon whether they desisted or proceeded, and the terms were absolute. There could be no compromise, only a choice between totalities. They could protect their lives and keep everything, or risk themselves and forfeit everything. Probably none realized, that in the power of that momentous interlude on the holding pad, each one's fate was to be decided, and decided by him. Except for the children, any one of them could have forced his own release. If they went, there would be no other chance, no other time when the full situation could be both apprehended and altered. Each group would be on its own, unable to know the other and to grasp their combined destiny until they again came together, but then there would be no choice in the outcome.

United 718 swung around and oriented itself parallel to TWA 2, on their left, while TWA 2 released their parking brakes and rolled forward onto runway 25R, halting in position for takeoff. The local controller called TWA 2 on the radio and said, "TWA Two, cleared for takeoff, contact departure radar on one-twenty-one-one prior to Del Rey."

With this, Flight 2 opened up its throttles and replied, "TWA Two going, on the roll, one-twenty-one point one after . . . prior to Del Rey." (The speaker really did say, ". . . After . . . prior . . ." He corrected himself.) The tremendous engines roared, and the *Star of the Seine* rapidly accelerated. They were going. In fate they were already gone. Their last choice had been made, and their last chance to turn back had passed. At 10:01 a.m. PDT, TWA Flight 2 left the earth, never to return.

The crew of United 718 could have watched the beautiful, white Constellation glide up into the sky over the ocean, but they were performing their own last-minute checks. Surely they at least noticed TWA 2 taking off down the runway; maybe one of them even had a moment's pause, feeling some unusual significance in the sight.

United 718 finished their own run-up and checklists and called the tower, "United Seven Eighteen, ready for takeoff."

The local controller responded, "United Air Lines Seven Eighteen, number two for takeoff, standby one moment." It had been a minute or two since TWA 2 took off, and another flight had finished readying itself in the meantime and was to take off ahead of United 718. After it did, the local controller came back with the instruction, "UAL Seven Eighteen, taxi into position two-five-left." The following brief dialogue ensued:

"It's into position for Seven Eighteen on two-five-left?"

"Roger. Are you closer to two-five-left?"

"Sure am."

"Roger. Taxi into position two-five-left."

United 718 was questioning the clearance, not just repeating it to confirm it. The tower's response was an example of the customary tact and diplomacy with which controllers elicited the cooperation of flight crews. The local controller discreetly persuaded United 718 to draw their own conclusion that 25L was preferable simply by asking,

"Are you closer to two-five-left?" Surely he knew that they were in fact closer to 25L than 25R—he could see them through the tower cab windows.

Normally 25L was used for landings and 25R was used for takeoffs. This was primarily for safety; 25L was farther from the ramps, so in the terrible event that an incoming plane crashed on the airfield while attempting to land, the resulting cavalcade of debris would be much less likely to harm any people or aircraft near the busy ramp area. Takeoffs and landings were the most dangerous phases of flight, and the prospect was a realistic concern, however rare such accidents were. The threat to people at the ramps posed by planes taking off was minimal, simply out of the fact that any flight experiencing a problem would almost certainly be well beyond the ramp area, westward toward the ocean, by the time they were in serious trouble. Another safety reason was that by designating 25L the primary landing runway and 25R the primary takeoff runway, departing planes did not have to cross the landing runway to get to the takeoff runway. This minimized the chance of departing planes accidentally crossing the paths of inbound planes, nearly eliminating the risk of an incoming flight colliding with a plane taxiing across the runway threshold area.

It was not rare for flights to take off from 25L, just unusual, so United 718 questioned it. I find it peculiar and interesting that there was that ruffle in their departure. Maybe they queried the local controller because it had already shaped up to be an odd day, and they were becoming incredulous or resistant to more unexpected happenings. The copilot First Officer Harms had been swapped in at the last moment, they had departed behind schedule, they had jumped the gun at the ramp and begun rolling before being cleared to move, and now they were being directed to the oddball runway instead of the usual one. That's enough in one hour to make anybody object.

It was also possible that whoever was on the radio, probably Harms, was beginning to sense that something was wrong.

CHAPTER 4

UNITED FLIGHT 718 was cleared for takeoff, and at 10:04 a.m. PDT they were streaking down the dashed centerline of runway 25L at over 130 mph. The crew eased back on the control yoke, completing the transfer of the *City of Vancouver's* fifty-three tons from its wheels to its wings, and they became airborne.

Both flights climbed out over the Pacific Ocean through a thin coastal overcast, and each in turn contacted the departure radar service for assistance in leaving the area. Seated before a radarscope, a controller in the tower used short-range radar equipment to monitor air traffic in the vicinity, which he could "see" in about a thirty-mile radius of the airport represented as blips on his fluorescent screen, even through clouds or at night. His job was to continually scrutinize the overall traffic and, with his comprehensive picture, guide pilots in maneuvering through the congestion near Los Angeles. In this capacity, he advised TWA 2 and United 718 of when to make two ninety-degree turns in succession, bringing both of them fully about heading back toward the beaches. At 10:03 TWA 2 broke out of the cloud layer in crystal-clear skies at an altitude of about 2,400 feet, bound for Kansas City. At 10:06 United 718 emerged from the overcast in the clear at an altitude of 2,900 feet, bound for Chicago. (All altitudes in this book are above mean sea level, m.s.l. for short.)

The tragedy that was only an hour and a half away was shaped and brought about by many things, none more evident than an early change that TWA 2 made in their flight plan en route, placing them at United 718's altitude. TWA 2 filed for a cruising altitude of 19,000 feet, and

United 718 filed for a cruising altitude of 21,000 feet. Cruising is the predominant phase of a trip, involving long-duration flight at a specific altitude; while altitude is changing, a flight is said to be ascending or descending, not cruising. TWA 2 in effect proposed spending most of their time at 19,000 feet, and United 718 in effect proposed spending most of their time at 21,000 feet, but as one of a collection of changes, TWA 2 ascended to 21,000 feet instead and remained there. This established one of the necessary conditions for the disaster to take place: namely, that the two planes were on the same level.

This cannot be said to have caused the accident, anymore than setting one number in the combination of a safe can be said to have opened it, but it was obviously one of the contributing factors. Had TWA 2 cruised at their originally planned altitude of 19,000 feet, the accident could not have happened. Little was known for certain of either flight's movements in the last half hour before they collided, which distinguished TWA 2's changing altitude all the more as one of the few definite factors.

What did seem known at the time, and never in reality occurred, was that the two flights were to have crisscrossed each other's courses in close proximity, a short distance beyond the eastern end of the Grand Canyon; their flight plans spelled out crossing courses, and because of happenstance delaying both of them at the airport, unequally, they would meet there rather than miss by a wide margin. This in itself seemed supremely dangerous to most people, despite being far less hazardous than crossing even a regulated intersection in a car. (See Appendix 3 for a map of their proposed courses.) Unfortunately, in the context of this portentous coincidence in their flight plans and in their luck or fate, any maneuver that would place the two flights at the same height appeared deadly, and that made TWA 2's ascent the prime candidate for the active cause of the accident. At the time, it was one of the only things that people could latch onto in their efforts to explain or understand the tragedy, and because of this it acquired an undeserved and exaggerated importance.

Even in the circumstance where their course eventually crossed that of another flight already at the new altitude, TWA 2's changing altitude was an ordinary maneuver executed harmlessly a hundred times a day. In this singular instance, however, the fate of all aboard both planes partly hinged upon it. It had a dual character: it was both trivial and instrumental, not one-sided, nor pivotal, much less one-sidedly pivotal as many at the time regarded it.

*　　*　　*

In 1956 the en route control of air traffic was administered from twenty-six centralized facilities called Air Route Traffic Control Centers (shortened to centers), distributed throughout the nation coast to coast. Correspondingly, there were twenty-six large territories constituting the whole United States, in which the centers had authority over air traffic. The centers were operated by the Civil Aeronautics Administration, forerunner of the FAA, and each one was responsible for the safe and efficient movements of flights along the major routes in its own territory. As a body rather than individually, the staff at one or more centers was called Air Route Traffic Control (ARTC). Primarily, a center's job was to prevent midair collisions and to facilitate an unhindered flow of traffic, the latter to optimize commerce and travel by air. ARTC routinely prevented problems by providing supervision, control, and safe spacing, and because of this they only occasionally had to contend with any serious conflicts.

Information on the identity, plans, and progress of a flight was relayed by proprietary telephone and Teletype lines from one center to the next along the flight's route, heralding its approach. The centers also received notices of this sort from airport departure control, airline dispatchers and radio operators, and special commercial and government radio service stations set up expressly to communicate with flights. Controllers in neighboring centers would confer over the phone with each other about pending decisions pertaining to some of the flights that would travel between their adjacent territories. The centers had radio equipment, too, with which they could talk to flight crews en route, but they used it for this purpose only sparingly. Long-range radar, with which the centers could have reliably fixed the positions of the actual planes in the sky, in a concrete and immediate way akin to seeing them, had been conceived but not yet built. Aside from three rudimentary, semireliable installations that served civil aviation in the eastern third of the country, long-range radar was a military device, and the centers operated without it. They relied instead on calculations that could be off by several miles, to plot the locations of aircraft.

At each center, controllers printed vital information about each flight within or approaching their territory on a small piece of paper called a flight progress strip. At their workstations, they had specialized bulletin boards that were designed to help them keep track of many flights at once, by systematically displaying these pieces of paper. The boards were organized so as to schematically represent the center's territory, and as a flight progressed, the controller correspondingly repositioned its flight progress strip to represent the movement. This enabled him to spot any possible conflicts at a glance, and from that to safely redistribute the traffic.

*   *   *

First TWA 2 and then United 718 reported to departure radar control that they were on top of the overcast, and both were instructed to contact Los Angeles ARTC on another frequency, in order to receive their en route clearances. An en route clearance amounted to express, itemized approval of a flight plan, possibly with alterations. ARTC cleared both flights' plans as filed.

Each flight's route followed what were called airways for a time and then broke off to follow a nearly direct line to the ultimate destination. The airways were imaginary, precisely defined aerial highways, ten miles wide, which could be drawn on a map and accurately followed by navigation. They were marked out in the sky by invisible radio beacons, analogous to the visible dashed line down the center of a road, which could be detected by navigational radio equipment aboard a plane. In terms of freedom of movement, the airways differed significantly from terrestrial roads in that they were three-dimensional spaces rather than flat surfaces; an airway was shaped like an elongated box. A plane could be at any number of altitudes and still be on the airway, so long as it stayed within the confines of the imaginary box.

The airways were named with a word followed by a number, and all of them were straight or segmented paths connecting navigational reference points to each other. On a map the whole country appeared to be randomly sprinkled with dots and crisscrossed with straight lines connecting the dots in a complex, abstract geometric figure. The lines were the airways, and the dots were the reference points. Many of the navigational reference points were VHF navigational radio stations, the latest equipment in the 1950s. The airways that connected these modern stations to each other were called victor airways, "victor" being the radio communications word standing for the letter "V," which in turn signified VHF. These airways were named Victor 1, Victor 2, and so on. The remaining airways were given the names of colors followed by a number.

United 718's plans were to follow an airway called Green 5 eastward for about 125 miles to the airspace over Palm Springs, California, where they would turn off and leave the airways to fly "off the road," directly to and beyond the airspace over Needles, California, at the state line between California and Arizona. TWA 2's flight plan called for them to follow Green 5 eastward from Los Angeles for about thirty miles, where they would turn onto another airway called Amber 2. They would then take Amber 2 for roughly ninety miles northeastward to the airspace over Daggett, California, where they would turn and leave the airways, to fly directly to and beyond the airspace over Lake Mohave, near the place where California, Nevada, and Arizona meet. (These mileages and all others in this book are in ordinary statute miles, not nautical miles.)

Immediately after receiving their en route clearance from Los Angeles ARTC, however, TWA 2 requested a change in the route they would follow to Daggett. They asked for Victor 210, a single segment to replace the two segments on Green 5 and Amber 2, and ARTC granted them this without a hitch. Taking the shortest path rather than the dogleg from Los Angeles to Daggett saved them five or six miles, or about two minutes' flying time at their comparatively low forward speed while climbing. For about the next seventeen minutes, TWA 2 made no further radio contact and simply proceeded toward Daggett.

Other than at the beginning or the end of a trip, flights did not usually contact ARTC directly. At the time, ARTC lacked both the communications facilities and the personnel to inaugurate a cross-country radio network directly linked to all of the flights in the sky—at any given moment there were simply too many of them. Instead, flights would contact ARTC through an intermediary, and in the case of TWA 2, this was their own company radio operator. Before reaching Daggett, TWA 2 called their company radio operator at Los Angeles International Airport to request a clearance for a new cruising altitude of 21,000 feet, two thousand feet higher than the altitude that ARTC had cleared in their original proposal. The radio operator in turn telephoned the Los Angeles ARTC Center to relay TWA 2's request. The time was 10:21.

To understand the situation that developed, it is necessary to have an understanding of the rules by which flights were conducted, and the corresponding responsibilities of ARTC. Most fundamentally, there were two ways to fly an airplane: namely, by piloting it visually, which is where flying began, and by following the indications of instruments, which came later. No doubt the first instrument any pilot used was a simple magnetic compass, and this innovation probably came right after the first time one of them got lost, which couldn't have been far behind the first time that one of them dared to fly beyond the boundaries of his ability to see where he came from. Eventually, pilots had amassed a collection of enough instruments that, aside from taking off and landing, they could fly without being able to see where they were going.

As flying grew, so did government regulating of it, and two sets of rules developed, one applying to visual flight and the other applying to flight that for some portion of the trip might be done blind, using only instruments. Plainly enough, these were called Visual Flight Rules and Instrument Flight Rules, and the flights to which they pertained were called VFR flights and IFR flights. The rules stipulated that the crew of a VFR flight be able to see what was around them all of the time, throughout an area large enough that the flight could be safely conducted solely through visual means, and required them to consistently ensure this by conforming to a set of standards that defined "an area large enough." IFR flights were allowed to proceed on instruments alone and so were not required to be able to see where they were going all of the time. For example, an IFR flight could pass through a cloud even though once inside they were flying blind or nearly blind, like driving in a fog. In such a case they needed to be kept apart from other planes by someone who could "see," and that was ARTC.

Because VFR flights were always able to see where they were going, they didn't strictly need any help in avoiding colliding with other planes. They were able to take care of themselves and were permitted to be on their own for most of their trip. In keeping with this, ARTC was not responsible for VFR flights, so ARTC normally took no active steps to predict or prevent collisions involving VFR flights, not even those that might occur on the airways, and not even those that might involve an IFR flight as the second plane. One exception to this was of course that if there seemed to be even a small threat of a collision, they would do everything possible to avert it. This situation was exceedingly rare, however, because most of the time ARTC had no way of knowing, and usually did not even pay attention to VFR flights. In one respect, when a crew asked for VFR status, they were implicitly requesting permission to fly without supervision or aid, and when ARTC granted them VFR status, they were condoning this request.

Most airline pilots, however, wanted a little supervision, for the greater safety it afforded them and their passengers. By the 1950s the days of brazen, audacious flying had already passed, primarily because there was no longer a need to be daring. In the early days of commercial flying, pilots took great pride in just reaching their destinations—it was fairly common for pilots to become lost, especially in bad weather and at night. Sometimes they would run out of fuel before re-establishing their bearings and would have to land on a country road or in a field. There were even instances of a plane landing on the streets of a town. In that era, pilots were a rougher breed that would have been in good company with explorers and frontier trappers. As time passed, however, progressive improvements in aviation made flying less of an experiment and more of an organized enterprise. Due to sophisticated navigational instruments attuned to stations on the ground, and due to two-way radio, it had become difficult to get lost. Also thanks to two-way radio, the hazard of flying into unknown weather or weather at odds with the forecasts had nearly been eliminated, since flight crews could ask for and receive weather updates en route. And pressurized cabins had made it possible to fly over most bad weather during the cruising phase of a trip. Precariously plowing through storm clouds and being pelted with hail or tossed about by strong turbulence were things of the past. For the most part, flying was no longer dangerous, and for the pilots, it was no longer an adventure most of the time. It had become uneventful and routine, and although most pilots had retained their independence and self-reliance, they had also become somewhat conservative. For them foolishness had never been a substitute for bravery, and where there was no need to take a risk, they avoided it.

This is where IFR flights came in. Most airline pilots filed IFR flight plans most of the time, because ARTC accorded a valuable measure of protection to IFR flights. During the time on a trip in which an IFR flight was on the airways, rather than in the uncontrolled airspaces between the airways, ARTC would keep them safely spaced apart from all other IFR flights in their vicinity. ARTC was responsible only for the airways and the immediate areas around airports, not the uncontrolled airspaces, and so except in the rarest of cases where there seemed to be a significant possibility of a collision, they made no active efforts to prevent collisions in uncontrolled airspace, not even when both planes were IFR flights. The meaning of uncontrolled airspace was, literally, airspace in which ARTC exercised no control.

This state of affairs was not nearly as dangerous as it sounds. The first responsibility of every pilot was to fly his plane safely, to the utmost of his independent ability, irrespective of whether or not anybody was helping him. Secondarily, most of the time there was no need or use for any help from the ground, because the skies were usually clear enough to permit seeing other planes in plenty of time to avoid them, and wherever the skies were *not* clear enough to permit observation, VFR flights were barred from going. In conditions of poor or nonexistent visibility, IFR flights were in danger only of other IFR flights, and on the airways this was addressed by ARTC.

Off the airways, if an IFR flight entered weather that prevented them from seeing where they were going, they were taking a significant risk: another IFR flight might be nearby, also blinded, and no one would realize it—not the crew because they couldn't see, and not ARTC because they weren't looking. ARTC would not be actively involved with them again until they re-entered controlled airspace. For these reasons, only very rarely did the captain of an IFR flight elect to fly blind off airways. He might fly blind on the airways, but off the airways he would maintain his visibility. To quote a retired TWA captain from the era, "You would never fly through a cloud off airways, even IFR, because some *other* idiot might be in there."

Both TWA Flight 2 and United Flight 718 were IFR flights. ARTC was unable to approve TWA 2's request for 21,000 feet because it could not ensure their safety at that altitude. Los Angeles ARTC could have made the decision by itself, but conscientiously in turn called Salt Lake City ARTC on the phone to ask their opinion, since TWA 2 would soon exit Los Angeles' area of responsibility and enter Salt Lake's.

Salt Lake ARTC was concerned that Flight 2 would have what was termed ill-defined separation from another IFR flight, while crossing the ten-mile width of an airway called Red 15. That other IFR flight was United 718.

Red 15 ran southeastward from Las Vegas, Nevada to Prescott, Arizona, and was at that moment about 200 hundred miles distant from both flights, but both of their proposed courses crossed it. Both flights had been cleared for flying direct for major portions of their trips, predominantly traveling very long, straight-line routes to their destinations rather than the circuitous, multisegmented routes along airways. What this meant was that for the most part each would be flying in uncontrolled airspace, where they were free to do pretty much as they pleased, including changing course. There were several expanses of uncontrolled airspace between Red 15 and the places where the two flights were to leave the airways, comprising roughly 125 miles of off-airways flying for each of them, so even though they would both have to cross Red 15 somewhere, it was impossible to predict where.

Were both flights to follow the most obvious courses, namely the direct routes they suggested in their flight plans, they would cross Red 15 at spots about thirty miles apart, and probably not even simultaneously, but with TWA 2 exiting Red 15 just as United 718 was entering. The trouble was that there was no practical way of knowing if the two would do what was most obvious. Both of them would have to be queried as to their intended maneuvers, and because TWA 2's request was not an emergency, this would be done through the awkward, time-consuming method of using the intermediary radio operators.

The only simple way that the Salt Lake controller could ensure, for his part, that TWA 2 and United 718 would not collide on Red 15, was for him to disapprove of their being at the same altitude. He did not yet have any authority over either flight, but the Los Angeles controller agreed, and called Los Angeles TWA radio back on the phone to say, "Advisory TWA Two, unable approve two-one thousand," almost as though he were speaking to a member of the crew rather than a middleman.

The TWA radio operator replied, "Just a minute, I think he wants a thousand on top . . . yes, a thousand on top until he can get it." Evidently, the TWA radio man wanted to double check his own record of what TWA 2 had said to him; some minutes had passed since then, and he had surely been busy with other communications in the meantime.

The phrase one thousand on top referred to a special altitude clearance available to IFR flights, which required them to stay at least one thousand feet above any and all clouds that they flew over, for as long as they followed the airways, but it did not specify any particular altitude. The clearance also authorized them to change altitude at their own discretion on the airways so that they could fulfill the requirement.

Los Angeles ARTC asked the TWA radio operator, "Is he a thousand on top at present?" to which the operator simply responded, "Yes." ARTC then said to him, "ARTC clears TWA Two maintain at least one thousand feet on top. Advise TWA Two his traffic is United Seven Eighteen, a DC-7, Needles direct Painted Desert direct Durango, estimating Needles 0957 PST." This conversation ended at 9:32 PST in the standard time used in aviation, or 10:32 PDT, the Daylight Saving Time on the average person's watch in California. The TWA radio operator had initially called ARTC on behalf of TWA 2 at 10:21; it had taken eleven minutes to work out a change in altitude clearance for TWA 2. The radio operator relayed the clearance, and Flight 2 repeated it to him verbatim. He also gave Flight 2 the information about United 718, to which Captain Gandy replied simply, "Traffic received."

The radio operator later testified that in addition to ARTC's traffic advisory about United 718, he told Flight 2 that the United flight was at 21,000 feet, which he had surmised. ARTC did not include this point in its message, for one because it was incorrect: United 718 was still climbing at that time. But what really matters here is that with the cruising altitude included, the traffic advisory could only have conveyed a complete, accurate impression to Captain Gandy of where and when to expect United 718.

ARTC tape recorded all of its vocal communications, both what controllers said and what was said to them, whether over the telephone or over the radio, so the dialogue between Los Angeles ARTC and TWA radio was perfectly preserved. However, TWA radio did not tape record its own communications, and airliners did not have cockpit voice recorders. The dialogue between the TWA radio operator and TWA 2 was recorded only in the form of being one-sidedly typewritten. Using a typewriter, the radio operator transcribed whatever was said to him by a flight and by ARTC, but he did not ordinarily type what he himself said—his function was to relay messages, not originate them, and he typed what he received only in order to have it exactly right when he passed it along. He then simply read it over the air to the flight it was for, or he relayed it by telephone to ARTC. Were he to have routinely typed his own vocalizations, he would only have produced a monotonous and useless string of redundancies, typing everything twice. When the flight or ARTC responded, he typed that, too, and that was all. This documentation later showed that TWA 2 repeated the new altitude clearance as ARTC gave it. Unfortunately there was no physical record of what exactly the operator told TWA 2 about United 718, except in the implicit sense that he typed what he *should* have told them. What would have proved that he read ARTC's message to TWA 2 exactly as given was TWA 2's verbatim repeating of it, which he would have typed, but that never happened. Captain Gandy did not repeat the message, as he had done with the clearance. All that survived was the radio operator's *recollection* of what he himself had said, and the typed record of Gandy's two cryptic words, "Traffic received."

This is a crucially important point. With the full advisory information about United 718, Captain Gandy should have been able to easily determine that he and they would be in close proximity near the eastern end of the Grand Canyon, which is where they collided. To believe that Gandy had the full advisory makes it all the more incredible that the tragedy occurred, and conversely, the fact that the tragedy occurred makes it compelling to believe that Gandy did not have the full advisory.

I am not implying or suggesting an answer, nor do I even have one firmly in mind, but the questions have to be asked because they are so important: What exactly did the radio operator tell TWA 2 about United 718, and what exactly did Captain Gandy hear? Lamentably, because there is no record of what was said, much less of what was heard, and because there never was, it appears that uncertainty will remain the only overriding truth in these two questions. No one can ever discover for certain what was communicated, so that in this respect it will remain a mystery how the accident was able to happen. The haunting possibility that Captain Gandy did not have all the information on United 718 will linger forever. The one thing that seems certain is that the captain listened directly to the advisory, whatever it contained, if not also the clearance. According to the TWA radio operator's later testimony, referenced in the CAB report, he recognized Captain Gandy's voice as the one saying, "Traffic received." Apparently Gandy was letting Ritner do the flying ~ probably for more experience ~ and operating the radio himself.

* * *

Clearances applied on the airways, not in uncontrolled airspace. ARTC had authority over the airways, as the name Air *Route* Traffic Control denotes, but not over the uncontrolled airspaces. More specifically, ARTC had the authority to issue or deny clearances to do this or that on the airways, not in uncontrolled airspace. Because of this, a clearance for a particular cruising altitude was in reality merely a clearance to fly at that altitude on the airways, with the implication that the flight would probably maintain it in the uncontrolled airspaces between the airways. That implicit meaning was not binding, not through the clearance or through any regulations—off airways, a flight could choose its own altitude, at its own discretion.

Altitude clearances, whether for a specific altitude or for one thousand on top, applied only to IFR flights. A normal, specific altitude clearance authorized an IFR flight to occupy a particular level on the airways and obligated them to stay at that level for as long as they remained on the airways. It also required them to be at the cleared altitude whenever they entered an airway from the uncontrolled airspace between the airways, whether to merge into it and follow it, or simply to cross it. Irrespective of their altitude clearance, once an IFR flight left the airways, they were entitled to choose their own cruising altitude from among several established options and to keep it for as long as they did not re-enter controlled airspace.

The one thousand on top clearance extended an IFR flight's freedom of choice to the airways themselves, affording them the same series of consecutive altitudes from which they could choose off the airways, while they were still *on* the airways, outlined according to what was called the Quadrantal Rule. The Quadrantal Rule was named in reference to the four quadrants of the compass, and it delineated permissible cruising altitudes as follows: odd thousand-foot altitudes for flights with magnetic compass courses between zero degrees and eighty-nine degrees; odd thousands plus five hundred feet for flights on magnetic courses from ninety degrees to 179 degrees; even thousands on courses from 180 degrees to 269 degrees; and even thousands plus five hundred from 270 degrees to 359 degrees. All IFR flights, regardless of altitude clearance, were required to conform to this scheme off airways, as were IFR flights operating under a one thousand on top clearance, even on the airways. The freedom to choose an altitude was also the obligation to choose one, and to select it from the very small group of very specific options designated by the CAA.

Flight 2's course was roughly forty degrees magnetic from Los Angeles to Daggett, and it was to have been roughly sixty degrees magnetic from Daggett to Kansas City, putting them in the first quadrant for the whole trip; their choices were 17,000 feet, 19,000 feet, 21,000 feet, 23,000 feet and so on, both higher and lower. Much higher, however, and the airplane would have handled poorly. Much lower, and the air might have been turbulent, discomforting the passengers. These four altitudes were generally the most desirable ones for flying a 1049 Constellation in the first quadrant.

The performance of an airplane depends largely upon the density of the air in which it flies. In thicker air the propellers produce more of an impetus, because they have more to push on, and the ailerons, elevators, and rudder or rudders are more effective for much the same reason. As an airplane ascends, the air becomes thinner, and the plane gradually loses its performance, with one important exception: in the thinner air it can fly faster at a given power output, because the air offers less resistance to an object moving through it. To achieve this on a prop liner, the pitch of the propeller blades has to be altered so that they take a bigger bite out of the air, to compensate for the air being a less substantial medium on which to push. On the other side, a pertinent example of the decline in a plane's capabilities is that as it climbs, it progressively loses its ability to climb. The higher it is, the harder it is for it to lift itself any higher.

One measure of a plane's capabilities is called its service ceiling. This is the upper limit of its useful performance. In rough terms, its service ceiling is the altitude by which it has forfeited nearly all of its sea level climbing ability. It could still climb even higher, but so slowly as to serve little or no practical purpose. The service ceiling of the 1049 Constellation was 23,000 feet, with this qualification: the plane was rated in terms of what were called standard atmospheric conditions. These were global, annual means of temperature, pressure, and density for the air at any particular altitude.

On the day of the accident, the high-level atmosphere in which TWA 2 cruised was forecast to be warmer than standard air of that altitude. Assuming that this turned out to be correct, the air was correspondingly also less dense than standard, on the principle that heating a body of air causes it to expand (unless it is sealed within a rigid container). Captain Gandy expected this because he had read the forecasts at the dispatch office. The air surrounding TWA 2 while they cruised would be of a density associated with standard air at an altitude higher than theirs. They would incur the deficiencies in performance that characterized their service ceiling, without having to ascend that high. Knowing this in advance may have been enough by itself for the captain to rule out 23,000 feet from the outset.

Captain Gandy may also have been more particular than the average pilot. He was a veteran flyer, having accumulated a total of 14,922 flying hours in his career. He had conducted over a thousand flights in just the model 1049 Constellation, representing nearly half of his total flying hours. He must have been familiar with its every nuance, no matter how subtle. He must have known intimately how responsive the plane should be, how crisply it should turn, how willingly it should move under his touch when he trimmed it, and so on. In his refined sense of discrimination, he might well have avoided 23,000 feet routinely, not just when the air was especially rarefied.

One way or another, he eliminated 23,000 feet, and of course 17,000 feet was out because he wanted to ascend, not descend, and 19,000 feet was the level that he decided against in the first place. This left only 21,000 feet as a reasonable cruising altitude, the very altitude he had wanted from ARTC to begin with. Incredible as it may seem, Captain Gandy was free to choose this altitude, despite the fact that ARTC had just declined to approve it. The regulatory scheme by which this seemingly bizarre situation could have prevailed, and the sense that it actually made, is examined in Chapter 6.

The problem Captain Gandy faced was that his flight plan clearance to cruise at 19,000 feet authorized him to cross the airways only at 19,000 feet, and it required him to cross them only at that altitude. To abide by that he would have to repeatedly vary his altitude in order to cruise higher in between the airways, or entirely forsake the higher altitude he honestly wanted in order to keep his cruising altitude consistent. Of the options available to him off the airways, 21,000 feet evidently best suited his purposes, so he sought to be cleared for this altitude *on* the airways. This would have enabled him to steadily maintain 21,000 feet from California all the way to Missouri. ARTC was unable to give this to him, but they were able to grant him a one thousand on top clearance, under which he was entitled to adopt 21,000 feet on the airways of his own accord.

At the time of the accident, newspapers all across the country promulgated the view that TWA 2 had asked for 21,000 feet, and then for one thousand on top, in order to get above the clouds and the turbulence that was typically in or near them. This was a reasonable explanation, because weather did account for most requests for the one thousand on top clearance. But Captain Gandy did not volunteer his motive to justify his request, nor did the TWA radio operator question him, nor did ARTC ask what his reason was, so there was no record expressly showing why he wanted to change his altitude clearance. The sensible belief that weather was the reason was actually just an assumption, and it was probably an incorrect assumption.

First of all, a clearance for a higher altitude could not have helped Flight 2 until about the time they were in the immediate area of Daggett, because they could not have attained their originally proposed altitude before that, and thus could not have begun making use of the freedom to climb any higher, until then. When they requested a cruising altitude of 21,000 feet, they were over fifty miles from Daggett, at an altitude of about 14,000 feet and still climbing. If weather was a factor, it had to have been the weather east of Daggett.

The weather reports for the region encompassing TWA 2's course from about midway between Daggett and Los Angeles, all the way to the eastern edge of California, indicated clear skies and unrestricted visibility, with only a few patchy altocumulus clouds near 15,000 feet in the southern part of the Mojave Desert. It is possible that one or more of these characteristically small formations was along Flight 2's course past Daggett, but it is highly unlikely because there were very few of them. And even if one or two were present, it should have been easy to fly around them because they were small, or over them because of their modest altitude.

Flight 2's proposed route across northern Arizona would keep them just to the south of the Grand Canyon, but it was typical for flights passing nearby the canyon to detour over it for sightseeing. These brief side trips, adding at most a few minutes to a flight's time in the air, were so common that they had become tradition and were expected by passengers and informally planned by crews, even though they were not indicated in written flight plans. In TWA 2's particular case, a sightseeing detour would likely not even add two minutes to their time in the air, because they would not be going out of their way. Flight 2 was behind schedule, and Captain Gandy may have decided to skip the sightseeing to conserve their time, but assuming that he at least left the possibility open, the weather over the Grand Canyon was important to him. Most probably the area that interested him was a west-east corridor, about forty miles wide, encompassing both the canyon and TWA 2's proposed course. At 10:21, the time they were asking for 21,000 feet, there were no buildups anywhere in this corridor; the only clouds that existed of any type were nearly a mile below 19,000 feet. Even if they could have seen halfway across northern Arizona from their location in California, there was nothing to see.

In my opinion, their motivation for requesting 21,000 feet was not the weather, and their motivation for requesting one thousand on top was fairly obviously to be able to cruise at 21,000 feet.

This leads to an even more important question than what motivated their ascent: why did Flight 2 especially want to cruise across the country at 21,000 feet rather than 19,000 feet? Throughout Arizona, the weather was not a problem. There was a lower overcast covering a large area far beneath them during the last ten or fifteen minutes for which they were in flight, with its top surface at 15,000 feet, but that was irrelevant. The only buildup that manifested on their path in Arizona was a cumulonimbus cloud that formed gradually near the eastern end of the Grand Canyon *after* TWA 2 asked for 21,000 feet. Except for at this far end, the entire corridor of interest to them remained clear at their altitude, and for over a mile below, for the whole time they were flying in it. And as already discussed, the weather in California wasn't a problem either.

I believe that they wanted to fly higher in order to save time.

Flight 2 had departed at 9:55, twenty-five minutes behind their scheduled departure time of 9:30, and this of course promised to make them equally late in arriving at Kansas City unless they did something about it. As already noted, up to a point the higher an airplane flies, the faster it flies, at a given power setting. The thinner air offers less opposition, so the plane speeds up. By cruising at 21,000 feet instead of 19,000 feet, Flight 2 stood to gain five or six miles per hour, which would save them another four or five minutes over the entire cruising phase of their trip. They could gain this advantage without pushing their engines any harder. But this, even combined with the two minutes saved by taking the shortcut of Victor 210, only began to be worthwhile. Saving six or seven minutes out of twenty-five was an improvement, but still not nearly enough.

I believe that they had a third strategy, already planned: using more than standard cruise power once they leveled off into the cruising phase of their trip. This was allowed by company policy in order to keep schedule. To quote the TWA Constellation Flight Crew Operating Manual from that period, "Up to maximum cruise powers may be used on scheduled continental operation, SCD, to maintain schedule." SCD stood for subject to captain's discretion.

At maximum cruise power, their speed would be increased by 4 percent over that at standard cruise power, for a fixed altitude. At 21,000 feet, their speed would be increased by 2 percent over that at 19,000 feet, for a fixed power setting. The product of the two factors was about a 6 percent increase in speed. Applied to a cruising phase of normally just under four hours in their five-hour trip to Kansas City, they could save about thirteen minutes, which combined with the two minutes saved on Victor 210 would save them fifteen minutes, putting them in Kansas City only ten minutes late.

This was a worthwhile improvement.

It would satisfy the crew's pride in their professionalism, it would satisfy the dispatch office at Kansas City, and it would satisfy the passengers. It would also prevent a frustrating or embarrassing cascade of late arrivals. The new crew taking over at Kansas City could not have made up the lost time on the shorter legs to St. Louis and Washington, D.C., no matter what strategies they might have employed. Reducing their burden to ten minutes would satisfy them, too.

But why did Captain Gandy make so much importance of changing his altitude *clearance*, when right after passing Daggett he would be in uncontrolled airspace and free to choose whatever altitude he wanted anyway? Flight 2 achieved 19,000 feet only about four minutes before reaching Daggett. Like a car driver harmlessly beginning to speed up a short distance before he reaches a speed limit sign indicating an increase, they might have tentatively continued ascending over the next four minutes in anticipation of leaving the airways and being free to keep climbing. Thus a new clearance wouldn't have affected what they were doing then. And if they had strictly adhered to regulations, the more likely possibility, they would have leveled off and held briefly, until they left the airways, after which they could have resumed climbing. After a pause of only about four minutes, they could have finished going up to 21,000 feet.

The answer must be that they wanted to be able to *stay* there once they got there. For this they needed either a specific clearance for 21,000 feet or a one thousand on top clearance. Without either of these, they could still have ascended to 21,000 feet after passing Daggett, but they would have had to return to 19,000 feet before crossing the airways that ran north and south near and along the juncture between California and Arizona. The next airway they would come to was Red 15, and the stretch of uncontrolled airspace between it and the state line was narrow enough in that area that they likely couldn't have regained 21,000 feet within it, before having to begin their descent back to 19,000 feet to cross Red 15, so they probably would have resigned themselves to remaining at 19,000 feet until they were past Red 15. After crossing Red 15, Flight 2 could have ascended again and flown the next expanse of uncontrolled airspace at their preferred altitude, only to have to descend again to 19,000 feet before crossing the next airway after Red 15, and so on. Besides being clumsy, this vacillating would cost them much of the time they were trying to save. Each time they crossed an airway, they would lose speed due to flying in denser air, and they would be slowed even more in climbing back up to 21,000 feet. And on top of this, the passengers would be discomforted and inconvenienced each time. It was just a bad idea, all the way around. Silly as it might seem, this rollercoaster ride was the only way they could legally cross the country at 21,000 feet if their clearance stood at 19,000 feet.

Surely Captain Gandy wanted to cruise across the country at 21,000 feet in order to save time, but this conclusion cannot surpass the facts and inferences from which it came. He stood to save quite a bit of time by flying at that altitude, he undoubtedly realized that he was behind schedule, and he certainly cared to try keeping his schedule—but what else might have motivated him? The external considerations were clear, but his attitudes and his other thoughts were his private domain and might have influenced his decision as much as anything else.

This point was very aptly put by a retired TWA captain named Robert C. Sherman, a contemporary of Gandy's who helped a great deal in this book. He was a very astute, pragmatic man, with a great faculty for deftly cutting through complexity and confusion with common sense that astounded me, not so much because of his insightfulness, even though that was impressive, as because of the fact that it had never occurred to *me*. The captain also had a wonderfully subtle knack for unobtrusively weaving sarcasm into his rhetoric, and a wry sense of humor that anyone with even a little bit of cleverness could truly relish. After long discussions of the subject, the captain simply and sincerely suggested, "Maybe Gandy just liked that altitude."

CHAPTER 5

AT 10:34, FLIGHT 2 passed Daggett, California, leaving the airways and entering uncontrolled airspace. Their altitude was then 20,000 feet, and they were still climbing. These facts the flight reported to the TWA company radio operator at Los Angeles, who relayed the information to Salt Lake ARTC two minutes later. At about 10:39, TWA 2 achieved what was to be their en route cruising altitude, 21,000 feet. They leveled out and for a short while cruised at climb power, transferring energy from the work of lifting the airplane to the work of accelerating it forward, to build up speed. The crew then eased back on the throttles from climb power to maximum cruise power or perhaps a little less, and they settled in for what was to have been about a four-hour steady trip to eastern Kansas, where they would have begun a gradual descent toward Kansas City, Missouri.

The "fasten seatbelt" and "no smoking" signs were normally turned off at some time during climbing on any airliner, unless there was some hazard such as bad weather or mechanical trouble. The weather was fine and the plane was operating perfectly. Once the signs were turned off, many passengers lit up cigarettes and some left their seats, even though it was more decorous and sensible to remain seated until the plane reached cruising altitude, because turbulence was more likely at the lower altitudes even in clear skies.

On the way up everyone's hearing became gradually dulled, while concomitantly the subtle and familiar yet strange sensation of lightheadedness caught them by surprise and slowly mounted; then their ears popped and their hearing was restored. The cabin pressure was maintained at about the equivalent of 7,000 feet above sea level in cruise, and the change from sea level pressure took place gradually in climb with much the same effect as that of driving up into the mountains. By the time they reached cruising altitude, the experience had subsided and nearly everyone felt nearly normal, though still a touch lightheaded.

Soon afterward, Miss Armbruster and Miss Davis began serving the midmorning snack that was customary on Flight 2. Many passengers probably welcomed the refreshment after their somewhat taxing delay of nearly half an hour on the ground. It consisted of cookies or biscuits or sweet rolls, served with a beverage of coffee or tea, or just plain water if anyone wanted it. Milk was also available for the children.

Most of the passengers felt relieved through being entirely free to get up and through the enjoyment of their snack, and that prompted a good deal of friendly, happy conversation and activity—people moving to the lounge or readjusting their seating positions, retrieving things from the overhead baggage racks, trading seats in order to give or to receive a better view of the sky, and so on. Many of them probably also felt elated in the special way particular to that era, which came from simply taking note of where they were: on an airplane, flying. Flying was regarded as special, as a privilege and an honor. Most people dressed up for a trip by air in their best clothes.

Flight 2 was perfectly balanced. Exactly half of the passengers were female, and exactly half were male. Seventy persons had gotten on at Los Angeles, of whom five were the acting crew; one was a crewmember as a technicality and had no duties, and sixty-four were passengers. Eleven of these were children, ranging from three weeks old to fourteen years old.

The Kite children, nine-year-old Sharon and six-year-old Linda, probably had no end of excited things to say to each other, to their parents, and to other passengers about the vacation they and their parents had just had at Disneyland. The girls had looked forward to the trip for months; it was the dream of every child to go to Disneyland,

and they were fortunate enough to have had the chance. The Kite family was from Prairie Village, Kansas, adjacent to Kansas City, Missouri, on the opposite side of the state line. Joseph Kite worked for TWA in Kansas City as an administrative assistant in construction and design. Peachie Marie was pregnant with what was to be their third child.

Mrs. Lois Laxton and her five-year-old son, Michael, were flying together to St. Louis, from where they were going to the town of Cape Girardeau, Missouri. The Laxton family had formerly lived there and was planning on moving back once Mrs. Laxton could find a house for them. She and her husband, Howard, had suffered a terrible heartbreak seven months earlier, around Thanksgiving of '55, when their three-month-old baby died, but they had had the courage to persevere in building a family; Mrs. Laxton was pregnant again.

Richard Payne was TWA's reservations agent-in-charge at Los Angeles, and was taking his two children, nine-year-old Monica and fourteen-year-old Richard, to the farm of their grandparents in Iowa for a summer vacation. Originally, Mrs. Payne had intended to escort the children, but the plans were changed and Mr. Payne went instead. The family was from Kansas City and had moved to the west coast five years before. Mrs. Payne's parents, Mr. and Mrs. Lester Nelson of Slater, Iowa, near Des Moines, were looking forward to a wonderful time with their grandchildren, but instead they would live through the most horrible scenario that could be conjured, and eight days hence they would travel to Flagstaff, Arizona, for the funeral of their daughter's whole family.

Helen Crewse had been a cook in the TWA flight kitchen at Los Angeles since 1950. She was working that day, preparing meals to be put aboard outbound flights. Her husband, Chester, and preschool daughter, Helen, were on Flight 2, flying free of charge on passes granted to members of TWA employees' families. The family lived in Redondo Beach, California. Later in the day Mrs. Crewse was told at work that her husband and daughter's plane had disappeared, and she started screaming uncontrollably.

Mr. Ira Braughton was a TWA aircraft mechanic at the company's overhaul base in Kansas City, and he had been with TWA for ten years. His wife, Esther, and their two daughters—Connie, age six, and Linda, age nine—were flying home on passes, returning from a vacation they had spent in California.

David and Geoffry Robinson, ages eleven and nine, were on their way to visit their father in Kansas City, chaperoned by their mother, Jeanette Robinson. She was divorced from the boys' father, and she and her sons lived in Santa Barbara, California.

Howard Maag was an infant, only three weeks old, and was on board with his mother and father, Claire and John Maag. The Maags were taking their new arrival to meet his grandmother in Sappington, Missouri, just outside of St. Louis. It would have been her first time seeing her new grandson. The Maags were from Los Angeles, where Mr. Maag was a real estate broker, and they were exceptionally nice, friendly, enthusiastic people. Mr. Maag was thirty-nine and his wife was thirty-seven.

Of the sixty-four passengers on TWA Flight 2, an extraordinary total of twenty-six were flying free of charge on company passes. Of these, eleven were TWA employees and twelve were members of employees' families. Three had no direct connection with the company.

A twenty-seventh person was flying for free on a status called ACM, which stood for additional crewmember. He was a thirty-four-year-old TWA flight engineer named Harry Allen, who had been based in Kansas City and was in the process of moving his family from Prairie Village, Kansas, to Los Angeles, where he had transferred. Even though he had no duties on the flight, he occupied the extra seat on the flight deck. Mr. Allen was on his way home to his wife, Norma, and their son, Harry, Jr.

Including Mr. Allen and the five crewmembers on duty, seventeen employees were on board, which combined with the employees' family members, made the staggering total of twenty-nine people intimately associated with the company. The tragedy that was only an hour away would shake TWA as perhaps no airline had ever been shaken before.

The three nonrevenue passengers not connected closely with TWA were Almeda Evans, Robert DeLonge, and Robert Sanders. Mrs. Evans was the wife of an airline captain who flew for Ethiopian Airlines, a company that had contractual ties with TWA. Mr. DeLonge was thirty-seven and lived in Sun Valley, California, with his wife, Theda, and their three sons, Michael, Thomas, and Stephen. He was an aeronautical engineer and worked for Lockheed Aircraft Corporation in Burbank, California, the company that had built the plane in which he was riding. The DeLonges had lived in Kansas City until a year before, and Mr. DeLonge was on his way back there for a job interview with TWA, hoping to be hired by their engineering department. Evidently the company was enthusiastic, as demonstrated by the fact that they had paid his way to come and talk to them.

Robert Sanders was from Atchison, Kansas, about forty miles from Kansas City, and he was returning home. He was twenty-one years old. He had studied radio and television at the University of Kansas and was planning to attend UCLA that fall. Sanders was full of the youthful excitement, daring, and mischief of his years, and he was flying on a pass illegitimately, impersonating a young friend of his from Kansas City whose father worked for TWA. Under the alias Miller, he had signed the pass and boarded Flight 2, taking a real chance, though probably unwittingly, because any number of people on board might have known the employee Miller and even his son. Most of the passengers who were connected with the company were from Kansas City. TWA's headquarters, in Kansas City, was relatively small at the time, and most of the employees knew each other. Large as it had become in the framework of the 1950s, TWA was still small enough and people oriented enough to have a family atmosphere. To his growing chagrin, Sanders probably found out en route that like any family, regardless of size, strangers could not for long infiltrate the group without being discovered. Hopefully nobody made him squirm too much for his prank.

Like the flight engineer Harry Allen, Thomas Ashton, Jr., was in the process of moving his family from Kansas City to Los Angeles. He was thirty-four years old, the same as Allen, and had a wife, Barbara; a ten-year-old son, Thomas III; and a daughter, Jennifer, age seven. TWA had just promoted Mr. Ashton to the job of supervisor of industrial relations for the western region. He was well liked by nearly everyone, and in just twelve years he had worked his way up from junior passenger agent to this level through several promotions.

Gloria Townsend was also thirty-four years old. To compound the shame that most divorcées felt in those years, she had the exceptional circumstance of not having custody of her child. Her ten-year-old daughter, Jannatta, nicknamed "Jinx," lived with Gloria's ex-husband and his new wife. Gloria had been chosen as Miss Kansas City in 1940 and had joined TWA in 1941. She had quit and been rehired since then, and she had transferred back and forth across the country several times. She was currently a Teletype operator in reservations at Los Angeles and was on her way to Kansas City to pick up her daughter and bring her back to Los Angeles for the summer.

Dennis Phelan worked for TWA in Kansas City as supervisor of engineering dynamics. He had been with the company only since February of that year, when he and his wife, Dorothy, and their two-year-old daughter, Mary Ann, had come from St. Louis, where Mr. Phelan had worked in engineering for McDonnell Aircraft Corporation. Mr. Phelan earned a master's degree at MIT and had served as an officer in the navy. He had been in San Diego working on a TWA jet development program, and he had curtailed his trip to be with his wife for the birth of their second child. Suzanne Marie was born the following day.

Of the thirty-eight passengers to whom passes had not been issued—excluding Sanders, who was issued one surreptitiously and would have made thirty-nine—thirty-seven had paid for their seats, and one was riding for free without the formality of any paperwork. Any one child under the age of two, accompanied by an adult paying full fare, was given free passage but not a seat. Howard Maag rode in his mother's lap and in a baby basket on the floor in front of her; he had no need of a ticket or a pass.

Miss Lillian Estelle Carple was an elevator operator in Los Angeles. She was thirty-nine years old and up until 1953 had lived in Kansas City. Miss Carple was black, which made her an exceptional figure on an airplane. Air travel, especially first-class air travel on transcontinental luxury liners, was still the province of whites. This was the day when blacks were expected to sit at the rear in public busses and even to give up their seats for whites. It was the time when public places had segregated restroom facilities for blacks and whites, labeled "White" and "Colored." The Montgomery, Alabama, bus boycott took place in '56, and full civil rights for blacks were still eight years away. American society was shamefully divided into three social classes, not just two: adults, children, and blacks. Black adults were often accorded less respect than white children. Miss Carple must have been something of a sensation, not only being black, which would have been ample, but also clearly being confident enough—perhaps cocky enough—to travel alone rather than under the wing of a man, and on top of that being from the cultural and economic lower class rather than a black woman of sophistication, wealth, or renown.

Even more surprising, Miss Carple was not alone in race on the airplane. Another black woman had also boarded Flight 2 at Los Angeles, named Esther Sharp. She was forty and was on her way home to East St. Louis, Illinois. She would have stayed on Flight 2 until it landed at its second stop, St. Louis, Missouri. She was a corresponding secretary for the National Association for the Advancement of Colored People, the NAACP. Maybe the two pioneers introduced themselves to each other and sat together. On the other hand, maybe each of them relished her self-reliance and savored the experience of being sufficient in standing alone in the white world, and thus on equal terms with it.

Donald Flentie was thirty-two years old and was the county agricultural agent for Leavenworth County, Kansas. He wrote a weekly column of farm news for the *Leavenworth Times* and made daily farm broadcasts on station KCLO. He had also been an instructor in an on-the-farm training program for veterans. Mr. Flentie had a wife, Marion, and a four-year-old son, Mark. He was on his way home to Leavenworth via Kansas City.

Another person on board from Leavenworth was Miss Sally Cressman. She was twenty-two years old and was a sweet and affable young woman. She had completed a training program in nursing at the University of Nebraska and was to start a new job as a nurse at the VA Hospital in Leavenworth the following Monday. Miss Cressman was also engaged to be married to a young man from Lincoln, Nebraska. She was on her way home from a vacation in California, visiting a cousin. Flying with her was her aunt, Virginia Goppert, with whom she had been visiting Mrs. Goppert's daughter, Nancy. Mrs. Goppert was forty-six years old and lived in Kansas City with her husband, Clarence, a prominent banker. The Gopperts had two adult children, Nancy and a son, Richard. Mrs. Goppert was to have the tragic distinction, five days hence, of being the first TWA victim to be identified.

All five members of the crew, the two hostesses and the three flight crewmembers, were from the Kansas City area and were going home. Tracine Armbruster was thirty years old. She had joined TWA in 1950 as a student hostess. Hostesses were typically attractive, and she was prettier than most. She had a lovely, happy smile and warm eyes. Like all flight attendants, she was unmarried.

Beth Davis was originally from Richfield Springs, New York, a small town in about the center of the state. Her parents still lived there and her brother lived in Albany. Miss Davis was twenty-five years old and shared an apartment with another hostess named Janice Heiser, who happened to be one of her passengers that day on Flight 2. Miss Davis had been awarded a Ford Foundation Scholarship to continue her studies beyond the bachelor's degree she had already earned. She planned to quit being a hostess after that summer and do graduate work, with the goal of earning a master's in education. She had been with TWA for three years, ever since graduating from college.

Flight Engineer Forrest Breyfogle was thirty-seven years old and had a wife, Evelyn, and two children: John, age five, and Jane, age two. He had graduated from Parks Air College in East St. Louis, Illinois, and started work for Mid-Continent Airlines in 1941 as a mechanic. In 1945 he joined TWA. Mr. Breyfogle was content being a flight engineer and had no plans to advance to copilot. His brother Ralph, on the other hand, was a copilot for United Air Lines; he was domiciled at Chicago and went on to become a captain.

First Officer James Ritner was thirty-one years old and had worked for TWA as a copilot since 1952. Mr. Ritner had a wife, Audrey; a son, Jimmie, age eleven; and two daughters, Terri, age seven, and Kimberley, six months old. He had accumulated nearly 7,000 hours of flying time, of which 825 were in 1049 Constellations.

Captain Jack Gandy was the only member of the crew that did not live in Kansas City itself. He was from Mission, Kansas, a small town just a few miles across the Missouri River. Mr. Gandy had a wife, Jane, and four children: George, age fourteen; Harriet, age eleven; Mark, age nine; and Sue, age five. He was forty-one years old and had been with TWA since the day after Christmas, 1939, when he was hired as a copilot. He became a reserve captain in 1942 and was promoted to regular captain in 1945. During the war, he was on an extended leave of absence from TWA to serve with the Naval Air Transport Service. Mr. Gandy had flown nearly 15,000 hours, of which over 7,000 had been on the type of plane he was flying that day. Gandy was respected throughout the line as a sagacious flyer and an honorable man. He had a strong moral character and respected the principles of law and religion. He was an elder in his church.

* * *

Unlike TWA flights, which reported to their own radio operators at various major airports across the country, United flights made their position reports to operators at installations of a company called Aeronautical Radio, Incorporated (ARINC). The acronym for this company was pronounced "air ink" in the industry—not quite right, but much nicer to say than "a rink." ARINC served under contract as United's company radio, performing the same functions as TWA's literal company radio operators. At the risk of confusing the situation, ARINC actually owned TWA's facilities and leased them to TWA, but it was TWA employees that operated the equipment, not ARINC employees. In the case of United, ARINC employees did the communicating on ARINC equipment, and United employees were not involved.

At 10:24, Flight 718 reported to Los Angeles ARINC that it was at Riverside and had reached an altitude of 12,000 feet, still climbing, and anticipated Palm Springs at 10:37. True to their forecast, United 718 was over Palm Springs at 10:37, having climbed to 18,000 feet and still climbing.

Daggett and Palm Springs were each other's counterpart, being equidistant from Los Angeles and major turning points for TWA 2 and United 718, respectively. TWA 2 had veered rightward 18 degrees at Daggett at 10:34, and there had left the airways. United 718 turned off the airways at Palm Springs three minutes later, veering 30 degrees leftward. The two flights were 70 miles apart at 10:37 and right together in their easterly motion. The new courses they took up when they turned off the airways were nearly parallel, with only 13 degrees separating them, and crisscrossed each other 300 miles farther on.

The crisscrossing of TWA 2's and United 718's courses was plain to see in their combined proposed flight plans, as was the likelihood that they would be close to each other near the intersection, if they both conformed to their proposed plans. But this would happen over 400 miles from Los Angeles about an hour and a half after takeoff, giving both crews plenty of room and time to make elective, arbitrary course changes—and to see and avoid each other if they ever did wind up in close proximity.

At about 10:50, eleven minutes after TWA 2, United 718 leveled out at their identical cruising altitude, 21,000 feet. After picking up some speed, the crew reduced power a little on the engines as the TWA crew had done, easing back for the part of a trip least interesting to flyers, the cruising phase. They expected about a four-and-a-half-hour trip to western Illinois, where they would have begun a descent toward Midway Airport at Chicago.

Soon after they leveled out, the stewardesses of Flight 718 began serving refreshments. Like TWA's Flight 2, United's Flight 718 included an excellent lunch suited to first-class fares, but unlike Flight 2, not also a snack, so the refreshments consisted simply of beverages. Miss Kemnitz and Miss Shoudt served coffee and tea, and probably milk for the children.

Nancy Kemnitz was twenty-four years old, and like all stewardesses, she was single. Miss Kemnitz lived on the south side of Chicago, in the Marquette Park neighborhood, about two and a half miles from Midway Airport. Her parents still lived in Moline, Illinois, where Nancy had been a high school cheerleader. She had been a United stewardess for over two years.

Margaret Shoudt was twenty-six years old and lived on the north side of Chicago. Her parents, a sister, and a brother lived in Philadelphia, where she was from originally. This was to have been Miss Shoudt's last trip for a time, during which she would have been on reserve duty status. She had been a United stewardess for just under two years. Miss Shoudt gave the impression of being a warm and friendly person.

Girardo Fiore was a small, thirty-nine-year-old man and was, of course, Italian. He was not far removed from his family's immigrating to the United States—his parents spoke English only poorly. Mr. Fiore was single and engaged to a girl in Italy. He lived in Torrance, California, roughly a ten-mile drive from Los Angeles International Airport. His first love was the mechanical aspects of airplanes, more so than the experience of flying, and United had hired him as a mechanic in 1948. Fiore was promoted to flight engineer in 1951 but still dabbled in aircraft mechanics in his spare time and was restoring an old private plane. He was a fun-loving, jocular guy, well liked by pilots. People called him Gerry.

First Officer Robert Harms was thirty-six years old and lived in Burbank, California, with his wife, Marge, and their five-year-old daughter, Linda. He was tall and lanky and somewhat taciturn. Harms had been with United since 1951 and was qualified as captain on DC-3 airplanes. Harms had about 4,500 hours of flying experience, over 200 of them in DC-7s.

Captain Robert Shirley was forty-eight years old and lived in Palos Verdes Estates, California, near the beach, about the same distance from the airport as Fiore. In fact, they were almost neighbors. Shirley had a wife, Mary, and a daughter, Linda, age ten. He had been with United for nearly twenty years, having been hired as a copilot in 1937. He had been a captain since 1940 and was qualified on various aircraft, most recently the DC-7. He had over 16,000 hours of flying behind him and was accordingly one of the most experienced captains on the line. Over 1,200 of these hours he had spent in the DC-7s alone, which also distinguished him as one of United's most experienced DC-7 captains, because that total was quite a lot for the short time (about two years) for which the airline had used that type of plane. His reputation as an outstanding flyer and a gentleman was widespread. Captain Shirley's passengers were in good hands. In fact, when news of the tragedy later reached United's ramp office in Chicago, one of the pilots standing there at the time exclaimed, "Not Shirley! Me, I could understand, but not *him!*"

Unlike TWA Flight 2, United Flight 718 had over three times as many males onboard as females: forty-four males and only fourteen females. Fifty-eight persons had boarded Flight 718 at Los Angeles, five crewmembers and fifty-three passengers. Five of the passengers were children, ranging from three months old to fifteen years of age.

Jeffrey Crider was five years old and was flying with his mother, Elizabeth Crider, to go visit his paternal grandparents in Detroit. When Jeffrey was just a baby, his parents and he moved from Detroit to Granada Hills, California, where his dad opened a tool shop. This was the first trip back "home" for Jeffrey and his mother, and it was to have been the first time for Jeffrey to meet his grandparents, whom he had not seen since he was a baby, too young to understand who they were. And it would have been the grandparents' first time of meeting Jeffrey the child, the person he had become, rather than Jeffrey the infant, too new to have developed a personality.

Fred Staecker was from Long Beach, California, and was eleven years old. He was flying alone to Chicago to join his grandfather for a special fishing trip to Michigan. Fred had broken his leg playing football the previous December and had recovered well enough to be ambulatory, but he still needed to use crutches. The trip was to be a consolation for his losses while he was laid up. Fred's parents took him to the airport in Los Angeles and waved good-bye to him from the observation patio when he appeared at one of the port windows of the DC-7. They had asked the airline to take special care of him. By the following day these proud parents, watching their young son achieving a milestone of independence as a young man, were both under a doctor's care for grief.

Peter Whyte was fifteen and was from a prominent family in Detroit. He had been in California visiting a friend of his who moved away. The trip was a reward to Peter for doing extremely well in school in the 1955-1956 school year, and although he could have extended his stay through the Fourth of July festivities as far as his parents were concerned, he had chosen to come home that weekend to start a job on Monday, July 2. Peter was a fine young man with character and ideals, and he intended to keep the commitment he had made without any alterations. He also planned to return to his honorary job of water boy for the Detroit Lions football team, whom he had served the previous season as number "00."

Carol Jean Church was on her way to the Chicago area to spend a summer vacation with her grandparents, Mr. and Mrs. Albert Vogt, of the suburb of Evanston. Mr. Vogt was personally bringing her from her home in San Diego. It was Carol's turn for this privilege, which her older siblings had had in previous years. She was the only little girl aboard the plane, and was six years old.

The youngest child on board was three-month-old Stephen Bishop. He was in the care of his mother, Rosemary Bishop, of Camarillo, California. Stephen was probably oblivious to everything but the basic distinctions between hunger and eating, cold and warmth, discomfort and comfort, and the absence or presence of his mother. Though he couldn't have known it, little Stephen must have been a delight to many on board.

There were forty-eight adult passengers. One of them was Mrs. Phyllis Berman. She was the national volunteer chairman of auxiliaries for the City of Hope. She had been at a meeting with the officials of the City of Hope in Duarte, California, and was returning home to Milwaukee, where she lived with her husband, Fred and their eleven-year-old son, Jimmy. She was forty-six years old and was an exceptionally caring, giving person. In her face one could see the depth of her humanity. She was an inspiration.

The oldest person on board was Mr. Hugo Pekruhn, of Steubenville, Ohio. He was eighty-three and had immigrated to the United States from Germany around the turn of the century. Mr. Pekruhn was a widower and was returning from visiting his daughter in Redondo Beach, California. He had sold automobiles from 1915, when they had balloon tires and wooden spoke wheels and were just becoming popular, until his retirement in 1936.

Mr. and Mrs. Walter Fuchs were returning to their home in Detroit from a convention in Los Angeles, at which Mr. Fuchs was awarded a plaque for fifty years of outstanding service in his industry. He was seventy-five, and his wife, Stella, was seventy-one. Mr. Fuchs was president of the Multi-Color Company, a pioneering blueprint photography company that he founded. He became a widower in 1940 and had three adult children from his first wife—a son and two daughters. Mrs. Fuchs had been a widow up until her marriage to Mr. Fuchs in 1948, and she had two adult sons from her first marriage.

Albert Vogt, the grandfather and chaperone of Carol Jean Church, had turned fifty-nine just the day before. He was senior deputy U.S. manager of Zurich General Accident and Liability Insurance Company. He and his wife, Lili, had a daughter, Mrs. Peggy Church, Carol's mother. Mrs. Vogt would be waiting that evening at Midway Airport for him and her granddaughter. My mom was standing near her when the terrible news came that the plane was missing, and fifty years later she was still able to vividly recall Mrs. Vogt's immediate and impassioned outpouring of anguish.

Like Albert Vogt, Francis Johlie II lived in the Chicago suburb of Evanston. He graduated from the School of Business at Northwestern University in that township and went on to become an executive of the Supermarket Institute, based in Chicago. Mr. Johlie had served as a navy lieutenant in the South Pacific during World War II, aboard a ship named the *Boxer*. He had been in California making arrangements with supermarket owners for the Institute's next conference and was on his way home. Mr. Johlie was thirty-two years old and had a wife, Ann; a four-year-old daughter, Gay Ann; and a two-year-old son, Francis III.

Carl Matland was thirty-nine years old and married. He was a research scientist for Westinghouse and lived in Pittsburgh, Pennsylvania. Like any genuine scientist, Mr. Matland was both humble and capable of inwardly rapturous insight, a dual quality that showed in a subtle glow in his eyes, corresponding uniquely to that special consciousness in which a person cannot help but revel in profound intellectual understanding.

Roberta Wilde was thirty-two years old and unmarried. She lived in Hollywood, California, and was a market research analyst. Miss Wilde was on her way to LaGrange, Illinois, via Chicago, where she was to have visited her parents and her brother.

Russell Shields, Jr., was from Highland Park, Michigan, a suburb of Detroit, and worked for Bendix Aviation as a research engineer. Bendix manufactured aircraft brakes and other components, and it was one of the companies with which Jack Groshans did business on behalf of Lockheed. Uncle Jack had probably visited the Bendix plant several times prior to that day to confer with engineers about Lockheed's requirements. He and Shields may have known each other. Mr. Shields was thirty years old and a bachelor, and he lived with his widowed father.

Traveling with Mr. Shields was Noel Gottesman, who was also thirty years old and was a mathematical analyst for Bendix Aviation. He was considered to be one of the nation's leading mathematicians and had been working on a group project in California. Most of the others took a plane back to Detroit the night before, but Mr. Gottesman wanted to make movies on a day flight, probably of the Grand Canyon, so he waited for Flight 718. He had a wife, Elizabeth; a son, David, fourteen months old; and a daughter, Lisa, who was five.

Christopher Balsat was nineteen years old and was a seaman third class in the navy, stationed on the west coast. He was on his way home to Fostoria, Ohio, a small town south of Toledo, and he would have transferred to another flight in Chicago. Mr. Balsat was on emergency leave, making an urgent trip to see his father, who was hospitalized and in recovery from an operation and scheduled for another. Instead of the elder Balsat receiving therapeutic encouragement from his son, his convalescence would be reversed by news of the tragedy, and in shock and grief, his condition would deteriorate to critical.

Dwight Nims was a buyer in outside manufacturing for Lockheed Aircraft Corporation in Burbank, California. He was thirty-six years old and lived in the nearby town of Granada Hills with his wife, Juanita, and their daughter, Jennifer Jean. He was traveling with my uncle to assist him in problems at Lockheed's purchasing office in Cleveland, Ohio, where Uncle Jack was in charge. The two had worked together in the Burbank plant in the previous two days, which was what had brought Uncle Jack to California, and they were to have continued their collaboration in Cleveland. Before they boarded Flight 718, Uncle Jack persuaded Mr. Nims to purchase trip insurance at the airport. Later, Nims' widow would express her gratitude for this to Uncle Jack's widow, my Aunt Joyce. Jack Groshans was a virtuous, caring man, and nearly everyone who knew him felt privileged. True to his character, one of his very last acts on earth turned out to be of great benefit to someone in need.

These and many others, 128 altogether, flew away into the mist at the edge of the world and never came back.

CHAPTER 6

ARTC WAS UNABLE to approve of 21,000 feet for TWA 2. In the public view, ARTC's position obviously meant that something was wrong with what Captain Gandy wanted, and many people were sure that this implication was as clear to him as it was to them. They believed that he knew, and yet he ascended to that very altitude—and at that altitude the collision occurred.

This outraged many people, and it seemed to them that he was absolutely in the wrong. On the surface it appeared that Captain Gandy had committed a grievously irresponsible act, and upon hearing what he did, people were astounded and indignant and then angry. His passengers had entrusted him with their lives, and it seemed clear that he had betrayed them. This notion transformed the public's anger into anguish and then into resentment. People believed that Gandy's ascending to 21,000 feet was what had caused the accident, and this unfortunate interpretation was compelling and obvious, and appeared incontrovertible.

Many people had misunderstood the facts.

Too much importance was made of Captain Gandy's decision to cruise at 21,000 feet. It was one of many contributing factors, all of which taken together conspired to bring about the disaster. The collision occurred about an hour after Gandy ascended, three hundred miles distant, and at a location substantially removed from both flights' proposed courses, after each had performed major detours. It took only a simple vertical movement of 2,000 feet to place the airplanes at the same altitude, but it took two complex, winding, perfectly coordinated movements, sprawled out across three hundred miles, to bring them to the same map coordinates at the same time. Numerous intricacies were involved in producing the exceedingly specific, total movements of each of the planes. The subtle adjustments to correct small discrepancies in course; the particular locations at which each flight left its proposed course; the precise timings, extents, and directions of the specific series of turns each made outside of its proposed course; any adjustments to engine power; and a host of other small manipulations were all combined to produce the terrible meeting in space. In view of this it makes no sense to regard Gandy's move to 21,000 feet as decisive.

It might as well, and just as poorly, be said that taking off was what caused the accident. Sincerely speaking, it too was a maneuver without which the accident could not have happened.

Part of why it was compelling to believe that Captain Gandy's ascent to 21,000 feet was a fatal maneuver was that it was a significant deviation from the original plan; he didn't do what he said he would do. In viewing this in the atmosphere of the terrible wrong that occurred in the Grand Canyon, it was easy to infer that he violated some moral obligation to stick to the plan. All he really did was change his mind. His flight plan was a proposal, not a promise. However, once morality was imposed on the change he made, it readily appeared that Gandy did something wrongful. In the most important sense, whatever caused the accident was something that shouldn't have been done, and if Gandy "shouldn't have" ascended to 21,000 feet, then this act fulfilled the minimum criterion for being the cause. Or so it seemed.

To understand the ensuing confusion, it is important to understand the differences between a course and a path. A course is just a line drawn on a map to represent the desired or planned movement of a flight. It is two-dimensional, and it is the crew's ideal in how they would like to get to their destination—but it is almost never realized. It is practically impossible to so perfectly perform a flight as to make its actual track over the map absolutely identical to its course. A path occupies three dimensions. It is represented by an imaginary line drawn in three-dimensional space and accounts not only for movement ahead and side-to-side, but also vertically. A path is the actual trajectory that a plane follows through the air, between the starting point and the destination on the ground.

In the first days following the accident, two stories purporting to describe the circumstances of the collision were circulated, one factual and the other fictitious. The misconstrued version was at least based on the facts and in effect described what might have happened had the flights not detoured from their proposed courses. It asserted that the combined flight plans filed by TWA 2 and United 718 amounted to "collision courses," a term that means something in sailing, where a course and a path can be the same because the boat never leaves the surface of the water—but it has no meaning in aviation because it doesn't account for altitude: if the planes are not at the same altitude, they cannot collide. The story suggested that the disaster had been unwittingly devised and had taken place at the intersection of the two proposed courses, but it overlooked the fact that they were not collision *paths*—if the flights kept to their filed plans, then as viewed from the side rather than from directly above, they would pass with TWA 2 underneath United 718 by over a third of a mile. The story also overlooked the fact that the planned courses would have had the planes over the map coordinates of the intersection point only at *about* the same time, even if they both flawlessly performed their plans once they finally took off, which was not when they had planned anyway.

The story also sadly disregarded the fact that the wreckage was found about thirty miles west of this "intersection" spot, back in the direction the flights were coming from, so that it did not make sense to believe that the planes had collided where their proposed courses crossed.

In reality, both flights left their planned courses well in advance of reaching the "paper intersection" point, and they collided in a place about twelve miles north of TWA 2's proposed course and twenty miles north of United 718's. This was the situation described by the other story. It showed that any complete, three-dimensional collision paths that might have in effect been in the works had dissolved, and that the planes never got anywhere near the intersection point. But the impression that Captain Gandy's movement to 21,000 feet had supplied the final, missing ingredient was compelling and convincing. People adopted it even though the true story showed that his detour had rendered his ascent irrelevant. It had not sealed their fate; in fact, once TWA 2 left their proposed course, they and United 718 were definitely no longer on collision paths with each other, if they ever had been. They weren't even on crossing courses anymore, and so their occupying the same altitude then became as innocuous as it would be for two cars, headed in divergent directions, to both be at street level.

Even people who believed the correct story, however, tended to regard TWA 2's cruising at 21,000 feet with exaggerated significance, because it was the only concretely known maneuver made by either flight in the whole complex of maneuvers they jointly made after leaving the airways. It was the only definite feature of the unique, convoluted, and otherwise unknown paths each of them had followed to the other, and so it was the only material scapegoat.

People were also shocked and angry that ARTC could have approved flight plans that outlined crossing courses for the two flights, no matter which story they embraced. Naturally, the people who believed that the planes collided along their planned courses were considerably angrier as a group than those who believed the correct story, because it appeared that the disaster was ARTC's fault. It looked like ARTC had obliviously authorized fatal courses, and despite having over an hour to recognize their own error and correct it, they had never noticed it—or worse, had noticed it and done nothing. They seemed guilty of the most appalling incompetence or negligence. People were stunned by the apparent ineptitude and irresponsibility of ARTC. The point they saw was of course that ARTC should never have approved such dangerous plans, whether an accident resulted from them or not. The fact that TWA 2 was originally supposed to have flown 2,000 feet lower than United

718 did little to mitigate their alarmed impression that the filed and cleared plans would have brought the two planes too close together.

All of this was yet another of what would be many misunderstandings of the tragedy. It was actually not rare off airways for flights to crisscross each other's courses in close proximity. Nor was it unusual for flight plans to be approved that, in conjunction with each other, effectively called for this to happen. ARTC did this routinely, a hundred times a day. Furthermore, controllers had the authority and the responsibility to disapprove only of flight plans that entailed some hazard within controlled airspace, where they had jurisdiction. Neither flight plan posed any such problem, so both plans were routinely approved. ARTC would not have approved of plans that would bring the planes so near to each other on the airways, but what might happen out in the middle of nowhere was not their responsibility to regulate or control, and in fact it was illegal for them to attempt doing so.

This was much safer and much more reliable than the public took it to be—in the whole history of aviation up to that time, there had been many millions of airline flights worldwide, but only about twenty of them had ended in a crash precipitated by a midair collision.

Many people were also angry with the U.S. government as the ultimate authority and governing body behind its instrument, Air Route Traffic Control. It seemed clear that the government was responsible to make sure that the rules administered by ARTC were adequate to make flying safe for the public, and yet these rules had in effect allowed TWA 2 to cruise at 21,000 feet, despite the fact that ARTC had been unable to approve it. Even if this had not caused the accident, it seemed wrong. It seemed crazy that ARTC could legally have set TWA 2 free to choose any altitude they wanted, including the one that they, ARTC, had declined to approve. The one thousand on top clearance appeared to provide the most glaring of loopholes, and this suggested in turn that the regulations had been formulated by idiots. In allowing themselves to sink to the indolence of such a blatant oversight, the rule makers had been criminally inept, or so it seemed. Far worse than this seemingly disgraceful conduct itself, of course, was the appearance that the disaster had actually resulted from it, and people blamed the U.S. government for allowing such a fiasco.

The key to the whole misunderstanding was the fact that being protected by ARTC was an option. In asking for the one thousand on top clearance, Captain Gandy was implicitly offering to release ARTC from any responsibility to keep him away from other IFR flights, including United 718. The protection given IFR flights was actually slightly more restrictive than thus far outlined. It was ARTC's duty to separate only those IFR flights on airways from each other that had specific altitude clearances. One thousand on top was not specific, and so if ARTC granted this clearance to TWA 2, then they would no longer be obligated to protect them, even on the airways. This only makes sense: ARTC could not be expected to protect a flight from collisions if they didn't know on what level the plane was.

Technically, a flight could remain IFR and adopt an amended one thousand on top clearance, forsaking ARTC's protection but retaining the right to reclaim it later at any time that they would again accept a specific altitude clearance. It was sort of like remaining employed but being on leave of absence. This was TWA 2's situation; ARTC would keep room open for them so that they could be fitted back into the picture, whenever they were ready to take up a designated altitude that ARTC could approve. In the meantime, TWA 2 would be fully responsible for themselves in avoiding other aircraft, even while crossing or following airways.

In order to do this, TWA 2 would have to remain in clear skies so that they could see where they were going and what was coming. At the time of the disaster, the erroneous story that TWA 2 had changed over to a VFR clearance was widely publicized, out of confusing TWA 2's responsibility with their clearance. Their clearance was still IFR, but they were flying under Visual Flight Rules while on the airways. It was a little confusing, not just for laymen, but also even for some of the officials who were involved later in the accident investigation and hearings.

If TWA 2 had switched to a VFR clearance, they could just as well have selected 21,000 feet for their cruising altitude, but there would have been no guarantee that they could regain the protection of an IFR status later, since in the meantime, someone else wanting an IFR clearance might in effect usurp their place in the workload. So Gandy asked for one thousand on top, not a complete changeover to VFR, and ARTC gave it to him. They were able to give it to him because in the same stroke they were no longer obligated to ensure that he and United 718 would be safely separated on Red 15, or anywhere else. Contrary to how it appeared, the situation was not so much that ARTC allowed TWA 2 to do something that they thought the flight shouldn't, as it was that the system allowed for TWA 2 to fly under ARTC's guidance and protection or without it, as the flight chose. One could live inside the castle and abide by the rules within its walls, or live in the forest and do as one pleased.

One issue that naturally arose from this, but which was overshadowed at the time by the dramatic apparent folly in TWA 2's changing altitude and received little attention outside of the hearings on the accident, was the question of whether it wasn't dangerous to relinquish ARTC's protection. It appeared to some that Gandy was imprudent in asking for one thousand on top, because the request entailed losing ARTC's help. It correspondingly appeared that ARTC was remiss in granting it for the same reason, or that the regulations had built into them what might be called an "adventure clause," a provision that allowed for unwarranted or unwise risk taking. To some extent each of these impressions was valid, but only with respect to flying on the airways. Trading a specific altitude clearance for a one thousand on top clearance, or an IFR clearance for a fully VFR clearance, would cost a flight a little bit of safety on the airways, but that applied very little to TWA 2. They would be flying almost entirely in uncontrolled airspace while they had the one thousand on top clearance, where ARTC would not assist them anyway. Basically, Gandy was forfeiting nothing but an idea, and a couple minutes' worth of protection per hour that were as empty of benefit as the sky was of conflicting traffic.

Where the one thousand on top clearance and the collateral loss of ARTC's help would have been a significant problem, though still not grave, was near Kansas City, where a tangle of airways for TWA 2 to cross over or fly along would collectively hold quite a few other aircraft. Here, being kept apart from other IFR flights by ARTC was a real asset, and this must have been in Captain Gandy's plan. By his own words, he intended to take up the specific altitude clearance for 21,000 feet as soon as he could get it, and certainly he would have accepted *any* specific altitude near Kansas City, for the sake of regaining ARTC's protection. There simply isn't any evidence here to support the idea that Gandy's request for one thousand on top was imprudent. In fact, it seems that he had everything covered.

For the same reason, it is unreasonable to assert that ARTC's decision to grant the one thousand on top clearance was anything but sound, and in view of this, the regulations and the ultimate government behind them probably can't be criticized either.

Against the impressions that the U.S. government in general, or ARTC in particular, had in one vein or another been lax, people also had the much more valid impressions that the regulations were well designed and that ARTC had done a competent job of attempting to keep TWA 2 and United 718 from harm. From this opposite pole, it again looked like the onus of responsibility and blame for the tragedy rested on TWA 2. Captain Gandy became the scapegoat, because it appeared that he had spurned ARTC in his decision to cruise at 21,000 feet.

It is clear that he did make full use of the regulations to get what he wanted. Obviously he knew that ARTC would decline to approve 21,000 feet only if there was a safety concern with that altitude. Yet he decided in advance to go there even if they did decline, provided he could maneuver around their judgment. Captain Gandy anticipated

ARTC's position and countered it by attaching the second approach, the one thousand on top clearance, to his request in the first place, and he got what he wanted. To some this seemed obnoxious, but all it implied was that he was determined and had handily exercised his rights and privileges.

Unfortunately, many people had the mistaken notion that he was obligated to acquiesce to ARTC's judgment, as a respectful son might submit to his father, and because of this misapprehension Gandy appeared to have been insubordinate or even antagonistic. Actually, he had no such obligation in this instance: first and foremost the flight was *his* responsibility, not that of someone who wasn't even on the plane, and commensurately Gandy's authority and judgment were preeminent. If anything, ARTC might have been required to assent to Gandy's judgment. Captain Gandy was entitled to claim the altitude he wanted within the provisions of the one thousand on top clearance, and he was entitled to ask for this clearance, so there was nothing wrongful in his asking, at least not on the surface.

Harm is probably always done when people use a rule to obtain something that it was not intended to afford them. The rule becomes a parody of itself, and people gradually lose faith in it and respect it less. The rule is undermined, and assuming that it is an honorable code of conduct designed to encourage and preserve the well-being of the group it serves, the group is harmed in proportion. The one thousand on top clearance was created to enable pilots to fly above known bad weather, or above clouds that might contain storm cells or strong turbulence even while appearing to be tame. Captain Gandy had neither of these needs and instead used the clearance to fly higher for other reasons. This could legitimately have angered the public even though it was minor and not relevant to the accident, but at the time, no one knew that he had taken this questionable advantage.

One of the saddest things about the aftermath was that beyond the raw, unexplained fact of the disaster, what angered people were falsehoods, not the truth.

Many people had adopted yet another falsehood: they had presumed that in ARTC's judgment, 21,000 feet was unsafe for TWA 2. This was the obvious meaning in ARTC's declining to approve of that altitude, and it was also incorrect. It was a case of the classic error in which the absence of a thing is misconstrued to be the presence of its opposite. ARTC had been unable to certify 21,000 feet as being safe, which was a far cry from calling it dangerous. Their true opinion was that it would in all probability be exceedingly safe.

At the time TWA 2 was requesting a new altitude clearance, they and United 718 were about forty miles apart and diverging from each other. They were to turn at a distance of about seventy miles from each other and head into nearly empty, uncontrolled airspace. Shortly afterward, they would cross airways in California and Arizona, the last of which was Red 15. This one was in Salt Lake City ARTC's area, and the controller there who would soon be handling the flights could not be certain of how far apart they would be on that airway. In his estimation, based on knowing their flight plans, they would be amply far apart, but he could not verify this. How to respond to the situation was a matter of judgment, and he decided to make abundantly sure of their safety by disapproving TWA 2's request to ascend to United 718's altitude. He had the latitude to approve or disapprove because there was no clear-cut risk; it appeared safe, and based on experience with many other flights in similar circumstances, it *was* safe.

Beyond this, on their new headings the flights' proposed courses would cross after about an hour, in uncontrolled airspace three hundred miles away. Although this was a more important concern, it was not ARTC's concern, because ARTC had no authority there. Even if they had, the most important fact in regard to safety was that traffic in the vicinity of the two flights at that time would be sparse, and without distraction they should be able to see and avoid each other. Besides this, both flights normally diverted for sightseeing over the Grand Canyon, as did all airline flights that skirted near it in those days, and it would have been very unusual if neither did. The crossing of their planned courses was about twenty-five miles beyond the canyon, so in all likelihood both flights would make detours well in advance of this riskier area. The Salt Lake City controller who was involved in the decision not to approve 21,000 feet for TWA 2 knew all of this, and he later testified that he was unconcerned for their safety even though he noticed the coincidences. In terms of the conventions at the time, there was no perceptible danger, and his attitude was appropriate, not remiss.

Notwithstanding this, the newspapers implicitly maligned him. On Saturday, August 4 of that year, he testified at the official investigatory hearing held by the Civil Aeronautics Board in Washington, D.C. The same day, the press badly distorted what he said. The syndicated story, written by International News Service (INS), began by saying, "A Salt Lake City air traffic controller testified Saturday that he knew two airliners were on converging courses over the Grand Canyon last June 30, but was too busy to warn them before they collided, killing 128 persons."

Obviously the controller could not have been juggling several other life-threatening emergencies, so that if he had been too busy, it would have been with routine work. The press had patched together fragments of his testimony from widely separated contexts, fabricating a meaning that the controller never intended. On top of this, they had essentially invented the idea that the controller was too busy. He knew that the flight plans called for converging courses, and he said so at the hearing. Elsewhere in his testimony he also explained that ARTC was not responsible to give advisory information to flights in uncontrolled airspace, and that it had neither the manpower nor the equipment to do so comprehensively, so that as a matter of policy this was avoided. The press excerpted these disparate lines of questioning and concocted a false accounting of his testimony that might as well have blatantly charged, "He knew they were going to destroy each other but did not want to upset his routines to warn them." He knew no such thing—no one did, and no one could have, because it never happened on those courses.

Neither was he too busy to warn them. ARTC provided a substantial service, not a tenuous one. Controllers didn't sit around playing cards between successive flights coming their way, as they might have done in the late thirties. Commercial air traffic really boomed after the war, like many industries, and by the fifties there were a great many airliners in the sky every day. Controllers were productively occupied most of the time. They were busy. As a result, they had to concentrate on the services most likely to make flying safer day by day, the services that proved to be most beneficial in the long run. So usually they did not send out traffic advisories to flights in progress in their areas. If ARTC had had any concrete reason to believe that Flights 2 and 718 were in danger, they would promptly have warned them. For example, if they had been flying at night with their lights off, as in wartime.

Because of the gravity of their responsibilities, ARTC could not afford to use their resources on extreme improbabilities. Nevertheless, from the testimony that there was not enough manpower to institute a new and nearly 100 percent superfluous service, it was derived that the controller involved in the tragedy couldn't be bothered to save 128 lives. The story also disregarded the pertinent fact that the same controller's extra caution, in discretionarily disapproving TWA 2's request for 21,000 feet, materially demonstrated that he was in reality conscientious, not lax.

Maybe this monster evolved in a cumulative series of warpings, quickly volleyed back and forth between unbalanced reporters in a newsroom, like the cascading distortions in propagating rumors. On the other hand, maybe the writer and his editor made no effort at all to understand or sensationalize the story, and they were just incredibly stupid or unfeeling people who were satisfied with face value and failed to realize the terrible implications of the phrasing. No matter how this travesty came into print, it was the worst kind of journalism.

Three days after printing the defaming story, the controller's hometown newspaper at least printed part of a Civil Aeronautics Administration official's defense of him, disputing the erroneous story, but the paper framed it with implicitly detracting commentary. Still, it was probably better than nothing. By then, however, many people in Salt Lake City and all across the country believed that he had been criminally negligent. Some of his neighbors must have pointed and vocally condemned him in front of their children, imparting their views to them; this is nearly always the route by which children acquire "adult" opinions or attitudes. The wound inflicted on the controller by the scorn of some of his own neighbors may never have fully healed, but what resulted for his family was probably even worse. His children were repeatedly harassed by cruel other children, who taunted them and shamed them for having the father who "made the planes crash."

His family was not the only one badly hurt by dishonest or unintelligent journalism, and by the public's belief in the libelous articles that were printed. Once ARTC's decision to disapprove TWA 2's request for 21,000 feet was incorrectly taken to mean that 21,000 feet was unsafe, then it was only a small additional step to infer that their declining to approve must have unequivocally conveyed this implication to Captain Gandy. People embraced this false impression and compounded his family's grief with the spurious tragedy of blaming him. Many people wrongly concluded that Captain Gandy had knowingly made an unsafe move, and they were outraged at what they correspondingly took to be his recklessness and arrogance. Much of their misapprehending of him was understandable in those emotional circumstances, but because they had a choice it was still inexcusable, and the guilt and shame resultantly foisted upon his family when they most needed support were unforgivable.

It was a mess, as the complexities of this chapter surely have illustrated—if not by elucidating some of the tangled conflicts between truth and illusion with which people wrestled shortly after the accident, and hopefully resolving some once and for all, then at least by engendering enough confusion to set the atmosphere in which people operated.

In the aftermath of the tragedy, as people tried to understand what had happened, they shared a pervasive sense of confusion. Next to the overriding awfulness of the disaster, this was one of the predominant moods characterizing nearly everyone's interest. It was astonishing, baffling, incredible, and confusing. There had never been a commercial air disaster like this before, not a midair collision between two large airliners, and not an airliner crash of any sort with such a tremendous loss of life. The only other midair collisions where both planes were commercial airliners carrying passengers had occurred between very small craft decades earlier, in foreign countries; probably not even one person in a thousand had ever heard of them.

There had been more recent midair collisions between an airliner and a military or private plane, involving a great loss of life, but even in the worst of them, not half as many people had perished as in the Grand Canyon tragedy. The worst prior airline accident of any kind had involved only one plane and had taken seventy-four lives. The Grand Canyon accident was beyond anything that had come before it, and people were reeling.

There was something especially horrifying about a midair collision. Planes were machines and were expected to occasionally break down, and sometimes even to crash as a result. Pilots were human beings and were expected to occasionally make mistakes, and once in a great while to crash as a result. But for two airliners to ram each other far up in the sky felt almost evil, almost diabolical, almost like murder. It electrified the skin of anyone who suddenly pictured it. It was too awful to be accepted, and too awful to be believed, and people tried in vain to fathom it.

CHAPTER 7

SHORT SIDE TRIPS for sightseeing were commonplace on cross-country airline flights that passed near the Grand Canyon, and typically passengers on TWA's regular Flight 2 to Kansas City and United Air Lines' regular Flight 718 to Chicago would be treated to that incredible spectacle. On June 30, 1956, however, both flights departed significantly behind schedule, especially TWA 2, and thereby had a motive to forsake the usual sightseeing detour. Furthermore, sightseeing was normally done on these flights over the eastern third of the canyon, but on this day, the eastern third was almost totally obscured from the air by an extensive low-level overcast. These facts leave ample room to wonder what actually brought the two flights over the canyon that day.

At 10:55 Flight 2 passed the intersection of two airways that met near an artificial body of water called Lake Mohave, situated along the state line between Nevada and Arizona. (TWA 2's proposed course cut through a minute section of Nevada at the "sharp point" of its southern tip, where it met California and Arizona. They did the vast majority of their flying over California and Arizona that day, and for most purposes the very brief piece over Nevada can be ignored.) Lake Mohave amounted to a giant flood pool, which formed when the Colorado River rose out of its banks as a consequence of the contemporaneously completed Davis Dam, downstream. The dam had slowed the river, causing it to swell upstream and to redefine its shape. Lake Mohave was merely a manmade bulge in the river, and though it was beautiful in itself, it was also grotesque in its implications and its origin, like a gall on the stem of a wildflower.

Because of its proximity to the lake, the intersection of these two airways was named, obviously enough, the Lake Mohave Intersection. Even though the flight did not pass through the intersection, it passed nearby enough that it was a useful checkpoint. At 10:59 the crew called in to Las Vegas TWA radio and reported that they had passed the intersection four minutes earlier, at 10:55.

Checkpoints were places from which flight crews would check in with people on the ground, reporting their locations. These brief reports were called position reports. Originally, the main purpose of position reports was to enable dispatchers and controllers to follow a flight's progress, so that if it disappeared, search parties could be sent out with at least a rough idea of where to look, starting with its last known position. A refinement in this was that crews would also advise from where they expected to make their next position report and when they estimated being there. This gave the authorities a second boundary to confine a search if a flight was not heard from again, and with the time estimate they also had a good gauge of when to start worrying. In fact, the standard became five minutes after the estimated time of arrival at the checkpoint. The system was that a crew would call in by then even if they had still not reached the checkpoint. If they did not call in by then, ground personnel would attempt to contact them, and if this were unsuccessful it would then be assumed that the flight was in some sort of trouble.

As time passed and air traffic increased, position reports acquired the second purpose of enabling controllers to determine the locations of various aircraft in relation to each other, so as to maintain a safely spaced, efficient flow of traffic. Commensurately, a flight plan was required to stipulate a complete series of checkpoints covering the whole trip a crew proposed making. This way both the crew and ARTC would have, in advance, the whole outline of where (and in effect roughly when) the flight should report.

In their position report from near Lake Mohave, TWA 2 also advised that they were cruising at 21,000 feet, and estimated that they would cross what was called the Painted Desert Line of Position, or Painted Desert LOP for short, at 11:31. The Painted Desert LOP was an imaginary line extending north-northwest from Winslow, Arizona, to Bryce Canyon, Utah. It served as a broad navigational locator, like a coastline, for flights passing through the desolate territories of northern Arizona and southern Utah. Here there were no natural checkpoints, like navigational radio stations or intersections of airways, and the line served as a catchall, identifying flights along its length as being in the middle of nowhere. This was better than nothing, but it gave no indication of where along this line a flight was, and so it was almost like a ship radioing that it had landed on the Pacific Coast. Beneath the line lay the huge Navajo Indian Reservation, and more narrowly, that part of the reservation that was the Painted Desert. Immediately to the west of this was the Grand Canyon.

The Lake Mohave position report from TWA 2 was the last message that was ever heard from them.

Immediately before TWA 2 was on the air talking to their company radio operator at Las Vegas, United 718 was talking to the radioman at a government installation called the Needles Interstate Airways Communications Station, or Needles INSACS for short. This was a sort of outpost facility located near the town of Needles, California, at the state line. It was one of many similar, isolated radio stations dotted throughout the country. These were operated by the Civil Aeronautics Administration and served flights in progress that otherwise might be too far from their own radio service stations to get through. Along with the manned two-way radio communications station there was also a navigational radio facility in that area, which, by the signal it continuously broadcast, served as a radio beacon and checkpoint for flights passing over it, much as a lighthouse marks its position visually for mariners sailing nearby. At 10:58 United 718 reported to Needles INSACS that they were at that moment passing this checkpoint. They also advised that they were cruising at 21,000 feet and estimated reaching the Painted Desert LOP at 11:31. No other normal radio contact ever occurred with United 718.

Despite taking off only three minutes apart, and also largely because of it, the flights were now in effect estimating arriving at the Painted Desert LOP together, down to the minute. Normally, if the Constellation took off only three minutes ahead of the DC-7, the DC-7 would have pulled out ahead of it by several minutes over the span from Los Angeles to the Painted Desert LOP; the DC-7 was just that much faster a plane. And were things to be entirely normal, with the Constellation taking off ahead of the DC-7 by fully the fifteen minutes forecast in the two schedules, the DC-7 would still be several minutes behind when the Constellation crossed the Painted Desert LOP. But this day the two flights estimated crossing the Painted Desert LOP simultaneously. They were both still on their proposed courses, and by another of the incredible series of coincidences or fated designs, these courses and the Painted Desert LOP all crossed each other within a very small area—only a few square miles.

Salt Lake City ARTC was not entirely surprised when they received TWA 2's position report from Las Vegas TWA radio and United 718's position report from the Needles INSACS, with both estimating the Painted Desert LOP at 11:31. The controller who received the reports was the same one who was involved with the earlier decision to disapprove TWA 2's request to be cleared for cruising at 21,000 feet, and so he had already consulted the large route map he had in front of him, depicting their courses and those of other flights, in order to form his opinion. He doubtless had already realized that the proposed courses would crisscross at about the same time, very near the Painted Desert LOP. In fact, he had even communicated to his counterpart at Los Angeles ARTC, that, "Their courses cross, and they are right together." There was nothing unusual about this, and also nothing certain about it, because it was likely that one or both flights would deviate from their proposed course and make the typical sightseeing detour over the Grand Canyon. As a consequence, they might cross the Painted Desert LOP at spots altogether different from the one that was in effect planned. The line was about 175 miles long, resembling nothing like a discrete location, and so the fact that the two flights would cross it, even simultaneously, did not in itself mean that they would ever be anywhere near each other.

But now he knew that the two flights were anticipating crossing the Painted Desert LOP at exactly the same time, not about the same time. In other words, if they stayed on their proposed courses, then TWA 2's and United 718's time estimates were as good as a forecast that the two would meet. The controller also knew that they were at the same altitude, so that if they *did* stay on their proposed courses, then in effect, the forecast was actually for approximately full collision paths. He noticed the coincidence and puzzled over it for a moment, but he was not alarmed. The situation was simply not dangerous, because even in the worst case the two should easily see each other. And again, the flights were likely to leave their proposed courses and randomly fly over the canyon, annulling their impending convergence. On top of this, in the frame of reference of weighing only the circumstances, not knowing what the incredibly unlucky and improbable outcome would be, it would have been silly or even absurd for him to try dissuading either flight from its course, about on the order of trying to persuade a farmer to stay home rather than drive to town, on the strength that a second farmer is driving to town on a different road and might pose a collision hazard somewhere within the city limits.

In the narrow perspective passively defined by the existence of the man, it was simply irrational. The sum of what he saw and felt was excised from the whole picture by his learned knowledge, his insight, his sense of identity, and his sense of purpose. It had been subtracted from the totality as a prime requisite of his being an individual, a person less than the totality, and that was good. It was necessary and inescapable, and it was not only tragically sad but also tragically forgivable that he saw no farther and did no more. Far from a superfluous or vain or hysterical effort, however, in the larger view it would have been momentously valuable, possibly supremely valuable, for him to alert the flights. A different set of influences could not have failed to produce a different outcome, and so a warning would have changed what was to be. It might even have made enough of a difference to prevent the accident. Even though both flights ended up leaving their proposed courses rather than following them straight to the Painted Desert LOP, a warning about what could occur if they stayed on them might have served to make them just a notch more keenly aware and alert for other aircraft. This will never be known. Whether or not it would have helped cannot be known, and if history can unfold in only one way, then the question does not even have any meaning. In ignorance of the full dynamics of how reality transforms as time passes and events progress, however, a more important observation is simply that a warning *might* have helped. It remains a possibility that everyone could have been saved, and knowing this must have been a terrible burden for anyone who could have done anything about it at all.

Despite knowing that his actions were impeccable, or that what befell others wasn't his fault, how does a thinking, feeling, decent person accept that he failed to see, at the most crucial moment in the lives of those who perished? How does he reconcile knowing that the signs were there, intuitively perceptible in their full import, with the fact that he chose not to attune himself in favor of unconsciously presuming that everything would be ordinary? How does he decide to believe that he wouldn't have had enough intuition at that moment to grasp what was coming anyway, even if he had attuned himself? Some people become stronger by living through such a personal crisis, because of the monumental effort it takes for them to believe in themselves in the face of their own disastrous limitations. Others are crushed by their guilt and unrelenting self-reproach, and give up on themselves, at best living failed lives of permanent despair and passing through life like ghosts. And some, who appear to have come out of it stronger, are in reality only harder. Though they have survived, their humanity has not.

*   *   *

After crossing the region where California and Arizona meet each other, neither flight ever notified anyone again of their locations or courses. Not one detail of their movements in Arizona airspace is known for certain. Once they finished their position reports at the state line and got off the air, it was as though they became invisible and entered a realm that was for them alone, a space in life that only they could inhabit. For the next half hour, which was to be the final half hour of their lives, they vivified that narrow niche, and then it closed up, leaving nowhere for them to be at all. What they did and what happened to them was their secret; they flew in utter isolation from mankind, in a tragic privacy that came to a halt but will never be broken. Their secrets are theirs alone and will be forever, but it is possible, based on the evidence that survived them, to form some reliable conclusions about what their last movements were. (See Appendix 4 for a diagram of their probable paths.)

Captain Lionel Stephan flew for American Airlines. American and National Airlines shared an interchange program during the spring, summer, and fall months, from April to November, when passenger traffic was heavy. This program involved crewmembers from one airline sometimes flying the aircraft of the other, and such was the case for Captain Stephan on June 30, 1956. He departed from Oakland, California, at 9:00 a.m. PDT in command of a National Airlines DC-6, headed for Dallas nonstop, with a cruising altitude of 19,000 feet. At 11:06 he passed over Las Vegas. According to his flight plan he was to have taken airway Victor 105 southeastward from there to Prescott, Arizona. Over part of its length Victor 105 was superimposed on Red 15, and had he followed Victor 105 he would have passed over the wakes of TWA 2 and United 718 about five minutes after they crossed the airway. Instead, Stephan diverted from his planned course, staying on a compass course of 74 degrees, a true course of exactly due east in that area. He had observed that the weather ahead was clear over the nearby Grand Canyon and had decided to show his passengers the sights.

On this course, he flew over about the western two-thirds of the canyon and then at 11:33, at a spot about twenty-five miles west of Grand Canyon Village, he turned roughly southeast, to head directly for Winslow, Arizona. (Grand Canyon Village is situated at the area called the South Rim and is about twenty miles west of the canyon's eastern extremity.) Captain Stephan had been persuaded to turn rather than complete the trip over the canyon by both common sense and necessity. It no longer served any purpose to fly over the canyon, because the clouds 4,000 feet below him had increased from sparsely scattered to broken to almost totally overcast as the flight progressed eastward. His passengers had experienced the Grand Canyon amply, and this had been curtailed by the thickening of the cloud cover far below. More importantly, directly ahead of him Captain Stephan was confronted with a massive cumulonimbus cloud protruding from the lower cloud deck, which thrust vertically to more than a mile above his own altitude. The giant cloud appeared to be a thunderstorm in the making and was centered over Grand Canyon Village.

Captain Stephan's course from Nevada took him over Lake Mead, eastward along a line of latitude seven miles to the north of Grand Canyon Village's latitude. The captain later testified in investigatory hearings on the accident and said that the giant cloud was right in front of him before he turned, and also that it was centered over Grand Canyon Village. One combined effect of these two statements was that the huge cloud in his way had to have been at least fourteen miles wide, north-to-south. How he ascertained the location of the village while the ground was obscured by the expansive cloud cover beneath him is another matter, leaving room initially for wondering if perhaps he only guessed. Of course, if he knew where he was, then he knew where the village was in relation to him and to the cloud ahead.

There is another way to gauge the cloud's size that is more concrete and may be more accurate. According to his log, Captain Stephan passed over Grand Canyon Airport at 11:39 and determined this by actually seeing the airport beneath him through a break in the lower cloud deck. He said that while passing over the airport, he skirted the southern edge of the cloud from only about two miles away. In 1956, Grand Canyon Airport was located fourteen miles south (and two miles east) of Grand Canyon Village, and this places the southern edge of the cloud twelve miles south of the village. Figuring its northern edge to have lain at least seven miles north of the village, based on his measured course while he approached from the west, the cloud had to be at least nineteen miles in north-to-south breadth, and possibly as much as twenty-four miles if it was literally centered over the village, as viewed from the west. It was truly a giant and may have formed by the coalescing of several smaller clouds that grew nearby each other.

The Civil Aeronautics Board Accident Investigation Report was released a little over eight months after the accident and paraphrased Captain Stephan, claiming that he had observed a towering cumulus cloud situated over Grand Canyon Village. The report said this once, and every other time, interspersed throughout, referred to that cloud with the general term "buildup." Captain Stephan never referred to the cloud as anything other than a cumulonimbus cloud or a buildup, both of which he said numerous times in his testimony. I believe that the CAB's use of the term "towering cumulus" was an error—a misnomer, a misquote, or a misprint. Unfortunately, decades later in interviews for this book, the captain could not clarify this. He was unable to recall his visual memory of the cloud, not too surprising considering that at the time, what mattered to him was the disaster itself, and the ominous fact that the cloud he saw in the area could very well have posed a deadly barrier between the flights, steering them around it and into each other.

A towering cumulus is generally proportioned as a tower, a buildup that is striking for its tallness, not for its breadth, whereas a cumulonimbus is generally proportioned horizontally oblong, and is striking for its breadth more so than its tallness, although the latter can be tremendous in the fully mature stage. If Stephan used the term "cumulonimbus" correctly, then that cloud could easily have been many miles wide. On the other hand, if he misspoke every time he said "cumulonimbus," and the CAB's usage of the term "towering cumulus" was correct, then the notion that the cloud was wide enough to stretch from miles out over the literal Grand Canyon, the gorge itself, southward to Grand Canyon Village and for miles beyond, is incorrect.

The average veteran pilot's grasp of weather conditions was second only to a meteorologist's, and in practical experience it far exceeded it. For this reason alone it is implausible that Captain Stephan repeatedly misspoke; moreover, if Stephan really meant "towering cumulus" every time he said "cumulonimbus," then he also grossly misjudged where he was in relation to Grand Canyon Village as he approached the area from the west, and he grossly misjudged how close he was to the cloud while he was passing the airport. This is truly far-fetched. Taking his testimony on face value is overwhelmingly more plausible, while holding it suspect entails complications that are somewhere between confounded and obtuse. For these reasons this book emphasizes the belief that the buildup was a cumulonimbus, and more to the point, that it was laterally extensive.

The cloud's size borrows its importance primarily from its location, or more precisely, the locations that it encompassed simultaneously. It extended like a giant wall almost as far south as Grand Canyon Airport from the area of Grand Canyon Village and points north of there. TWA 2's proposed course skirted the southern edge of the Grand Canyon midway between the village and the airport, meaning that with a great margin for error, the line of their proposed course cut through the cloud, where it stood at 11:39, about four or five miles into its mass laterally from the southern edge. If the cloud had already grown to nearly the proportions that Captain Stephan observed, by the earlier time TWA 2 reached it, then it was right in TWA 2's way and could account for why they detoured over the Grand Canyon.

The high altitude winds in the area were blowing almost exactly toward the east, at twenty-three miles per hour, so the cloud was moving in that direction and at that speed. Because TWA 2 was on about a 76-degree true course, pretty much eastward itself, and because the wind speed was only moderate, the cloud's translational motion due to the wind was not a dramatic factor in its gradually encroaching on TWA 2's course. If there was a dramatic factor, it had to be the cloud's growth rate, but this is another dead end because the rate at which the cloud was growing cannot be determined from the evidence.

Because not even one of its dimensions is clearly described for two clearly defined times, there is simply no way to calculate even an average rate. Its length north to south is well pinned down for 11:39 but for no other time; its height is clear at an unspecified time while Stephan was flying over the Grand Canyon toward it, before he turned, and ambiguously specified as the same at exactly 11:39; and the captain was unable to estimate its width east to west in 1956, let alone decades later, probably because by the time he could have seen the cloud in that aspect, from its southern side, the cloud's size was not especially important to him. How near he was to it mattered to him, but how big it was did not, because it no longer posed an obstruction for him to assess and get around. He had passed it. It is impossible to extrapolate backwards in time to show that the cloud blocked TWA 2's proposed course.

Still, a lot can be learned from a simple approach using no calculations, no times, and no distances.

United 718 was not affected by the giant cloud no matter how expansive it was when they were near it. It couldn't possibly have been in their way, because it was still north of their proposed course even when Captain Stephan flew past it to the south, which was well after United

718 was there. From the west side of it, they could not have seen any breaks in the lower cloud deck from their proposed course even if there were some, because of the distance, and by the same token they were impractically far from the canyon at that time for a sightseeing venture anyway, so they had no good reason at all to turn northward then.

Grand Canyon airspace was defined as the airspace directly above the rocky gorge itself, not also above the forested rim or the surrounding plateau. United 718 must have entered Grand Canyon airspace on the *east* side of the cloud, and purely for the sake of sightseeing.

If TWA 2 diverted from their proposed course in the area of the canyon's eastern end, then the giant cloud *had* to be in their way. They couldn't have flown northward into the canyon on the far side of it, the eastern side, or they and United 718 would have been so near to each other that they would undoubtedly have seen each other, and there would have been no accident.

Disregarding the fact that they had no motive to do so, it could still be argued that United 718 might have entered Grand Canyon airspace from the west side of the cloud while TWA 2 flew on the east side, but then United is on the left and TWA is on the right when they meet, contrary to their relation when they collided. This would require that they crisscross, very nearly colliding, and then come back together, but they certainly would have seen each other in the crisscross and would not have collided after that.

TWA 2 must have flown out over the canyon to the *west* of the cloud. From their course, much nearer the canyon than United 718's in the neighborhood of the cloud, they could have seen the lower overcast stretching westward out from underneath of it well enough to determine that there were only few and small breaks, or no breaks at all; ergo, the only sensible, compelling reason for them to have flown there is that they were forced by the cloud's barring their way along their proposed course.

This doesn't prove that the cloud was in their way; rather, it proves that *if* they entered Grand Canyon airspace at the canyon's eastern end, it *had* to be. They might have left their proposed course to fly out over the canyon much sooner, out of expecting trouble ahead or simply out of wanting to ensure that they could show the sights to the passengers.

These are the primary possibilities, and probably no more needs to be said to outline them. More detail can be given to these simple conclusions, however, to bring them to life and to better illustrate the fateful movements of both flights during their obscure journey through the wilderness of northern Arizona.

If TWA 2 crossed over into the canyon at its eastern end, then the giant cloud had to have been in their way. As already examined, they could not reasonably have flown along its eastern face. This also means that they couldn't have veered around it to the south and arced northward from there, which of course would have put them on the east side. Moreover, practicality likely dissuaded them if they considered the longer way around: to circumnavigate the cloud to the south was inefficient, because Kansas City was to the north component-wise. The eastern third was covered over by the lower cloud deck, and they were probably resigned to nature having refused them sightseeing, since they surely saw that the coverage was total or nearly total, but in trying they would at least have a chance.

In the opinion of many captains at the time, the best views of the Grand Canyon were those from the area of one of its side canyons, called Havasau Canyon, eastward—or to put it another way, from about 112 degrees, 40 minutes west longitude eastward. On their proposed course, TWA 2 would have reached 112 degrees, 40 minutes west at about 11:17. Here they would certainly have been able to perceive that the cloud was going to be trouble for them on their proposed course. The canyon was impractically far north of their particular course at that time, irrespective of how beautiful it might have been, so if they turned here it was to avoid the cloud well ahead of time, and sightseeing was secondary. Maybe they left their proposed course in this area, or maybe they flew on for a few more minutes, ten or fifteen miles nearer to the cloud, and then turned. The Grand Canyon was significantly closer to TWA 2's proposed course at that distance eastward, but it was also more thickly socked in with the lower cloud deck.

The other major possibility is that TWA 2 flew out over the canyon before reaching the eastern end and the vicinity of the cumulonimbus cloud. At about 11:09 they reached a part of the Grand Canyon called Lower Granite Gorge, where the Colorado River lay only about five miles off their proposed course, to the north. This general area is the canyon's overall southern extremity and spread all the way to TWA 2's proposed course and beyond, to the south. Their course crossed over a side canyon called Peach Springs Canyon, which they could simply have followed northward to Lower Granite Gorge. And in all likelihood they *were* still on their proposed course at 11:09, because before that there was no good reason to leave it.

Lower Granite Gorge did not offer quite the spectacular sights that could be had at the eastern end, but it was magnificent in itself and well worth seeing. In this area and for another fifty miles eastward, only scattered to broken lower clouds floated over the canyon, and excellent sightseeing could have been done from the air. Beyond fifty miles to the east, the canyon was covered by the thick overcast that spread westward from the area of Grand Canyon Village. From his altitude Captain Gandy could hardly have discerned that the cloud cover fifty or more miles away had not quite sealed itself over and still had a few modest breaks in it. Being only just over a mile higher, his line of sight angled downward toward it at only about one degree. It would be like lying prostrate on a sidewalk and trying to judge from that vantage point how cracked and chipped the sidewalk was fifty feet away. One could see the sidewalk, but not its features, and although Gandy could see the carpeting of clouds, he surely could not see its features either. However, he could see the building cumulonimbus cloud at that distance, smaller than it would be by the time he reached it but already big. This dubious picture might have encouraged him to take the sure bet and do the lesser but guaranteed sightseeing.

And if it was not enough by itself to decisively influence him, then the beautiful vista to his left probably was. He could see perfectly that the huge area in and beyond nearby Lower Granite Gorge was filled predominantly with open sky, and that there the canyon could be viewed from above. It was simply logical to take the known opportunity for sightseeing rather than gamble on the chance of having a better opportunity farther on—logical, that is, if he judged he could afford the time for sightseeing. A modest detour might have cost two minutes, but no more and probably less, because it would be conducted northward and eastward, and Kansas City lay in both of these directions. On the other side, sightseeing was traditional and expected on Flight 2, and perhaps he never seriously entertained skipping it.

In this scenario TWA 2 left their proposed course and flew about five miles northward to Lower Granite Gorge, probably through Peach Springs Canyon, and then followed the Colorado River northward and then northeastward, which in effect amounted to following the canyon in those directions. They may have performed a couple "S" maneuvers along the way, arcing gently leftward for a half minute or so and then equivalently rightward, dipping the left wing and then the right wing in succession to drop them out of the way of passengers' views on alternate sides of the plane. The "S" was a popular sightseeing pattern, because it gave equal time to passengers on each side and enabled even passengers seated over the wings to see below, and because the plane left the figure headed in the same direction it was going when it entered it. Of course, with the meandering of the Colorado River, following a straight course down the center line of its wavering would have given passengers on both sides equal opportunity anyway, except for those seated right over the wings.

Whatever pattern they flew, they probably rolled out on an eastward heading at roughly the middle latitude of the Grand Canyon's eastern third. This was the latitude on which they and United 718 collided some miles farther on; contrarily supposing that TWA 2 ventured farther north, they would have had to backtrack southward to wind up there. This is unlikely because it would have been inefficient time-wise, being that Kansas City was northward. There is another reason for which they would have wanted to roll out on an eastward heading at about the canyon's middle latitude, which is more concrete but also somewhat esoteric; this issue is taken up in Chapter 9.

Concisely, TWA 2 entered Grand Canyon airspace either near the longitude of Havasau Canyon, out of the necessity of avoiding the huge, building cumulonimbus cloud, or through Lower Granite Gorge, for the sake of sightseeing. There are other lesser possibilities, but these two stand out as by far the most likely, because they are the only ones that provide a clear motive.

Whichever way history played itself out on that tragic flight, the crisscrossing that was by chance or by fate built into the combined flight plans of TWA 2 and United 718 was dissolved as soon as TWA 2 diverted from their proposed course. Once they turned off, the "hazard" that had loomed ahead for the whole time they were in uncontrolled airspace vanished, and both they and United 718 were free of it, as safe as any two flights could have been.

Of course, their new total safety was both short-lived and completely lost on them, vanishing without benefitting them at all. The only person in the world who could have benefited from the detouring never did. It could have been at least some small vindication of the Salt Lake City controller who handled the two flights. Both flights' position reports were forwarded to him, but he did not receive United 718's from Needles INSACS until 11:12. Even though United 718 radioed it at 10:58, the interphone circuits between the INSACS and Salt Lake ARTC were tied up, causing a delay of fourteen minutes. (The man at Needles had successfully relayed the report to Albuquerque ARTC at 11:00, but Albuquerque was not required to relay it in turn to Salt Lake ARTC because Albuquerque's area *followed* Salt Lake's, not the other way around.)

Assuming that TWA 2 turned off their proposed course at 11:09 to head for Lower Granite Gorge, a simple conclusion directly follows:

namely, by the time the Salt lake City controller knew that both TWA 2 and United 718 were expecting to reach the Painted Desert LOP at exactly the same time and could have warned them, the collision risk implied in their original flight plans no longer existed. He couldn't have known this, because he couldn't have known that TWA 2 had turned off, but that's beside the point: the original risk at the Painted Desert LOP was gone. As he later testified, such warnings would normally be of little use and might have caused more confusion than anything else. Unfortunately for him, the possibility that TWA 2 diverted at Lower Granite Gorge was never connected with his refraining from warning them. He would still have been criticized, but the likelihood that the danger had passed would at least have mitigated the public's opinion.

*   *   *

United 718's movements over Arizona are also conjectural because, like TWA 2, they sent no messages indicating what they were doing, and they had no flight data recording equipment. Likewise no one saw them, at least not anyone who came forward. Nevertheless, two major details emerge as highly probable. Despite the overcast covering the eastern third of the canyon, there is every reason to believe that they left their proposed course to fly out over the canyon only for the sake of sightseeing, and that they turned off to do this at the far eastern end. In complement there appears to be no good reason to believe anything different from this.

The cumulonimbus cloud that likely encompassed TWA 2's proposed course near Grand Canyon Village was not in United 718's way; their proposed course passed about three miles south of Grand Canyon Airport, or likely over five miles south of the cloud. Consequently the cloud's presence cannot explain the fact that United 718 turned and headed out over the canyon. They could simply have flown past it, with a very wide berth to their left and without straying at all from their proposed course.

The possibility that there was yet another huge cumulus cloud up ahead and in their way over the Painted Desert, immediately east of the canyon, can be ruled out because Captain Stephan later described the sky east of the canyon as being clear of buildups. He noted that there were two or three more buildups to the northeast of the giant one and spoke of no others, but these were over the canyon itself and were considerably north of United 718's proposed course. These could not possibly have forced them to turn, much less to turn in the direction of the canyon. Weather was not a factor in what brought them to the Grand Canyon. The only possibility this leaves is sightseeing.

United 718's proposed course ran to the south of TWA 2's across Arizona all the way to the Painted Desert LOP, twenty-five miles east of the Grand Canyon, where the two courses crossed each other. United 718 passed too far away (fully thirty miles) from Lower Granite Gorge for a sightseeing detour there to be practical, and they did not come closer to any other part of the canyon until they neared the eastern end. As they neared the giant cloud, coming to roughly its longitude, the canyon veered closer to them in its undulating layout below but still remained too far away for a sightseeing jaunt to be conservative, about twenty miles. Also from that distance, the crew could not reliably have discerned any but the largest breaks in the nearly total overcast that obscured the eastern end of the canyon. The overcast was about a mile thick, and though there might have been a few holes in it, they must, by definition of "overcast," have been modest and therefore too small to make out clearly from a shallow angle twenty or more miles away. From here the crew could not have distinguished a pothole in the cloud deck from a shaft of open sky that ran clear through it.

A few minutes farther along, United 718 passed the giant cloud, and then the only remaining area fronting the canyon from their side was the eastern South Rim. This was also the southernmost extremity of the eastern end, and thereby the area that came the nearest to United 718's proposed course. Here they were only about eight miles away and fairly likely could have discerned even modest breaks in the lower cloud deck. The eastern South Rim was their last chance to fly over any part of the canyon.

Again, the east-to-west dimension of the huge cloud is unknown, but in very rough terms it was probably substantial given its north-to-south massiveness, leaving room to wonder if the sky over the eastern South Rim was clear or not at United 718's altitude. However, as previously noted, Captain Stephan saw more buildups to the northeast of the giant one as he passed it to the south. These were over the canyon, which extended no farther eastward than its South Rim did. Had the giant one extended over most of the South Rim, he could not have seen the others from his vantage point south of it. And because he mentioned no additional buildups, it is safe to assume that there were no others over the South Rim area. Still more directly, the fact that United 718 wound up over the canyon at all pretty much proves that the huge cloud did not cover the whole South Rim—and more to the point, that the sky there was visually navigable. This in turn means that sightseeing was possible. Somewhere along the eastern fifteen miles or so of the South Rim they entered the Grand Canyon.

*　　*　　*

Even the time at which United 718 reached the longitude of the eastern South Rim and turned off their proposed course to head for it can be reliably estimated. By at least two independent schemes of calculation, drawing from the time at which they were over Needles, the time at which they expected to cross the Painted Desert LOP, their probable true airspeed, and the winds aloft in their area, United 718 made their northward turn toward the Grand Canyon at about 11:24. Less than seven minutes later they collided with TWA 2.

Whether the crew of United 718 decided to detour for an exploratory excursion to the north in search of a break in the lower cloud cover, or because they actually saw a break from their proposed course, what really counts is that United 718's detour placed them and TWA 2 on opposite sides of the giant cloud, headed *toward* each other again.

Whether TWA 2 got there on a short, direct detour path northward beginning near Havasau Canyon, or on a long, indirect path northward through Lower Granite Gorge earlier and eastward from there, they would have arrived at the north end of the giant cloud at the same time, almost exactly. Either way, TWA 2 was abreast of the northwest quadrant of the giant cloud, or roughly ten miles west and ten miles north of Grand Canyon Village, at about 11:24, the very time that United 718 was turning off to head for the canyon—a turn which placed them abreast of the southeast quadrant of the cloud, diagonally opposite from TWA 2.

Once TWA 2 resumed flying eastward, whether near the cloud's north end or way back at Lower Granite Gorge, then for their part they set the stage for a new disaster. When United 718 turned northward to head for the canyon, they completed this altogether new collision hazard. The planes were once again on converging courses, and more precisely, full collision *paths*, both headed for the airspace over a place within the canyon called the Walhalla Plateau, each from about twenty miles away.

This must have happened even if the "huge" cloud was only big, say, five or ten miles across north to south. It was still over Grand Canyon Village or nearby, just to the north—Captain Stephan could not reasonably have mistaken that it was right in front of him as he flew eastward over the canyon. More reasonably speaking, he might have misjudged his distance from the cloud when he flew over the airport, although surely not by many miles. Or there could have been a numerical, typographical error at that spot in the transcript of his testimony. For example, printing "2" instead of "12," leaving out the "1," would make it appear that he said he was two miles from the cloud, when what he really said was, "Twelve." That of course would mean that the cloud was actually a great deal smaller. How likely a disastrous typographical error like that might be is anyone's guess, but it is very unlikely, simply on the strength that nearly every character in any official, printed document is correct.

Taking the cloud to have lain over the village or nearby north of it, which is very reliable testimony because Stephan could hardly have been mistaken on both the point that it was in front of him and the point that it was over the village, a smaller version of it can be conceived as the northern quarter or third of the hypothesized "huge" cloud. Before reaching the immediate area of this reduced cloud, the flights would have been too far apart to see each other, and by the time they could reliably have seen each other, the cloud would have been in between them. In essence, their circumstances are not changed, and envisioning their courses correspondingly the same as if the cloud had been huge, the entire situation is the same in all important respects but one.

If the "giant" cumulonimbus cloud over Grand Canyon Village was actually much smaller than thus far portrayed, big but not huge, then there is no substance to the belief that the cloud blocked TWA 2's way along their proposed course. If they passed up their chance for sightseeing at Lower Granite Gorge, then for lack of another reasonable opportunity, they in all likelihood just kept flying along their proposed course until they reached the area of the big cloud. In that area their course passed by the Grand Canyon closely enough for them to see that there were only scanty breaks or no breaks at all in the lower overcast adjacent to the big cloud, on its west side. Disregarding the previous reasoning in this chapter for the moment and starting over, if they entered Grand Canyon airspace at the eastern end, then it would seem to be a foregone conclusion that they did so on the far side of the cloud, after passing it. To skirt its western face would have served no purpose. But there are two problems with this: first, TWA 2 and United 718 then do not come around the cloud from opposite sides, so there is no concrete indication of anything obstructing their view of each other, and they should not have collided; and second, they must have flown northward together on the east side of the cloud—presumably to avail themselves of the last chance to find any breaks in the lower cloud deck—with one of them only a mile or two behind the other, or else the trailing one could not have caught up soon enough for the accident to occur over the Grand Canyon. But from so close, the one behind would certainly see the one in front and avoid running into it. Again there would be no collision.

This greatly fortifies the supposition that TWA 2 turned off their proposed course to head into Grand Canyon airspace at about 11:09 after all, at Lower Granite Gorge. It also fortifies the odd notion that if TWA 2 did divert from their proposed course at the eastern end of the canyon, then they must have flown northward along the *west* face of the cloud, despite the cloud not barring their way and forcing them to turn, and without any intention of sightseeing. The latter scenario apparently amounts to suggesting that they flew over the canyon for no reason at all. The best that can be done with it is to rephrase it: they went there for reasons utterly unknown. This is vacuous, and it is also invalid, because it asserts that there was a reason without any concrete evidence to support that there was.

It all comes down to this: if the cloud that was over Grand Canyon Village was not laterally gigantic, then almost beyond doubt TWA 2 ventured into Grand Canyon airspace at Lower Granite Gorge, and for no other reason than sightseeing. And the latitude at which they turned eastward remains unchanged—the cloud is still over Grand Canyon Village, the desirable middle latitude of the eastern canyon is of course the same, and their esoteric motive for following that latitude eastward had nothing to do with clouds, as will be discussed in Chapter 9.

As for United 718, their situation remains exactly as already portrayed even if it turns out that the cumulonimbus cloud was actually modest in size or not a cumulonimbus at all, but a towering cumulus, tall but not especially expansive laterally. It was still over Grand Canyon Village and still served as the signpost around which they turned and flew out past the edge of the world. Their first reasonable chance for sightseeing came only after they coincidentally passed the cloud's longitude and were on the east side of it. Then in contrast to the circumstance west of it, they could see the cloud deck at 15,000 feet in enough detail to discern some of the breaks in it, if there were any. And if there weren't any to be seen, then simple hope must have carried them. United 718 went out there only to see the sights, crossing over into canyon airspace at the eastern South Rim, at about 11:26.

And unfortunately, tragically, the terrible rendezvous near the Walhalla Plateau, TWA from the west and United from the south, with the obscuring cloud between them, is unchanged. The cloud is smaller, but no less disastrous an intervening obstruction.

It was as though their ends were predestined. Every move they made seems to have had no determinative bearing on the outcome. They had been chosen for sacrifice, and the decision had been made without them; they had been reduced to irrelevancies in their own destinies. There had been the coincidence of the original flight plans collectively spelling converging courses; and then the coincidence of both planes being held up on the ground so that they took off only three minutes apart rather than fifteen; and then TWA 2's ascent to 21,000 feet, turning the converging courses into actual collision paths; and then the nullifying of the impending disaster by TWA 2's northward detour, wherever they made it; and then, as if in obeisance to the principle that fate cannot be revoked and must be satisfied, the two had separately turned from their benign courses, TWA 2 from their northerly detour course and United 718 from their proposed course east-northeasterly, to again converge on each other.

They were helpless—helpless because they were unaware, helpless because every path they could take led to the same place, and helpless because they had no voice in the decree.

Somewhere over the wilderness of northern Arizona, they left the known and assumed and predictable world behind them. They left the familiar world of human endeavors and of mundane laws, and they entered the dominion of the heavens. Destiny may be preordained from eternity, or decided only at some definable moment in time and only thereafter irrevocable. If it is as most of us conceive of it—impossible to alter once it has been set, whether decreed from the beginning of creation or only just a moment ago—then it defies material laws, which always allow for what is impending to be changed. Obviously if there is any time remaining at all before an event, then it can be averted by the application of force, and there is no limit to how much force may be impressed, nor to how comprehensively what would have been can be rewritten. This is simply a matter of observation. Or is it? No amount of evidence consistent with a given belief can prove that it has no exceptions.

When inexplicable events occur, it is only humble and honest to surrender and call them destiny, and to defer their cause to a vague, intangible, all-encompassing will, which has been given the name fate. As the motive power behind events that seem to have an unlimited capacity to carry themselves out, because they resist or elude any and all of our efforts to prevent them, fate becomes undeniable and absolutely convincing. It seems as real as anything tangible, and no doubt it is. Fate is axiomatic—its reality is inescapable, and it is a timeless theme in which mankind has believed throughout history.

Given that there is fate, then its laws operate outside of physical laws to unfold destiny; and yet because fate is impressed upon and expressed within material reality, its laws must operate within and through physical laws. A plane crashes not by the Earth rising to strike it, but by falling to the ground, in conformity with the laws of aerodynamics and gravity. But because fate has made its absolute pronouncement, no physical force or object or act can stop it. A limited physical thing, the plane, would thus seem to have been imbued with infinite power, or to be shielded from the laws of cause and effect that govern the entire material universe, both of which are impossible; and yet there appears to be no denying that fate is real. Fate, in its collusion with material reality, becomes a paradox, breaking physical laws by preserving them. The freak of nature that results is at once undeniable and unbelievable, a thing that is both whole and broken at the same time, like an intact vase lying shattered in pieces.

On a midsummer day in 1956, two groups of air travelers imperceptibly slipped from this world and entered onto a frame of reference where they were hardly more than metaphors. They existed for a time in a paradoxical place that was real even though it couldn't be, a space that gained its principles from a paranormal volition that manifested them or dissolved them to suit its designs. Though they were not yet absolutely gone, they were also definitely no longer here. They had been removed to a place unlike any natural place, somewhere as figurative as it was literal, from which it was impossible to exit. They were *elsewhere*.

CHAPTER 8

IN THE DAYS and weeks following the tragedy, evidence was discovered suggesting that Captain Shirley was not in his seat when his plane collided with Captain Gandy's. This apparently was never publicized, and whether judiciously or fortuitously, it's a good thing that it wasn't, because it would almost certainly have been immediately and widely construed to mean that the disaster was Captain Shirley's fault, for having been away from his station at the crucial moment. It would have been another tragedy for his family and friends, and a cruel compounding of their suffering: in their grief they would also have to have endured the anguish of the public blaming and condemning him. The pilots were almost always prejudicially blamed, but with "concrete" evidence backing up the public's opinion, their criticism would have been especially cutting. It was enough for the man to lose his life. It would have been criminal for his reputation, and his memory, and the good standing of his name to have spuriously died with him.

It was obviously safer to have two pilots at the controls and keeping lookouts than to have just one; this cannot be sensibly disputed. Whenever either of the pilots left the cockpit, his flight was temporarily more vulnerable. From Captain Shirley's seat there was a better view of the sky to the left of the DC-7, the side from which the 1049 closed in on them, than from anywhere else on the flight deck. But Captain Shirley had no obligation to continuously remain in his seat, and he did have a customary obligation to leave it and go meet the passengers. This was a tradition that, for airmen, was analogous to a seafaring captain's having dinner with some of his passengers. He may have been doing this when the planes collided, and if he was, then the accident was something that was done to him as much as it was to the passengers, not something that he caused.

What could be questioned is the custom itself, and if his absence was in fact partly to blame for the disaster, then if anything, it would be better to condemn the custom than to blame the man, and more meaningful. It may not even be sensible to find fault with the custom. Every act entails a risk. The world has not been improved by doing away with the captain's visit. It may be slightly safer, but it's not better. The captain recognized that his passengers were all entrusting him with their lives—a very powerful statement of their confidence in his capableness, and in him personally. The two could not be separated, and he felt honored. They gave him this and he felt grateful, and in return he wanted to thank them. The most genuine, sincere way he could do that was to go back and personally meet them, one at a time. By showing them face-to-face who they were trusting, letting them see his character in his eyes, he gave substance and legitimacy to their judgment. In turn they felt affirmed and more confident in their decision to fly, and in him. They could see his sincerity and he could see theirs, and the small personal bond that this small act of kindness engendered made the whole experience brighter.

People were more honored when the captain walked back into the passenger compartment to meet them than they are by the stricter code that has supplanted that charming tradition in the name of their safety. One simple principle in life seems to be that ultimately, the better way is to follow the options that have a heart, and there is no heart in the crew sequestering themselves behind a door. To the intellect this precaution may appear more logical, and it is, but a higher logic follows the greater good and produces a world with more heartfelt value. There was heart in the captain's visit, and if it was deemed necessary to make piloting practices safer, then a new custom could have been added to support the old one, rather than to displace it. For example, the flight engineer could have taken the captain's seat and his lookout.

At most it could be asked why Captain Shirley did not forsake tradition in the name of the greatest possible safety, but he can hardly be regarded as culpable. For Captain Shirley to reject the etiquette that was expected of him, which was considered safe by an industry-wide consensus, would have required him to be a man of unusual sensibilities, and no one can be faulted for being less than extraordinary, except possibly for someone who *is* extraordinary.

Seeking someone to blame would run blatantly in conflict with the purpose of this book; the motivation behind such a goal cannot help but be judgmental, punitive, and heartless. Had my research revealed anyone to be culpable, that person would be identified in the text, but with a grave and respectful tone, not a condemnatory one. No one emerged even as suspect, let alone clearly negligent or incompetent. I was dedicated to finding the cause of the tragedy no matter what it was—nature, machine, or man—and fortunately I was spared the sorrowful task of having to defame anyone. No matter how I would have handled it, that would have become a contradiction in the book's spirit: harming a human being as an expression of the value and dignity of human life.

The spirit of this book is the conviction that people matter. In the case in point, the importance of the captain's whereabouts in the final minutes is that any particulars of his actions, even those developed by inference, serve both to memorialize him and to indicate what might have been the circumstances of the other crewmembers, and of the passengers. Except for a meager few details, all of those people vanished from life in total obscurity, and it can only honor them to tell some portion, any portion, of their story.

When the *City of Vancouver* crashed, it hit a natural, solid rock wall head-on and disintegrated. At the speed they were going, not only was survival impossible, but on top of this, everyone on board was subjected to damage carried to an extreme well beyond fatal injuries. The terrible truth was that, regardless of how much aircraft structure surrounded and lay in front of a person to absorb some of the impact and diminish the destructiveness that would be inflicted upon him, almost everyone was severely rended, and some were outright annihilated. The amount of protection a victim had did make a difference, but not much. Still, many escaped obliteration partly due to having the shielding of a lot of compressible objects and materials in front of them, and partly due to having relatively little of unyielding objects or materials behind them. Also, flukes in the incredibly complex multitude of individual motions, during the split-second ground breakup sequence, caused a few of them to be thrown clear of the paths of greatest destructiveness.

The very front of the airplane afforded neither of these circumstances. There was practically no shielding in front of the flight deck, and it was right on the path of greatest destructiveness. The nose had nowhere to go, and by the time the flight deck could have been thrust anywhere, it had disintegrated. Furthermore, behind it lay almost the entire fuselage. Behind the flight deck was the maximum extent of unforgiving objects imposed upon anyone on the plane. Of the three flight crewmembers, only Captain Shirley was ever identified. Four persons aboard were spared the worst rending and the fire. He was one of them. Reasonably speaking, he must not have been with Harms and Fiore when the plane hit the ground.

Just before that, First Officer Harms sent a mayday message, which was picked up by the ARINC station at Salt Lake City. It was brief, but Harms held the microphone for a comparatively long time after he finished speaking, still squeezing the send button on it and thereby continuing to transmit. Unlike TWA stations using leased ARINC equipment, ARINC stations recorded their radio communications, just like ARTC. Harms' whole transmission was tape recorded by ARINC, and in playing it back later, a second person could be heard in the background yelling, "Pull up! Pull up!" while Harms was speaking, and making other desperate utterances after that while Harms was silent. Friends of Flight Engineer Fiore later identified the second person's voice as his when listening to the tape, just as friends of First Officer Harms identified Harms' voice as that of the sender in the mayday message. But there was no third voice on the recording. Captain Shirley's voice could not be found, not even through laboratory analysis.

It seems implausible, if not incredible, that the officer in command in a mortal emergency, having his hands full with a crippled airplane and needing all the help he could get, would not utter a single word for the extended time of this transmission. The captain might have shouted orders to Harms or Fiore, or vocally coaxed the machine as though it were alive with phrases like, "Come on, baby, come on!" But he would not have been *silent*. The absence of Captain Shirley's voice on the tape recording has to mean that he wasn't there.

One dissenting interpretation of this with at least a shred of credibility is that Captain Shirley was unconscious. The Constellation came from the left and imparted a sharp, rightward impulse momentarily to the DC-7. With the airplane that was carrying them being their stationary frame of reference, the United crew and passengers experienced this relatively as being thrust bodily leftward. It is possible that if he was in his seat, the jolt of the impact banged the captain's head against the side window to his left, possibly even forcefully enough to knock him out. It is also possible that if he was just leaving the flight deck when the collision occurred, the same jolt threw him against the radio rack on the port side, or caused him to stumble and fall. Either of these could have knocked him out. In all three cases, however, it is very unlikely—with such tremendous masses involved, the impact forces did little more to the planes than destroy the areas of them that struck each other. Both planes were jolted but probably not severely, and so the hypothetical effects on Captain Shirley would not have been severe either. He may have fallen or hit his head, but not hard enough to knock him out. Unfortunately, the fact that Harms and Fiore were conscious afterward says nothing about how the captain may have fared, because there were no structures immediately left of their seats to deliver blows. And because they were required to be wearing their seatbelts whenever they were occupying their seats, they could not have been thrown out of them.

Considerably less likely is the possibility that Captain Shirley was resigned to the situation being hopeless and had fallen silent, dissociated from the peril they were in. He may have been convinced, if he was present, that the airplane could not be stabilized, especially because with his sixteen years as a captain and roughly two hundred trips flying DC-7s, he of all people should have been able to judge by feel whether or not his airplane was mortally wounded. But being by character a man of life long decisiveness, he would valiantly have tried everything he could. If he could have paused to think, a man of his sort might have thought, "As long as I'm alive, I have a chance." He could have been positive that it was hopeless without being resigned to it, certain that it was the end yet struggling still to save everyone. Irrational as this might be, it would be far crazier to do nothing. Only a fool would use his head rather than his gut and not even try to save himself. Captain Shirley would have hung on and would have spoken, if not to his crew or his machine, then at least to express his fear to the open air. This may be a feeling as much as it is a reasoned opinion, but it stands to reason all around: few captains ever freeze in a crisis, and few human beings ever give up on their own lives.

In another vein, irrespective of the captain's voice lacking on the tape recording, it might be argued that Harms' sending of the distress call suggests that he was not piloting the airplane alone after all. Even in normal situations, let alone in an emergency, there were only infrequent exceptions to the convention that someone other than the pilot doing the flying would send the messages. In normal conditions, this gave another crewmember that might otherwise have been temporarily idle something to do, and it relieved the one flying of the awkwardness of doing two things at once. In an emergency, of course, it was imperative that the one flying not split his attention. If Captain Shirley were absent, leaving Harms in command flying the airplane, Harms would tell Fiore to make the call, so on the surface it looks like the captain must have been there. But Fiore was beside himself. As will be shown in more detail in Chapter 10, he was nearly hysterical. Harms probably did order Fiore to send the message, and in the incoherence of his panic, Fiore was unable to comply. Harms would have to have sent it himself, even while desperately trying to control the plane.

If Captain Shirley had been present and in control, Fiore would almost certainly have been his first choice, too, because this would leave Harms entirely free to help the captain try to fly the crippled airplane. With Fiore unable to function, however, the captain would have had Harms send the message rather than doing it himself, and this is consistent with what is known to have happened: Harms did send the message. But the fact that Harms sent it means nothing about whether the captain was actually present or not, because Harms would have been the one to get on the radio either way.

One more point: it does seem implausible on first examination, that Harms would have operated the radio while trying to control the perilously unstable plane. But Harms knew they were going to crash, as he made plain in his message, "We are going in," and he must have realized that if he managed a crash *landing*, there would be survivors, many of whom would be gravely injured, with death imminent. He must have realized that it was imperative for him to alert Salt Lake City to this, so that a search and a rescue could occur as soon as possible, and the injured victims could be saved. Harms had the ultimate duty of saving everyone aboard, and there were two ways he could act to that end: flying the plane and calling for help. He did both.

In all probability Captain Shirley left First Officer Harms and Flight Engineer Fiore, and in the last minutes Harms was flying the airplane by himself, with Fiore in the central, engineer's jump seat. It is highly doubtful that Fiore moved up into the captain's seat, on the left, to help keep the lookout for other planes while the captain was gone. For one thing, the captain would not have exited if he had judged there to be any appreciable hazard, like problematic clouds up ahead that could not be easily circumnavigated. The fact that he left, assuming he actually did, shows that he probably had no concrete reason to ask Fiore to change seats and help Harms watch the sky. By the same token, Harms probably had little or no reason to ask Fiore to move up, even though in the captain's absence he had the authority.

Even with a good reason, Fiore would certainly not have presumed to change seats of his own accord, any more than the royal cook would take the throne in the king's absence. As one retired captain from those days gravely put it, "You could lose your head that way." The command structure in a flight crew was not casual or informal, but divided firmly into a hierarchy whose levels were large steps apart. To illustrate this point, ordinarily whenever two captains met by chance at the ramp office, accompanied by their copilots, the captains greeted each other and conversed exclusively with each other, as though oblivious to the presence of their inferiors. They might nod once to the copilots or even say a few token words to them, and the copilots were expected to return the nod or to respond with only a respectful minimum of words, and never to venture initiating any further dialogue. Even a copilot would never have dared to take the captain's seat without permission, let alone an engineer.

There was also a difficult political situation between United Air Lines' pilots and flight engineers, which had evolved into an artificial etiquette that tacitly prescribed standoffishness between the two groups. Pilots and flight engineers alike had become resolved to preserve the distinction between pilots' duties and engineers' duties, or more plainly, the distinction between pilots and engineers.

Since just after World War II there had been conflict between the two groups, chiefly through their respective unions, centering predominantly on the issue of whether or not engineers should also be qualified pilots. Starting in 1948, United's management had repeatedly taken the position that they should, and it had insisted on this in negotiations with the flight engineers' union each time the contract between the union and the company neared the end of its term, only to back down each time in reaction to counter maneuvers made by the engineers' union. Management proposed replacing the flight engineer's position with a new title called second officer, and using only employees that were qualified both as engineers and copilots to fill this position. The company offered free copilot training to its pure flight engineers, as well as higher pay as second officers than they were accustomed to earning as flight engineers, but as a group the engineers did not want the change, primarily because both in background and at heart they were mechanics more than flyers.

United's pilots, on the other hand, were opposed as a group to there even being a third crewmember on the flight deck, whether flight engineer or second officer, because in their estimation the Douglas aircraft, including the DC-7, could be flown perfectly well by two people. These planes had in fact been designed this way, unlike Lockheed's Constellations, which required three, but government regulations promulgated in 1948 had foisted a flight engineer upon the pilots for safety reasons. Most pilots refuted these reasons, because they addressed possible emergencies that had largely been precluded by subsequent design changes in the aircraft. Moreover, United's pilots took the position that if they had to tolerate a third crewmember crowding them, then let it be one of their own breed, a flyer rather than a mechanic.

The pilots were also concerned that with the bigger, faster aircraft that were progressively becoming available, the numbers of flights might be reduced, and the flying times of many trips would certainly be reduced. Fewer flights could carry the same number of passengers, and between this and getting there faster, there appeared the grave prospect that many pilots would lose working hours and thus receive less pay. Consequently, they hoped to compensate for this eventuality by ensuring for their part that only pilots could qualify for the third job on the flight deck. They sought to exploit the average flight engineer's disinclination to become a pilot and counted on many resigning rather than earning promotions to second officer. This would create a decline in the flight crew workforce, corresponding with the decline in the available work hours, with the effect that the flying time allotted for the average crewmember who was already working as a pilot would be little changed. So in their own union contract negotiations with the company, the pilots pressed United to press the engineers.

The result was a lot of animosity, which went both ways. The friction between the two groups had been long and repeatedly re-enlivened, causing a generalized atmosphere of disdain or at least alienation between them, which most crewmembers sublimated into a sort of stoic forbearance that prevailed no matter how much they might like or respect one another personally. It was both subtle and firm.

On the other side, whether they knew each other personally or not, most pilots and flight engineers at least tolerated each other's ambitions and philosophical differences, no matter how maddening, and on duty they put them as far aside as they could. In most groupings they worked well together as a team, nearly as they would have done had there been no conflicts, with the primary exceptions that pilots were careful not to encroach on engineers' territories or impose any pilots' duties on them, and engineers were careful not to add any pilots' duties to their own if they could help it. Keeping the lookout was a pilot's duty and had to be done from a pilot's seat, so in all likelihood neither Captain Shirley nor First Officer Harms asked Flight Engineer Fiore to do it, and Fiore didn't volunteer.

*　　*　　*

The captain's seat was surely vacant in the last moments before the disaster, and he was somewhere in the back, probably visiting with the passengers. Of course there is no way of knowing whether Captain Shirley was in fact visiting just before the end, much less with whom, but I like to imagine that he was talking to the five-year-old boy on board, Master Jeffrey Crider. I picture the captain presenting him with a complimentary pair of junior wings, making him feel like a big shot with a badge to prove it, and affectionately asking Jeffrey, "How do you like the clouds?"

Jeffrey, first beaming with enthusiasm and then frowning in the gentle disapprobation with which only children can object to things not being the way they're supposed to be, replies, "They're big! But I don't see any angels." At this the captain and a couple of passengers seated immediately around Jeffrey chuckle benevolently, and Jeffrey's mother, sitting next to him, smiles and blushes, feeling charmed by her son and slightly embarrassed.

I see the captain, after a moment's pause to regain himself, saying, "That's right, they must be on some other cloud today."

Jeffrey, looking entirely pensive, nods emphatically and says, "Yes, they're bowling on some other cloud." Captain Shirley, Mrs. Crider, and the other passengers nearby laugh out loud and feel warmhearted, protective affection for Jeffrey in his innocence. This story may be purely fanciful, but I'm sure that Jeffrey Crider was one of the chosen ones who did see the angels that day.

CHAPTER 9

A SECOND CLOUD may have been the next element in what caused the disaster. Captain Stephan saw several other cumulonimbus clouds that morning to the northeast of the giant one, and he also observed that there were no buildups east of the Grand Canyon, over the Painted Desert. He could not recall the scene with any more precision than that, which is not surprising because when he was there, it was not important to him. I don't propose to try establishing where exactly these clouds were, but only to indicate where one of them could have been. Straight off, however, their location can be rephrased more meaningfully: all of them were over the canyon.

Insofar as things are most substantially located wherever their centers lie, "northeast" means that the center of any one of the additional clouds was approximately to the northeast of the giant cloud's center. In this scheme a cloud significantly smaller in girth than the giant one could be located to the northeast of it without extending any farther northward than it did. (See diagram in Appendix 5.)

The concrete significance of this is that another cloud, one of the other ones that Captain Stephan saw, could have been positioned so that it interposed a visual barrier between TWA 2 and United 718 just as the giant one did. This is really not far-fetched at all. No matter where the north edge of the giant cloud was, TWA 2 flew a course north of that, to pass it; on the same course, they could as well have passed to the north of one of the other clouds, on the backside of the giant one, because one of the other ones could have been confined to the same side of their course the giant one was on and still have satisfied the description that it lay to the northeast. United 718 was also on the backside, the east side, of the giant cloud, flying northward from the South Rim. Simply put, if the second cloud was there, the two flights could very well have passed around opposite sides of it, TWA 2 to the north of it, and United 718 to the south and east, in a scaled down reprise of their motions around the giant cloud. This of course would prevent them *again* from seeing each other. (See diagram in Appendix 5.)

As noted in Chapter 7, the giant cloud was centered over Grand Canyon Village, so in rough but concrete, convenient terms, the other clouds were somewhere northeast of the village. So was a place called the Walhalla Plateau. The Walhalla Plateau is an approximately thirty-square-mile, peninsular protrusion of the North Rim of the Grand Canyon. Erosion has progressively defined its perimeter throughout the ages and in the process has cut it off nearly completely from the main land mass. In geological time, it will soon become an island. The plateau is forested like the rest of the North Rim and slopes gradually downward from north to south, extending from the elevation of the main land mass to about that of the South Rim. The Walhalla Plateau is centered about thirteen miles northeast of Grand Canyon Village, or about ten miles west of the crash sites and the confluence of the Colorado and Little Colorado rivers. Measured northeasterly, it is situated about halfway between the village and the Nankoweap Rapids area of the Colorado River. The river basically demarcates the eastern end of the canyon, so all of the additional buildups were strung out along or near the same northeasterly line. The pertinent effect of this is that the chance is good that at least one of the additional buildups lay between the giant cloud and the plateau.

In a different aspect, a second cloud located near the giant one to its northeast would also have been one good reason for United 718 to resume their eastward progress and head out of Grand Canyon airspace as they neared the plateau, because any lofty cloud formation in their path would in effect have steered them.

Whether there was one of these clouds in this approximate location or not, United 718 almost certainly did turn eastward no later than when they reached the area of the Walhalla Plateau. The most obvious reason to believe this is that the collision occurred only a few miles to the east of the plateau. This by itself is strong enough evidence, but there is more. Fifty miles east of the Grand Canyon was the western boundary of a government territory through which both flights' proposed courses ran, called the Albuquerque Air Defense Identification Zone, or Albuquerque ADIZ for short. At the time, there were seven ADIZs in the United States, each of which served the purpose of preserving national security. Within these zones all aircraft in flight had to either be identified as friendly or forced to land, to prevent attacks on the country by air. Both seacoasts and the borders with Canada and Mexico were covered, as well as three interior regions, one of which was roughly centered over Albuquerque, New Mexico. Each ADIZ was a huge territory; the Albuquerque ADIZ, for example, was as big as the state of New Mexico, covering most of its home state, part of southeastern Utah, and most of southwestern Colorado and northeastern Arizona.

With radar, air force personnel manning the Albuquerque ADIZ would spot United 718 as they entered the zone and would compare their entry time and location with a list outlining whom to expect. Each ADIZ was notified in advance of all flights that would enter it, so the Albuquerque ADIZ personnel already had information on both United 718 and TWA 2. If either of them entered the zone at a place or time not expected, they would immediately be hailed by radio. If this failed to establish contact, and possibly even if it succeeded, fighter jets would be scrambled to visually inspect and identify the aircraft. Even the lesser of these military actions was embarrassing, so airline crews made sure to either enter ADIZs on time and on their proposed courses, or to advise their companies or ARINC of any changes far enough in advance so that notice could be relayed to the ADIZ before they got there. Normally these changes were avoided because the time it would take for the required revision to be relayed to the ADIZ was not reliably predictable. The first choice of most captains was simply to keep to their original plans with respect to any ADIZs they encountered.

If United 718 took up an eastward heading at any latitude occupied by the Walhalla Plateau, they would intercept their originally planned course where it crossed into the ADIZ, to within a few miles, which was close enough. By another of the incredibly many coincidences in their flight plans, it was likewise true that if TWA 2 headed eastward at any latitude of the plateau, they would intercept their own originally planned route where it crossed over into the ADIZ, give or take a few miles. Each would also arrive at the ADIZ within a couple minutes of the time they had forecast, which was again close enough. There would be no need for either flight to advise anyone of any changes because with respect to the ADIZ there would not be any, and considering neither flight sent any messages, it seems clear that both of them did in fact intend to re-establish their original courses before they got there. This was TWA 2's esoteric motive, alluded to but not explained in Chapter 7, for rolling out on an eastward heading at roughly the middle latitude of the canyon's eastern third, way back near Lower Granite Gorge (if they entered Grand Canyon airspace there). The rough middle latitude of the eastern third of the canyon is coincidentally also the middle latitude of the Walhalla Plateau.

Of course, because the collision happened just inside the Grand Canyon, fifty miles and nine minutes' flying time from the Albuquerque ADIZ, either flight could have been intending to radio a revision that they never got to send, so it remains possible that one or even both of them intended taking up new courses from the Grand Canyon to their destinations. However, these new courses would be nearly 100 percent as long as the alternative of simply proceeding eastward and rejoining their original courses. It would serve almost no practical purpose to change their plans in this way, saving each of them not even a whole minute, but it would definitely saddle them with impractical purposes, like risking being tied up with the ADIZ. There is no way to be certain, but one simple observation can clear most of the muddle: usually people do the simplest thing that will get them where they want to go, and the simplest thing was for the two flights to get back on their planned, cleared courses.

During all of the final minute before the collision the two planes were within visual range of each other, no matter what combined courses they were following. They had to be, because at the speed they were going, each was covering about five miles a minute, fixing their maximum distance apart at ten miles, just barely within the discernible range. But being near enough to see does not necessarily mean having a line of sight on which to do so. For example, with one of them about a hundred yards directly above the other, neither of them could have seen the other.

The CAB did an extremely thorough analysis of each crew's ability to spot the other plane during the last two minutes before the collision, which they published in their official accident investigation report, offering excellent diagrams and written descriptions of their findings (not of the mathematics to get there). The report examined where the other plane would have appeared to be in all the classes of possible joint flight paths, as they defined them, and from each of the four pilots' seats. A "class" was, for example, both planes flying straight, examined from various angles of convergence, or one plane flying straight and the other in a turn of any of a number of radii. The CAB concluded that with no obstructive, intervening cloud between them during the final two minutes, one pilot or the other, or both, depending upon the class, would have had ample or sufficient opportunity to spot the other plane in every case, and that with a cloud between them their opportunity could have been as brief as twelve seconds, which the Board considered to be insufficient.

Because it mattered as much as it did to me, I independently analyzed the situation, deciding to do this for the period of only just the final *one* minute before the collision, using a differently defined set of classes of possible combined flight paths, and different constraints. I came to essentially the same conclusion. In my analysis the overwhelming truth, applying to nine out of the ten classes I defined, was that for at least half of the final minute, enough time to spot the other plane and take successful evasive action, each plane could have been seen from one or both pilots' seats on the other, depending again upon the class, *unless something prevented them.*

There may have been some sort of minor emergency on the flight deck of one of the planes, like one of the pilots spilling coffee all over himself or dropping the ember of his cigarette down in between himself and his seat, or something equally unusual and distracting. But the idea that there were separate, concurrent emergencies in both cockpits is difficult to feature. Of course, the tragedy itself was one in a million. It is a principle in the mechanical conception of cause and effect that the cause of an event cannot be more common than the event. When every condition necessary to produce rain is present, for example, rain cannot help but come forth, every time. The full cause of the accident, the product of all the elements, had to be at least as rare as the accident itself.

Maybe there were simultaneous mishaps on the flight decks of the two planes, but it is much more plausible that there was an intervening cloud obscuring each crew's view of the other plane for much if not most of the final minute before the collision. It can easily be shown that unless the giant cloud had a very particular, very unusual contour in its northeast quadrant, being either squarish or drawn to an acute-angled edge pointing eastward there, rather than rounded and clumpy, it could not have lain between TWA 2 and United 718 during the final minute; they would have come around it with ample time to see each other. To illustrate the principle, if two people are walking around a very large circular building toward each other from opposite sides, they will see each other from far apart, in plenty of time to politely step out of each other's way. But if the building is rectangular and their timings are such that they will reach one of its corners at the same time, they won't see each other until they run into each other at the corner. On the other hand, if the building is circular but is small, like a silo on a farm, they will see each other before they collide, but they may not have enough time to get out of each other's way.

If there was a cloud between TWA 2 and United 718 during the final minute before they collided, then it had to be one a lot smaller around than the giant one. In other words, it had to be a second cloud, one of the smaller ones that Captain Stephan saw to the northeast of the giant one. This circumstance is much more likely than the giant cloud having a rare contour at its northeast quadrant. Moreover, assuming that the giant one had no such rare contour, the smaller intervening cloud is almost certainly necessary for explaining how the two flights could end up hazardously close together without seeing each other beforehand. If United 718 had performed a typical, slow right turn eastward near the northern end of the giant without there being a smaller built-up cloud between their arced path and TWA 2's path from the west, then there would have been plenty of time, likely over a minute, for each crew to notice the other's airplane. But with a small cloud between them, United 718 might nearly have completed its turn and been very close to TWA 2 before the two passed that cloud, setting them up to collide and allowing only a small amount of time remaining in which they might see each other (diagrammed in Appendix 5).

This picture is little changed even if the "giant" cloud was actually only big—it was still over Grand Canyon Village, and as shown in Chapter 7, they must have flown around opposite sides of it irrespective of its size. The second cloud, lying nearby northeast of it, would still have compelled United 718 to turn eastward in that area, veering around it on the south. If TWA 2 did enter the canyon at Lower Granite Gorge, then they were approaching the area from the west, and if from this perspective the second cloud were only partially exposed, they would have adjusted their course so as to veer past it on the north. If TWA 2 entered the canyon near the big cloud, and the second one was again only partially exposed on the backside of it, then as they rounded the big one, they would still have flown around the second one on its north. And of course, no matter where they entered the canyon, if the second cloud were entirely hidden behind the big one, they would have passed the second one on its north. Only if the second cloud were entirely exposed would TWA 2 have passed it to its south, the side that United 718 was on, and in this case they would have seen each other. The smaller the big cloud was, the more likely this becomes, but there is hardly any difference in likelihood from the case where the big cloud is actually gigantic.

Basically the second cloud must have been very near to the larger one and not fully exposed as viewed from the west, or they would have collided somewhere else and not crashed where they did (or they wouldn't have collided at all).

Plausible as it may be, the belief that a second intervening cloud blocked their views of each other until it was too late to avert the impending catastrophe is not without problems. Pilots gravely recognized the capacity of clouds for concealing other aircraft, and they were solemnly motivated to keep a good distance laterally from them. That way, if another plane suddenly burst from the interior of a cloud or came rapidly around a cloud from the other side on a collision path, there was enough time to spot it and get out of its way. On face value, it seems that both TWA 2 and United 718 must have passed any buildup lying between them from a generous distance off for the sake of safety, yet the fact that the accident happened at all contrarily indicates that they were closer in. It appears that as they came around the cloud, they did not have enough time to save themselves.

The recommended safety standard was to keep a minimum lateral separation of 2,000 feet, about three-eighths of a mile, between a plane and any clouds abreast of it. Being an un-amended IFR flight, United 718 could have disregarded this, but pilots usually observed it whether they were required to or not, because it was sensible. Moreover, if First Officer Harms was in fact flying the DC-7 alone, and Flight Engineer Fiore was not helping him keep the lookout, then he probably wanted to stay even farther away from the cloud than the recommended minimum.

Normally two crewmembers were watching the sky together, so that one of them could safely afford to keep his attention on the cloud and the open sky immediately surrounding it while the other watched the rest of the sky. With only one crewmember up front to look for other aircraft, exclusively or predominantly scrutinizing any one area outside of the windows also meant continually or primarily disregarding the rest of the sky—obviously a deadly proposition. If Harms was alone up front, he must have wanted to give himself a greater margin of time to spot aircraft coming from the area of the cloud, so that he could afford to watch that area only intermittently, scanning the remainder of the sky in between times.

What's really puzzling is that if he did increase his margin of safety, say to a mile or more, he should have seen TWA 2 in time to prevent the disaster. By the same token, if he instead flew to within 2,000 feet of the cloud, then he likely asked Fiore to take the captain's seat and help in the lookout after all, because there was then a special need. Again the tragedy should have been prevented. Something else was involved. It had to be.

It must be said that coincidence was prevalent in the tragic events of that fateful day. The two airlines' terminals were adjacent at Los Angeles International Airport, and the two planes were parked next to each other on opposite sides of the ramp. Both flights had significant last minute problems on the ground, TWA 2 with a mechanical discrepancy in the airplane and United 718 with a crew scheduling change, resulting from mechanical trouble with Harms' other airplane. They both departed late and wound up right alongside each other on the run-up pad. Their original flight plans called for effectively simultaneous crisscrossing of their courses in northeastern Arizona. With so many coincidences at play, it seems that coincidence was a generative theme rather than a quirk. It seems that the compounded improbability normally associated with yet another coincidence must actually have been inverted, and that more coincidence was preposterously *more* likely. When strangeness is the rule, it becomes normalcy, and the usual becomes the odd. In view of this it seems plausible that there were in fact mishaps on both flight decks in the final minute.

But because of their habitual awareness of the danger in ignoring the sky, minor cockpit emergencies could not have kept everyone in both cockpits from looking out of the windows for a whole minute running. They must have looked while the second cloud was still between them, or late in what remained of their last minute after they passed it, or both—but not immediately after passing that cloud, or else there would have been no collision. The compelling thing about this is that the moment of passing a cloud, and the first seconds right afterward, were among the most critical times for a crew to be keeping a lookout. The risk of a midair collision during that brief span was the greatest of any time other than when they were in the congestion of flights near a big airport. Each crew ordinarily would be very motivated to scrutinize the open sky at their altitude surrounding a cloud, and yet apparently neither followed through and did this. Something had to have disrupted or overridden their instincts to watch out, if only for just a handful of seconds. There must have been mishaps in both cockpits during at least the crucial brief period immediately following their passing the second cloud. Like the second cloud, this too, seems necessary.

Compelling as this may be, it all serves to demonstrate the belief that they didn't see each other until it was too late, which at its core is still only just an assumption. It is a sound belief and is the reason for which nearly all midair collisions have happened, but it is still speculation, categorically different from knowledge. In another realm of circumstance it is tragically possible that they did see each other in time to prevent the collision, and they reacted with maneuvers that actually kept them from missing each other rather than driving them apart. For example, if they both climbed to fly over each other or both dived to fly under each other, they might only have preserved or even reinforced their convergence. Or they may have made emergency maneuvers that simply fell short of saving them, like evasively turning when they should have dived or climbed.

No clues were found in the wreckage to suggest anything at all about the latter, but as to the possibility that they both dived to fly under each other or both climbed to fly over each other, the collision evidence actually indicated the contrary. The angles of dents and scratches on pieces of wreckage showed that there was about a ten-degree difference in pitch between the two planes when they struck each other, with United 718 being pitched nose downward in relation to TWA 2. The evidence suggested nothing about their orientations relative to the ground, anymore than the slant of a line drawn across a sheet of paper can reveal whether the page was aligned obliquely or perpendicularly with the edge of the desk on which the drawing was done. It is possible that both were diving, with United 718 doing so more steeply, or both were climbing, with TWA 2 doing so more dramatically, but it's unlikely.

There was no evidence whatsoever to suggest any reason for which either of them might have wanted to descend, outside of diving to avoid the other. Outside of a desperate attempt to loft themselves over the other plane, there was one barely plausible motive for one or both of them to have been ascending: namely, to surmount a cloud, but this is exceedingly unlikely in their circumstances. For one thing, they were near or at their working service ceilings, because the air around them was warmer and less dense than standard air at their altitude. Ascending would be slow going, so any appreciable ascent would require planning well in advance. It would be necessary to begin ascending while any cloud in their way along their course was still far up ahead. Being a great distance from it, they could simply veer very slightly from the course they were on and pass to one side of the cloud, while adding almost nothing to their distance from its longitude. For example, if they changed direction twenty-five miles from a cloud five miles in diameter, turning from a course that would have taken them squarely through its middle to a course that would just skirt past one side or the other, they would need to change direction by only six degrees, requiring only a feather touch to the flight controls. Rather than twenty-five miles, the trip would then span twenty-five and an eighth miles. At three hundred miles per hour, it takes only one and a half seconds to fly an eighth of a mile. That's all the time they'd lose!

On the other hand, were they to start climbing from twenty-five miles away—say, in order to ascend two thousand feet at their sluggish vertical pace—they would gradually lose a good measure of airspeed. They would have to divert some horsepower to laboriously lifting the airplane, taking that power away from the job of maintaining their forward speed against air resistance, which in turn would gradually slow them down. They would lose comparatively a lot of time, unless they opened up the engines to climb power, which would waste fuel. Neither way made any sense, when simply veering a hair to one side was so easy and would use only immeasurably more fuel. Besides this, with so few buildups in the area, it bordered on idiotic to climb over one, about like climbing over a picnic table in one's path on a walk through an otherwise empty field, rather than simply stepping around it. The only exception to this was the giant cloud, or the biggest cloud in the lot if it was only big. It was likely much wider than any of the others, so flying around it would lean toward being an imposition, less practical than flying around any of the others. But it also extended to 25,000 feet, well above what either flight could reasonably have attained no matter how far ahead of time they began ascending.

In sum, it seems clear that they flew around whatever might have been in their way—the small buildups because they were modest in diameter and thereby easy to circumnavigate, and the biggest one because even if it was cumbersome to fly around, it was too tall to fly over. That eliminates the only plausible normal motive for ascending, and the only normal motive for changing altitude regardless of in which sense.

Obviously somebody was changing altitude, because they could not both have been flying level. Ruling out normal maneuvers to explain this leaves only emergency ones. Ascending or descending, the fact of any vertical movement proves that at least one of them saw what was coming, and saw what was coming soon enough to take action. But it was evidently not soon enough for them to save themselves. For want of a second or two, all those lives were lost.

The supposition that they were both evasively climbing or both evasively diving requires that *each* of them saw the other. But if one of them dived or climbed ahead of the other by enough time to account for the difference in pitch, then the other should have been able to perceive the movement and do the opposite; on the other hand, if they dived or climbed simultaneously, there should not have been so large a difference in pitch. More reasonably speaking, the difference means that either United 718 was attempting to dive under TWA 2, or TWA 2 was attempting to climb over United 718, or both. This rules out the possibility that they had the tragic mishap of making identical moves to avoid each other.

There is yet another category of circumstances, sadder and more dreadful than the others, that would epitomize the meaning of tragedy: they may not even have been on collision paths. In a terrible irony, they may have misjudged each other's motion, falsely perceiving a collision threat that did not exist, and taking evasive action that was precisely what thrust them into each other. A major accident of this sort did happen once, when the crew of one plane misjudged the altitude of the other. The other plane was actually 1,000 feet higher, but an optical illusion supported by a sloping cloud deck below made them appear to be at the same level. The crew of the lower plane pulled up drastically to fly over the higher one, only to hit it instead.

The difference in pitch at the moment of impact actually says more than that somebody was reacting to the emergency, but it says it ambiguously. Obviously, whoever had changed pitch was also actively changing altitude, and had been for some small time, at least for however long it took to pitch the fuselage from level to its inclination or declination at the instant the planes collided. The serious question is: by how much had they changed altitude?

More than a little would mean that before they took action, there was enough space in between the planes vertically that, had they done nothing, they wouldn't have collided. Equivocally, the difference in pitch could have been produced fast enough that there wouldn't have been time for the planes to appreciably move vertically. In this case, if they were already on collision paths before they took action, then all that their emergency ascent or descent changed was which areas of the planes would strike each other.

The collision evidence favors neither possibility; rather, the "sinister" fact here is merely that it is *consistent* with the possibility that one or both crews actually caused the accident. But so is all of the evidence, insofar as none of it demonstrates that the crews could not have caused the accident. The pitch evidence shows that at least one of them saw what was coming, and that at least one of them was changing altitude in response when they hit each other, and that's all. I see no reason to make more of it than that. There are other combinations of major maneuvers that might actually have brought about the disaster and that could be considered, but what ties them all together is that there was no physical evidence to support either believing them or disbelieving them.

Most accidents are just that: accidents, no one's fault. They are caused primarily by circumstances and only instrumentally or incidentally by someone's error. Once in a great while, someone makes a mistake grave enough to be called the driving factor in whatever ensued; for example, someone arms a bomb when he meant to disarm it. The resulting disaster is more his fault than the bomb's. But almost always the human element is the smaller. For example, a man forgets to plug in his weather radio, and during the night, while the family is sleeping, an alarm is sent out to which his radio cannot awaken him. Fifteen minutes later a tornado destroys the house and the family.

Here, the disaster is the tornado's fault, and the man's mistake is only sad and tragic.

In face-value view of this, it is unlikely that anyone made a grievous error like climbing to avoid an illusory collision only to cause a real one instead. Besides, they were flying at the same altitude, insofar as the precision of their altimeters and the meticulousness with which they had manually set these instruments allowed. With the equipment and maintenance standards of the times, and the carefulness of the typical crew, they should both have been extremely close to 21,000 feet, if not right on. This pretty much rules out any optical illusion of their being at the same altitude: the appearance would have been correct. Of course, they might have had the illusion that they were *not* at the same altitude, and fatally delayed reacting. One eerie fact in this vein is that the Walhalla Plateau is tilted, with its northern edge at an elevation about 1,000 feet higher than its southern edge.

*   *   *

The enigma of what really happened to all of those people is very challenging. Because the people who lost their lives matter, it matters to try to solve the enigma, and by the same token, it is important to start with looking at the fullest possible picture. Having done that, it then becomes more important to simplify the inquiry, in the hope of narrowing it down to the truth. There are two ways that an idea can be complicated: namely, it can be difficult to believe or difficult to understand. Assuming that the idea is clearly phrased, these difficulties are particular to it, not the fault of how it is conceived. The idea is inherently incredible or complex, and that's why it is hard to believe or to understand. In these terms, to free this examination of its complications means eliminating the possibilities that are incredible or complex. Fortunately in this instance, the natural inclination toward ease is harmonious with the fundamental purpose of seeking the truth—the bias toward ease is more focusing than blinding.

The truth is almost always uncomplicated. Credibility, simplicity, and accuracy usually go together. In this vein, the same captain who said, "Maybe Gandy just liked that altitude," also said, after equally long discussions about how they could have run into each other, "The simplest explanation is usually the correct one." Taking his observation as advice and implementing it, my thinking becomes clear, direct, and decisive: Why did they collide? Because they didn't see each other in time. Why didn't they see each other in time? Because they couldn't, or they weren't looking. Why couldn't they? Because they were too near an intervening cloud. Why weren't they looking? Because they were preoccupied with trouble on their flight decks.

Somebody made a mistake. Most mistakes are merely insignificant flaws, minor discrepancies between what is intended or should be intended, and what is actually done. They are harmless and have no practical importance—ordinarily. Harmless or not, however, mistakes open up new avenues for harm to be done and thereby make it more likely. Ordinarily there is no disaster poised to attack if only given the chance, so nothing comes of the increased vulnerability. A pilot looks for slightly too long at another aircraft off in the distance, ignoring other areas of the sky for slightly too long in the meantime, but no third airplane appears from out of nowhere in front of him while he isn't looking. Another misjudges his height above the ground on final approach to land and sets down beyond where he intended to, but there is enough extra length of runway for him to safely come to a stop. Errors on this level are common, and the low incidence of accidents shows that on the whole these mistakes are really not very dangerous. But one time in a million the runway is extra short, or the pilot looks back ahead only to find the horror of another plane coming right at him, near enough that he can see its crew.

I don't know what happened, certainly not all of it. I have thought about the parts I don't know and finally decided what to believe about most of them. Beyond this I have chosen to believe myself, and because of this secondary act of trust, I have faith in my beliefs about the accident, despite knowing that I may be mistaken. Faith is a type of contentedness pertaining more to oneself than to its external object; it is an intuitive feeling of adequacy.

I have faith in my work because I have chosen to trust that in the framework of my own values, the effort I made to understand this story is good enough. I am content with what I have accomplished, because I am content with myself as the person who accomplished it. I did as much as my own caring compelled me to do, and so I am able to rest in my beliefs about the tragedy, not in faith that they are correct exactly, but rather in faith that they are sufficient. This is what it means to be sure, and being sure is the best that I can hope to achieve. For me to have absolute, honest certainty, I would have to see the truth empirically and infallibly, and I would need the insightfulness to penetrate any illusion and see it for what it is, no matter how deceptive. A limited consciousness is obviously incapable of this because it requires limitless perceptivity. Knowing a thing in its entirety and absolutely distinguishing between fiction and fact are beyond mortals. In our limited viewpoints, illusion can be as realistic to us as reality, and reality always runs deeper than we can see. The best we can achieve is to be sure. In this context our only decisive freedom is to decide to believe ourselves, or not.

I believe that the Grand Canyon tragedy was caused by an incredibly particular, compounded chain of bad luck, which found its final, decisive opportunity to strike in an inconsiderable mistake. Fate concocted a progressive series of circumstances culminating in a deadly situation, and there stopped short, leaving the outcome undecided. It persuaded both flights into a trap whose final signpost was the smaller, second cumulonimbus cloud. At that place fate granted each crew one chance to extricate themselves from the predicament into which it had placed them, and if its will was tempered with any compassion or respect for life at all, it then relented and permitted them to determine for themselves how to use it. They failed. They had one chance to unlock their plight and set themselves free of it, and each did something else instead. And for them it didn't matter what, because everything other than the solution was a mistake. It might have been spilling coffee; it might have been flying too near the cloud; it might have been a moment's daydreaming, or looking for too long at a third airplane way off in the distance. Both crews made a mistake, because if even one of them had done what it would take to avoid the other, there would have been only a close call, not an accident. Incredible bad luck was allowed to run its full course, rather than being curtailed at the last moment, because a minor flaw in the performance of one or more crewmembers on each plane precluded their realizing in time what had to be done. The only question I have is this: was fate behind *all* of it, not just all the bad luck, but even their failures to make their last chance be their salvation?

CHAPTER 10

THE CLOUDS BELOW glowed in the sunlight to the edges of the visible world. They were suffused with an extraordinary resplendency, upturned to the sun, that terrestrial man never saw, a divine brilliance that seemed to emanate from within them in rejoicing. As an infant in his mother's arms beams his rapture back up into her loving eyes, so also the clouds seemed to radiate their ecstasy in return to the source of light and warmth.

The air was cleaner than cold rain, and the sky was a richer, clearer blue than most of the passengers had ever seen. It seemed to sparkle with an exquisitely subtle prismatic aura, as though seen through a flawless lens.

In their immensity, the vaulting cumulus clouds nearby cast man's diminutive stature in thrillingly humbling perspective. They gave man the joy of knowing himself, the joy of knowing his place in the grand scheme of existence, a minute corpuscle of wondrously self-aware life, floating in a tremendous, inanimate world, both infinitesimal and infinitely blessed. In finding himself man was finally home, and it was curious for such a grounding feeling to be discovered in a place so far removed, in space and in character, from the ground on which he lived.

The clouds awakened man's soul and charmed his heart and mind, affirming his uniquely human imagination and flair for symbolism. Like a loving parent, they did not always teach but also played. They told stories, appealing to man's love of make-believe. They were the substance of fairy tales. Scenes of great mythical castles, inhabited by giants or by the gods, took form in them without need of the will to bring them about, as though it were they that impressed their imaginative appearances on the mind and heart, rather than the other way around. The dreamer and the dream became transposed, and the lands of the sorcerers manifested fully as real, impressing the observer for a timeless moment with the tremulous sensation that it was he that was surreal. The supernatural became the natural, and in ecstatic liberation, man's heart reawakened to the childlike wonder of all things being possible.

This divine beauty formed the boundless, enchanted atmosphere in which the two tiny craft advanced. This glorious place in the heavens, and the scintillating spirit it instilled and evoked in man, were the setting and the mood in which a history-making tragedy was about to occur. How could the splendor of their surroundings and the opulent ease of their passage through the sky be reconciled with the horrific abuse that the people aboard were to suffer? It was incomprehensible how either of these antithetical realities could even succeed the other, let alone become it. All of those people would be thrown from their earthly heaven and their childlike openness, straight into a hell as dire as the spiritual inferno has ever been conceived to be.

A spot three miles up in the sky, to all appearances like any other spot, unmarked and as a thing invisible, made only of the air, was to become the site of a great wrong. Whether it had a penchant for malice, like the cold spot that is the locus of evil in a bedeviled house, and drew the two planes into its spell, or merely had the capacity and the pliancy to host such a catastrophe, this invisible place was to become a memorial to tragedy. And being a place made only of the atmosphere, reposed far up in the sky, it would never decay nor be dismantled nor covered over like terrestrial shrines. It would also remain in utter solitude and isolation, never to be visited by anyone. Somewhere in the airspace between the Walhalla Plateau and the confluence of the Colorado and Little Colorado rivers was the place where the terrible event would happen.

Whether they were too near the smaller, second cumulonimbus cloud, or had passed it and had only just looked up from distractions in the cockpits, the following portrayal is likely nearly how it was for them.

For a split-second of stunned disbelief, the pilots caught sight of each other's planes. Each plane had the unreal aura of an apparition that had come from the ether and materialized instantly in corporeal form in empty space, at once splendorous and ghastly, beautiful in appearance and hideous in meaning and intent. And then their emotions caught up with their vision, and suddenly the same planes loomed astonishingly large and near, as though instantly translocated closer. Each pilot who saw was jolted with electric alarm and then horror. All of this had occurred in less than a second. Death had been thrust upon each crew in the form of a giant rushing at them with merciless speed, giving no quarter for them to recover their balance and escape. Probably every pilot yelled in shock.

Each crew reacted very fast and in the extreme, but either too late or in error. In the last second or two all they could do was watch themselves collide. For a moment, each pilot felt like a driver sliding helplessly on ice, watching his car heading into the accident that he is about to have. The driver immediately grasps what the outcome will be and the fact that it is inescapable. He is alarmed and yet somehow detached, removed in a sense, perhaps by the partial suspension of his will as an involuntary response to realizing that he cannot stop the accident. For a moment the driver is an observer in his own life, not a participant, impossible as definition and logic claim this to be. But for the pilots in the Grand Canyon tragedy, this self-transcendent experience must have been the extreme of its own paradox: along with their calm inner detachment, they surely were also alarmed to the ultimate degree of knowing that the collision would be fatal to them. It was not merely an accident into which they were inescapably sliding—it was the end, and they knew it right away. All pilots lived in mortal fear of three things: structural failures, in-flight fires, and midair collisions. Through their training and countless discussions with their peers, and their own private thoughts and fears, and in some instances through the electrifying mishap of nearly colliding with another plane, pilots had developed their own esoteric creed about midair collisions. Like schoolchildren reared to regard kidnappers and the devil with terror, pilots were conditioned with such deeply held impressions and preconceptions of a midair collision that when it happened, they immediately, intensely, instinctively knew it was death.

Some of the passengers must have seen what was coming also, some on the left on the United DC-7 and some on the right on the TWA Constellation, those that just happened to be looking out of the windows at that moment. People gasped and in the next second regained their voices and the volition to act, the capacity to yell from their seats to the crew to save themselves. Simultaneously the cabin lurched out from underneath them and toppled them toward the windows on the side facing the horror, or left them falling like a roller coaster accelerating into a plunge. Some of the passengers yelled for their lives. Both planes recoiled as though from the sight of each other, as though in revulsion to something unspeakably ugly. People and machines as one were willing the thing not to happen, and then it was all over.

With a terrific crash the rear end of the Constellation and the outer left wing of the DC-7 destroyed each other and themselves. The collision, the entire sequence of contact between the two planes, was over in a split second. They had crossed paths and were hastily diverging from each other, as though in horrified retreat from an enemy that had mortally wounded them. They had more than struck each other— they had passed through each other and were grotesquely disfigured. The DC-7's left wing had been ripped off from just outboard of the left-most engine, leaving behind a jagged stump where it had been attached. The Constellation no longer had a tail, and the rear of its passenger compartment was open to the sky at what had been the back wall of the lounge; its ceiling was split open from the lounge to nearly the main entry door.

The noise heard aboard United 718 was probably a very forceful bang, loud and muffled, transmitted through the metal structure of the left wing and through the outside air, yet dampened by the extent of wing structure and sound-insulating fuselage sidewall through which it had to travel to reach the passengers. The impact jolted the whole plane for an instant, casting it into a sudden, momentary rolling movement. The underside of the outer left wing had hit the upper right side of the Constellation's rear fuselage, with the effect that the DC-7's left wing was relatively propelled upward. After a second of this rolling with the left wing rising, the rotation reversed itself, rolling the DC-7 the other way, with the left wing dropping for lack of lift on that side to counterbalance the lift force on the right side: over a third of the wing was missing. Harms probably had no choice but to go with this motion, converting it into one component of an involuntary, descending left turn, a turn he could influence but not countermand.

The bang heard aboard TWA 2 was thunderous, both deeply sonorous and sharply cracking. The impact took place largely inside the passenger compartment, so there was no sound-insulating airplane structure between the sound source and the passengers. Furthermore, the cabin was explosively decompressed at the instant that the DC-7's wing passed through it. The two sounds resounded deafeningly together in that terrible moment between the unconscious certainty of life, and the conscious certainty of death. As though lightning had struck the airplane and divided the sky with a tremendous, "Crack!" inside the cabin, the thunderclap divided these realities from each other and, in its malevolence, transformed the one into the other.

For an instant the impact jolted the Constellation sharply leftward and downward at the rear over small distances. The immediate decompression blew almost everything in the rear half of the cabin that wasn't dense and wasn't tied down out the gaping hole at the rear end, in a gust like that of the worst windstorms. Even the crew felt the outrush of air, all the way forward in the cockpit. Dirt and dust in every hidden recess behind and under control panels blew out of every crevice, and some of this maelstrom of grit probably got into the crew's eyes. The exceedingly rapid depressurization also severely chilled the remaining cabin air in a split second, on the same principle, though much more rapidly expressed, by which the contents of an aerosol can become progressively colder as the can is sprayed. In turn, the dramatic chilling caused a fog to form and fill the cabin, just as each warm breath a person exhales outdoors in the winter becomes a cloud, in the fraction of a second it takes for it to be chilled by the surrounding cold air. Everyone must have had intense, sharp pain in their ears from the pressure difference between the inner ear and the cabin air, and this, combined with the terrific bang, the rushing gust, the cold, and the fog, had to have been utterly bewildering and overwhelming. Some people probably thought they had been shot or hit over the head from behind.

Some passengers in the lounge and anyone in the attached lavatory may mercifully have been killed instantly by the DC-7's wing as it passed through the cabin, or by structures of their own plane crushed by it. There was one window on each side of the lounge, and the seats next to these windows faced away from them, toward the other side of the lounge. Whoever was seated on the port side likely could have seen the DC-7 out the starboard lounge window if no one had drawn the curtains. The sun was very bright on the starboard side, and someone may have. Hopefully no one killed outright by the collision ever felt the trauma of seeing the DC-7's wing coming right at him. One moment he was conversing or reading or playing cards, and the next he was gone, punctuated only by the surprise of the airplane shifting in the last couple seconds, if even that.

On the other hand, in a monstrous antithesis of this, some people in or near the rear may have been blown out of the airplane through the huge opening. Thankfully no evidence of this was ever reported, but then most men of any decency among the numerous investigators that searched the crash area would have concealed a fact as atrocious as this from the public. To have revealed that a particular victim fell from the sky, perhaps from as much as three miles above the ground and possibly alive, would have been a criminal act without need of any law to make it so. Everyone had a need to know the truth of his loved one's final moments, but for many people, learning a truth such as this would have been far more cruel and destructive than beneficial. Even a report that an unnamed victim, never to be named, was found some distance removed from the main concentration of victims would have cruelly alerted the families of all of the victims to the possibility that it was their loved one. Fortunately, the word publicized stated that all of the TWA victims had been found concentrated in one small area, indicating that no one was blown out of the plane and further, that no one fell out even as the Constellation fell to earth.

Only a couple of seconds had passed. For most of the people aboard the Constellation, life stood precariously balanced for an eternal instant in the fog, as though to seize it and keep it were still an option. Their situation lacked the realism that could be bestowed upon it only by their own belief. Most were stunned and did not realize that this was the end, and so for them it was as though still undecided. They were unharmed and had not yet fallen over the edge of the abyss. The airplane was still flying almost normally, cruising almost as it would have been had it not lost its huge triple tail, though it was beginning to hunch forward. And then their moment of irresolution exempt from the decisive laws of cause and effect passed, and the airplane began clearly pitching nose downward and falling. The crew fought this dive in total futility, because the elevators that they needed in order to bring the nose up to level were gone with the rest of the tail. As the crew frantically tore at their useless controls, the Constellation pitched fully into a nosedive, rushing earthward. It kept right on pitching past the vertical as it came down from the sky, tumbling end over end toward the ground.

Throughout the whole plane, from the cockpit on back, there was utter havoc, sheer panic to the extreme of nearly immediate insanity for most if not all of those who were still alive and conscious. Crew and passengers alike probably knew for a moment that it was death and then entered the mindless grip of raw terror and madness. Everyone not strapped in was thrown violently around inside the plane, and although the flight crewmembers on the flight deck were strapped in, the tremendous, chaotically changing forces probably flailed them around by the waist. Certainly after the first few seconds they never did anything purposeful or sane again.

With nothing to hold it up in the air, the Constellation fell rapidly, as if it had been dropped. It plummeted, arcing forward parabolically with the momentum it still had from before the collision, covering a little more ground eastward. It tumbled and twisted in the ghastly, chaotic manner in which a bird that has been shot dead in flight, obscenely gyrates in its rushing fall to earth. The Constellation plunged straight into hell, carrying with it the undifferentiated mass of screaming, raving, primal humanity that only a moment before had been a multitude of sensitive, thinking human beings. It was as though their personhood had already been destroyed, and only the lesser assault of taking their bodies could still be inflicted upon them. Mercifully, because of the extreme strain and lack of oxygen, probably most of them quickly blacked out.

In cruel contrast to this careening mayhem, coats and pillow cases and napkins that had been blown out of the plane were lazily floating to earth, carried gently toward the Painted Desert by the moderate easterly winds aloft. Like a band playing a happy, popular tune in the midst of a battle, it was a crazed combination, a dichotomy straight out of a sadistic lunatic's mind. It was as though the procession of litter drifting toward the ground mocked the mental and emotional razing of the people aboard the Constellation and mocked what was to be their ultimate fate, in a demented parade that flaunted how much better it was to be a napkin than a person.

While TWA 2 rushed earthward in their solitary nightmare, United 718 descended along a leftward-winding corkscrew path. As the DC-7 swung around in its first revolution, the dead Constellation with its living cargo came into view ahead and below, visible to the crew and to the passengers on the left side. Even in the midst of their own peril and alarm, some of them must have witnessed the horrific spectacle. Undoubtedly they reflexively denied what they were seeing, because it was too terrible to believe, or because it was part of their own situation, which was itself too terrible to believe. This and the titanic scale of the scene must have cast a glaze of unreality on the image of the falling Constellation. Yet as those who saw this helplessly watched the splendid white and silver plane tumbling far below, like a much nearer toy plane falling in slow motion, the undeniably vivid reality of it all—undeniable partly because it was too bizarre to be a concoction of the imagination—must have made it positively clear to them that this was death, not only for the people in the surreal plane below but for themselves.

And then TWA 2 disappeared in the clouds. The people aboard United 718 were alone, isolated from their accidental comrades and from all the rest of humanity. In private they descended; in private, Harms wrestled the DC-7 while Fiore hung on and desperately watched. Again the focus of those who had been engrossed in the appalling sight of the Constellation returned to their own plight. Like coming up into the air from beneath the water, they were suddenly reabsorbed in the cacophony of their own group. Everyone was terrified and many were shouting. The fact that the airplane was still in a sense flying, still maneuvering and following a simple, semi-ordered path rather than a chaotic one, helped only little to assuage their fear, because they were nonetheless in a dramatic descent and not pulling out of it. They were *falling*, and they were helpless to stop it.

In the collision, the DC-7 passed primarily underneath the Constellation, with only minimal contact between the two. This was accomplished partly by the ten-degree difference in pitch between the planes at the moment they struck each other. It was also accomplished partly by a twenty-degree difference in roll, with the DC-7 rolled relatively right wing down, which the wreckage revealed. The absolute orientations of the planes, their attitudes in relation to the ground, were again unknown, but for the sake of visualizing how the planes could have escaped slamming into each other more squarely, as with major areas of their fuselages colliding, the relative picture is all that is needed. With the DC-7's right wing down and its left wing correspondingly up, it is not hard to see how it could have passed so cleanly from right to left under the Constellation, hitting it principally with the raised left wing as the two sideswiped each other.

As the DC-7 passed underneath the Constellation, the outer ends of three of the four blades on the propeller of its number one (left-most) engine cut in succession into the underside of the Constellation's rear fuselage. In the process, all three penetrating blades were bent, throwing the propeller hopelessly out of balance and propagating a continuous vibration in the whole DC-7; the blades may even have broken off. The engine was undamaged and still running. Harms, or Fiore at Harms' order, must have immediately shut it down, to keep it from shaking itself to pieces and further damaging the airplane or starting a fire. When the outer left wing was destroyed, the fuel tank in it ruptured and released a deluge of over six hundred gallons of fuel instantaneously, and yet miraculously there had been no fire. Had the number one engine been running on this fuel tank when the collision occurred, it would have starved for fuel and died, relieving the crew of its menacing shaking. But it was running on another tank at the time, and so it would have to have been shut down.

The DC-7 had eight fuel tanks, four mains and four alternates, all located within the wings. Normally an engine was supplied with fuel by a tank within its own half of its own wing, although almost any connections could be selected in flight from a comprehensive bank of fuel selector valves in the cockpit. Thus the left outboard engine usually ran on either the left outboard main or the left outboard alternate. Numbering systems parallel with the scheme applied to the engines were used for the tanks, so this amounted to saying that the number one engine ran on the number one main or the number one alternate. It was the number one main that was destroyed in the collision.

Fuel was not expended arbitrarily, but rather in conformity with a standard fuel schedule, involving switching tanks en route. Accordingly, all four mains were used for takeoff and for the first twenty minutes or so of flight, and they were to be used again during the second half of the trip. At about 10:20, near Riverside, California, Fiore switched over to using all four alternates, shutting off the mains. There was nothing magical about twenty minutes or Riverside; it was just that by then a prescribed amount of fuel had been drawn from the mains, two of which, number one and number four, were in the outer ends of the wings, and to optimize the handling of the airplane some weight would be left out there rather than draining these tanks, for the time being. United 718 was running on alternates when they collided with TWA 2 and would have continued drawing fuel from these tanks for about another half hour had there been no accident.

The number one alternate tank was behind the number one engine and was far enough inboard that it escaped direct damage when the outer twenty feet of the wing was torn away. Possibly this tank was damaged by structural members or control cables that were wrenched away by pieces of the outer wing as it disintegrated and tore free. It may have been leaking, but it was probably still feeding the number one engine. So Harms and Fiore had to contend with that, right in the midst of their initial intense alarm, even before they could fully grasp what had been done to them, what damage had been inflicted, and what could be done about it to save their lives. Like a blind person aware that an intruder is in his house, frantically struggling in blackness to protect himself or to escape, they pathetically struggled in shocked ignorance, feeling their way to survive. And as his darkness hampers the blind person and intensifies his fear, the bewilderment in which Harms and Fiore operated amplified their terror to the verge of panic, but Harms caught hold of himself, and for the moment so did Fiore.

In losing an engine, Harms lost some of the power with which to control the DC-7. And in losing the outer third of the left wing, he was operating at critically deficient lift on that side, along with increased drag due to the jagged end. He also had no left aileron, because this control surface was hinged to the absent outer left wing. Here, too,

Harms was handicapped in producing any lift on the left side to bring the wing up to level and stop the turn. He must have had severe control problems. All of this and much more he hurriedly juggled, in a life-and-death contest to keep the airplane up in the air by trial and error.

As Harms desperately worked to find a solution, United 718 reached the level of the cloud deck. They had surrendered over a mile of altitude and were still descending. They probably penetrated the clouds and became immersed in them, rather than having the luck of passing down through a break. It must have been too much for many to bear. To be lost in the formless whiteness could only have heightened everyone's terror, passengers and crew alike. At least Harms and Fiore had the altimeter, and a rough knowledge of the elevation of the eastern rim of the canyon and the buttes near it, with which to judge whether or not they would hit the ground, but those in the passenger cabin had no way to gauge where they were, and so no way to judge the degree of their peril. For many this surpassed the extreme limit of their tolerance. Engulfed in the whiteout, some of them became hysterical, and others were overcome by the strain and fainted. There was cruelly ample time for either of these reactions to be forced out of them. The cloud deck was over a mile thick; it probably took about half a minute for them to pass through the cloud layer.

By the time United 718 emerged beneath the clouds, TWA 2 no longer existed.

The Constellation had disintegrated in a dry wash at the base of the northeastern slope of a place called Temple Butte, at an elevation of about 3,400 feet, over half a mile below the eastern rim. The exact spot was about a quarter mile inland from the west bank of the Colorado River, and about one and a half miles downstream, southerly, from the confluence of the Colorado and Little Colorado rivers. Everyone alive on board had perished instantly. The plane had come straight down from above and struck the ground upside down, on its back. A great blaze was raging at the crash site, and as United 718 spiraled down into the canyon from a mile higher up, many people on board probably saw the fire and the thick black smoke billowing out of it. At the sight of the other airplane's destruction, those who realized that there had been a collision must have been aghast in the certainty that their own fate would be the same. Those who saw the fire and did not know that there had been a collision could not have construed the inferno on the ground below to be an airplane. They never understood what was happening, and in their bewilderment, the frighteningly alien, harsh, and inhospitable landscape of rock and fire must have filled them with dread. Some of them probably believed they had died and entered hell.

In the cockpit Harms, now convinced that he could not pull out of the descent, began sending his mayday message to Salt Lake City ARINC. The time was exactly 11:30:53 a.m., MST (the same time as PDT), which was determined later from time checks incorporated into the routine tape recording that ARINC made of the communication. Fiore was by then in a panic, yelling, "Pull up! Pull up!" and could not send the message. Maybe Harms never even wanted him to, feeling that a message that grave must be sent by the one in command. It was not a plea for help, and it was more than a proclamation that they were going to crash. It was a pronouncement of death. Harms' whole message was only nine words, and yet it summed up the entire lives of fifty-eight human beings: "Salt Lake . . . ah . . . Seven Eighteen . . . We are going in." It was the end, and Harms knew it. To crash was inescapable, as he had plainly declared in pilots' jargon with the phrase, "We are going in." And to crash in the Grand Canyon, with nothing but solid rock carved into the endlessly varied shapes of buttes and peaks and slopes, with their promontories and gullies and no flat surfaces anywhere larger than the airplane, and moving at three or four hundred miles per hour, was beyond doubt to die. Harms knew, and one can only admire the tremendous courage and dignity of the man, with which he maintained his composure and performed his duty to send the message. Despite being terrified, he didn't just blurt out his predicament. He spoke in standard procedural form, addressing whom he was calling, then identifying himself, and only then stating the gist of his reason for calling. What is more, instead of resorting to contractions to expedite speaking and saying, "We're going in," as nearly anyone else under a similarly monumental strain would have done, he used the best grammar, saying, "We are going in." I can only marvel at Robert Harms.

No one ever responded. His transmission was severely garbled, both faint and static-laden, poor enough to be unintelligible to the Salt Lake City ARINC operator who received it. To be deciphered, the tape recording of the message had to be played back, but due to the eerie coincidence of the playback feature malfunctioning, this could not be done right away. For the time being the operator did not even know who had called, let alone why, and so he never responded. They were utterly on their own, already cut off forever from the rest of mankind. Harms held the microphone send button pushed in, continuing to transmit after he finished speaking, which also prevented him from receiving incoming messages. Maybe he squeezed the microphone tightly to hang on, to keep his message live and unfinished, as though it could be changed or amended so long as he did not release it. Maybe he willed for there to be more, something more he could say, so that his pronouncement would not be the final word and the final reality.

It was the end, but Harms was not likely resigned to it. There was one remaining chance, however minute and unrealistic, which a desperate person who had nothing to lose and the whole world to gain might try: a crash landing on the river. They had spiraled in over the Colorado River, where the Little Colorado flows into it. If Harms could maneuver past the buttes at the confluence of the rivers and head northward, he would have miles of river in front of him to gradually descend to. And if he could pull up enough at the last moment to just about level off, the plane would skim across the surface of the water. Rapids could complicate the problem, or more precisely, the *causes* of rapids could complicate the problem: boulders under the surface, ancient lava flows, steps in the riverbed. However, the nearest rapids far enough away that United 718 could descend to them from their altitude were 51/2 miles upstream, allowing plenty of room to land on the water and stop before getting there. Harms had no way of knowing in advance where the rapids were, but hazards hardly mattered: it was a *chance*.

Notwithstanding the fact that the Colorado River became fortuitously straight in that area and stayed that way for several miles approximately northward, precisely aiming the erratically moving machine along the course mapped out by that narrow band of water below him would be extremely difficult. Even if he could manage it, a river landing would almost certainly end abruptly in disaster. The Colorado River averaged only about three hundred feet wide in that area and for the next several miles to the north, adequate to accommodate the DC-7 but just barely, especially considering the undulations in the banks. Three hundred feet was only three times the truncated wingspan of the DC-7. To stay between the river's banks once they were on the water would require the luck of cutting a nearly straight line down the middle, unlikely even in an airplane that was whole, let alone one that was seriously unbalanced from missing a big piece of a wing and the fuel that was in it. And to try the narrower, winding Little Colorado would be certain suicide. Even on the wider Colorado, surely the plane would veer straightaway into one of the rocky banks, or one of the wings would dip and catch the water, sending the plane into one disastrous motion or another. Harms would also have to find a way to dramatically reduce his speed before touching down without losing what little control he had, a contradiction in terms because his meager lift force was in proportion to his speed. Otherwise the water itself would destroy the airplane even with a perfect landing, just as a fire hose might strip the aluminum siding off a house.

Maybe he held out this slim hope, and maybe, insane as it was, it never even occurred to him. But it was not to be. The rivers were a quarter mile farther down into the gorge from the place where United

Flight 718 ended. Harms needed either more control of his airplane or more space in which to maneuver. It was hopeless.

As if in profound testament to this, poor Fiore was now wailing, "Holy Mary, Mother of God! We're going to crash!" These pathetic words were also recorded on the ARINC tape, while Harms was still pressing the microphone button. Fiore's voice was considerably elevated in pitch, to a degree even higher than that of a normal female voice. During his mayday message Harms' voice was somewhat elevated in pitch also, but it was still within the range for males. Harms was obviously in great distress, but the much greater increase in Fiore's pitch, by orders of magnitude, showed that he was far more acutely terrified than Harms. He was scared to death, and that would be his last reaction to life. Everyone hopes that when the time comes, he will be content with himself and what he has accomplished, and at peace with death, but Fiore had one of the cruelest ends anyone could have. His final impression of himself was that of a crazy man, and he faced his death not with peace but with abject terror. It was deeper and crueler than the ultimate fear of dying—it was the terror of being human, the terror of being so vulnerable. His life would end as it began, not in the fear of leaving, but in the primal fear of being here.

Fiore was helpless. He was in his own seat, not the captain's seat, and he had nothing to hang onto. With no flight controls in front of him, he could not steer the plane or pull back to try making it climb. There was nothing he could do to try saving himself. Harms on the other hand had the reassurance of holding the control yoke, having the copilot's wheel in his hands, and he was able to maneuver with it at least a little. Having a modicum of control must have dulled the sharp edge of his fear and given him a sense of resoluteness rather than helplessness overlaid on it, no matter how afraid he was. But Fiore had no control. His helplessness accentuated his fear to an unbearable intensity, and the poor man lost himself.

Fiore's trauma became a record of the situation on the flight deck. He paid a terrible price to leave behind a historical legacy showing that he was in his own seat. Just as the premise that he was there explains the degree of his emotion, so also does his acute terror place him in the engineer's seat rather than the captain's seat. This in turn means that Fiore could not have been helping Harms keep the lookout when the collision occurred. Through his terrible ordeal, Girardo Fiore left one of the only definite clues about how the accident had been able to happen.

Of all the people aboard the *City of Vancouver*, only Harms had a measure of control over his peril. In having some ability to maneuver the airplane, he was in a unique position: he could directly act to save himself by trying to keep the plane from crashing. Harms alone had this asset, as well as the invaluable bolstering of his mental and emotional wherewithal that it conferred. Harms was fortunate, if there can be any validity in the idea that two persons facing infinite loss can be unequally bad off.

On the other hand, by being in the singular position of having partial control over the airplane, Harms was also the only person who was de facto responsible and bound to perform a miracle, rescuing his passengers, himself, and his airplane. It was up to him and only him. He was blessed with a special diminution of his fear that was granted no one else, and by the same token, he was also beset with an extreme demand, an ultimatum incumbent upon no one else. If he was more than vaguely aware of the fifty-seven other people behind him that were depending on him and his actions for their very lives, he must have felt a strain that can scarcely be imagined. His coherence during the mayday message, however, contrarily indicates that he had blocked out everything but flying the airplane.

The passengers' situation was entirely different. Besides being helpless to control the plane, they were helpless to face the situation they were in. Most blatantly, they couldn't see where they were going, like Harms could, because they could look out of only the sides. Secondarily, few of them were aviators; most were naive about the real risks involved in flying, and having only a sketch of a realistic mental and emotional predisposition, they were caught utterly defenseless. An aviator might have thought, in immediate recognition, "It has finally happened!" but the average passenger at best could have desperately thought, "What in God's name is happening?"

The passengers were unprepared because they had placed their trust and their lives in the care of the airline and the crew. They had trusted that there would be no emergency, and that on the one in a million chance that there would be, the crew would cope with it and keep them safe. The passengers were supposed to have been free of needing to do anything to keep themselves alive, and the shock of discovering that they had been betrayed had to have been like finding out that they had been murdered. They were falling unrelentingly, as though they had been abandoned and no one was flying the plane. They had been tricked and were helpless to save themselves. The passengers had freely walked right into a death trap and unwittingly surrendered their own lives, and now having realized their mistake, they were fighting desperately and hopelessly to escape. They fought without having any means to fight, by yelling and hanging on, willing the horror to cease. Surely some poor souls were overcome and rendered mindlessly incompetent. With no chance at all, the others tried to protect themselves. They buckled in and braced themselves. They shielded each other bodily. Some probably even stopped resisting and found the self-possession to accept their end and to pray for spiritual protection, or for God to help and protect their loved ones, who were going to lose them.

The stewardesses may have been able to maneuver well enough to help some of the passengers prepare for the crash, fastening their seatbelts or instructing them to cover their heads. It was their duty to think of the passengers first, even to the point of forsaking their own safety, and it was in most stewardesses' characters to be courageous in an emergency. Their jobs and their responsibilities were similar in principle to those of a nurse, who has vowed to help her patients even at the risk of her own health or safety, or even her life. (In fact, stewardesses were required to be nurses in the earlier days of passenger flight.) The stewardesses had to be ultimately self-sacrificing. They had to do everything they could to save strangers, and when they were put to the test, most of them were that noble. Nancy Kemnitz and Margaret Shoudt probably gave some of the passengers the last care they ever received. They probably also managed the pandemonium to some degree by being voices of authority and hope.

In that extreme crisis, with so many people to care for and such rampant fear amongst them, certainly neither of the stewardesses ever sat down and strapped herself in; they gave aid to the terrified passengers right up to when the plane hit the ground. No one but Harms, and Fiore if he was still looking, could see that that was about to happen, because no one else could see ahead. In the last moments, United 718 approached the fatal rock formation from the southwest, heading in approximately the same direction they were when they crashed, and the summit of the butte that was to be their final destination could be seen nearby to the left, out the passenger cabin windows on that side. The ground below was visible out both sides of the plane and still lay a quarter mile down. This gave the illusion that they were still far from crashing. Probably everyone in the passenger cabin, Miss Kemnitz and Miss Shoudt included, was spared the final horror of realizing that in their unique predicament, it was not the ground below that was their mortal enemy, but rather the ground in front of them. They never knew what they hit.

Captain Shirley may have helped the passengers too, but much more likely he was single-mindedly intent upon getting back to the cockpit. In that mortal emergency he would not have delayed unless to directly save someone's life. He must have unconsciously and instinctively realized the futility of helping anyone if he could not level out the plane. It was also ingrained in his identity to be in charge and in control. It was his plane and his territory above anyone else's, and it was his second nature to bend every effort to reassert his command when it was threatened. Taking it as fact that he was not on the flight deck when the DC-7 crashed, something evidently prevented him despite how strong and certain his will was.

One man's choice is another's fate. Fate had conjured an epic set, and whether it gave Harms a minor determining role or took all of those lives to their conclusions itself, controlling even Harms' final actions, the effect on Captain Shirley was the same: his circumstances had been entirely decided for him. At the most crucial moment of his career, he was thwarted and beaten—not by a worthy adversary like the power of a great storm, which might have made his failure admirable or even legendary, but most probably by something as tragically absurd as the collision having thrown too many people into the aisle to crawl over in time. At least Captain Shirley was able to try, which was more than his counterpart on the TWA Constellation had been able to do.

Immediately to the northeast of the place where the hellish abuse of everyone aboard the Constellation ended is a place called Chuar Butte (pronounced choo-er). Chuar Butte is situated on the west bank of the Colorado River, at the area where the Little Colorado flows into it. Like most buttes, it has several major ridges that radiate laterally from a higher central area and drop off. These are defined by more or less peninsular cliff faces and can be termed shoulders, after the analogy that they are to a butte as the shoulders of a figure are to a bust. From far above, Chuar Butte looks vaguely like an amoeba, with its graceless, asymmetrical pseudopods (its stubby, misshapen "legs") protruding at odd intervals around its circumference. These legs are the shoulders. At their bases the shoulders are surrounded by talus slopes—fanned out, sloped skirtings of fallen rock. Over the aeons, chunks of stone have cracked off the shoulders and fallen to the ground below, often breaking apart when they struck it. The resulting rocky debris has piled up in the probabilistic shape of a cone, the only shape it could pile up in, surrounding each of the shoulders.

One of the shoulders of Chuar Butte points to the east-southeast, directly at the confluence of the Colorado and Little Colorado rivers, from just under half a mile away. Its talus slope rises from the Colorado

River bank at an angle of about thirty degrees, climbing from the river's elevation of 2,700 feet to an elevation of 3,400 feet. From there, at the top of the talus slope, the shoulder thrusts upward over 650 feet higher, nearly vertically, to its crest. United 718 struck the top edge of this promontory at an elevation of about 4,050 feet, only ten feet below the crest, about a hundred feet inland from the crest's eastern extremity. This location is at the top of a steep gully feature on the south face of the shoulder, which directs falling rock and rainwater from the crest downward a couple hundred feet and then over the cliff face. The plane came in on an east-northeast heading, pitched about twenty-five degrees nose down and rolled about ten degrees right wing down. These particulars were ascertained from careful examination of the wreckage distribution and from marks left on the rock face, with the final heading corroborated by the one cockpit navigational instrument that was found reasonably intact. It read forty-five degrees magnetic, equivalent to sixty degrees true heading in that area in that year. (The magnetic north pole gradually moves, and correspondingly the disparity between magnetic and true bearings gradually changes.)

One thing strikingly indicated by the manner in which the DC-7 came to earth was that Harms might have managed a good measure of improvised control after all. When the plane made contact with Chuar Butte, it was rolled with its right wing down by ten degrees, suggesting that Harms had found a way to stop the involuntary left turn imposed upon him by the collision damage. He may even have regained enough control to navigate the canyon. Of course, it may be that in its tendency to roll leftward the DC-7 had rolled nearly all the way over. It might also be that Harms had made it do this as the only way he could maneuver the plane into a right-wing-down attitude. The intriguing possibility, however, is that Harms was engaged in a nearly normal right turn when the end came, nearly normal mechanically that is. The purpose of the turn would have been anything but normal: namely, to miss Chuar Butte, and maybe to follow one of the rivers. Whether by design or by chance, his final heading was aligned well with the course of the Colorado River, as it stood laid out for a mile or so behind him. Maybe he had been following it.

The Colorado River arced gently in its circuit around the base of Chuar Butte. In order to follow it upstream northward from there, Harms would have to start a left turn immediately after passing the confluence of the rivers. An undamaged DC-7 was capable of a far sharper turn, but more pertinently, because the *City of Vancouver* was already bent on turning left, it should have been feasible for it to turn leftward quickly enough to follow the river's curvature, even badly damaged.

Opposite this pathetically hopeful picture, though not necessarily in contradiction of it, other evidence indicated a disastrous final few seconds by showing that immediately before the DC-7 crashed, its elevators and horizontal stabilizers tore free. Horizontal stabilizers are the fixed horizontal tail planes, and elevators are the tilting flaps hinged to the rear edges of the horizontal stabilizers. The elevators are used primarily to make an airplane ascend or descend. When the elevators tore off, they damaged structures that held on the horizontal stabilizers, which in turn tore free because they were no longer strong enough to remain attached. Had the elevators remained in place in their hinges, the whole tail would have remained intact, but as it was, only the vertical fin and the rudder hinged to its rear edge stayed on the airplane all the way to the ground. Even in the lightning-fast succession of events during the split-second ground breakup, the destruction of the fuel tanks in the wings preceded the destruction of the tail, fifty feet behind, by enough time for the fire to erupt and for the tail to be singed as it sailed through the fireball. The vertical tail fin and rudder were found with the corresponding telltale black smudges, but the other tail components, the horizontal stabilizers and the elevators, were found clean. The only way for them to escape passing through the fireball or coming to rest within the ground fire was for them to come off the airplane before it crashed, and to follow divergent paths to the ground. These parts were found nearby enough, however, to indicate that their paths were only slightly different, showing in turn that they separated from the airplane no more than a couple seconds before the crash.

Assuming that the elevators were still useable after the collision, there are two possibilities as to what Harms was doing with them right before they came off: using them to control the pitch of the airplane, and less likely, leaving them in a "neutral" position. If Harms was making the elevators do work to maintain level flight, against an unnatural tendency of his damaged airplane to pitch nose downward, or if he was using them to pull out of a descent or enter a climb, then when they tore free, the DC-7 must have pitched nose downward. On the other hand, if Harms had miraculously found a way to fly level without making the elevators do any work, leaving them in a neutral position, then when they came off, no appreciable forces affecting the attitude of the plane were lost, and the nose of the plane didn't significantly drop.

The elevators were relatively light, and losing them didn't affect the balance of the plane dramatically, but the horizontal stabilizers were quite a bit heavier. The plane pitched nose downward when they subsequently tore off, because of the loss of their balancing weight at the rear. Also, the horizontal stabilizers generated a nonadjustable downward "lift" force all the time in flight, like small upside-down wings. This force of course vanished with the horizontal stabilizers, letting the rear end rise, with the corresponding relative effect of the nose pitching downward. These principles had already been horribly demonstrated by the Constellation when it went into a nosedive, wholly caused by losing its own tail.

Inasmuch as Harms was probably using the elevators to try to pull up in the last moments, the DC-7's pitch was probably directly affected when they came off, possibly to a disastrous degree. Whether it was or not, however, it was the event that ended everyone's lives. By giving out, the elevators caused the horizontal stabilizers to tear off, and that secondary reaction was fatal. Irrespective of the elevators, the DC-7 descended more sharply and rapidly in the last couple of seconds before the crash because it had lost its horizontal stabilizers. Had this not occurred, United 718 would not have struck Chuar Butte, which they only just barely clipped. Instead, they would have retained just a little bit more altitude, and would have over flown the promontory that pointed at the Little Colorado River, low enough to raise the dust.

When the DC-7 hit Chuar Butte, it was pitched nose downward twenty-five degrees, pretty steep but not terribly steep for a plane that had lost its horizontal stabilizers. When the stabilizers came off, the plane pitched very rapidly, so it wouldn't have taken long for it to tip to twenty-five degrees below level, from whatever inclination it had right before. This indicates that the DC-7 was coming down only very gently, if at all, up until the stabilizers came off, because its pitch immediately prior to that must have been significantly shallower than twenty-five degrees. In fact, Harms may have been holding the plane level or even climbing. First Officer Robert Harms must have done a magnificent job of regaining control of the airplane after the collision. He had probably done as good a piece of emergency flying as anyone ever had; through his skill and his presence of mind, the *City of Vancouver* was not in a deadly fall. At the worst it was gradually sinking, like the weakened machine that it was, unable to fully support itself though far from defeated.

This is not to say that without the plane beginning to come apart, and without it hitting Chuar Butte, Harms could have saved everyone. With such serious damage severely handicapping maneuvering, United 718 would likely still have crashed in the Grand Canyon. They were 2,000 feet below the East Rim, and it would have taken a long time to climb that far with nearly half of a wing missing and one engine out. In the meantime Harms would have to have navigated the canyon, following the Colorado River with impaired maneuverability. Hard as it would have been, it does appear from the meager evidence that he was trying to do just that. Besides, from a level two-thirds of the way down into the depths of the canyon, flying over the Colorado River, there was no good alternative but to follow the river because he was walled in. And if he could not climb out of the gorge, which is very likely, then it's back to the impossibly hazardous river landing.

United 718 would still have had a chance if the tail had not begun to come apart, and it seems that they came extremely close. Structures called elevator center hinge A-frames were retrieved in the ensuing on-site investigation. These components were deeply gouged in a way characteristically indicating that just before breaking free, the elevators were severely oscillating. In fact, this uncontrollable, violent flapping motion was in all likelihood what tore them off. Harms had evidently nearly leveled out from a steeper prior descent when the elevators came off, which he probably could not have accomplished without them. The elevators presumably then had been usable, which is to say controllable, until nearly the end, meaning that their flapping became violent only just before the crash.

The severe oscillating was probably a consequence of excessive airspeed, perhaps aggravated by some form of structural damage that was inflicted upon one or both elevators by flying debris in the collision itself. If Harms had in fact basically leveled out, then his speed had reached a peak, not a plateau, and would momentarily have begun dropping back to something reasonable. If only the elevators had held for a few moments longer, their flapping would have begun to subside, and they might never have torn off; on the other hand, if only Harms had been able to level out just moments sooner, his airspeed might never have reached the critical level that destroyed the elevators. From either perspective, he nearly made it. United 718 nearly made it. Everyone on board nearly made it.

Some of this is of course highly wishful thinking, yet unrealistic as it may be, it is fundamentally humane to think it and wish it. A hundred times I have imagined their last moments, and with exquisite frustration wished that there could at least have been some chance, some way out, even though they did not take it. Somehow their fate would seem a little less cruel if it was not of itself absolutely unyielding. Obviously the tail had to come apart at the point it did, but I have to wonder if there might have been some way to prevent reaching that point. Harms did a fabulous job and almost saved everyone. It only makes him more admirable to suppose that there was a way for him to have succeeded. It would make it true that at the end of his life he was purposefully trying to solve a legitimate problem, rather than pointlessly trying to wrestle an alternative from an innately single-sided and irremovable reality, trying to solve a riddle that was only a dirty trick with no solution. He would have been trying to open a door, not a solid wall. One meaning of his final endeavor, over and above its inspiring courageousness and heart-rending inadequacy, would then be that he died in a way befitting his dignity: he died with fate respecting him rather than mocking him.

Harms tried everything he had time for, and then there was no more room for United 718. Their airspace ran out, and in a flash their lives were gone. The magnificent, shining airplane that had carried them in comfort, safety, and luxury folded up, disintegrated, and exploded in a horrific fireball. It vanished all in the space of a fifth of a second, from the instant its nose touched the stone. The absolute rending of that airplane and the human beings aboard it was accomplished in literally just the time it takes to snap your fingers. Snap! And their lives were gone. Snap! And the DC-7 had become a hurtling, fulminating cloud of shredded junk. Many fragments were flung over the crest of the promontory, and tumbled through space or down the cliff face on the other side. Most of the wreckage cascaded down the impact gully, pursued by a racing flood of flaming aviation fuel pouring down its slope, and came to rest within it. A small multitude of fragments rolled and bounced the full length of the gully and sailed over the sheer cliff at its mouth, careening in a tumultuous shower through the open air to the narrow ledges and the talus slope far below.

Within ten or twenty seconds all of the multifarious motions had ceased. A raging fire roared in the gully, made all the more vehement by burning on a nearly vertical surface, enabling it to draw oxygen into itself from below through its own rising draft like a chimney. Of all the things in the gully, only the fire's diaphanous form stirred of its own accord. Its violent blustering caused sheet metal to quiver and buckle, and fabrics and papers to ascend like burning leaves, carried high above the fire by the rapidly rising, blisteringly hot air. A few things slid farther down the gully as the fire freed them by consumption from the rocks. Everything else kept still as it submitted to the fire's power and melted or turned to cinders.

The worst accident in commercial aviation history had just occurred, and the scope of the catastrophe was rudely proved by what lay in the combined disaster area, and by the sheer incomprehensibility of it all.

Two fierce fires, leaping high into the air and spread over areas as big as football fields, were blazing on top of solid, barren rock, in a place with hardly more indigenous flammable materials than it would take to make a campfire. It was a scene from the time when creation was hardly beyond its Ideation, the dawn of a primordial landscape, with flaming gasses rushing from fumaroles in rock formations that were still hot from their forgings in the subterranean furnaces. Reason was of no use against its fearsomeness, and to attempt fitting the phantasm into a rational frame could only compound it. The inferno had to be the doing of man, not nature, and not an act intended to be beneficial, nor even a calculatedly malicious act, but wholly some terrible error.

No mortal eyes beheld this Vulcan spectacle, not while it was anywhere near its full fury. It was rendered in a desolate place, remote from mankind, and it vanished into the unattainable, ethereal past before anyone could capture it. From a distance a few Navajo Indians at the reservation to the east saw its black spirit, two columns of sooty black smoke rising in the west, but not its will, not its fire, half a mile down into the Grand Canyon. From their uncomplicated perspectives they could not have guessed the significance of what they saw. For them, the mysterious smoke was only a sign of the foolhardy activities of the white man.

The persons who lost their lives on TWA 2:

Harry Harvey Allen
Tracine Elizabeth Armbruster
Thomas Edward Ashton, Jr.
Robert Vernon Beatty
Martha Ann Beck
Stephen Robert Bishop
Connie June Braughton
Esther Ellen Braughton
Linda Kay Braughton
Forrest Dean Breyfogle
Lois Klein Brock
Lillian Estelle Carple
Lawrence Zay Chatten
Sally Ann Cressman
Chester Arnold Crewse
Helen Colleen Crewse
Beth Ellis Davis
Selma Louise Davis
Robert Earl DeLonge
Almeda Evans
Donald Lloyd Flentie
Jack Silvetus Gandy
Virginia Elizabeth Goppert
Janice Tracy Haas
Mildred Rogene Crick Hatcher
William Wallace Hatcher
Janice Mae Heiser
Harry Robinson Holman
James Joseph Jang
Wayne Gardner Jeffrey

Sidney Roland Joslin
Catherine Kennaley
Joseph James Kite
Linda JoAnn Kite
Peachie Marie Kite
Sharon Marie Kite
Marie Jane Klemp
Lois Marie Laxton
Michael Anthony Laxton
Mary Ellen Lytle
Claire M. Maag
Howard John Maag
John Otto Maag
Donald K. MacBain
William H. Markey, Jr.
Rosalie Maude McClenny
Alice Emma Meyer
Andrew Jackson Nasalroad
Robert B. Nelson
Marietta Thompson Noel
Richard Curtis Noel
John Walker Payne
Monica Jean Payne
Richard Darling Payne
Richard Michael Payne
Robert Farley Perisho
Dennis Joseph Phelan
Neal Alan Power
Edward Merrill Reaves
James Henry Ritner
David Karn Robinson
Geoffry Brian Robinson

Jeanette Karn Robinson
Robert Ernest Sanders
Esther Fair Sharp
Robert Frank Sontag
Gloria Kathleen Gipson Townsend
Bessie Whitman
Carolyn Ruth Wiley
Elizabeth May Young

The persons who lost their lives on United 718:

Christopher E. Balsat

John A. Barry

Phyllis G. Berman

Rosemary Bishop

Stephen John Bishop

Gertrude Coyne Book

Frank C. Caple

M. Barry Carlton

Carol Jean Church

Frank H. Clark

L. David Cook, Jr.

Elizabeth Crider

Jeffrey Crider

Elizabeth Frances Doering

Thomas W. Doyle, Jr.

Girardo X. Fiore

Stella B. Fuchs

Walter M. Fuchs

Noel H. Gottesman

Jack Brothers Groshans

James Hadfield

Lillian Ruth Hahn

Robert W. Harms

Eugene B. Hoffman

Russell Charles Huber

Francis Robert Johlie II

Donald F. Kehl

Nancy Lou Kemnitz

Dee D. Kovack

Ted M. Kubiniec

Ray Oliver Lasby

Sally Lou Laughlin
Joseph M. Levis
Theodore Henry Lyman
Carl G. Matland
John J. Muldoon
Gerald Murchison
Dwight B. Nims
Floyd A. Nixon
Elsie W. Osterbrock
Hugo Pekruhn
John George Reba
Alexander Eugene Rosenblatt
Russell A. Shields, Jr.
Robert F. Shirley
Margaret Ann Shoudt
Carl J. Snyder
Fred Staecker
Thomas J. Sulpizio
James W. Tobias, Jr.
Albert Vogt
Stanley Jerome Weiss
Peter Whyte
Albert E. Widdifield
Roberta E. Wilde
Donald L. Winings
Weslau G. Wright
John E. Yaeger

CHAPTER II

ALL OF THE victims had perished in utter obscurity. Not a living soul knew what had befallen them. A few unusually intuitive persons probably knew vaguely by clairvoyance but did not understand their own perceptions. Most people hadn't the least inkling that anything had gone wrong, and those who had were far from sure. Even the Salt Lake City ARINC operator who received United 718's distress call did not know.

For the whole world, even for those who had lost a loved one, it was as though nothing had happened at all, as if the rhythms of life had not been altered even minutely or upset by even the least tremor. The most catastrophic destruction had just occurred in the lives of a thousand people, family, and dear friends of those who had died, and yet it had produced not the slightest tangible impact.

At the same time that the horror in the Grand Canyon was both outdoing itself and consummating itself in the second crash, an air traffic controller named Stuart Halsey was opening the brown paper sack that held his lunch. He was the watch supervisor on duty at the Salt Lake City Air Route Traffic Control center, and he sat alone in the austere, somewhat shabby lunchroom at the facility. Ever since about 10:49, six minutes before leaving California airspace, TWA 2 had been in Halsey's area; and ever since about 11:08, ten minutes inside Arizona airspace for them, United 718 had also been in Halsey's area. The huge territory for which he was responsible included all of the Grand Canyon; much of airway Red 15; most of the Painted Desert, including the Line of Position that ran through it; and most of Utah and Nevada.

The flight progress strips for TWA 2 and United 718 were on the board of Lynn McCreary and indicated that each expected to reach the Painted Desert LOP at 11:31. McCreary was one of several controllers working under Halsey and was also the Salt Lake controller who had earlier been involved in the decision with Los Angeles ARTC to disapprove of TWA 2's request for a change to cruising at 21,000 feet. He knew that the two proposed courses crossed and that the planes were nearly neck and neck, or that they at least had been an hour earlier. However, he was not particularly concerned because the situation was common.

11:31 passed without either flight's radio service or one of the INSACS advising that they had received a position report, and McCreary began to wonder and then became concerned. After the five-minute grace period expired without either flight having been reported, his uneasiness surpassed the indefinable barrier between concern and worry. It was not unusual for telephone tie-ups to delay a position report, but for two reports to fail to come in at the same time from separate facilities using separate phone lines, regarding airliners that would be in close proximity to each other in uncontrolled airspace, was not only odd but unsettling. McCreary sought out his boss, who was sitting on the lunchroom couch eating his sandwich, and apprised him of the situation.

Halsey knew right away what it had to mean. In his own words, "It's a rather strange affair to not have two airplanes report over the same place at the same time, or approximately the same time, and I was immediately alerted to the fact that this very well could have been a midair collision." At about 11:40, Halsey initiated efforts to locate the two flights. He telephoned the Las Vegas and Albuquerque TWA radio installations and the Salt Lake City facilities of ARINC. TWA had not heard from Flight 2 and had not been able to reach them. Similarly,

ARINC advised that they had not heard from United 718, though this was actually false.

Halsey also called the INSACS in the area in case they had heard from either flight, and again the answer was negative. He then telephoned the Albuquerque ADIZ to ask if they had spotted either plane on their radar equipment, and of course they had not; neither flight ever made it that far. He asked them if they would watch for the two flights and let him know if either one turned up, and they assured him that they would.

Salt Lake City ARTC also made numerous, persistent attempts, on a wide range of frequencies, to contact both flights directly by radio, all of which were fruitless. In the meantime, TWA radio at Albuquerque telephoned Albuquerque ARTC to ask if they had received a position report from Flight 2. This would have been unusual, because normally flights had no direct contact with ARTC en route; in fact Albuquerque ARTC normally depended on Albuquerque TWA to relay progress reports to *them* by phone, not the other way around.

Halsey held a joint telephone conference with his counterparts at the ARTC centers in Los Angeles, Albuquerque, and Denver. These were the centers overseeing the areas where the flights had originated, where they should have been by then if they were still airborne and where they would be next. Both would already have left the Salt Lake City ARTC region if they were still flying. The four men decided that the Salt Lake center would coordinate communications as liaison between the various concerned parties—the centers, the two airlines, and others—partly because they all knew instinctively that the planes were down and that they had come to earth somewhere in the Salt Lake center's area.

Halsey's next move was to set up a joint telephone conference with the dispatch offices of United Air Lines and TWA at Los Angeles, and with the United States Air Force. The dispatch offices were responsible for the two flights inasmuch as they had overseen and coordinated the planning and preparations for them and had been monitoring their progress, and the air force would be responsible to conduct an aerial search if it came to that. The officials involved in this conference came to the consensus that the radio and radar searches ought to continue for the time being.

TWA 2 had upcoming designated checkpoints at Farmington, New Mexico, and at Trinidad, Colorado; United 718 had upcoming designated checkpoints at Durango, Colorado, and Pueblo, Colorado. The conferees decided that if either flight had still not been found by the time it should make the second of its upcoming position reports, then the air force would launch a full-scale aerial search and rescue mission. If either flight missed these position reports, then it would have missed three in a row, starting with the Painted Desert LOP. Also, Trinidad and Pueblo were right at the eastern boundary of the Albuquerque ADIZ, Trinidad just inside of it and Pueblo just outside of it, and using these as the demarcating points in the wait had the added advantage of giving the air force the maximum chance to locate the planes on the radar equipment that it employed to watch over the zone. The flights would have to pass fully through the ADIZ from west to east in order to reach their checkpoints at its eastern edge, and there was no more chance that they could do this undetected than an enemy bomber could.

Over an hour passed between the time ARTC first regarded the flights as unreported and the time that the all-out search began. This was ample time to find them if they were still in the air, more than enough even if by an incredible coincidence both of them had simultaneously lost the use of all of their radio equipment. In fact, some people in the industry were appalled and condemned it as being excessive to the point of unconscionable, considering that if the planes had crashed or crash-landed and there were survivors, some of them might well be critically injured and fast approaching death. Their view was that the aerial search ought to have begun immediately in case the planes had crashed, rather than be postponed in case they hadn't. This of course was the more humane position, the one more clearly on the side of saving lives.

Unfortunately there were protocols that had to be followed. The tremendous expenditure of resources entailed in an all-out aerial search and rescue mission had to be regulated, in order to ensure that those resources would not be uselessly exhausted, and that they would be applied for the greatest good overall, saving the most lives in the long run. In other words, it was essential to be conservative given limited means. One stipulation implementing this principle was that those in charge of conducting a proposed mission had to be sure that it was necessary. Naturally if "sure" were not defined, at least by guidelines, then the principle would have hardly more value than no principle at all, so standards were developed amounting to a series of procedures that would be followed in order to locate a missing aircraft or, by elimination, to qualify it for an all-out search. Still, one has to ask why more money wasn't allocated for this invaluable lifesaving service, so that it could have been initiated sooner in general, using a less cautious sieve to catch false cases.

Even within the system as it stood on June 30, 1956, one has to ask: Given the extreme improbability of two aircraft disappearing in the same area at the same time unless they had collided, why was it not more readily assumed that there had been an accident, so that the aerial search could begin? The standard procedures ought to have been relaxed or even waived.

While they waited for Salt Lake City ARTC to officially declare the flights to be missing rather than only unreported, both airlines prepared for the worst. They both knew from experience that a missing airliner in modern times nearly always meant that there had been a disaster. Twenty years earlier it would as likely have meant either that the crew was lost or that they had had a forced landing in a field, but mishaps like these were rare by the 1950s.

At 12:51 p.m. MST, Stuart Halsey received the dreadful word that both flights were still unreported, and he issued the official Missing

Aircraft Alert. One hour and twenty minutes had passed, and now a tremendous search and rescue operation began getting under way. There was no one to save, nor had there been for even a moment. All of them had perished in a split-second when the planes came to earth, if not beforehand, but no one in the world knew that, and a massive movement began to take shape in the urgent yet restrained hope of finding survivors. Everyone involved realized that the chance was slim, but they were dedicated to the ultimate principle that human lives might be saved.

* * *

Analogous to its sub-dividedness as the individual states, the whole country was parceled off into the areas over which the various ARTC centers were responsible. There were only about half as many of these as states, or looking at it the other way around, most of these were about twice as large as a state. Overlaid on the ARTC map were the ADIZs. Unlike the states and the ARTC territories, these zones were discontinuous patches. An ADIZ might irregularly overlap portions of several ARTC areas, but then also major regions of the country were not within any ADIZ. A third aviation map overlaid these, dividing the nation into nine regions according to yet another scheme. These nine together composed the whole country and were the regions of responsibility of the Air Rescue Service, the branch of the U.S. Air Force that conducted aerial search and rescue missions. Like ARTC areas and the ADIZs, these regions were delineated in correspondence with their own independent considerations and criteria, and so they overlapped the former only irregularly and by happenstance, not by design.

A particular air force base within each region had been designated as the permanent headquarters from which aerial search and rescue duties would be administered in that region, but the sense in which an elected base was responsible was only supportive and passive. It was actually specific air rescue squadrons stationed at these bases that were responsible, just as it was not literally a town that was responsible to rescue victims and put out fires in its vicinity, but rather the fire department stationed in the town.

From the west coast to the state line between Arizona and New Mexico, the proposed courses of both TWA 2 and United 718 lay entirely within the Air Rescue Service region whose headquarters were at March Air Force Base. March AFB was situated about sixty-five miles east of Los Angeles, and its region consisted of southern California, small portions of southern Nevada, and all of Arizona but for a northern slice cut off along a line that divided the Grand Canyon and the Painted Desert into north and south halves. Both planes had disappeared within March's vast region, inasmuch as they had both last reported their positions from within it and had both subsequently failed to report from within it at the Painted Desert LOP.

The 42nd Air Rescue Squadron (ARS) was stationed at March AFB at the time, and accordingly the squadron was responsible and in charge of the search. Their first move was to set up emergency headquarters at the airport in Winslow, Arizona, in order to conduct the operations from there. They had a rough idea of where to start looking for the missing aircraft, and Winslow's airport was the nearest one to this area that had modern runways and a modern VHF navigational radio facility. Winslow also had high-octane aviation fuel available to keep their aircraft flying, though this was not strictly an advantage because tank trucks could have been driven to any airfield they chose.

The 42nd ARS was to receive major assistance from the 41st ARS, stationed at Hamilton AFB near San Francisco. Hamilton was the headquarters for Air Rescue Service operations in the huge area adjacent to March's, to the north. Each squadron was responsible for half of the Grand Canyon and unequal but huge areas of the Painted Desert, so of course it only made sense to have the 41st ARS involved from the outset. In addition to the primary air search and rescue squadrons, pilots and medics from transport and medical squadrons at Luke AFB, near Phoenix, had also been committed to the effort. These would go in on the ground via helicopter once the crash sites were located.

As was policy in civilian aviation accidents and mishaps, the Civil Air Patrol (CAP) was also called in on the search. The CAP was a group of volunteers who served as a civilian air force, originally with the purpose of bolstering national defense should the need ever arise; during peacetime, among other duties, they helped in aerial searches for downed aircraft. The CAP was a legally chartered component of the U.S. Air Force and had its own squadrons domiciled at a great many airports and air force bases, including March AFB and Hamilton AFB. There were many private pilots and their airplanes in the fold, and the CAP had previously been instrumental in numerous rescues.

By mid-afternoon a great many civilians and military men had mobilized and were preparing to head for northern Arizona or were already en route. It was to be quite a show of humanity and nobility, and yet as if in sad mockery of this virtuous effort, the massive search was actually superfluous. The mystery of where the planes were had already been solved, though the man with the answer did not yet realize he had it.

Mr. Palen Hudgin was eating his lunch at about 1:00 p.m. and telling his wife of the dense, black smoke he had seen rising out of the canyon about half an hour before. He was part owner of Hudgin Flying Service, the one aerial sightseeing company operating in the Grand Canyon at the time. With his brothers, he also owned what was locally known as Red Butte Airfield, situated fourteen miles south of Grand Canyon Village. It took its name from the geographic feature nearby and was also known as Grand Canyon Airport. Here the brothers had two dirt airstrips, a hangar, an office building, and several houses. At about 12:30 Hudgin was flying near the confluence of the Colorado and Little Colorado rivers with a group of tourists. He saw the smoke, and though its denseness and sootiness seemed odd to him, he assumed that there was a brush fire somewhere down in the canyon, probably started by lightning in the storms the day before. (An appreciable amount of vegetation grew along the riverbank, but not where the planes had crashed; he didn't see the fires themselves, and so he did not realize that they were burning in places higher up, where his supposition made little sense.) After returning to Red Butte Airfield and parting from his passengers, Hudgin simply walked over to his house to eat. He had no idea that anything was wrong in the canyon, or that two airliners were missing, and he simply continued the normal business of his day.

*   *   *

Between all of the airlines operating flights throughout the southwest, many flights passed right through the region. TWA and United Air Lines, and their associated competitors, asked the crews of these flights to watch for fire on the ground below. A fire from the crash of even a small, private plane, let alone a very large, four-engine airliner, would be visible even from high altitude, wherever clouds did not obscure the ground. Unfortunately, none of the airline crews that looked for Flights 2 and 718 saw any fire from the air. Some of them flew right over the eastern end of the canyon, and even these failed to see the blazes at Temple Butte and Chuar Butte, which raged all afternoon; the lower overcast must have hidden them.

Meanwhile, United's flight operations department in Denver contacted Mr. Francis Shamrell, manager of Flagstaff Municipal Airport in Flagstaff, Arizona, to explain the situation to him and to ask his permission to make use of a hangar. He agreed without hesitation, and a United Convair 340 loaded with equipment for backpacking and mountain climbing flew in from Denver that afternoon, carrying a group of company men unfortunately experienced in disasters. Every airline that had been around for a while had had accidents, with only a couple of exceptions, and those were as much a gift of good luck as a product of excellent safety standards. United Air Lines and TWA were among the oldest and the largest airlines in the country, and despite good safety policies and practices, they had had their share of tragedy. Both had had recent accidents in very rugged terrain, and they were still fresh from those ordeals. Only nine months before, a United DC-4 crashed at Medicine Bow Peak in the mountains near Laramie, Wyoming; a year and four months prior to the Grand Canyon accident, a TWA Martin 404 hit Sandia Mountain near Albuquerque. In both cases there was terrible and total loss of life, and both wrecks were exceedingly difficult to reach.

Like United Air Lines, TWA flew to the area near where Flight 2 was thought to have disappeared. A special plane loaded with equipment and knowledgeable personnel, including some executives, was flown from TWA's Kansas City headquarters to Winslow that afternoon. Why TWA went to Winslow and United went to Flagstaff is probably lost to the past, because most of the people who made the decisions are gone, and these decisions were not important enough to have merited keeping permanent records of them. Perhaps it is enough to say that Flagstaff and Winslow were roughly equidistant from the initial search area, and though Winslow's airport was superior, Flagstaff's was fully adequate to accommodate any of the smaller twin-engine airliners. From the perspective of either airline, the two airports could well have seemed equally suitable. The primary difference of any significance to them was probably that the air force was to be headquartered at Winslow for their air search and rescue operations. In one vein this was an asset because of the close communication that sharing a base with the air rescue squadrons facilitated; in another vein it was a problem, because combining forces at a single small airport entailed some crowding both on the ground and in the airspace over the airport. Which one to choose may have been an educated toss-up.

Three other groups bound for the area from their various offices across the country were officials of the CAA and the CAB, who would conduct the on-site accident investigation and attempt to preliminarily determine what had happened, and newspaper reporters, who would inform the public of everything that was being done.

Collectively, the reporting comprised three categories: short biographical pieces on the victims, most of which were sensitively written and gave the reader a clearer grasp of the meaning of the tragedy by illustrating the personal, human terms of how much was lost; articles about the people who were crushed by the tragedy through losing a loved one, portraying them in the settings of the airport terminals on the day of the accident, and at TWA's mass funeral soon thereafter, most of which were sensitive, respectful, and accurate; and articles about officials performing their duties in various settings such as the crash sites and the subsequent hearings, many of which were just the opposite: insensitive, disrespectful, or just plain incorrect. The human-interest articles generally were well written, both compassionate and informative—a real benefit; the articles about what the officials were doing at the crash sites and how they were interpreting the evidence to determine how the disaster came about were largely garbled "crime scene" and "witch hunt" exposés, many of which were insincerely or selfishly conceived and grossly misleading—a real disservice. As a measure of this, one crash scene investigator, TWA Captain Jasper Solomon, who I interviewed many times for this book, said that the newspaper stories he read while in the midst of his work out there were so far removed from what he and his colleagues were actually doing that he honestly, actually, literally believed that there must have been a second midair collision in the area. Some stories meant well but were written naively or carelessly, and thereby they proffered falsehoods along with truths, misinforming the readers who did not realize this, and confusing and frustrating everyone who did. Fortunately, some of the sincere reporters checked their facts and made the effort it took to incisively understand them; as a result their stories about the official responses to the tragedy were meaningful, authentic, and beneficial. But all of this was still to come.

With the exception of early reconnaissance jets, the air force search and rescue aircraft had not yet reached the search area even by the time that TWA Flight 2 was scheduled to arrive in Kansas City. At 3:25 p.m.

CST, equivalent to 2:25 p.m. in Arizona, or only about an hour and a half after the official Missing Aircraft Alert was issued, a large group of people had gathered at the TWA terminal at Kansas City Municipal Airport to wait for Flight 2 to come in. Nearly two-thirds of the people aboard were bound for Kansas City, and of them, twenty-nine persons were TWA employees and family of TWA employees, most of whom lived in or near Kansas City. Through the kindness of insiders at the company, a few of their families had been advised that the plane was missing, and some of them waited at home, having faith that through their connection with the company they would be notified at least as soon as anyone at the terminal whenever there was any word. People associated with the airline realized that if a missing flight turned up safely, there would be plenty of time to get to the airport, and that if it did not, there would be nothing they could do at the airport—and a lot to do outside of it. Unlike those not affiliated with the airline, whose only means of feeling connected to those in authority in a crisis was to wait at the terminal, employees and their families were relatively secure in their involvement even at a distance.

Whether they were connected with the company or not, most of the people waiting at the TWA terminal for Flight 2 had not been advised that anything was wrong. It was impossible to forewarn them all, and the company had not even tried to forewarn the families of unaffiliated passengers. It was better all around to wait and tell family members in person in the official surroundings of the airport terminal. There they could see the airline official's sincerity, earnestness, and regret, in his eyes and his face, which helped them to trust him and the airline and to have faith that the airline was doing everything possible to find their missing loved ones.

Were it even possible to have notified them all over the phone, the first reaction of most would have been to go to the airport terminal and confront whoever was in charge, to get him to confirm and explain what they had been told. They would all have wound up there anyway, but with predispositions of alarm and mistrust, and in some cases also indignation that the airline had given them such terribly distressing news in an impersonal way. The airline would have set them up to have attitudes obstructive to their own comprehension and faith, both of which they needed as much or more than ever before.

Everyone coming to the airport would be in the company of others, and in camaraderie with those strangers they might find the courage to face the situation they were all in. Yet in the irreducible brutality of what was happening, it seems inhumane that they were left having faith that everything was all right, until some ultimate moment when they were present at the terminal, rather than being told sooner, and then, for lack of any unthreatening way to reveal it, were shockingly, abruptly given the awful news. It had to be abrupt no matter how gently and gradually it was drawn, because there was no way to become prepared to hear it, but postponing telling them seems almost to have made fools of them, almost like having humored them, albeit with a benevolent rather than disrespectful motive. It was cruel to have made the bottom fall out for all of those people in that way, not cruel on the part of the airline or the airline personnel at the terminal exactly, but just plain cruel, a cruel reality, a cruel situation that was possibly as kind as it could have been made and was yet severe.

Shortly after 3:25 an announcement came over the loudspeaker system requesting all persons waiting for Flight 2 to go to the north end of the terminal lobby, where they were escorted into a private room. It was there that everyone was told. A doctor and nurse had already been summoned and tended to those who felt faint or panicky, giving them smelling salts or sedatives, and reassurance. Robert Helmer, a public relations man, and John Bailey, a district sales manager, disclosed to the group the vague, ominous, terrible fact that Flight 2 was missing. They tried to answer questions though there was little that they could say. The flight had disappeared and nothing more was known. There in that small, comfortable lounge, the unsurpassed grief and agony that were to be suffered together by a thousand people were released. No more were these feelings confined to the few who had been forewarned and had held them in relative private. The crisis was now public, and soon the anguish of the people in the lounge would spread to their community, and to other groups of as yet unknowing souls at other airports in succession to the east and west coasts. The nightmare had started. An ocean swell of destruction rose and heaved and surged across the land, lifting one person after another and large groups of people together, throwing them into a tumbling chaos as it swept out from under them in its haste to overtake others. Immediately behind it was a tidal wave of alarm and following that, wave after wave of unmitigated woe. The evil had been conjured, and with an awful, supernormal verity that was unbelievable because it was more vivid than reality, it swiftly afflicted everyone who cared for anyone who had been lost.

*　　*　　*

Exactly an hour after TWA 2 should have arrived at the gate at Kansas City Municipal Airport, United 718 should have pulled up to the gate at Chicago's Midway Airport. It was 5:25 p.m. CDT in Chicago, and a throng of people had gathered at United's terminal. The flight board behind the counter still said "On Time" next to the listing for Flight 718.

I was a toddler, riding piggyback on the shoulders of my grandfather, Guy Groshans, as we walked around the terminal building in Chicago. I was fascinated by the sounds of the air conditioning machinery and repeatedly steered Grandpa toward the various vent and utility compartments from which the sounds came, using my hands on his cheeks to push his face in the direction I wanted to go, like a rider uses the reins to turn a horse. My mother was with us, carrying my three-month-old sister. We were there to meet Flight 718, which was supposed to bring Uncle Jack to us. We were going to take him to Grandma and Grandpa's house for dinner. It was going to be a celebration of his thirty-third birthday, which had come three days earlier while he was on business in California. The following day, Uncle

Jack was to have flown the rest of the way home to Cleveland, Ohio, where he lived in the suburb of Parma with his wife, my Aunt Joyce, and their daughters, my cousins Carol and Claudia.

I was too little to understand what was about to develop, and so I was insulated from it. The adults would become sad and discretely scared, and because of this I would become sad and vaguely scared, in the way that children sympathetically reproduce whatever the adults around them feel, even though they cannot understand. My lack of sophistication protected me, but Grandpa and Mom were exceedingly vulnerable, as was everyone there old enough to know the value of life and the meaning of its loss. At most they might postpone, in some cases, realizing that their own lives had been destroyed. For all of them at the terminal, the first hint of the tragedy was at hand. The hour had passed 5:25, and there had been no announcement of Flight 718's arrival. My grandfather felt a subtle twinge of apprehension and remarked to my mother, "The plane is probably on the ground already," alluding to the possibility that it was somewhere far out on the airfield, taxiing toward the terminal building from the end of the runway on which it had just landed. Whether his purpose was more to reassure her or himself, he abandoned it a moment later in reaction to a voice on the loudspeaker system, which asked for all persons awaiting Flight 718 from Los Angeles to come to the ticket counter.

This was a relief and a comfort to some who had begun to worry, but for the more astute it was a shock. A simple delay would be announced over the loudspeaker, so it could only be serious and therefore threatening, that everyone was being summoned to be told something discreetly and face to face with whoever would tell it. Something was wrong, and those who were more acutely aware, whether by character or just in that unfamiliar circumstance, instinctively knew it.

To some of them, the physical space between themselves and the ticket counter, and the few seconds that it would take to cross it, instinctively felt like a limbo in which they themselves held the power over fact and could forestall an imminent reality taking shape, or make an already manifest reality vanish and return to the realm of ideas. It seemed as though whatever the bad news awaiting them at the counter might be, they could annul it simply by lingering or turning away. Over there was danger, and anywhere else was safe. The safety and security of their familiar lives seemed tangibly reposed in the chair they had just vacated, and it seemed to be calling them from the everyday world outside of the terminal. Yet in realism and courage, the ones who felt some inkling of this sensation crossed the void, along with the others who feared without any urge to leave, and the few who were naive.

Once they had gathered, the group was directed to a room nearby. Now the astute were sure, and the naive were afraid. It was obvious to all of them that this was exactly what would be done if there had been a crash.

Inside the room the ground was gently and undeniably pulled out from under. United Air Lines' passenger service supervisor, Stanley Mills, told everyone that the airline did not yet know what had happened, but Flight 718 had not been heard from since about noon. An elderly, well-to-do woman in the group immediately broke into tears and began sobbing. She had come to meet her husband, Albert Vogt, and their granddaughter, Carol Jean Church. It was Miss Church's turn to spend a summer vacation at her grandparents' home in the Chicago suburb of Evanston. Mr. Vogt was bringing her to Evanston from her family home in San Diego, where she lived with her sister and brother and her parents, the Vogts' daughter and son-in-law. Mrs. Vogt was holding a gift of a very large, beautiful rag doll, the size of a three-year-old, for her granddaughter. Maybe in her helplessness Mrs. Vogt felt like a little girl lost in a crowd of strangers, carrying a proportionately smaller doll of her own.

Some people asked questions, among them my mom. She asked, "Might there have been a bomb?" She was thinking of the sabotage of a United DC-6 only eight months earlier, wherein a demented individual hid a bomb in his mother's luggage, in order to collect on her life insurance benefit. Despite the fact that in the DC-6 bombing the plane went completely out of control, breaking apart in the air, she imagined only a small hole in the fuselage of her brother's plane and pictured the pilots safely making an emergency landing somewhere in the wilderness. Her supposition that there was a bomb also could not explain why TWA had a flight missing in the same area, an ominous coincidence of which Mr. Mills had informed everyone. My mother's question was childlike in its naiveté, and maybe that's more of a point than an observation. The circumstances awoke and evoked the child within her, and she reverted to her more original, less capable self. Her fear washed away the layers of maturity and confidence that had successively overlaid her youthful self as she grew and learned. That severely alarming situation represented a wholly new principle, outside the scope of her experience, and she was again a novice, innocent and vulnerable, needing guidance and protection.

While this was happening in Chicago, people waiting at TWA's terminal in Lambert-St. Louis Municipal Airport were becoming increasingly anxious. St. Louis and Chicago were on the same time system, Central Daylight, and up until 5:30 p.m., the time that people waiting for Flight 718 at Midway Airport were called to the United ticket counter, the flight board at TWA's terminal in St. Louis had displayed the message "Late" next to Flight 2. Family and friends had been arriving since about 5:00 even though Flight 2 was not due until 5:57, and most had inquired at the ticket counter about how late Flight 2 would be. They were given only the disquieting, cryptic answer that no more information was available and that more was expected soon, but then around 5:30, "Late" was replaced with the chalked-in message "More Information at 7 p.m." This was a truly frightening promise because it obviously meant either that the airline did not know where Flight 2 was, or that they knew and were withholding the information, pending deciding how to reveal it. Either way, something was seriously wrong.

At 5:40, the chalked-in message was erased from the flight board, leaving a blank line next to Flight 2, and the TWA employees who had been present retreated to a room behind the counter. For some of the people waiting, the bottom must have fallen out right then. It was the third indication that something was wrong, and the most dramatic and portentous of the three. Then at 5:45, about the time that Lorraine Nelson was asking about bombs in Chicago, Mr. Edgar Willer, a TWA passenger service representative, emerged from the little room behind the counter. In a tone almost as apologetic and remorseful as if it were his own fault, he addressed the group waiting for Flight 2 and said, "I'm sorry folks, but there's some bad news. Flight 2 from Los Angeles has not been heard from and is apparently lost."

People gasped. Many of them immediately blurted out their alarm and their helplessness with terse, desperate exclamations like, "Oh no!" and, "Oh my Lord!" Some people in the group looked around at the others for the confirmation or denial that they knew would be in their eyes. Those who had come with a friend or another family member implicitly trusted their companions, but in a way the attitudes of the strangers around them had more meaning. Despite having no bond of faith with these people, their judgments and feelings were in some respects more credible than those of familiars, because the strangers were not biased by any devoted urges to be supportive and had clearly separate consciences. Family members tend to duplicate the feelings of their kin, through the empathy inherent in the closeness of their relationships, or to disagree in a compassionate attempt to undo the other family member's pain by undermining its foundation, rather than disagreeing on the basis of appraising the facts. Friends initially lean the same way in a crisis. Either way, the attitudes of friends and family are seldom truly independent or forthright, and as a result they are tenuous as concurrence or dissent, despite the people themselves being trustworthy. They care more about the person than about the truth generally, and that is probably as it should be. Strangers are not influenced by intimacy or loyalty, and so even though they are also not privileged to be personally trusted, their impressions are very convincing. Still, what friends and family lack in freedom from bias, they make up for in the faith they uphold and convey by their love and commitment, and the result was that no matter whose eyes a person queried, familiar or stranger, he could hardly help but believe what he found in them.

Whether they looked to their companions or to people unknown to them, most of the people in the group found only anxiety and deadly serious fear, the same things that they themselves were feeling. Most became more entrapped in their plight rather than being reassured that it was only some mistake. Innumerable times throughout their lives, most of them had at least in passing dreaded the prospect of being in such an awful situation someday in the future, and now it had finally become a reality. This was it, and most of them knew it.

As by the swift water upstream near a waterfall, they were being drawn to some calamity, and there was no way to step aside of its pull. Something very powerful was happening, and yet it was still largely concealed. It had not yet become a dramatic turmoil like the rapids immediately before the falls. The placid surface of the current somehow made it appear gentle and benign, even though its momentum toppled anything that stood to obstruct it, and this illusion gave some people the calmness to try to understand. Some of them asked questions, the obvious and vital ones like, "What has happened? Where are they? Has there been a crash?" The only answers that Mr. Willer could give them were that no one knew yet, and, "We have had no word for many hours. There is a possibility that the plane may have had a forced landing." Despite his kindness, most people read this as crash landing, or simply crash.

While many maintained a grave composure, others could not bear to have been seized and lost their reason quickly, as their fear escalated to panic or shock. Mrs. Shirley Jeffrey had come to the airport to meet her husband, Wayne Jeffrey, who had been in California on business. She suddenly began screaming, crying out uncontrollably over and over again as though she were being repeatedly stabbed. With help she staggered to the back room, and a doctor was immediately called. Terror overcame Mrs. Robert Lacy, who had come to meet her half sister, Bessie Whitman. She was wide-eyed with fright and was in shock, and she called out, "I feel like I'm going to faint." A man nearby held her up and walked her to the back room. Others were near collapse, and several wept. It was a dreadful, heart-rending, overwhelming scene. They had now joined their counterparts in Chicago and Kansas City.

In the midst of this agony, people were still arriving there to meet Flight 2. They were like unsuspecting patrons walking in on a bank robbery in progress, who in disbelief see the other patrons lying on the floor and are then hastily taken hostage themselves by the robbers. They were consumed by the devastation and sorrow in that space the moment they walked in, conquered and taken by it before they could muster a defense, and they could only give their own grief or fear or despair to the pool of anguish they had joined.

In Chicago a bus waited in front of the United terminal to take the group across Cicero Avenue to United's headquarters building, to await further news. Here they could be more comfortable than in the cramped quarters of the small lounge, and they were less exposed than they were in the public terminal lobby. This landmark building faced the airport from the immediate east and had a beautiful, two-story, cylindrical glass stairwell enclosure in front. It was artistic and distinctive, but in passive testimony to the meaninglessness of material things against the prospect of the loss of a loved one, it might as well have been a sheltered bus stop for all anyone who went there that evening cared. Everyone was ushered into an auditorium inside, where off duty United stewardesses offered sandwiches and coffee and any assistance they could. My mom asked a stewardess to heat my sister's baby bottle, and while the milk was being warmed, Grandpa went to telephone Grandma.

Grandma had been cooking dinner, happily looking forward to seeing her son and listening to music on the kitchen radio. When Grandpa reached her to relay the terrible news that Jack's plane was missing, she was already in shock. Just moments before, she had heard a special report about it, interrupting the music. She told Grandpa that the radio was already saying that the planes were down, and she implored him to come home right away. Probably the radio had actually said that the planes were feared down, since neither crash had been discovered. In her own fear, Grandma may have unwittingly exaggerated, but whether she did or not, her words conveyed nothing more than the truth.

By this time, families all over the country were finding out. In Los Angeles there were as many families with loved ones on the missing planes as anywhere else—those of Robert Harms and Robert Shirley as well as the numerous passengers on both flights who were leaving home rather than going home—and the awful news was reaching them. Insiders at the airlines advised some of them, in particular the families of crewmembers, but most heard of the disappearances of the planes on the radio or on television, and were desperately calling the airlines to find out if the stories were true.

Which source was more distressing depended more on the person receiving the news than on anything else. For some of the people connected directly with the airlines, getting the news from insiders that they had known for years was more threatening than being told by a stranger would have been, because it was so much more persuasive. A close family friend of Robert and Marge Harms, who was also a pilot at United, courageously visited her at her home that afternoon and told her in person that her husband's plane was missing. Even with a source that credible and trustworthy, she refused to believe what she was hearing. Her husband hadn't telephoned her that morning to let her know that his flight had been changed. But then, why would he have? The destination remained the same, and he still planned to layover at the same hotel in Chicago. Mrs. Harms was adamant that her husband flew 732, not 718, and she insisted, "You're crazy! Bob's already in Chicago. I'll call the Del Prado Hotel right now and prove it to you."

Everyone approaches an overwhelming tragedy in his own way, according to his own unique knowledge, values and needs, and sense of identity, and this makes it utterly personal. But there are themes that tie people together and make them the same in their struggle to face the terrible new truth of their lives. Some people fight; some run; some stand their ground with their eyes open; some sit down and close their eyes. Some people go it alone, and some seek the help of others. Marge Harms first fought and then escaped into an unreality, dissociated from her authentic life. Day after day she kept believing impossibilities, like that her husband was alive somewhere in the Grand Canyon, stumbling around lost and utterly disoriented, or that Indians had found him and taken him to their dwelling to nurse him back to health. She believed that he had amnesia and couldn't tell them who he was or where he had come from.

Everyone needs to forestall facing tragedy until he can honestly choose to face it, but no longer. Facing it by force can so traumatize a person that he is rendered incapable of healthily, effectively working through the crisis, and waiting too long can make him crazy. How each person needs to approach that choice is a consequence of the totality of who he is, and it depends only partly on how strong he is and how sound of mind. Some people open themselves directly to whatever the truth may be, choosing immediately to face the tragedy; some insist on being sure that it is real before choosing to face it; and some need to be sure that they need to be sure. The last group needs to see how harmful it is for them to go on refusing the truth, before they can become willing even to open their minds and hearts to the bare fact that the tragedy has really happened. Only then can they become convinced that it has, and only after that can they take the next step of choosing to face the full reality, the full meaning and consequences of it in their lives. Mrs. Harms was a strong, substantial person who needed to wait, and she gained the time she needed by embracing desperate hopes. It was about two weeks before she finally began to believe that Bob was gone.

It was just after 6:00 p.m. CDT, and the four of us left the auditorium. How we got to the car is a minor mystery—we may have just walked, but my mom doesn't remember. The car was parked near United's terminal, which was just inside the airport grounds at 58th Street. United's headquarters building was right on the sidewalk on the other side of Cicero Avenue, at 60th Street. The walk was only about three city blocks, two along Cicero and one inside the fence, but Grandma was in desperate need, and Grandpa was in a hurry, so my guess is that we got a ride.

As Grandpa drove us across town, people were arriving at Detroit's Willow Run Airport to meet Flight 718, which was due there at 7:00 p.m. EST, Detroit time, equivalent to 7:00 p.m. CDT, Chicago time. The trip from Midway to Willow Run took only an hour, gate to gate. *The City of Vancouver* would have left the gate at Chicago at 6:00 p.m., thirty-five minutes after arriving, with a fresh crew. Instead, the crew that was to have taken the plane onward from Chicago all the way to Newark, via Detroit and Philadelphia, flew out of Midway with a substituted DC-6B, for the sake of those passengers that had tickets for Flight 718 with Chicago or Detroit as their embarkation points. The substituted plane taxied out onto the airfield on time. In eerie reference to it rather than to the *City of Vancouver*, the flight board in United's terminal at Willow Run predicted "On Time" next to the notation for Flight 718.

At about 6:30 Grandpa drove us down the alley behind the house at 520 W. Marquette Road, also known as 67th Street, and pulled the car into the garage. Grandma and Grandpa lived in the Normal Park neighborhood, about three miles from the South Shore area and Lake Michigan. It was the house in which Uncle Jack and my mom grew up. The children had grown up and moved away, but this was still home. Grandma and Grandpa's house was home for the entire family, as it had always been, and family members were always welcome to come and stay as long as they wanted or as long as they could, throughout the year. Every Thanksgiving Grandma served her traditionally fabulous dinners to a large group.

We entered the house from the rear, walking up the wooden back porch steps and through the small vestibule, which opened into the kitchen. My mom was in a daze and took my sister and me directly into the living room. She cannot remember having seen her mother in the kitchen as we passed through it, but Grandma was there. All through the long ride across town, Grandpa had been strong and dignified, a gentleman chivalrously keeping his composure and doing the driving, not revealing how scared he was, but when he entered the kitchen and saw his wife, the two of them rushed to embrace each other, and they both caved in, sobbing.

In her own mounting fear and soaring need, it wasn't long before my mom thought to call my dad. He was the custodian at our church and was at work. Though she had dialed the number countless times, both on church business and to talk to him, she was so disoriented that she couldn't remember it. She got out the telephone directory to look up the number and was at once lost among its pages. Every literate person knows how to use a phone book or a dictionary and can do it as second nature, but even though she was more literate than many and had taught grade school up until just before I was born, she could not comprehend the alphabet. She could not get enough of a grip on herself to recall what came before or after the letter "C".

Grandpa phoned his daughter-in-law, my Aunt Joyce, in Parma, Ohio. My cousins were old enough to be away from their own yard after supper; Carol was ten and Claudia was eight, and both girls were outside playing in the neighborhood. Only Aunt Joyce was there. Grandpa hadn't said much to her before she recognized that this was the kind of phone call everyone dreaded the most, and she immediately became defensively angry and irrational, inwardly rejecting everything that he said though outwardly maintaining her politeness. With indignation that was as much a defense of herself against the terrible threat as it was a defense of her husband, she insisted to herself, "How thoughtless it is of him to call long distance, to tell me that Jack's plane is missing! How can he even suggest that there may have been a crash when everyone knows it is impossible for anything to have happened to Jack? How rude it is of him to burden me with this ridiculous concern and to scare me. They must have landed somewhere!"

When Aunt Joyce hung up after the call, she was vividly alone. She was acutely aware and isolated, and it occurred to her that maybe there was something to what Grandpa had said; maybe it was real. She reached for the knob on the television set in case there might be a special report, but she couldn't bring herself to turn it on. Then she went back to the phone to call a friend of hers and dialed the number, but she was unable to speak when the friend answered. She just hung up. She was petrified, and in a growing daze went to the front door and saw a couple of the neighbor ladies across the street standing out in the yard chatting casually, as neighbors often did. They saw her, and still mute with fear, Aunt Joyce desperately motioned for them to come to her. One of them did; her name was Mrs. Testa, and she lived in a duplex across the street that she and her husband split with her parents. Reassured by the nearness of another human being, Aunt Joyce found her voice and was able to say, "Jack's plane is lost." Mrs. Testa was horrified, and the two of them went inside to talk. After a time, they went down into the basement where Aunt Joyce had been fixing Carol's jacket in preparation for summer Girl Scout camp; Carol was going to leave for camp the next day. Aunt Joyce began ironing while she and her friend continued to talk, and soon she was feeling somewhat reassured and comforted by the familiar, safe chore. Everything would be all right, as it always had been. To her it seemed that as long as she didn't admit it, nothing was changing, and as she resolutely rejected what she knew, she also desperately conceived and embraced the faith that her husband was safe and that nothing terrible had happened.

Mixed as it was with a great need to deny the evidence and with the irrational will to control a reality that was entirely beyond her control, her faith was in a sense pitifully fanatical rather than sound, despite her profound sincerity, humility, and earnestness. It also contradicted itself. It was a fervent belief in goodness and mercy founded in part on disloyalty to the truth—this was crazy, and that's part of what was so sad. Here was a wonderful, virtuous, sensitive, intelligent woman who had unwittingly compromised a part of her character in order to deceive herself and survive for another hour. She was deathly afraid. Her fear had compelled her to cower, and she had submitted.

Almost everyone under a similar strain yields in one way or another. Some people smoke profusely; others take a few drinks, or a lot of drinks; some forsake their dignity to become aggressive and forceful with officers of the airline to get results; still others are rational about it all in order to dispel the truth rather than disclose it, demonstrating with reasoning the improbability of a disaster to assuage their fear. Aunt Joyce came the nearest to the last stratagem. Her attitude was slanted but was not pure avoidance—it was also wise. From her perspective the crisis had only the proportions of a terrible rumor, a fairly credible rumor, but still just a rumor. The information from Grandpa was at least secondhand, perhaps third or fourth, and "missing" had not been defined. No one in authority, as far as she knew, was saying that any disaster had occurred, or even any mishap like an emergency landing in the wilderness. She had been given a terrible shock and no proof, and she was caught between honestly believing that things were okay and being convinced that they were not, unable to choose between them. She needed to resolve the impossible conflict to clear her head; she needed the relief at least momentarily, and to obtain it she blindly went to one side, the side she desperately needed to be real.

Because it had grown later in the day by the time they left their homes or businesses for the airport, some of the friends and relatives of United passengers bound for Detroit from Los Angeles had already heard on the radio that the plane was missing, or they had been telephoned or visited by someone who had. They were prepared, if anyone could be, for United personnel at Willow Run Airport to have only the same news for them. Others heard nothing until they reached the terminal and were horrified like so many before them. One or a few at a time, people were escorted to a private lounge behind United's ticket counter as they approached to inquire about Flight 718. In that room, Passenger Relations Supervisor Jack Hendrickson had the grim task of informing everyone, whether for the first time or as confirmation, that the plane was missing. He also explained that the plane on its way to Willow Run was a substitute and was not the one that began Flight 718 in Los Angeles. This completed the picture of futility in waiting at the airport: not only was the right plane missing, but a replacement for it was coming instead. The substitute plane would be a tangible reality signifying the absence of the original plane, making it physically, undeniably real that the right plane was not going to appear.

The substitute DC-6B that was performing Flight 718 from Chicago landed in Detroit and pulled up to the gate at about 7:00 p.m. EST. Most of the people that had planned to meet the flight had already quietly left to go home and pray and wait for more news. A few remained in the lounge, not knowing where else to go, and one large family group consisting of eight persons waited out in the terminal's public lobby rather than in private. They were relatives of Miss Lillian Hahn, who was making her first flight, and they had decided to meet the substitute DC-6B in the hope that Miss Hahn had taken some other flight to Chicago and had caught Flight 718 only there. They watched all of the Detroit passengers who had embarked at Midway enter the rear of the terminal building from the ramp, some of them joyously greeted by their loved ones. The reports that United Flight 718 was missing had been more than enough to scare almost anyone, no matter how clear they had also been that the missing flight originated at Los Angeles, not Chicago. The chance that this point had been misconstrued had worried many, and with glee or with tears of relief, or both, they received their loved ones. Lillian Hahn's family watched, with anguish that was only heightened by the joyfulness of these reunions, until the last passenger from Chicago had come and gone, and then in stunned gravity they retreated and left.

By this time, everyone who had come to Kansas City Municipal Airport to meet TWA Flight 2 had long since gone home. There was not a trace, not a vestige, not a hint of the tragedy anywhere to be found in the terminal. The scene was bizarre precisely for being entirely normal. Within the preceding two and a half hours, a great many people had been undone in that very space, and yet there was not a sign of their destruction. It was too easy. It was too convenient. Had they not struggled? Somehow it seemed wrongful that they could have been so grievously wounded without leaving a mark, without so much as the smell of fear or the scent of their tears lingering behind them in testament. It felt criminal, as though someone had shamelessly, profanely compounded the terrible injustice by expunging all evidence of it.

In Chicago, most of the people who had come to meet United Flight 718 had gone home, but a few remained in the auditorium. Despite the full lighting, the atmosphere in the large, gently echoing space felt like the subtly dizzying sensation of falling from this world into another that stirred just beneath the surface in a big theater as the lights were dimmed. It was part of the self-transcendence that made the theater so special and magical, but in the auditorium in United's headquarters, the feeling of being removed from the ordinary world supported no magic. It felt instead like drifting into the depths of purgatory; it only made people feel all the more tortured and disoriented.

In St. Louis there was still turmoil. It had been only just over an hour since TWA Flight 2 should have landed, and many people who had come to meet it were still there. Many were distraught, overwhelmed, and in tears. A few had left, having finally become convinced that the advice of TWA agents to go home and wait was sound, but the majority were still reeling. From time to time, people were recovering their balance and beginning to move away, to walk tentatively toward the door of the terminal. Some hesitated, half turning back as if the situation could be changed if only they stayed, and then in final resignation they departed. Others used their balance to plant themselves rather than to retreat to their homes. There is a companion to the instinctive sense that refusing to hear bad news can prevent it from becoming a reality:

the unreasoned, instinctive sense that once heard, it can be suspended or contained by postponing acting on it. As long as someone suspended *himself* to stay put and guard it like a sentry, the bad news could not become an independent, irrevocable reality. To walk out the door was to acknowledge that the plane would not be arriving; it was to act on it and to unleash that terrible reality. To cling instead to the airline felt influential, like the resolve of a man who refuses to leave his home against an oncoming flood, in the stubborn, utterly unreasoned belief that his will can prevent his house from being washed away. It was futile, but clinging was the only thing that some of them had. Like a painter high atop a falling ladder, they held on, even though this could not stop their own fall.

Irrespective of whether or not it accomplished anything, clinging was undeniably a way to care. Like a political demonstration that did not in itself change the law, it mattered to be assertive, it mattered to stay put and in that way stand for the people who were missing. It mattered to do what could be done, even if this was only a show of allegiance. For some there was no other way to care, and because of this the prospect of leaving felt to them like forsaking their lost loved ones, abandoning them to whatever fate had befallen them. Keeping a vigil at the airport was joining them in their trial; it felt like remaining involved. Yet the truth that they were not involved in any influential capacity kept reasserting itself. Despite their dreadful circumstances, the people waiting at the airport prevailed in clarity and realism and found their wisdom, letting it be the guide of their decisions. One by one they surrendered and at once knew more surely that the worst had happened. When they first heard it, the truth had hit them emotionally, and then they had countered, and now it could hit them rationally. This was a disaster. It was real. In grief, in dread or in guilt, they made their way out of the air-conditioned building and into the hot outside air, knowing that there was nothing they could do now but face what had come.

It was nearly 7:30 p.m. CDT in St. Louis, 8:30 p.m. EDT in Parma, Ohio. Aunt Joyce was feeling better in her fantasy, and then the distinct ringing of the telephone bell intruded startlingly on her sequestered world, bringing her back to a remembrance of the outer world and sundering her false security. It was her mother calling. After a greeting, Mrs. Lamb's first words to her daughter were, "Are you coming home?" meaning to the Chicago area where Aunt Joyce, like Uncle Jack, had grown up.

Up until that moment Aunt Joyce had successfully negated the whole thing, denied it entirely, and in mild rebuke she asked, "Why? Why would I come home?"

Her mother replied, "Oh . . . you don't know." That simple statement—in its momentously meaningful incorrectness, in the truth it alluded to, in the way it implied that her attitude was inappropriate because she actually did know, and in the trust it evoked because of who had made it—shattered Aunt Joyce's delusion, and then she knew that she knew.

She thrust the phone into Mrs. Testa's hand, unable to continue the conversation herself. She was falling into the whirlpool of her gathering trauma and was terrified and desperate about what was happening to her. She feared for her sanity, and when Mrs. Testa got off the phone, Aunt Joyce implored her to get the minister and the doctor, whom she telephoned immediately. Both of them came promptly, and soon after that other people came. One at a time the girls came home from playing.

Neither plane had been found. Like many others, Aunt Joyce intuitively knew what had happened, and feeling that she had to tell her daughter, she got on her knees and hugged Carol and said, "Your daddy's plane has crashed." Carol asked, "Will he be all right?" and with incredible tenderness her mother simply said, "No." As she held Carol and wept, Aunt Joyce could feel a shudder move up and down Carol's little body.

Most of what was going on is a blur in Aunt Joyce's memory, because she was oblivious to it at the time, like a little girl who has fallen very ill and is unaware of the actions and conversations of the adults around her, only tenuously identifying the images of their faces and not understanding the sounds of their voices, feeling the modulations of their tones without comprehending even the simple words that she ordinarily would. Many people were in the house, but for the most part they were a blur. She doesn't recall what happened next after holding Carol, and she can't recall telling Claudia. Her memory becomes clear again when she and the girls were sitting on the couch, one on either side of her, surrounded by many others in the room. The girls each put a hand on one of Aunt Joyce's knees and looked up at her with wide open, trusting eyes, placing their faith in her to make everything right. Her daughters were losing their father, for God's sake, and she was called upon to make *that* all right, to carry them through *that*? How could she keep them from their own unbearable pain and at the same time tell them the whole truth, the truth they would have to know? How could she do this alone, when in any other situation as traumatic as this, she would have depended on her husband to carry *her*? She just about lost it right there, and then from somewhere deep within her came the will to protect her children, and she gathered her incredible strength for them, thinking to herself, "I can't let go here."

From Aunt Joyce's mother, Mrs. Testa got information pertinent to securing emergency passage for Aunt Joyce and the girls on a United flight to Chicago, and she telephoned the airline to make the arrangements for late that night. To occupy herself and help ward off her tears, Aunt Joyce and the girls began doing practical things like dressing and packing for the trip to Chicago. She particularly remembered putting on her lipstick, looking at herself in the mirror, and thinking, "This is so silly. How can you automatically do these things when something so terrible is happening?"

Two hours had passed since Grandpa's phone call. In just two hours Aunt Joyce's life, which had taken thirty-three years to build, had been undone. Time seemed to be in a dizzying rush, unreeling events at a bewildering pace, like a film flashing through its frames and scenes in fast motion. Two hours had spanned a whole lifetime's worth of changes, because in those two hours her whole life had changed.

It was just after 9:30 p.m. in Parma, and night had fallen. It was dark. In Detroit it was twilight, and the sky was a deep blue, almost purple. In Chicago the sky was a brightly lit yellowish orange, filled with the warm glow of the sun, which was not far below the horizon. In St. Louis the sun had only just set, and in Kansas City it was still up, a great orange ball not yet made oval by resting on the horizon, yet very low in the sky. Just about this time the planes would have run out of fuel, and so there was no longer any doubt that they were down.

It had been over two and a half hours since the *Star of the Seine* should have arrived in St. Louis, and Mrs. Fred Huddleston and her daughter Aileen were just leaving the TWA terminal at Lambert-St. Louis Airport. They were the last to leave. Mrs. Huddleston had come to meet her brother, Robert Perisho, from Long Beach, California, unaware that the last time she had seen him was the last time that she ever would. Accompanied by her daughter, she walked out into the warm evening, ten minutes after the sunset, and with her, in a sense, the last hope in St. Louis flickered out. Everyone there had moved to another level of faith and doubt. The last of them had joined their unknown comrades in Detroit, Chicago, and Kansas City. No one remained at any of these airports awaiting Flight 718 or Flight 2. Soon the terminal buildings through which the victims should have come in life became eerily lit portals, glowing in the gathering darkness, through which only their spirits could pass.

Of all the cities in which either flight was to have landed, Kansas City was the first. It was the western most of them all, and by the same token it was also the last one to lose its daylight. Sunset that evening in Kansas City was at 7:48 p.m. CST. As the western sky gradually lit up with the beautiful colors that the sun, in its rapturous benevolence, induced in the atmosphere as it passed, the substitute United plane completing Flight 718 began descending over eastern Pennsylvania, on approach to Philadelphia. It was nearly 10:00 p.m. there and nearly 7:00 p.m. in the Painted Desert and the Grand Canyon. Search planes were still crisscrossing the Painted Desert, but some had already turned off to head for Winslow, where they would join many other aircraft that had been massed for a greater search in the morning.

After supper that evening, Palen Hudgin started up his gasoline-powered electric generator with the idea in mind of relaxing and enjoying a radio program. He tuned in radio station KCLS out of Flagstaff, 600 on the AM dial, but before long his comfort and amusement were abruptly curtailed by the terrible news that two giant airliners had been missing since about noon and were presumed to be down, somewhere in or near the Painted Desert. He was immediately jolted by the realization that the evil-looking black smoke he had seen earlier in the day must have been from the crash of one or both of the missing planes. It was in the right area, next to the Painted Desert. With the help of his brother Henry, Palen hastily prepared their small Piper Tri-Pacer for flight, to return to where he had seen the smoke rising out of the Grand Canyon. The time was about 7:15.

At about 7:40 p.m. MST the Hudgins came upon the disaster scene, from the south, and found the site of the TWA crash. Sunset that evening was only nine minutes away, and the sun was already so close to the horizon that there were long, deep shadows filling all but the highest elevations in the Grand Canyon. However, the brothers spotted the TWA wreckage with no difficulty. There were still several small fires burning in the dry wash where the plane had come to earth. The Constellation's huge, fifty-foot wide, white and silver tail was readily visible, lying in pieces on the boulder strewn slope about five hundred yards to the north, in the shadows between Temple and Chuar buttes. The Hudgins circled around and made a low pass over the area for a second, closer look, making the clear assessment that there were no survivors. It was obvious from the degree of the destruction that there could not be. They were also able to discern, on this pass, TWA's red logo and stripes painted on the white vertical tail fins.

Heightening the horror of Temple butte, the Hudgins could see sooty black smoke still rising at Chuar Butte, about a mile upstream along the Colorado River, but there was no time to investigate. Night was approaching, and flying down in the canyon was dangerous enough even in the full light of day. Powerful updrafts and downdrafts, invisible and unpredictable, invariably buffeted small planes and made them difficult to control. The problem was especially hazardous near the ground, since a plane might actually crash before its pilot could regain control. In semidarkness the risks were multiplied; with the dimming of color contrasts and light and shadow contrasts, and the overall darkening of the scene, it became difficult to judge where the ground was. Outside the canyon the Hudgins would incur another problem if they stayed much longer: once the sun set in northern Arizona, night fell rapidly. Sunset that evening was at 7:49, and they were risking a hazardous landing in the twilight—their rustic airfield had no runway lighting. For their own safety they needed to ascend from the canyon and head for home, and that is what they did.

While the Hudgins flew toward Grand Canyon Airport, all but one of the remaining search planes over the Painted Desert departed and flew away toward Winslow, where the airport had lighted runways. The search planes could have remained and still been able to safely land in the dark, but the sun had set, and the terrain below was becoming too poorly lighted for spotting anything but fire.

The Hudgins landed their small plane, jumped in their car, and drove hurriedly along the dirt road that led to the highway two miles west of their property. They turned right at the highway and sped fourteen miles northward to Grand Canyon Village, where there was a telephone. Palen Hudgin placed a long-distance collect call to the TWA headquarters in Kansas City to alert the company to his terrible discovery, but in an absurd complication, out of all proportion to his overall endeavor to help and to the importance of the message, the

TWA operator adhered to company policy and refused to accept the charges for the call, even after his purpose was explained to her. He paid for the call himself.

The world knew now. The Hudgins had privately held the knowledge for less than an hour, and now it had been relayed and imparted to the larger world of human society far outside their secluded, desolate, obscure world, released to an authority that would disseminate it, an authority bound to verify the truth and make it public. Inasmuch as no one, not even the Hudgins, had as yet seen the United wreck, United 718 was still missing. But the truth, at a higher level of validity than common sense can embrace, was that United 718 had in fact been found. In discovering the still-burning TWA wreck and witnessing the black smoke rising a mile away, like an evil straining to emulate its source and despoil the heavens that no evil can reach, the Hudgins had found the very soul of the disaster, far more real than its worldly forms. They had seen the living evil, still boiling in its own malevolence. They knew more concretely than any physical evidence apprehended in daylight could convey, whether they realized the full significance of their perception or not. The reality was foremost a nightmare, more spiritual at its core than material. To see it at twilight as fire and smoke in a vast, darkening gorge of stone, which had exhaled all the color of life and was shifting from the reality of this world to that of the netherworld for the night, was to see the nightmare authentically as the greater of the two realities, the supernatural vividly cast on the fading, comparatively intangible background of the natural.

The Hudgins had found TWA 2 and United 718 more surely than anyone else ever would, and in reality beyond reality, the search for the missing planes was over.

A blanket of darkness had drawn over the dead in the canyon. The victims were gone as souls, and now their physical remains, discarded in an alien world of stone, remote and forbidding, were hidden in blackness. The victims had wholly been taken, seized from out of elsewhere and stolen from this life, and as though to flout its dominance in excess, the force that was responsible had secreted the remains and would uncover them only with the returning of the sun. As if in submission, the lone remaining search plane scouting the Painted Desert looking for fire had been called off, and the sky was empty.

*   *   *

Mr. and Mrs. Testa drove Aunt Joyce, Carol, and Claudia to the United Air Lines terminal at Hopkins Airport in Cleveland. Aunt Joyce stood at the ticket counter and signed three special passes for herself and her daughters. Her doctor had given her a sedative to help keep her from repeatedly bursting into tears at every new experience, at every new turn that might make the singular reality she was facing more evident, and she was able to compose herself well enough to manage the rituals of checking in. The district sales manager who issued the tickets of course knew why she was being given free passage, and he was so nervous that he didn't even notice his rubber stamp was incorrectly set to June 29. He gave her three tickets marked, "Positive Space," meaning that even paying passengers could not take precedence and usurp her seats. The passes were for Flight 639, a first-class DC-6B flight to Chicago, scheduled to depart from Cleveland at 11:40 p.m. EDT. The trip would take an hour and thirty-five minutes, placing Uncle Jack's family at Midway Airport fifteen minutes after midnight, Chicago time. Meanwhile Mr. Testa bought about twenty cartoon and coloring books for the girls at the airport gift shop. He must have collected one of every kind they had, maybe two of every kind.

The plane that carried Aunt Joyce and the girls to Chicago had almost no one on it. She took an aisle seat and Claudia sat next to her, at the window. Carol sat on the opposite side of the aisle. Along the way, the stewardesses sat behind Aunt Joyce and Claudia in order to be continuously available, to provide any aid or comfort that Aunt Joyce or the girls might need or want. For example, they took the children to the restroom to spare Aunt Joyce the suffering of walking all the way forward and back past the few other passengers in her anguish, with her smeared mascara and reddened eyes.

During the trip, Aunt Joyce had a very private, very powerful experience, one that made the reality of her ordeal and her aloneness in it especially poignant to her. For a time, with the stewardesses seated behind her, she could overhear them softly, discretely speaking to each other in such subtle tones that their voices were hardly distinguishable as coming from outside of her. As if she were hearing her own conscience compassionately confirming her suffering, she overheard one of them quietly implore the other, "Will this night ever end?"

Midnight passed on the eastern seaboard, and like the great shadow of night that had preceded it, flowed westward, soon encompassing all of the cities in which the flights were to have landed, and finally the one from which they had come. In three and a half hours it crossed the whole country and passed out over the Pacific Ocean, into the abyss. The worst day in a thousand people's lives had ended and given way to Sunday, the first of July; the ceaseless progression of time had rolled on without them.

Most of them were adrift in an awful continuum of unparalleled anxiety, in which time did not exist except as the sensations of excruciating, interminable waiting and dreadful anticipation. Most could not sleep at all. Some wrestled fitfully in their beds or on their couches throughout the protracted night, as though bound and wracked by the delirium of a high fever; with eyes closed, they languished in tortured exhaustion or in stupor. Repeatedly images of their missing loved ones filled their minds in unsolicited and uncontrollable processions, sometimes turning in happy veins and sometimes in unhappy ones, sometimes memories and sometimes fantasies. For a few moments at a time these depictions were distracting but had the potential to remind them that their loved ones were missing and to confront them with the terrifying reality of their own helplessness, and many times they cried out and had to collect themselves. Some of the images were direct and explicit reminders, horrible scenes of their loved ones crashing, and they sat up in the dark with a start, breathing rapidly, turning on the light, and vowing to stay awake for fear of repeating the terrible experience.

Although they desperately needed the emotional and mental relief of escaping into unconsciousness, most of the people whose loved ones were missing were captives of their own trauma and were acutely, persistently aware. All night even drowsiness was impossible for them, much less sleep. They were hyper-vigilant as though their own lives were being threatened, and in reality they were. Besides fearing for their loved ones, they feared for themselves. It was the most singularly horrible night in most of their lives.

CHAPTER 12

AFTER AN INTERMINABLE night of lying awake in bed and sweating in the oppressive heat of midsummer, Lorraine Nelson gave up on sleep to face the fear that had tormented her in the dark. She arose just after sunrise and in dread forced herself into the real world. It was about 6:00 a.m. in Chicago, and she switched on the radio in hope and in fear of hearing some news of her brother's plane.

Soon, the announcer read a bulletin over the airwaves to the effect that wreckage, thought to be that of the missing TWA plane, had been found late the previous evening, and that no survivors were expected. The effect of this dire broadcast on my mom was that of an assault like none she had ever known. It hit her right in the stomach, doubling her over and nearly making her physically ill. Until that moment she had kept her composure, and there she lost it, crying and wailing in a delirium of anguish.

While my mom was disintegrating as a person, the Hudgin brothers awoke, thirteen hundred miles away. It was a little after 4:00 a.m. in the canyon area. The Hudgins arose in the dark and gravely prepared to return to the disaster scene that they had discovered the night before. By 5:30, just after sunrise, they were airborne in their small plane heading again for the area near the confluence of the Colorado and Little Colorado rivers. Soon they were over Temple Butte and were confronted with the same terrible spectacle that had stunned them ten hours earlier. In the new light of daybreak, even in the shadow of the East Rim, the debris that had been a magnificent airplane, its crew, its passengers, and its cargo was harshly real. Nothing was recognizable except for the tail, and because of the tail markings it was obvious that the wreckage was the remains of the missing TWA plane.

The Hudgins flew on to Chuar Butte and circled it, and there they found what they had feared: the second crash. Wreckage was scattered down the south cliff face of the high promontory that jutted out eastward directly toward the Little Colorado River. They saw the large burned area that spilled from the crest of the promontory downward, in which the rock was so blackened that it looked like a huge vein of coal. They saw nothing that could identify the debris as the remains of the missing United Air Lines DC-7, and yet it was absolutely clear what the disintegrated chaos was, clear because of the very fact that it was unrecognizable. The overwhelming singularity of the display left no room to doubt that it was the United plane; there was nothing else it could be.

By 7:00 a.m. many small civilian and military planes were circling the disaster area, while their crews attempted to grasp and assess the situation and looked for routes from which the wreckage might be reached over land. One of the planes was a single-engine air force reconnaissance plane called an L-20. It was a military version of the de Havilland Beaver, a rugged little plane that was the top choice among bush pilots and was affectionately known in their circles as the flying pickup truck. Captain Dean W. Lewis and Master Sgt. Albert W. Hessell, both stationed at Luke Air Force Base near Phoenix, were piloting the L-20. Lewis and Hessell made the first official identifications of both wrecks. For positive proof they used the TWA Constellation's tail, as the Hudgins had done the evening before and that morning, and the United DC-7's tail, which the Hudgins had not found. The vertical fin of the DC-7's tail was lying on the northeast talus slope, and on it could be read "TED" from "UNITED," and "-7" from "DC-7." The missing portions of these markings were painted on the rudder, which was not there. The fin had been catapulted over the crest with the rudder still attached, and had fallen down the backside of the crash promontory, hitting a ledge that girdled it about 400 feet below. The impact sheared off the rudder, and the fin bounced off the ledge and continued falling to the talus slope, finally coming to rest a couple hundred feet down it.

All across the country that morning, a thousand people suffered the trauma that Lorraine Nelson had, some before her and some after, in hundreds of variations. From the radio or over the telephone or through a friend at their door, they received the crushing news that wreckage had been found and that no survivors were expected. Their wife or husband or father or mother or child was probably gone forever, and in most of them exploded a nightmare worse than that of the agonizing night through which they had just lived. Their loved one was no longer missing, and instead of this being a glorious relief, it was overwhelmingly dreadful. The missing people had been located but not found, and were presumed to be dead.

Some poor souls had fallen into deep slumber during the night from total emotional exhaustion, followed by pleasant dreams near morning, and they awoke in panic remembering that their loved ones were missing. They emerged from the safe worlds of their dreams in complete forgetfulness of the crisis and were not prepared. It was as though they were for the first time being apprised of the situation, but this was worse because they were not protected by the company of other families or by the reassuring presence of airline personnel. There was no one in authority to carry part of the weight of responsibility and worry, and there were no strangers in the same plight with whom to share their fear. They had not yet reasserted their personalities and wills and convictions, as people do in the process of waking up, and they were still in the childlike simplicity and defenselessness of the metamorphosis from dreams to reality. They were without their adult sophistication and prowess, and they faced the truth unprotected and incapable of counterattack. They were devastated and they cried out or wept, and they trembled in their helplessness before the hope that remained to them brought them into possession of themselves again.

But whether they had slept and relived the shock of learning that something was wrong, or had lain awake all night never forgetting the situation, all of the people who had a loved one on one of the two missing planes suffered the incomparable anguish that morning of finding out that the destroyed remains of the planes had been discovered. For most of them, Saturday the thirtieth of June had been the worst day of their lives. Now mercilessly, Sunday the first of July had already exceeded it.

By midmorning, families had gathered all across the country to love each other and to wait together for specific news of their family members. In Chicago the air was already forcefully hot. The indomitable energy driving it to stifle everyone who breathed could be sensed almost as tangibly as distant thunder and with equal apprehension. It was a threatening spirit hidden within the air, and it was coming. The city was in siege, and it humbled everyone who intuited it. Of all the days for it to happen, the temperature in Chicago was well on its way to 103° F, which would make it the hottest day of the year there and the hottest July 1 ever recorded in the city. Very few people had air conditioning and so for most there was no escape. It was as if creation itself were bent on suffocating the people there who had a loved one in the tragedy, and had added its own oppressive misery to the hell that everyone was already in. At my grandparents' house the windows were all open, and electric fans were running, making their hypnotic, droning sound as they slowly swirled the air around the living room. The air was so hot that it carried the smell of the varnish on the furniture and the horsehair inside the sofa, even though all were long past new. It wafted everyone with heat as it moved, but at least in moving the air helped evaporate sweat.

Many family members were at my grandparents' house, including Aunt Joyce and the girls. Grandma and Grandpa had met them at Midway Airport around midnight the night before, to take them back to the house over east. It had been a frightful ordeal for Grandpa to drive back to the very place his hell had begun and walk for the second time in seven hours to the terminal where his son should have appeared. When he caught sight of Aunt Joyce and the girls walking toward him, it was like the first tanks in an invasion rolling into view at the horizon. It was really happening. It was no longer a report or a rumor or just a fear, but a manifest reality, and it was here.

*   *   *

At about noon Chicago time, 10:00 a.m. in the canyon, search and rescue teams from squadrons stationed at Luke Air Force Base arrived by helicopter at the TWA crash site. They had come in two Sikorsky helicopters of a type that the air force designated H-19, which had a single rotor and four wheels arranged in a rectangular pattern. They looked something like a bulbous, streamlined step van with a long tail, and they could each carry eight people. On the minuscule chance of finding survivors, each helicopter held only a pilot, a copilot, and a medic, so that there would be room for victims to be evacuated.

The wreckage was in the lower reaches of the butte near the river, where the butte leaned toward leveling out, and after careful examination of the terrain in order to ascertain the best landing spots and approaches, the six officers in their two machines set down nearby. They were Capt. James Womack and Lt. Miles Burd, pilots; Lt. Daryl M. Strong and 2nd Lt. Phillip S. Prince, copilots; and Capt. Sylvester J. Ryan and Capt. Don R. Hunter, medics. All of them were from squadrons of the 360th Combat Crew Training Wing, stationed at Luke.

The men walked a short distance to the crash, across the harsh surface of Temple Butte. The terrain was very rugged, mostly rocky, uneven, and sloping. Boulders of all sizes were strewn everywhere, having split off of the cliffs above and tumbled, often breaking apart into smaller chunks, rolling to their resting places one or several at a time in a ritual repeated over and over again throughout the aeons. It was a barren, desolate landscape, alien and nearly lifeless. On a grand scale it was like a deep stone quarry, more of an absence than a presence, made by scooping out all the life and even most of the rich soil that could support life. The ground was beige-colored stone sculpted in outcroppings of ledges here and there along its slope, interspersed with dense loam and sparsely dotted with scrubby tufts of small desert bushes.

In the midst of this wild lay something incongruous, something befuddling for the clash it posed. The wreckage was an anomaly of blackened, twisted, indefinable shapes unlike anything else in the surrounding land, so obviously foreign as to be unnerving. It did not belong. The group did not stay long. It was their job to save lives if possible, and it was immediately and incontrovertibly clear to them that no one could have survived. Based on the aerial observations, no one who had witnessed the disaster scene had held any realistic hope, but from the ground, because of the nearness and the stillness, any remaining doubts that no one was left alive there were immediately vanquished.

Captain Ryan described the scene at the time. "The first thing I saw was a white towel with TWA on it. Then we came to the burned area. It was about 150 yards long and 30 yards wide. The largest piece of plane I saw was a section of the fuselage, which contained six windows. The wrecked engines were right in the center of the burn. Then we saw the bodies. We almost walked right by them. It was hard to recognize them. They seemed to be piled on each other as if the plane had hit almost in a nosedive. It looked as if the bodies were stacked about three feet deep. We could count only fifteen, but we were sure the rest were underneath. We saw safety belts, shoes, children's clothing, and lots of black twisted metal. It was the worst sight I have ever seen."

The fuselage section he referred to with six windows was a curved outer skin panel with its structural ribs and stringers still attached, having the holes for six windows but no glass. It measured about twenty feet in length by five feet in height overall, and from one side it looked something like the inside of a frame wall in an unfinished, uninsulated garage. The circumference of the intact fuselage was over thirty feet, so this piece was vertically only about a sixth of the whole cylinder, and appeared almost flat. It was akin to a single section of the garage wall, torn off and standing free with the rest of the garage missing.

The six men climbed back into their helicopters and extricated themselves from the canyon depths and from the horror that they had found there. The time was about 10:30. Besides having accomplished their primary mission, the wind in the gorge had picked up to a blustery twenty-five miles an hour or more, driven by the sun heating the stone and causing sweeping convection currents. Flying in strong wind was precarious, especially for helicopters, and the team needed to leave before the wind became any stronger, which it usually did as morning progressed to midday. Like great fans the machines ascended, whipping the air with their rotors. Some of the men watched as the terrible scene below shrank and became just a small, nondescript dark spot. It seemed to lose the sharp edge of its horridness as it was diminished, but there was no relief in this because the substance of the horror transferred from the scene to the men. What they had witnessed had penetrated their minds and their hearts irremovably and was still unfolding within them, deepening its grasp on their souls. Lt. Prince later expressed it frankly. He said, "It was the most terrible, the most grim sight I have ever seen . . . It was a mess. When one of the guys in the Air Force crashes, we figure that's the breaks. But this—well, it's terrible."

No other landings were made that day at the TWA site, and none at all were attempted at the United site. By late morning, the air had become as dangerous to helicopters as rough seas are to a small boat, and there was a very real risk of rescue craft being shoved into the rock formations while closely approaching to land. Reconnaissance flights over Chuar Butte continued from safer distances, for the sake of hopefully discovering a route of ascent for climbers or a place for helicopters to land. All they sighted was one small, prospective landing area that appeared to be extremely perilous. The growing consensus that first day was that it might be impossible to reach the United crash site.

As was the case with the TWA site at Temple Butte, the primary purpose of an initial landing at Chuar Butte was to have been to search for survivors, sure as it was that there were none to find. If there were any at Chuar Butte, they would be near the crash site, high up on the shoulder that the DC-7 struck, not 650 feet below on the talus slope. For anyone to be found alive below, that person would have to have survived not only the crash but also a fall equivalent to that from the roof of a fifty-story skyscraper. If the word impossible had any practical meaning at all, that was impossible, and for that reason the task of landing near the base of Chuar Butte was ignored on Sunday.

The United victims were left for that day, in their solitude and in the privacy of their deaths. They remained isolated in a forbidding world, theirs alone until another day. Not one of them had as yet been seen.

In the midst of the little group gathered at Grandma and Grandpa's house back in Chicago, still hoping and praying that by some miracle Jack Groshans had been spared and was alive, my cousin Carol composed a poem. It went something like this:

Please help Dad, Lord.
Lord, please do.
I love Dad, Lord,
Yes I do.
Please help Dad, Lord,
See him through.

CHAPTER 13

BEFORE DAWN ON Monday, July 2, U.S. Army personnel at Grand Canyon Airport were busy readying three giant army helicopters for flight. The machines were called H-21s and had twin rotors mounted in tandem, one above the cockpit and the other above the rear end. They were about fifty feet long and had tubular fuselages that bent downward in the middle, where there was a large, sliding door for loading personnel and cargo. Because of the peculiar bend, the H-21 had acquired the nickname flying banana, even though it was painted olive drab rather than yellow.

By 6:00 a.m., the first of them lifted off and headed for the disaster area, twenty-eight miles to the northeast. The other two followed it closely in succession, and the trio plodded along, slowly enough that outside the bare fact that they were moving in a straight line, and from that presumably had a destination, they scarcely appeared to be going anywhere important. Stretching beneath them from the airfield to the canyon were the utterly unspoiled wilds of Kaibab National Forest, and as they passed overhead, their transit was a bizarre, incongruous sight. Three weird contraptions, alien in their form and intrusive in their noisiness, were putting their way across the low sky, impinging upon the pristine wilderness below them.

As the men passed from the forest to the canyon, the ground dropped suddenly out from under them and fell to a great depth below. They were captivated by the remarkable dual phenomenon of the dense, living habitat abruptly terminating and the vast, barren world of the tremendous gorge simultaneously opening up before them.

They were not prepared for the awesome totality of that instantaneous transformation. It was as though the earth, with its familiar greenery, had simply stopped, as though they had crossed over the fabled edge of the world. And contrary to legend they had not fallen off into the void but had discovered and penetrated the Creator's unfinished remainder of the world, entering upon a primeval landscape still unchanged by life, extending as far as they could see. Those of them who had seen the Grand Canyon only in photographs up until that moment were speechless. Its immensity was absolutely flabbergasting—they had no framework of experience from which to fathom anything that enormous, and the only possible response was, "My God!"

From any perspective, something extraordinary was going on, and of course this was the reality. A terrible wrong had occurred, a grotesque error, a situation that did not belong and yet existed. The crash sites rendered aghast all who beheld them for the first time, and even the second or the third. There was "nothing" there. At each place there was a huge black spot where, for a split second, an airliner had been. Each site was covered with soot from the fuel and other combustible materials that had burned there, and strewn with blackened shards of what once had been an airplane. Numerous small fragments of aluminum and other materials that had escaped the flames, or had been only partially consumed by them, surrounded the fire zones. For the totality of the destruction, each site was appallingly less than an airplane crash and looked instead like a garbage dump that had been poured over with tar and set on fire, abandoned to burn itself out. In fact, when one TWA investigator came upon the TWA wreckage from the air and saw it for the first time, he impulsively exclaimed, "Where's the *rest* of it?"

This was the sight that confronted and unnerved the men in the three helicopters. The TWA site was their objective, and they faced it in awe as they came upon it and descended to land nearby. They had come to retrieve the remains of the dead, and they quickly regained their composure and resolve, after being initially taken aback. The prospect of the gruesome task before them was even more sobering than the sight of the wreckage.

Army officers from Fort Huachuca, in southern Arizona, piloted the three huge helicopters. They were Capt. Walter E. Spriggs, Jr.; Chief Warrant Officer James P. Spearman, Jr.; and Chief Warrant Officer Howard Proctor. They brought in a large team of investigators and a good deal of equipment, including not only tools and body bags but also survival gear such as water, rations, cooking utensils, and sleeping bags, so that the team could remain in the canyon overnight. The strong winds expected once the sun heated the rocky canyon walls and floor made flying very awkward and dangerous. The average peak temperature on July afternoons in the Inner Gorge, the canyon's lowest reaches, was 106°F, and in the early part of July, before most of the summer rains came, the air frequently achieved the incredible high of 115°F. As it became hotter, the air also became progressively rarefied, making it harder for helicopters to generate the lift sufficient to leave or to descend gradually enough to safely land. The combination of the two undesirable conditions was expected to preclude safe flying within the canyon by midmorning, as it had done the previous day, persisting until after dark. In keeping with this, the team expected to remain at the site until Tuesday, so the plan was to work all day to whatever extent the heat would allow, irrespective of whether or not the H-21s could return before dark; otherwise they could get very little done and would have to leave after only about four hours.

By about 10:30 a.m. the heat and the wind had picked up hazardously, and the last of the three H-21s had to leave the TWA site. As if to confirm the danger and to dispel any remaining doubts some of the men might have had about the necessity of the helicopters leaving, a small scout plane and a helicopter nearly collided. For lack of predictable control, it took an unusual degree of concentration just to fly in a reasonably coordinated manner against all the buffeting, and this left the pilot little room to pay attention to anything else, like the whereabouts of other aircraft. Another midair collision, especially between two rescue craft piloted by men nobly attempting to contend with the disaster, would have been too much to bear, and all flying was called off for the day within the canyon.

Before the last H-21 left, the men had had time to attend to some of the victims. The helicopter lifted off with five body bags on board, the first remains removed from the canyon, and it left behind a group of twelve men. Contrary to the numerous sensationalized newspaper stories at the time, they stayed overnight by plan and by choice rather than by being stranded.

CWO Howard Proctor flew the remains to Grand Canyon Airport, where they were transferred to another army aircraft, a traditional airplane called a U-1A. This was the military version of the de Havilland Otter, big brother of the de Havilland Beaver. The U-1A was a stout, heavy-duty plane capable of carrying ten passengers and a crew of two pilots, and like the L-20, it had one propeller, in its nose, driven by a heavy radial engine. Like most small airplanes, its wing was on top of the fuselage rather than under it.

Under the command of Major Jerome B. Feldt, the army was responsible for removing the victims' remains, removing fragments of wreckage that might be indicative of what had happened, and transporting the investigators who would retrieve the remains and collect the evidence. Major Feldt flew the U-1A and its tragic cargo himself to Flagstaff Municipal Airport.

Only two days before, the things in the rubber sacks behind him had been living, breathing persons, with the exquisite emotional, intellectual, and spiritual awareness known only to human beings. They had had inestimable knowledge and remembered experience; they had had values and goals, desires and wishes and hopes, fears and concerns and doubts. They had loved and cared about other human beings. Two days before, the pitiful remnants had been people—dignified, well groomed, and well dressed—riding in comfort and luxury aboard a beautiful machine that was the culmination of their forebears' struggles for a thousand years, to understand the world and to invent implements with which to better survive in it. All of that effort had failed, and now, because of that, all that remained of them in this world were the inanimate, repugnant masses being hauled like cargo to Flagstaff. Valued members of society had been mercilessly subjected to such foul abuse that their enduring vestiges were unfit even to be near the living and had to be quarantined. People with names and identities and personalities had been reduced to the horrible objects that were now sealed impersonally in unremarkable, degrading packages behind Major Feldt.

At Flagstaff Municipal Airport the remains were transferred to an ambulance and driven to TWA's temporary morgue at Coconino County Fairgrounds, a short distance away. In the canyon, the team on the ground at the TWA site worked in blindingly bright sun and barely breathable, unbelievably hot air, recovering more remains. Some of the victims were underneath wreckage and had to be dug out. What the men at Temple Butte had to contend with was horrendous. It is very hard to grasp the extent of the devastation wreaked on human beings in an airplane crash. Most of us who have never seen for ourselves picture it being like a fatal car accident, but in fact the damage done to the victims in surface travel accidents is slight in comparison. An airplane crash is usually far worse, mainly due to greater speed and to fire.

The slowest that the Constellation could have been moving when it hit the ground was about 300 mph (its approximate horizontal speed in cruising just before it entered a dive), and because it fell about three and a half miles, it was probably moving much faster. Everyone knows that the faster a vehicle is moving when it crashes, the worse the accident will be, but the straightforward notion that doubling the speed will double the severity is oversimplified. The damage done in any crash is in part a result of the kinetic energy of the vehicle and its occupants, which is proportional not simply to the speed, but to the *square* of the speed. Airplanes cannot be equated with automobiles in any but the roughest of ways, but an analogy is still useful because most of us have a feel for cars. All other things being equal, a plane diving straight into rocky ground at 300 mph would inflict 25 times the damage on its occupants as a car running into a brick wall at 60 mph would do, even though the speed of the plane is only five times as great. In the automobile accident the people are grievously injured, but unless there is a fire (and usually there is not), they still look like people. In the airplane crash, it is as though a very powerful bomb encased in shrapnel exploded in their midst. Most of the remains are fragmentary and unrecognizable even if there is no ensuing fire, which there nearly always is. This was the case in the Grand Canyon at both sites, and the fires were not only tremendously hot, being gasoline fires, but they burned all day. Each plane took on a very large load of fuel at Los Angeles, enough to fly about three-fourths of the way across the country plus a reserve, and each had used only a fourth of the fuel with which it took off.

The United DC-7 wreck was about one and a quarter miles upstream from the TWA site, on the same side of the Colorado River (see map in Appendix 6). The area could be reached from Temple Butte by walking along the west bank and the talus slopes, difficult terrain but negotiable. Two members of the twelve-man team at Temple Butte made the trek to Chuar Butte around midday. The impact site high up on one of Chuar's promontories was clearly visible from the riverbed 1,300 feet below. Like the TWA site, the United site was marked by a very large, blackened area where the fire had been, contrasting with the much lighter colors of the rocky landscape. In United's case the burned area appeared to have been poured down the cliff from its crest, and it gave the unnerving impression of evil. It was Death taken shape and had flowed like black lava, violently growing from a seed of malevolence.

The two hikers had no difficulty in judging where anything from the crash site high above should have fallen, because the direction of the pouring effect was obvious. When they reached the immediate area, they walked up the talus slope, a very hard climb at about thirty degrees over unremitting rocky ground that in fact was nothing more than a huge rock pile. Near the top of the talus slope, beneath the blackened crash site, they found what they had dreaded, and their hearts sank. There before them was the body of a woman from the United wreck. She had surely perished instantly upon impact at the crash site like everyone else, but she had also rolled down the gully and over the cliff, tumbling hundreds of feet to the ground below. She had been spared the fire.

It was now fully real that the United passengers and crew were all dead, too. No one involved in the operations had had any honest doubt, but now there was tangible proof. The first of them had been found. Against their heartfelt caring for another human being and against their chivalrous feelings toward a woman, the men had to leave her there where they found her. They had not brought a stretcher or even a body bag, and without either of these it would have been hopelessly difficult for them to carry her even the short distance downhill to the river's edge, let alone for over a mile horizontally. So with chagrin, they refused their senses of what was right or decent, and they left her there.

After a time of investigating the area, the two men left and headed back downriver to rejoin their teammates at Temple Butte. When they returned they told the others of the woman they had found and what they thought might be a couple other bodies higher up, which they were not able to reach. By 6:00 p.m. the team had filled twenty-one more bags at the TWA site, and there was nothing more to be found. They had also collected a bagful of airmail, some of which was badly singed. Much of this mail was later sent on its way and ultimately delivered.

In the morning of that day, a helicopter crew had attempted to land on the shoulder of Chuar Butte where the United DC-7 crashed, but they aborted this because the pilots' instincts told them that it was far too dangerous. There was almost no level ground on the crest. Boulders were randomly scattered across the area, and farther inland from the point of the shoulder, the ground sloped upward rapidly to nearly vertical, forming the much higher central peak of the butte. Instead, the helicopter merely hovered while its crew looked for possible routes by which climbers might make the ascent from far down below.

A collateral but much simpler problem was that of how to get the climbers to that starting location in the first place. Chuar Butte was surrounded on all sides by impassable terrain. Like a great, jaggedly tiered wall, the other side of the gorge faced it from the east. The only opening in the wall was the equally forbidding gorge that straddled the Little Colorado River. To the north, the south and the west spread mile after mile of other buttes in a tortured, undulating, scathing landscape that seemed to extend forever, and in the prospect of traversing it by foot might as well have. The only approaches to the butte were from the river and from the air.

Reaching it from the riverbank by rafting down the Colorado River from upstream was entirely feasible; the real problem was getting from the base of Chuar Butte to the crash site high above. Whoever might come on the scene by raft would have to make the trek up the talus slope, ascending about 700 feet in the process, and then a vertical climb of another 650 feet in order to reach the crest. To give some familiar scale to this, if the Empire State Building could somehow have been transplanted to the giant sandbar at the confluence of the two rivers, an observer in its top floor could have gazed at the crash site at just about eye level, nearly half a mile away across open space.

Primarily because it appeared unnecessary, no one had embarked upon the river-rafting journey. Helicopter pilots had judged that it would probably be possible to simply land men at the base of Chuar Butte, on either the giant sandbar or one of the small sandbars next to the shoreline. No one had attempted this yet because landing up high at the crash site itself had not been ruled out, even though it appeared that at best it would be very dangerous. Beside this, no one had thus far been able to discover a route by which climbers could scale the vertical face of the promontory, and the consensus was growing that it might be impossible. Workers at the base would have the important task of searching for and retrieving telltale wreckage, as well as the vital task of recovering any bodies that might have fallen from above, but in the morning, before flying was called off for the day, no one knew that any victims had in fact fallen to the talus. In all respects, there was no concrete, urgent reason to get to the base of Chuar Butte, so no one tried it. At the close of the day Monday, no one in the United team had yet set foot on any part of the United crash area.

*   *   *

Since before the dawn of civilization, the place where the United plane crashed had been a sanctuary, an aerie so lofty and isolated that only purity had ever been able to alight there. With infinite patience it had evolved throughout the ages, never altered by man. Probably no one, not even ancient American Indians, had ever set foot there. And then in one terrible, panicked, rushing moment, a thing of man's design, carrying fifty-eight human beings against their wills and in terror, hurtled down from the heavens like some ghastly, menacing, artificial meteor and desecrated this untouched place with horrendous violence. When the fire finally went out and the last of its embers cooled and ceased to stir, the ancient stillness resumed unchanged, as though it had never been broken. The wind swept over the rocky promontory as it had done for uncounted millennia and took no notice of the new debris. Though the force of man had been impressed, man had not yet been there, and in that sense the defiled place remained untouched.

Night fell for the third time over the victims in the canyon. Those from the TWA flight had been covered by their caretakers and were not touched by the night this time, not by its fathomless darkness or by the light of its stars. Those from the United flight were once again speckled with starlight, immaculate and sublime, exquisitely exerting infinitesimal pressure by its touch, lighter than snowflakes yet tangible. Stardust rested on them, but not the dust of matter; rather, it was a dust that was starlight itself, the earthly cast of the multitudinous pinpoints of light. In the crystal clear air of that unpolluted desert wilderness, the sky was blacker than any black ever beheld in light. Myriads of glistening diamonds, radiating their splendor throughout the aeons, had come out on this particular night, of all the nights in the infinitude they had known, to grace and to honor the minute beings whose incredibly brief lives had been made even briefer.

Each in the privacy of his own thoughts, the men at Temple Butte drifted off into slumber. In the cooler air of the night and the relative comfort of their sleeping bags, stretched out on the stony ground, they found escape from the hardships of the day and from the singularly awful sights they had seen. These images could have driven them into nightmares, but they were exhausted and fell into deeper sleep instead. They rested and slept peacefully, among those who would rest forevermore.

CHAPTER 14

AT DAWN ON the morning of Tuesday, July 3, twin-rotor H-21 army helicopters took off from Grand Canyon Airport and chopped their way toward the disaster area. They had stood overnight at the rudimentary dirt and scrub grass airfield, and they had been refueled by a large gasoline tank truck that was parked there especially for the purpose. The primary missions for the day were to land a team of men at Chuar Butte, up high if possible, and to remove the bodies from Temple Butte. Once again a pilot attempted to land atop the United impact shoulder, and once again, because the terrain was so precarious and forbidding, he aborted it. Instead, the pilot set his machine down on a sandbar in the river far below.

At the confluence of the Colorado and Little Colorado rivers are two sizable sandbars, one well known and the other hardly known at all. On any large scale map of the area, one can see a huge, roughly triangular sandbar measuring about a quarter mile west to east and about an eighth of a mile north to south overall. No other sandbar is distinguishable in that area on most maps, but there is a second, much smaller sandbar flanking the shoreline at the west bank, and this is where the H-21 landed. The giant triangular sandbar was unsuitable because the rushing Colorado River separated it by about 200 feet from the shoreline at the base of Chuar Butte, and this water would have been difficult to cross, especially with equipment. On the other hand, the small sandbar was separated from the west bank by only a thin ribbon of shallow, gently flowing water about 40 feet wide, which was easy to cross. Despite being much smaller than the giant sandbar, the small one was plenty large enough for a landing pad, measuring about 300 feet north to south, parallel with the Colorado, and 150 feet west to east.

Aboard the H-21 was the counterpart of the team that had spent the night at the TWA site. A group of about ten men disembarked and waded across the shallow, intervening stream with their equipment. On the beach at the base of Chuar Butte, they began to set up the base camp from which some of them would attempt to scale the talus and the cliff face above it. Like the group at Temple Butte, they had come prepared and had no intention of leaving that day. They had tents and sleeping bags; hiking and climbing gear, including numerous tools and a great deal of rope; cooking pans and coffee pots; plates and cups and silverware; and plenty of food and water rations. They even had a charcoal grill.

Three of the men in the United team had been involved in a similar situation at Medicine Bow Peak, Wyoming, just nine months earlier. They were Carl M. Christenson, director of safety at United Air Lines; Robert A. Graham, staff superintendent of training for United Air Lines; and Capt. John Lovett, a pilot of United Air Lines. On October 6, 1955, a United DC-4 with sixty-six people aboard crashed into the mountain peak, leaving no survivors. The job of searching the crash site to retrieve the victims' remains and vital wreckage entailed climbing the mountain along an approach that was severely sloped and nearly vertical in areas, like the promontory of Chuar Butte. Christenson, Graham, and Lovett applied the experience they had acquired in that tragedy to the disaster they were facing, hiking up the talus slope in the general direction of the fearsome black spot high above.

It is difficult to imagine the ruggedness of the talus because it is so extreme, and because the talus itself is unlike almost any other place. If all the brick buildings and concrete buildings and marble buildings from the downtown of a large city were crushed by some fantastic pulverizing machine, making stone and masonry rubble of all sizes, from that of a pebble to that of a refrigerator, and if this tremendous volume of waste were mixed with half as much reddish, sandy dirt, and then the whole conglomeration were dumped over the top of a butte, falling to all sides and piling up around it at the base, the result would be like the talus. Adding a few scrubby green shrubs here and there and a few small lizards would complete the picture. There is scarcely a smooth or flat place to step, and most of the smaller rocks, say those from the size of a shoebox to the size of a small chair seat, are unstable rather than firmly embedded in the soil or wedged under other rocks. They tip and slide underfoot, throwing the climber off balance.

To get from the bottom to the top, the hikers had to scale the talus for a quarter mile along its inclined surface. They laboriously staggered their way up this jagged, repellent rock pile, roughly the steepness of the typical home roof and only a few degrees gentler than the average home staircase. Walking up even the best-crafted staircase a quarter mile long would be beyond many people, and for most that could do it, it would require several stops to rest. Most that made it would be left with pervasive muscle strain in their legs and persistent pain like that of deep bruises, which would not subside for several days or a week afterward. The talus was considerably worse because it had no convenient steps. Every footfall was unique, rather than a reprise of the forward and vertical movement of the last. Each step had to be planned instead of taken with the unconscious ease of the metered, regular stepping involved in ascending stairs.

The only consolations for the climbers were that the sun was at their backs and the rocks were not yet hot enough to oppressively irradiate and inflame their shaded faces. The air was hot and the rocks were hot, but it was early morning, and neither had reached its abominable, midsummer, midafternoon extreme. The men attained the top of the talus slope and for several arduous hours searched for a way up the sheer cliff above them to the wreckage site at its crest, but they found none. They returned to base camp, sweltering and frustrated. As if in testament to the strain and the futility of the climb, the only concrete result was that Captain Lovett's leather climbing boots were badly gouged and cut from numerous conflicts with sharp rocks.

The United team made some very important progress that day despite the climbers' failing to find a way up to the crash site. Other workers carefully removed the body of the woman who was discovered by the TWA team the previous afternoon, and they carried her to the beach. They found two other victims nearby and removed them to the beach also. Like the woman, they had escaped the inferno above. One was a marine, immediately obvious in the uniform that he wore, and the other appeared to be a businessman. Unfortunately, before these three victims were brought down the slope to the base camp, helicopter landings were called off for the day, due again to the wind and the heat. Despite the urgency of identification experts examining them, the bodies had to stay in the wild for yet another day before they could be returned to civilization. In the meantime they were remedially preserved with formaldehyde poured into the bags.

Earlier in the day, while the climbers at Chuar Butte were hobbling up the talus slope, H-21 helicopters landed at the TWA site at Temple Butte. By late morning they had transported most of the twelve investigators who spent the night there and had also evacuated all twenty-one bags of remains. The H-21s flew to Grand Canyon Airport, where the remains were transferred to an army U1-A and a TWA DC-3. A DC-3 was a medium-sized, unpressurized airliner with dual radial engines, normally configured to carry about twenty passengers. In the 1930s TWA introduced passenger service that utilized DC-3s, and the plane was popular for many years, but by 1956 it was pretty much obsolete as an airliner. The DC-3 that the company used in the Grand Canyon disaster was one of their last. It and the U1-A had the job of flying the cargo off-loaded from the H-21s to Flagstaff for identification.

The arrival of the planes at Flagstaff was a terrible scene, one that probably cannot be described in agreeable terms. When the doors of the planes were opened, swarms of flies poured out in wild disarray, like bees that had been alarmed by someone batting their hive with a stick. With the flies came forth the foulest, most threatening fumes, which rapidly suffused the area. The stench was indescribably awful and sickening, so bad that it was as if the very flies, creatures at home in the most putrid of places, had rushed out not in startled mindlessness, but in the desperate and willful need to escape it. The military men who had piloted the U1-A got out in haste and vomited. The TWA DC-3 later had to be fully reupholstered because the odor could not be shampooed out.

Everything brought to Flagstaff was driven in pickup trucks and an ambulance to the temporary morgue at the Coconino County Fairgrounds, and the work of identifying the dead got into full swing. Identification experts from the air force and the FBI joined with local officials and with TWA personnel to tackle the awful task. The men worked in shifts for very short periods, taking breaks outdoors in the fresh air.

In the early afternoon, shortly after United's climbers returned in failure to base camp on the beach, the United team radioed to a plane high overhead with the news that they could not climb the butte. The only ways they could communicate with the outside world were by radio and by word of mouth, and the latter would have to wait for the return of the helicopters in the morning. The trouble with radio, on the other hand, was that from nearly a mile down inside a "stone quarry," they could hardly transmit a signal horizontally to a station many miles away on the ground above; but they could send a signal straight up. So they radioed to airplanes.

Because of their altitude above the Coconino, Marble, and Kaibab plateaus that surrounded the eastern Grand Canyon, the airplanes could broadcast for great distances, like the tallest of radio towers. From an airplane, the United team's plight was relayed to Mr. Earl Isaacson, staff assistant at United's Denver Operating Base. Since Sunday, the day after the accident, Isaacson had been in communication with an organization called the Rocky Mountain Rescue Group (RMRG) to keep them apprised of the situation as it developed, in case their help might be needed. The RMRG was divided into three units, each one comprised principally of young mountain climbing enthusiasts who lived in the territory covered by the unit. The RMRG was founded for the purpose that its name suggested: to rescue people, predominantly other climbers, from the mountains. The physical and technical skills required to reach a crash site high atop a cliff, and to remove bodies, were essentially the same as those required to reach injured, immobile mountain climbers and to rescue them, and for this reason the expertise of the RMRG qualified them well for the job that needed to be done at Chuar Butte. Moreover, the group had been involved with two airplane crashes in the past, the more recent one being the DC-4 crash at Medicine Bow Peak, where they had worked for United Air Lines. In that tragedy the RMRG took the initiative and, based on the news over the radio, drove unsolicited to the accident area. They simply guessed which hotel the United officials might be staying at and went there to meet with them and offer their services. Not only was their guess correct, but also they actually arrived before the United officials did! United accepted their help at Medicine Bow Peak, and there the RMRG had proved themselves.

Now United Air Lines had taken the initiative and had called the RMRG. Just before two o'clock, Isaacson telephoned the Boulder unit of the RMRG to ask that two of their best climbers be at Denver's Stapleton Airfield, with equipment and ready to go, by 3:30. Two young men named L. David Lewis and Raymond Batson were chosen. The whole unit had been on standby alert ever since Isaacson's initial contact on Sunday, and it did not take long for Lewis and Batson to get ready for the short drive from Boulder to Denver.

It was the policy of United Air Lines to pay individuals and groups from which it received assistance in contending with a tragedy, and so Lewis and Batson were to be paid for their services. The work they would do was expected to be exceedingly hazardous, and commensurately the rate of pay was set at $150 a day apiece, quite a lot at the time, considering that the average suburban family was able to live comfortably on one income of about $30 a day. The RMRG would have unhesitatingly given their help free of compensation, but United insisted on paying, and that was the agreement.

David Lewis was the leader of the Boulder unit of the RMRG and was only twenty years old. He was a college student majoring in physics and lived at his parents' home in Boulder. Raymond Batson was married and was also a college student, majoring in geology. Both young men were outstanding climbers. By late afternoon Lewis and Batson were airborne in the skies over Arizona, in a United Air Lines Convair 340 heading for Flagstaff. They landed at suppertime and were driven from the airport to a motel, where they ate and retired for the evening. Instead of planning or receiving briefings about what lay ahead, the two prepared simply by getting as much sleep as they could, starting while the sun was still shining. A little after 3:00 a.m. they arose, cleaned up, and left their rooms. They were driven back to Flagstaff Municipal Airport in the dark, where they boarded a waiting United DC-3 for the flight to Grand Canyon Airport, fifty-six miles away. There they climbed aboard a waiting army H-21, which flew them into the canyon. David Lewis had never flown before at all, on any kind of aircraft, not even a balloon. In the first fifteen hours of his experience with travel by air, he had flown not only on two types of airplanes, but also on a helicopter, the latter something that most long-time fliers had never done.

The H-21 eased down on the small sandbar next to the base camp on the beach, and Lewis and Batson got out and readjusted their senses of balance to the still earth. Sunlight was slowly creeping down the east face of Chuar Butte toward the morning shadows at river level as the two young men waded across the shallow water between the sandbar and the shore. There could have been no more dramatic an introduction than for nature itself to gradually illuminate what they were facing, from the top to the bottom, and as they looked up in front of them, they got their first view of Chuar Butte. It was Wednesday, the Fourth of July.

CHAPTER 15

IN THE EARLY morning of Wednesday, July 4, the three bodies retrieved from the talus slope of Chuar Butte the previous day were loaded onto the helicopter that brought David Lewis and Raymond Batson to the sandbar, and were flown out of the gorge. They were the first United victims to be removed, and they would remain the only ones removed for the time being.

Two other expert climbers, from a group called the Colorado Mountain Club (CMC) based in Denver, accompanied Lewis and Batson on the H-21. Rather than rescuing stranded persons from the wilds, the primary purposes of the CMC were to promote the sport of mountaineering and to promote the preservation of the wilderness. United Air Lines had also been in contact with this group since Sunday, and as with the RMRG they had asked the CMC for help. Two of their members, Charles Pavlik and Fred Welch, both of Denver, had come in response. Pavlik was a chemist and Welch was an engineer, and both were married. Lewis was the only bachelor in the four-man team.

The opening plan was the most obvious one: namely for Lewis, Batson, Pavlik, and Welch to scale the talus and look for a way to reach the crest of the impact shoulder, as Christenson, Graham, and Lovett had done on Tuesday. It is difficult to really grasp the problem that they faced. The shoulder that they wanted to climb jutted out about a quarter mile eastward from the main body of Chuar Butte and was encircled on its three open sides by the talus. It was severely steep, almost vertical, narrowing to a ridge at its top. Its faces were rough and sculpted with numerous vertical channels and cracks, and it had countless small shelves and other footholds.

Many people had done aerial reconnaissance from very nearby, both by circling in airplanes and by hovering in helicopters, and a number of people had scrutinized the situation from the beach and from the talus slope. Photographs had even been taken and developed and studied, and yet no sure path had been discerned by any of the many people working on the problem. Common sense might suggest that the problem should be as straightforward as looking at an early twentieth-century skyscraper, with its numerous ledges and cornerstones and windowsills, and apprehending how to climb it, but in actuality it was much more involved. Following any course visually up the cliff was more like trying to trace by eye the path that an ant might follow up the maze of crevices in the bark of a tree trunk, without encountering a dead-end. The task is complex, tedious, and confusing even with the luck of selecting a path that leads all the way up. There are many forks in the crevice system and thus many turns to remember, and one crevice looks like another, so it is easy to get lost. The job is almost hopeless even sitting still at an optimum distance from the tree and intently concentrating—let alone if one is moving.

While looking at Chuar Butte, most of the observers were moving, in aircraft, but moving or still, all of them were either too near to the cliff face to take in the whole at once, or they were too far away to distinguish its smaller features reliably, except with binoculars, and that was optically equivalent to being too near again, narrowing the effective view and rendering it bewilderingly disjoined from the whole. There was no middle ground—the escarpment was so huge that to see all of it at once required being far enough back that the fuller intricacy of its contours was lost.

The people who studied the photographs, on the other hand, were at the great disadvantage of having only relatively tiny images to examine, and two-dimensional ones at that. Their depth perception was effectively hampered, and they could not alter their perspective by moving to one side as the people looking at the real butte could do. They also incurred a special problem peculiar to photographs: it is often difficult or even impossible to determine whether a rock formation in a photograph is a protrusion or a depression. The two frequently look alike, and what is more, shadows complicate the visual pattern, further confounding it and confusing the eye.

There was just no easy way to figure out how to climb up. The team suspected and hoped, however, that they at least had a part of the answer. A ledge encircled the shoulder about a quarter of the way up the sheer cliff face from the top of the talus, and it had been an object of great interest for all concerned since it appeared that climbers might be able to reach the lofty crash gully from a position on the ledge directly beneath it. Commensurately the team cast their objective in terms of finding a way up to the ledge. If they could achieve this they would go from there. As they ascended the talus slope, they looked for a reasonable way up the nearly vertical wall that projected heavenward from it, and they saw none. Near the top of the talus they did, however, begin finding something else. Crumpled and torn fragments of wreckage, few bigger than a small table, littered the ground. These displaced objects gave the situation a whole new order of reality. The men had already seen a few collected scraps at the base camp, but those had been removed from where they were found and laid with a measure of care in the composed and ordered world of the base camp. Now that the men had come upon undisturbed wreckage, they had entered the crash area. The wreckage around them lay exactly where the violence and chaos of the crash had flung it; the actual disaster had begun to show itself and was unnervingly real.

The four climbers walked around the base of the towering rock wall, at the top of the talus slope, making their way across the south face beneath the crash site, to the east face fronting the confluence of the two rivers, without finding any reasonable way up. They were not surprised, because the United climbers had covered much of this territory on Tuesday and found nothing, and so they persisted, gradually making their way around the east end and into the north side. It was on this side that they found it. There was a steep, narrow breach in the wall, a nearly vertical channel extending from the talus up to the horizontal ledge that wrapped around the entire circumference of the promontory. The channel was hardly wider than a man, but it gave them a way to the ledge high above as surely as a ladder.

The crack in the wall contained many footholds and handholds, and being experienced climbers, the men had little difficulty scaling it. From a layman's point of view, it is stretching the meaning of the term beyond its natural scope, but in the modest words of David Lewis the four essentially "walked up the breach." Most people would probably observe that they climbed, though without the use of ropes. (Newspapers across the country that evening and the next day printed the exaggerated and totally false stories that the men had pounded many rock drills and many pitons into the rocky cliff face, and had used these in conjunction with ropes to scale it. The truth was that they never used a single spike, and although they did use a little rope to progress horizontally once they were on the ledge, they never used any rope at all to get up there.) Soon they were on the ledge and began to walk in the usual sense back around the circumference of the promontory in the direction from which they had come.

From a distance it looked like there was but a single ledge, one discreet band where the girth of the shoulder reduced. The structure of the promontory looked in principle like the effect that would be produced if a box were centered on top of a slightly longer, wider box, creating a shelf all around at the juncture between the two. However, the ledge was actually a system of ledges, none of which by itself traversed the whole peninsular circumference of the promontory. Rather, they ran broken and stratified, close together vertically in a group around it. The ledge system was amply wide in most areas but uncomfortably narrow in others. In many places the ledges were piled with gravel that had fallen there and collected through the ages. It had accreted in the same probabilistic distribution as the talus slope, more toward where the pieces had come from and less outward, so that the piling on the ledges sloped downward toward the edge. Obviously the slant was disadvantageous, tending to divert a person overboard, but perhaps more important the looseness of the gravel posed the hazard of unstable footing. Even in the more roomy areas the cliff would forgive only very little misjudgment, but in the narrower areas there was almost no latitude in where to step. Each movement had to be right the first time, and so for average climbers the situation would have been deadly. Even for the expert climbers on the ledges the conditions were dangerous and sobering. The stakes were high: to fall would have meant a drop of about 150 feet and certain death. The men were not belayed, and so falling to their deaths was possible. As a measure against this, Lewis, who was in the lead, ran a length of rope behind himself along the ledge to serve as a makeshift handrail should one of his companions slip and need something to grab onto. Lewis himself had nothing for which to reach except loose rock and air if he lost his own balance.

The group walked cautiously and sometimes crawled on hands and knees around the cliff face. Like mites on a sandcastle, they were minute beings against the enormousness of Chuar Butte, specks so insignificant as to defy detection. A large distance in their world seemed a small distance in the world of observers half a mile away, and in crossing it even at a rate that seemed substantial to them, the specks appeared hardly to move at all. Their progress was like that of the minute hand of a clock, imperceptible so long as it is watched. It is known only through the magic of memory, which after a period of inattentiveness differs markedly from the position of the actual hand, revealing that it moved while no one was looking.

Not far along the northern ledges the climbers found the United DC-7's airspeed indicator and altimeter. These were cockpit instruments from the panel in front of the pilots and had been thrown over the crest from the other side where the plane hit. The men put the pair of clocklike devices in a knapsack to bring back, in case they might have been jammed at their final readings by the force of the crash and would tell something about what happened.

They stopped to rest when they reached the eastern extreme of the promontory. It had been slow going, and they had come around the ledge system to roughly the midpoint between the crack in the wall where they had climbed up to the ledges and the spot directly beneath the crash site. Less than a city block away along the southern ledges were a group of open vertical channels called chimneys that stretched from the ledges to the steep gully into which the DC-7 had crashed high above. The gully began at the crest and fell steeply for almost 200 feet to where it leveled out in a shallowly sloped, fanned-out apron that in turn spilled over the edge of the cliff. Between the apron and the ledges was a sheer vertical expanse dropping about 300 feet, notched by the chimneys. The climbers hoped that they would be able to ascend these three-hundred-foot-high chimneys all of the way from the ledges to the apron at the bottom of the crash gully.

The men sat in the shade on one of the eastern ledges and rested, and drank some water. Like ancient cliff dwellers they were invulnerable, secure beyond any ordinary proportions and most extraordinary proportions in their unassailable loft. Below them at the bottom of a precipice as tall as a twelve-story building was the nearest approach from that direction: the talus slope. At their backs the men were buttressed with a solid rock wall, immediate and impregnable, and on all sides in front of them spread titanic rock formations as far as they could see. There was no horizon in the usual sense, but only fortifications of rock in all directions, enclosing them ahead, and to the left and the right, from half a mile and more away and behind from only feet away.

A short distance down the talus slope lay several gigantic boulders, each the size of a two or three-story house. Through nature's indomitable will they had been moved, cracked off the cliff face, and pulled to the ground beneath it. For countless thousands of years the earth had incessantly drawn them, and the earth had finally won. How long they had lain on the talus was anyone's guess; they may have fallen and come to rest there while Neanderthal man painted the caves in the forests that became France.

At the bottom of the talus surged the great Colorado, flowing powerfully past in front of the men from left to right. It was muddy brown because it flowed forcefully enough to carry great amounts of silt in suspension. On the opposite banks rose other talus slopes, from which escarpments jutted almost vertically and then slanted jaggedly upward to the flat land of the Navajo Indian Reservation above the canyon. The tranquil, brilliantly turquoise water of the Little Colorado flowed gently toward Chuar Butte from the east, parting the great escarpments that confronted Chuar from that direction. It was a winding road to a paradise, supernaturally colorful and beautiful against the earth tones that bordered it, and it seemed to lead away eastward despite the fact that it was moving westward. Its water was perfectly clear because it flowed too slowly to carry any silt, and remained clean. It was a marvel that the two totally dissimilar rivers could meld so completely at their confluence, and a mystery where the radiant blue went in their union.

Their world was stone, river, and sky, and the true horizon lay hidden behind the elevated rim of the tremendous gorge that held them. The scene before them was beautiful and magnificent beyond description, as near to seeing God as material perception can be. It would have brought most people to tears of humility and awe.

It had taken long enough to reach this Olympian place that the four men had already consumed about half of their water. It was a point of no return, and consequently they had to consider their next move. Like the desert, with its blistering, stifling heat, the canyon was so hot during the day that a person could not safely do without water for even a few hours. At least they were in the shade, since the sun had passed its zenith and was in the southwest, obscured by Chuar Butte. They also had a breeze from the convection currents caused by the heat. It was warm rather than cool, yet it still provided some relief. Despite the shade and the moving air, it was nevertheless essential for the men to keep drinking water frequently, and there was no way for them to get more.

They thought about continuing to at least the chimneys, to prove to themselves that there was in fact a complete route along the ledge system. They also thought about scaling the chimneys at least part way for exploratory purposes, in the hope of ascertaining how best to attain the bottom of the gully, 300 feet above the ledges. The problem was that even the lesser of these endeavors would leave them with little or no reserve of water, and not nearly enough for the trip back to base camp in any case. As a complication it was late enough in the day that they might not be able to retrace their steps to base camp before dark if they spent much more time on the ledges first.

For both reasons, to continue would require their rappelling down the cliff face from the ledges to the talus, in order to get back before they ran out of water and daylight. The team had brought plenty of rope to do this, but it was risky, and they ruled out the shortcut on grounds of safety. At each spot where a climber would swing back to the cliff face, at the bottom of each short jump, he might strike a rock that jutted out, or twist his ankle in a crevice. These were hazards that often could not be seen from above; rappelling down an unfamiliar cliff was somewhat daring, like diving into water of unknown depth or parachuting at dusk. Retreating was the reasonable option, so the men decided to leave. Having come that far, they were optimistic and fairly confident that the climb could be made successfully all the way to the crash site, and they were determined to try again the following morning.

*   *   *

It was Independence Day, and all across the country people were making it a festive occasion. There were picnics on every block in every town. Men barbecued hotdogs and hamburgers on outdoor charcoal grills for their families and friends and neighbors to enjoy. Picnickers ate potato salad and baked beans and Jell-O with their hamburgers and hotdogs, using paper plates and napkins, and plastic forks and spoons. Children drank Kool-Aid or Hi-C from waxed paper cups printed with cheerful designs and colors, and many grown-ups had beer or mixed drinks. Adults and children alike drank soda pop and lemonade and punch, and everyone ate watermelon, gleefully spitting out the large black seeds all over the place. (There was no such thing as seedless watermelon back then.) Everywhere people were having a delightful summer holiday celebrating the birth of the nation and the birth of American Democracy, and just plain enjoying the food and the company of others. Scarcely a business was open, and most of those that were closed up early. Patriotism ran high and prevalently, and it made people happy to remember on that special day that they were part of a great nation, an honorable country devoted to the ideals of human worth. In the name of freedom, the United States of America had grown to become one of the leading powers in the world. We had made it, and our country shone for all the world to admire. We knew we had found the right way to live, and we were both humble and proud.

For the men in the canyon, however, Independence Day might as well have belonged to a long forgotten dream. To them there was no civilization, no society, no holiday. The Fourth of July festivities did not exist in their reality, and their world was almost as far removed from mankind as the earth had been before the dawn of man.

In a few hundred homes across the land there were people just as isolated, even though they were encircled by their neighbors and their towns. For many of the people who had lost a loved one in the canyon, the trauma of their ongoing ordeal was only intensified by the contrast of the society around them celebrating. Their pain and their aloneness were amplified by the joy and commonality and togetherness everyone outside their homes was having. They were acutely agonized, like a kidnap victim being marshaled at concealed gunpoint through a crowd of friendly faces, unable to reveal his plight to them.

Most of the people who had lost a loved one, however, were oblivious to what the rest of the world was doing. It simply did not matter. They were in their own disparate realities, with their own entirely valid precepts, and they operated from those principles as heedless of the merrymakers and their interests as anyone would normally be of a neighborhood cat and its pursuits. The smell of a dark corner and the spider under the porch were simply irrelevant to anyone but the cat. Its life was remote and unreachable, and the world of the merrymakers was equally alien and obscure.

A few of these tortured secondary victims were more fully aware of the Fourth of July holiday than in a quick, peripheral way, and they asked themselves if they should carry on, perhaps for the children, perhaps for their friend, perhaps for themselves. They wondered if they should make some effort to do normal things for the holiday, as a show of faith that their loved one would turn up alive, in case this brave act would impress God as a prayerful entreaty for a miracle. Some of them opened their kitchen cupboards and stared at the boxes of soda straws and sparklers and various other items that were there for the occasion, and they thought of what should have been and of who ought to have been there, and they wept. Most of them simply closed the cupboards.

*   *   *

Besides the rescuers, many other individuals and groups concerned in official capacities with the accident—medical examiners, army personnel, identification experts, airline executives, and crash investigators, to name a few—had also detached themselves from the holiday and worked right through it. Earlier in the day, Mr. Shelby McCauley, the coroner of Coconino County, Arizona, examined the United site from the air, hovering in a helicopter, and he concluded with certainty that everyone aboard the DC-7 had perished. The destruction was so total that there could not be the least rational hope of survivors.

McCauley was positive, and although he had not probed the wreckage searching for concealed survivors, he took the professional and moral risk of officially declaring everyone dead.

McCauley had already officially pronounced all of the victims at the TWA site dead on Tuesday, and the two determinations taken together constituted his vouching that there were no survivors at all. This ended the air force's obligation, which had been to search for survivors unless and until it were certified that there were none, and having fulfilled its obligation the air force officially withdrew. The Grand Canyon operations as a whole had been reduced from a search and rescue mission to a recovery mission, and the army took over coordinating in place of the air force.

Another major development was that the first identifications were made. Late in the day United Air Lines announced to the press that they had positively identified two victims: James W. Tobias, Jr., a marine corps captain from Philadelphia; and Carl G. Matland, a scientist for Westinghouse in Pittsburgh, Pennsylvania. These men of course came from the talus slope; there was nowhere else they could have been found, because no one had as yet reached the crest. United was discrete and dignified in not explicitly making that connection to the press, given the shocking, macabre nature of it, yet anyone following the stories at the time could easily have deduced it. After all this time, it is hopefully not inappropriate or insensitive for this book to reveal that awful fact; rather, it seems an honoring of the men to give the last circumstances or events of their lives, even if those events followed their deaths, which they surely did, and are only poetically parts of their lives. The woman who was found near them on Monday, by members of the TWA team that walked from Temple Butte to Chuar Butte, had been tentatively identified, but because a more conclusive proof was required to qualify as positive identification, her name was not revealed.

The United identification team at the Coconino County Fairgrounds had made remarkably swift progress considering that they had had the remains in their possession for examination only since that morning. Their success of course was a testament not only to their competence but also to the greatly superior condition of the remains when no fire was involved. As yet none of the TWA victims had been identified, even though some of them had been under examination since early Monday. This was no surprise, because none of the TWA victims had escaped the inferno. TWA's vice president of public relations, Gordon Gilmore, announced the sad failure, and he cared enough to courageously add that the airline did not want "to hold out the hope for identification to the relatives." It had appeared hopeless at the outset to the air force medics who examined the remains on Sunday, down in the canyon at the crash site; then on Monday the first were brought to the identification team at the fairgrounds in Flagstaff, and those experts had been awed at the daunting task and had added their own fears or convictions that it was impossible. From there the fruitlessness of two succeeding days of effort had demonstrated these impressions to be accurate, and the prospect had become even more dismal.

John Collings, TWA's executive vice president, announced that a mass funeral service and burial had been planned in consultation with the families for Monday, July 9 at 11:00 a.m., at Flagstaff Citizens' Cemetery. In part he said, "The instantaneous and complete nature of the accident has made it impossible to identify any of the individuals. Consequently, on the advice of State of Arizona officials and Coconino County officers, and with the approval of religious authorities, a single burial service was decided upon as the most reverent final tribute to the unfortunate passengers and crewmembers." There appeared to be no reasonable or decent alternative. If no remains could be identified, then to which families would they be sent for burial? Accordingly, work had already begun on a large plot measuring twenty-four feet by twenty-four feet. This may seem small for so many persons, and it was. The grave was conceived to accommodate all of the remains in individual caskets, corresponding with the individual bags that had contained them. There were only twenty-six bags, so only twenty-six caskets would be buried there according to the plan, not seventy, as things stood on Wednesday. The B. B. Bonner Construction Company of Flagstaff began that morning to prepare the burial site, using a power shovel with bulldozer treads and an articulated boom to excavate the huge hole.

*   *   *

In the canyon the on-site investigation of the wreckage at Temple Butte got into full swing on Independence Day. A large team of specialists labored at the TWA crash site to find clues in the scrap heap that might suggest what had happened. Some of the investigators were there even on Monday, but most arrived for the first time on Wednesday after waiting for the men who removed the bodies to finish their jobs on Tuesday. This was a new phase in the aftermath of the disaster, the first one that compelled no sense of urgency. The investigators could work calmly and deliberately, taking the time to pause and to try to visualize one aspect or another of what had occurred there. They were detectives, most of them highly trained in observing the physical evidence and in interpreting it, and they worked methodically and patiently to uncover the truth.

Many concerned organizations were represented, among them the two airlines, the Civil Aeronautics Board, the Air Line Pilots' Association, the Flight Engineers' Association, and Lockheed Aircraft Corporation, builder of the TWA Constellation. Irrespective of their affiliations they functioned as a team, without competitiveness or mistrust. They were there to find the truth, and the magnitude of the tragedy humbled them all, dissolving any petty rivalries or partisan loyalties. This was not a hunt for a scapegoat, nor even for someone to legitimately blame, but a heart-rending effort to uncover and face the reality of the tragedy.

Their first objective was to establish conclusively that a midair collision had occurred. Few people had any serious doubts about this because it was inescapably obvious that for two airliners to both crash in the same small area at the same time, out in the middle of nowhere, they must have run into each other. But it had to be proved, not just surmised. The team examined the Constellation's huge triple tail, which had fallen about a third of a mile north of the main wreckage. The distance made it incontrovertible that the tail had broken free of the rest of the airplane up in the air, but that did not in itself reveal the cause, which could have been structural or otherwise internal to the Constellation. A small portion of the fuselage immediately forward of the tail had remained attached to it and was deformed inward, yet it lacked the characteristic gouges that an impact with the rocky ground would have left inside the concavity; something else had crushed it. The deformed area was frightfully scuffed with red and blue paint. This was a very strong indication that the planes had collided—the Constellation had blue in its paint scheme in the minor areas of the American flags, but there was no reasonable explanation for how a piece of the fuselage with a flag painted on it could have struck the concaved area in flight. On the other hand, the DC-7 had blue prevalently in its color scheme, and there was already every reason to believe that it and the Constellation had struck each other in flight. It was easy to envision many ways in which this could have happened.

The team also found a piece of the Constellation's fuselage skin (i.e., the sheathing of curved sheet metal panels that makes up the outer surface) from the area of the upper right hand side just forward of the tail, measuring about one and a half feet by four feet, which was bent inward about 90 degrees and bore blue, red, and black paint smudges. Besides having blue and red in its paint scheme, the United DC-7's wings displayed its registration number in huge black characters, outlined in white. There were probably white scuffmarks, too, invisible on the white background of the Constellation's own paint.

Several pieces of the United DC-7's outer left wing structure were also found at the TWA wreckage site, most notably a section of skin from the underside of the wing, measuring about two feet by five feet.

On this piece of sheet metal was painted a portion of the numeral six and all of the numeral three, from the DC-7's registration number, N6324C. Scratches and scrape marks were evident, running diagonally aft and inboard through the black painted numerals, for the most part parallel to each other. A small fragment of TWA's cream-colored, cabin-headlining fabric was pinched in a tear in the skin, and running parallel with the scratches there were brown streaks of what was later identified as fuselage sealant used on the Constellation. It appeared that the outer end of the DC-7's left wing had struck and passed through the Constellation's aft fuselage just forward of the tail.

A compelling sidelight to this development concerned the enigmatic personage Howard Hughes. The appearance that the DC-7 had struck the Constellation in the rear, when combined with the facts that the DC-7 was the faster of the two planes and had left Los Angeles after the Constellation, made it enticing to jump to the conclusion that the United plane had struck the TWA plane from behind. On careless examination it looked like the DC-7 had overtaken and rear-ended the Constellation, which was totally false, and it would have made United solely responsible for the disaster. The fact was that the DC-7 had struck the Constellation *in* the rear, not *from* the rear. At the time, Howard Hughes owned the controlling interest in TWA and ran the company as much or more than its elected president did. One of his public relations men caught wind of the false notion, based on fragmentary news from the canyon regarding the specific damage that the DC-7 had inflicted on the Constellation, and contacted Hughes to relay the good news. Instead of being relieved or pleased, Hughes was offended and irritated, and he snapped, "Knock that shit off. I don't want either United or us blamed."

Unfortunately, the press also heard the rumors and, in the first days following the accident, published newspaper articles portraying United Air Lines as having caused it. These stories put forth the tale that the DC-7 had caught up with the Constellation and had rammed it from behind, and with the meager preliminary evidence, this impression was both obvious and compelling. The fact of the matter, however, was that the DC-7's outer left wing and the Constellation's tail and rear-most fuselage hit each other side-to-side, making the two of them equal perpetrators and equal victims. Through painstaking examination of the wreckage in the months that followed, investigators determined that, with United 718 on the right and TWA 2 on the left, the planes converged in a "V" configuration, about like a car on the expressway and another merging with it from the on ramp, with an angle of 25 degrees between their fuselages at the moment of impact. They sideswiped each other.

On the underside of the Constellation, just ahead of the main cabin entry door, was the loading hatch of the aft cargo hold. The investigators located this hatch and some of the framing that surrounded it, as well as some of the aft cargo hold flooring. All of these pieces bore long, curved gashes that were apparently propeller cuts. Along the edges of one cut were streaks of red and blue paint, consistent with the DC-7's paint scheme, in which the propeller blades were detailed near their tips with encircling red and blue stripes. It was later proved through laboratory analysis that the gashes were in fact propeller cuts, inflicted by the DC-7.

It was clear to the team that they had achieved their primary goal of proving, through physical evidence found in the wreckage, that the planes had hit each other. There had certainly been a midair collision. The same evidence had also answered half of the next most important question: did the collision by itself cause the subsequent crashes, or did the pilots also mishandle their damaged aircraft? In the case of TWA, it was absolutely obvious that the collision itself was enough. The DC-7's left wing evidently cut off the Constellation's tail, or perhaps more precisely, so seriously damaged the Constellation's fuselage just forward of the tail that the normal aerodynamic forces operating on the tail were able to tear it free of the airplane. Directly or indirectly, the collision had caused the Constellation's triple tail to separate from the plane, and without its tail the plane was uncontrollable; ergo the collision in itself made the Constellation crash. The fate of the DC-7 remained to be fully ascertained based on the wreckage at Chuar Butte, because the plane could conceivably have remained marginally flyable with a piece of a wing missing.

The team at Temple Butte was also intent upon discovering *why* the two airliners had collided. This was a much more difficult question to answer, one that might involve intangible elements like the quality of a given crewmember's attentiveness, or tangible but ephemeral elements like an erroneous evasive maneuver or an obscuring cloud, which left no trace of their existence in the physical evidence. Neither plane had a flight data recorder to reveal its final motions. Knowing that their prospects were not good, the team nevertheless exhaustively searched through the wreckage for any material clues from which even a part of the cause might be indicated.

It was possible that something went wrong on one of the planes just before the collision and became a contributing factor. Some control device may have malfunctioned, some electrical circuit may have shorted out causing a fire, the cabin may have lost pressurization, an engine may have blown, and so on. A great many possible problems could have been indicated by wreckage components that had not been utterly destroyed, or ruled out by the same or other evidence, and the team searched for anything they could find that might suggest what circumstances prevailed at the end. They found nothing indicative of any in-flight problems preceding the collision, and some evidence ruling out some possible problems, but not much of that. All the team was able to establish was that, on the basis of the evidence, the crew was operating the airplane under normal conditions. Much of the plane was simply not recovered and was presumed to have disintegrated in the crash or the ensuing fire. On the other hand, many components that the team did retrieve were too severely damaged to convey any significance. If some tragic mishap occurred aboard TWA Flight 2 prior to the collision, it was apparently destined to forever remain a secret of those who were aboard.

Another possibility was that the TWA crew had no clear line of sight to the DC-7, and so even in the best of conditions they could not have seen the plane. United might have been above or below or even behind TWA, making it impossible for the TWA crew to see them. The accident happened during the cruising phase of each flight, during nearly all of which a flight is moving straight ahead, not turning. Up until at most the last few seconds, when one or both crews might have spotted the other plane and made evasive maneuvers, the two planes most likely were moving in straight lines. And because neither could have changed its direction much in a couple seconds, the directions they were going when they hit each other were very close to, if not exactly the same as, the directions they were going just before they hit each other. This is the crucial point: most probably each plane had been flying steadily in approximately the same direction it had at impact, for some appreciable time before the collision.

The literal directions of the two planes—that is, their map courses—could not be determined from the collision evidence in the wreckage, but the *difference* in their directions could be. Most airplane collisions could be called instantaneous, because they happen so fast that the planes are in contact with each other for only a split second. A collision in which the planes come together flying in almost exactly the same direction, and skid along each other's surfaces for several seconds or even become interlocked, is extremely rare. In instantaneous collisions, the impact forces are much greater but are expressed for so brief a time that neither plane is appreciably turned by them. As a result, the damage that each one inflicts on the other is propagated in very nearly a straight line in each area of contact. The principle is the same as that by which a bullet fired at high speed into a densely compacted bale of hay passes straight through it, whereas a low speed bullet fired into the same bale of hay may be significantly deflected, following a curved path inside the bale and exiting at an angle quite different from the angle at which it entered.

The Grand Canyon accident qualified as an instantaneous collision. From a mathematical analysis of the propeller cut evidence, the rate at which the planes came together, called the closure rate, can be shown to have been tremendous—approximately 200 miles per hour at the moment they struck each other. That is, the side-to-side gap between them was closing at a rate of 200 miles per hour, shrinking at the equivalent rate of about one hundred yards per second. That's a football field per second. At this speed, the two planes passed straight *through* each other rather than bouncing off of each other. The DC-7's wing passed through the Constellation's fuselage, and the Constellation's fuselage passed through the DC-7's wing.

Because it follows a straight path, the damage done in an instantaneous collision has a direction that can be measured relative to one or another axis of the airplane. What's really interesting about this is the amazing fact that the line of sight between two planes shortly before they collide is parallel to the direction in which the collision damage runs across or through the planes, provided neither turns at the last moment. By measuring the angles of the scratches and tears and dents that each plane made on the other, investigators would in effect be measuring the angle of the line of sight to the other plane. Allowing for the fact that either plane might have turned at the last moment to avoid the other, these measurements would at least be close to the angle of the line of sight that each crew had shortly before the collision.

One way to visualize this is to imagine being an observer on one of the planes, looking out the window and watching the other plane approaching off in the distance. With respect to the point in the sky where the impending collision will take place, the planes are neck-and-neck with each other, because they will arrive there at exactly the same time. Along with flying in a straight line, the other predominant features of the cruising phase of a flight are that the plane holds a steady speed and altitude. Assuming that neither plane changes speed, they will remain neck-and-neck. The plane off in the distance outside of the window neither gains nor falls behind, and because both planes hold their altitude, it likewise does not drop or rise. To the observer, the other plane appears to be standing still in the sky—it holds its position outside of the window, like a speck of dirt adhering to the glass, and merely grows larger as time passes. If the observer could somehow witness the entire collision sequence, the other plane would appear to slide steadily sideways in the sky directly into his own plane, and to pass across or through it in the same line. Relatively speaking, the effect is the same as what would be produced if the observer's plane was sitting still on the ground, parked halfway across a straight, level length of railroad track, and the other plane was positioned sideways on a railroad flatcar rolling toward it at a steady speed. The railroad car simply delivers its airplane cargo directly into the observer's plane, at a constant speed, without veering side to side and without moving up or down.

If the observer is seated directly over the railroad track, then the other plane is coming right at him. His line of sight to the other plane is perfectly parallel to the track, which also makes it perfectly parallel to the line in which the other plane will inflict the collision damage.

This is as far as the analogy can be taken, because it implicitly treats the two planes as points rather than extended objects with three dimensions. Any observer is much smaller than the other plane, so of course it can never be true that every part of the other plane is coming right at him, no matter where he sits. At most, some spot on the other plane the size of the observer is coming right at him; and because it's a collision between two planes that we're talking about, not a collision between an observer and a plane, the truth is most directly and pertinently that at least one spot on the other plane is coming right at an equal-size spot on the first plane. This results in most or all observers' lines of sight, to most or all spots on the other plane, rotating rapidly in the last couple seconds before the collision, even if neither plane turns. But for most practical purposes this complication can be ignored. What counts is that the crew's line of sight to the other plane prior to the last couple seconds is approximately parallel to the direction in which the impending collision damage will be propagated.

For purposes of evaluating whether the crew had an opportunity to spot the other plane in time to evade it, it is the crew's line of sight prior to the last couple seconds, when they would have had time to get out of the other plane's way, that counts. In the last couple seconds an airplane that big could not be deflected substantially from its motion before that, so for the sake of determining how the accident was able to happen, all lines of sight, from any seat on the plane, up front or in the back, can be considered parallel to each other and to the direction in which the collision damage was propagated. Working backwards, the direction of the collision damage, projected outward from the plane, is the direction from which the other plane approached, growing nearer as it "slid sideways" in the sky.

The team at Temple Butte searched in the debris for pieces of the Constellation that had been damaged in measurable directions, so they could determine where the DC-7 came from. The band in which the DC-7's propeller cut the Constellation's fuselage ran laterally across the underside, showing that the DC-7 passed from one side to the other. An object moving from right to left had damaged the Constellation's tail, and also the upper right side of the fuselage in the rear, in the area between the propeller cuts and the tail. Metal had been crumpled leftward in both cases. Numerous other fragments were found bearing collision damage, but all of them were difficult to interpret with any precision. All that could be determined down in the canyon was that the DC-7 had come from the Constellation's right, not from behind, and right was only a rough idea, nothing like saying, "Ninety degrees right of dead ahead."

Another of the numerous peculiarities of this sad, bizarre accident was that wreckage at the TWA site told what the final moments were like for United, and not for TWA. Even though the overwhelming majority of parts were from the TWA plane, the few parts from the United plane that had fallen there told very precise stories. The scratched piece of the DC-7's lower, outer left wing panel was as good as a diagram of what had happened. The scratches ran diagonally aft and inboard, all basically parallel to each other, at an angle of about 25 degrees in relation to the lateral axis of the plane. This axis was defined by an internal wing structure called the center spar, which ran straight down the length of the wing, and it was with reference to this that the measurement was taken. The scratches were plainly caused by the collision, not by rocks as the fragment came to rest on the ground, and they eerily showed what direction the Constellation had come from: it had closed on the DC-7 from a bearing of about 65 degrees left of dead ahead. (See Appendix 7 for a drawing of how they collided.)

Instead of the evidence suggesting that one or both planes had come from a direction in which they could not have been seen, it showed clearly that United 718 should have been able to see TWA 2, and it strongly though roughly indicated that TWA 2 should have been able to see United 718. Each crew apparently had a clear line of sight to the other plane unless, that is, something else obscured it.

Wednesday had been another very long day for all of the men in the canyon. They had been up since before dawn. Late in the day some of the men at each of the two buttes bathed in the Colorado River to cool off and to wash. Just before dusk charcoal-broiled steaks were served to the men at Chuar Butte, at their river-level camp on the sandy west bank. That evening Lewis, Batson, Pavlik, and Welch formulated their plans for Thursday.

Batson, Pavlik, and Welch would follow the established route along the ledge system, accompanied by another mountaineer named Allen Auten, who was expected to arrive early Thursday morning. Auten was a member of the Colorado Mountain Club and was already en route. He would take Lewis' place in the four-man climbing team, while a helicopter took Lewis to the crest of the crash promontory. Because a landing had been ruled out, the plan was that the helicopter would hover 30 feet or more above the crest, and Lewis would climb down or be lowered from there. A spool of rope would then be dropped to him, and he would in turn lower this rope to his teammates on the ledge system below.

The helicopter pilots were apprehensive about the strong, shifting air currents that were sure to be flowing over the surface of the crash promontory and swirling in space nearby. These would make it difficult to keep a helicopter over the same spot, at a fixed distance above it – the machine would be buffeted in all three dimensions. There were several ways that Lewis could get from the helicopter to the crest of the shoulder: he could climb down a line of rope, he could climb down a rope ladder, and he could be lowered in a sling. If the H-21 were hit by a sharply impulsive gust in any direction but down, it would jerk the rope or the ladder in the same direction, and Lewis might lose his grip and fall. On the other hand, if Lewis were very near the ground in the sling, and the H-21 were shoved sideways, he could be dragged over rocks, because he could not simply let go. And if the helicopter were dropped by the wind, there would be no advantage in any means over the others, because Lewis would fall to the ground as though the equipment suspending him had been cut. No matter how it was to be done, it would be dangerous, and so the plan was to risk it with only one man, not all five. The others would climb up, the consensus being that this was safer and more predictable despite all of the loose rock on the ledges and in the crash gully.

*   *   *

It was an incomparably beautiful summer night, scintillating and magical. The men at Chuar Butte were on what could have been the ultimate campout, in the midst of the unsurpassed beauty of unspoiled nature. The gorge surrounding them was filled with the song of crickets, declaring their importance from the bushes along the river's edge. In the background the river whooshed like a steady wind in trees as it flowed unceasingly past. The air smelled of the water and of clean stone, and in the heavens were a million benevolent lights, reassuring all those who beheld them that they were loved by the universe. Sadly, most of the men only dimly felt these wonders. In the face of the reality that they were there to deal with death, most could hardly surpass a feeling of reserve and resolve. They were also exhausted, from the hardships of the day. Their work had been laborious and sweltering. Tiredness was the richest feeling that most of them had, and they rested until they fell asleep on the sand.

All across the country fireworks exploded and erupted in dazzling spheres and fountains of electric-neon sparks. Crowds in every town thrilled as the night skies lit up and crackled. It was dark and yet nothing was asleep, not even listless, not even the ground squirrels resting in their burrows to wait out the night. Every blade of grass seemed poised to move, charged by the urge to express its wakefulness though unable to act. The air itself was vibrantly alive with the energy of the midsummer heat. And then the heavens, too, came alive, leaving not even the void in tranquility. Everywhere life celebrated itself, and scarcely a living thing was unaware of the display. Summer danced in the streets of its own enchantment, and on that night Americans added their own festival to nature's exuberance.

Within the great and widespread jubilation there were other, lesser worlds that went unnoticed by most. Like the quiet, sequestered, alter-reality inside the fortuneteller's tent at a carnival, there were unobtrusive realities in the homes of the victims' families, right in the midst of the festivities and yet profoundly dissociated. Most of the people who had lost a loved one were oblivious to the Fourth of July and knew only their own grief and sense of doom, and the terrible truth that was gaining material reality in their lives. For a few of them, however, it was as though they had lost their minds. The alarming stimulation of the fireworks augmented their anguish, and the two together were overwhelming, so bewildering that they lost all perspective and fell into a surreal agony. It was as though they were being purged of sin by torture, stripped of all vanity and worldly ambition by the ordeal of pain and horror. Their trauma was like the madness of an excruciating injury, and yet in its crazed fervor it had the feel and the supernatural portent of martyrdom and spiritual transcendence. With each explosion of a skyrocket, bursting into a brilliantly colored globe of embers, it was as though the person himself had exploded, as though his mind had exploded and burst into some new and insane form, abandoning him to stand naked before God or before the devil. There was no fighting it; there was no hope of resistance, nor even the impulse to resist. Each had been taken and writhed but did not struggle to free himself.

Finally the fireworks desisted, and the torment of those few possessed souls began to subside. They were released from their mad hallucinations and were overcome by an oppressive relative peace, like that in the collapse of a convict when the whipping stops. But most of the people whose loved ones were aboard Flight 2 or Flight 718 took no notice at all of society's doings. They were not perturbed by the onset of the noise, nor relieved by its cessation. For them, the fireworks of the Fourth of July, 1956, never were.

Chapter 16

It was Thursday, July 5, the fifth day since the accident, and as the diffuse light of dawn illuminated the butte, revealing it once again to the men at the base camp, it towered above them in imposing indifference, still impregnable. The daily compounded indignity of the victims' remains decomposing in the open air was reaching atrocious proportions. It was a disgrace, and although no one could be faulted or blamed for how long it was taking to reach the crash site, many workers were beginning to feel a subtly shameful urgency, a pained sense of obligation to both the dead and their grieving loved ones. The delays and the failures had to stop, and if anything, most of the workers felt more determined, not discouraged.

Following Palen Hudgin's directions, search and rescue personnel had officially located the United wreckage on Sunday, and as the various workers came on the scene that day and on Monday, Tuesday, and Wednesday, they all saw exactly where it was. The advance party had landed on the sandbar at the west bank of the Colorado River just after dawn on Tuesday and had established a base camp on the beach. Ever since then, members of the United team had been stationed there and had only to look up and point at the spot to place themselves in relation to it. Literally and figuratively, they had been through long travels to be standing there and to be understanding what it meant to be there. In stages, each of them had progressed from having very little conception of the situation to ultimately apprehending the gargantuan scale of everything in the Grand Canyon, most especially the butte that towered before them asserting its greatness and its awesome power to exist, to endure, and to remain where it was. Its unmovable presence confronted all who began to grasp it with the unmistakable truth of their own inherent fragility, impotence, and mortality. They could be witness to its stature and its permanence while remaining forever removed, unable to partake of them. And in concordance, it appeared that the men would also remain materially removed from the butte. All of them had come there through circuitous routes, from far away, and each time they looked, it was more painfully obvious than the last that they could not cross the final, small space between themselves and their destination. They were very close but were stymied there, able to get no closer.

The problems associated with landing a helicopter near the crash site were numerous. As with airplanes, takeoffs and landings were the most dangerous phases of a flight in a helicopter. Very near to the ground there was little margin for error, because the helicopter could crash before the crew had time to react, or even before they recognized that they were in trouble. It was imperative to minimize any factors that could make the machine difficult or unpredictable to control, because so near to the ground, any instability could cause it to *hit* the ground.

One thing that could destabilize it was the wind. In proportion to its severity, a gust would rock the helicopter, tipping it back and forth, and the pilots might lose control. Far up in the air they would usually have time to effectively respond, but very near to the ground they might not. The alternative to regaining control was to crash, and even at the low speed of coming down to land, a crash could be fatal. The huge rotors would chop into the ground and become bent or broken, likely shaking the helicopter apart or cutting into the fuselage, which in turn could cause a fire and destroy the helicopter and its occupants.

As the helicopter neared the ground, the downwash of air from its rotors would become packed underneath them, in between them and the ground, creating a sort of cushion. If the ground was uneven, the cushion would be uneven, unbalancing the helicopter, and the pilots might have serious control problems.

And then there was contact with the surface to consider. If it were uneven, a coordinated touchdown would be difficult to manage, likely resulting in the wheels making contact out of order, complicating the procedure. The same unevenness would set the machine cockeyed at rest, once it was down. How serious either of these problems would be depended upon how uneven the ground was. Beyond a modest point, the helicopter could actually tip over. With the engine running and the rotors spinning, the results would again be catastrophic.

The prospect of landing up at the crash site was much more threatening than promising. Every area appeared too small, too narrow, too undulating, too arched, too sloped, or too beset with boulders. There was no good place on the crest of the shoulder, and farther inland into the main body of the butte, it was even worse. With wind compounding the other difficulties, it was somewhere between reckless and crazy to even try. In view of all of this, the army helicopter pilots had become resigned to settling for second best: hovering and lowering a man to the crash site from a safe position above it.

At about 7:15, Captain Walter Spriggs and his copilot, Chief Warrant Officer Howard Proctor, were hovering their H-21 over the United crash area. Aboard was David Lewis, who was preparing to climb down a knotted rope to the promontory 30 feet below. The plan was that Lewis would find a way down from there to the ledge system, trailing his rope behind him like an explorer opening a trail through the jungle. His fellow mountaineers would meet him on the ledges, and all of them would then use the rope to climb to the top.

As the helicopter swayed in the fluctuating breezes, a third crewmember, called the loadmaster, dropped a large spool of rope out of the open cargo door for Lewis to use in that endeavor. At the last moment before Lewis ventured into the open air, dangling from the knotted rope, Spriggs made the daring, spontaneous decision to attempt a landing. He boldly put the machine into a descent, and the ground began rising up to meet it. Beneath him was a small, uneven, tilted area, primarily free of rocky rubble. The ground they were over was bad enough to be a foolhardy choice, but it was the best to be had. Everyone tensed in that suspenseful moment, submitting to where he was going and fearing what was going to happen to him when he got there; they truly did not know if they were going to survive the attempt. And then they were down. To Spriggs and Proctor's amazement, they had not slammed into the ground. All in the space of a breath, their tension became elation, and they realized that the helicopter had not tipped over. It felt stable. In surprise and relief, Spriggs proudly said to Lewis, "Well, here you are, buddy."

Neither pilot had ever attempted a maneuver as hazardous, and later, both pilots were quoted as saying that it was the most dangerous landing they had ever heard of.

They had landed a couple hundred feet west of the main crash area. Spriggs left the engine running, and the helicopter's twin rotors continued to whip around deafeningly, at reduced power, while the loadmaster helped Lewis unload the rest of his gear. They wasted no time, recognizing that undoing the landing would be extremely dangerous, too, posing all of the same hazards in reverse. In a few minutes everything was unloaded, and the crew exchanged good-byes with Lewis. From their perspective, they were abandoning him on a virgin frontier, to face whatever dangers and trials lay before him in solitude. From his perspective, his last link with humanity was about to depart, leaving him more isolated than he had ever been. As Lewis ran to avoid the blowing dust and grit, the helicopter increased power and lifted off. He was alone. In his own words, he clearly knew the meaning of, "Burning your bridges behind you."

Finally a man was on top of Chuar Butte at the crash site. The feat that was thought impossible had been accomplished, by a method that was feared impossible. David Lewis was there, and no one had died getting him there.

The tremendous responsibility of searching for the victims of the world's worst civil air disaster rested for that moment on a young man who was not yet even legally a man. His youthfulness accentuated his peripheral feeling of insecurity about standing alone with such a monumentally important task ahead of him, and he felt his individuality keenly and with awe.

It may seem strange by modern standards that such a responsibility was delegated to so young a man, and in the larger sense, to an informal organization of volunteers. They were simply mountaineering enthusiasts who cared enough about others to have formed a club dedicated to rescuing injured or stranded campers and mountain climbers. They were not career professionals in their field, but these were the real experts, among the best in the whole country, as they had already amply demonstrated in the work they did at the Medicine Bow Peak crash. They were also Americans in the best tradition—civilian volunteers. They were like a militia: independent, dedicated, and competent. They dressed according to their own tastes rather than wearing uniforms, and they were not regulated by any federal standards. There was no need of regulating them or certifying them, and trying to make them all the same would have missed the point. They were accomplished largely because they were individuals, leading their own lives.

Among other things, Lewis had an olive drab regulation army safety can, filled with five gallons of water, two large wooden spools of white nylon rope, and a radiotelephone. His first objective was to establish radio contact with his teammates far down below, at the river. He sought a spot at the edge of the cliff from which he could see the base camp, the idea being that the same absence of obstructions that afforded him a clear line of sight would also permit him the best reception. Lewis walked along the crest from the landing area eastward, toward its extremity, carrying the radiotelephone with him. He had to pass the crash area in between, and as he walked along the upper rim of the gully in which the *City of Vancouver* had disintegrated, he came upon the first body. Right on the crest, removed from all of the other victims and from nearly all of the wreckage, was a lone body clothed in the uniform of a United Air Lines flight crewmember. Lewis could see the company shield and logo plainly on the belt buckle. It was Captain Shirley.

Lewis had seen death before and also had the peculiar attitude of disaster workers, wherein the horrors are regarded by the intellect, not the heart, and viewed as business to be attended to rather than as human tragedy. For both reasons, his composure was hardly ruffled. He began to feel something but walked on. There was nothing he could do with the body for the time being, and he needed to make contact with the men at the base camp.

Lewis stopped near the eastern end of the promontory and unburdened himself of his very heavy radio equipment. Standing at the edge of the cliff, looking down, he could see the tiny images of the other men. He set up his radiotelephone, turned on the power switch . . . and nothing happened. The radio didn't work. Without a radio Lewis was totally cut off, by himself in a place where probably no other human being had ever been, with no way even to communicate with his fellow man. The emotional numbness that shielded him from the terrible fate suffered by the crash victims did not protect him from feeling his own circumstances, and having been caught unprepared by the surprise of his equipment failing, Lewis could not help but be distressed.

The helicopter crew felt encouraged by their successful landing and had decided on the spot to go back down to base camp and get Raymond Batson, Lewis' friend and close associate in the RMRG, to fly him up to the crash area to join Lewis. Batson would be there directly if all went well, because there was no time to delay. The pilots regarded their success as improbable good fortune, which would certainly not be repeatable if even one of the factors were to become less advantageous or more adverse, and they were anxious to make use of the opportunity while it existed.

In the meantime, Lewis began to look around. He walked back across the upper rim of the gully, the top edge of where nature had chiseled the gully away from the promontory, and appraised the wreckage from the immediate west. Thousands of mangled fragments of the *City of Vancouver* littered the gully, from the top all the way down to where it turned so steeply that it dropped out of sight over its own cliff. It was very strange—there was no *color*. The gully was an anomaly of silver and black.

Lewis walked into the top, central area of the sloping field of junk, where the grade was only moderate, and examined one of the few identifiable bits of wreckage, the remains of the nose landing gear. The nose gear mechanism was still fairly well together and lay on top of a neatly stacked pile of thin gauge steel wire hoops a little over three feet in diameter, the vestiges of the steel-belted front tire after the rubber had burned away.

For all its clutter, the tilted landscape of the gully was barren because it was almost entirely devoid of objects of any perceptible function, present or past. Like a field of nothing but broken rocks, none of the shapes could be said to have any purpose, nor could they be traced to lost purposeful origins. There was nothing there, a tremendous lot of nothing.

Most of the substance of the *City of Vancouver* and most of the human beings aboard it had lodged in the gully. Some aircraft debris had been cast over the ridge to the northern face of the shoulder and had fallen to the ledges or the talus below. Some of the wreckage, and three of the victims, had rolled down the gully to its mouth at the south cliff face and had kept right on going, falling to the talus slope far below the crash site. Some of the wreckage that fell down the south cliff face landed on the ledges and stayed there. Some debris—and possibly some victims, though the latter was never proved or disproved—fell into the chimneys whose tops were at the mouth of the gully, rather than sailing over these great vertical channels. But very little debris came to rest on the ridge, immediately outside the top end of the gully, and only one victim. At the highest elevation in the crash scene, in the only basically clear area, was where the captain prominently lay. It was as though he had been put there deliberately, as to proclaim and decry the horrible reality below him.

Lewis' solitude lasted for only about twenty minutes; it ended with the return of Spriggs' helicopter and the arrival of Raymond Batson. Without delay the machine was airborne again, leaving Batson behind in its rotor wash. No other landings would be attempted that day. As the H-21 wheeled off in the distance, the first thing that the two friends did was to try getting their radiotelephone working. They soon discovered that the problem was a faulty power switch, fortunately about the simplest thing that could have gone wrong. Even though no one had anticipated this contingency, and consequently no one had prepared for it, they managed to get the radio apart enough to expose the bad switch and rig a temporary repair. How they did that was the really incredible thing.

The DC-7 was a masterpiece of engineering complexity and ingenuity. Like the human body it had skin and a skeleton and numerous organs underneath, with a variety of utility systems spread throughout that controlled it and enabled it to function, most of which were arranged in bilaterally symmetrical configurations. There was a left aileron and a right aileron, a left generator and a right generator, a left flux-gate compass and a right flux-gate compass, and so on, analogous to all of the paired, left and right side features or organs of the human body. There was a hydraulic system and a fuel system, each pumping fluids to wherever they were needed, and there were air scoops that channeled fresh air to the engines so that they could breathe. There were fantastically complex systems of steel cables and turnbuckles and pulleys and levers, for controlling everything from remote fire extinguishers to the rudder, like muscles and tendons that would tighten or loosen and engage or relax them. And like a human being's nervous system, there was also a phenomenally intricate and extensive electrical system. A DC-7 was among the most profusely, versatilely wired of man's inventions. It had the better part of a hundred cockpit instruments, several radios, numerous cockpit warning lights and passenger cabin lights, electric facilities in the galley, a music system, an intercom, a PA system, and on, and on, and on. *The City of Vancouver* was outfitted with roughly 90,000 feet of electrical wire, enough to have strung the length of the fuselage 900 times!

The shambles of the wreckage was terrible, everything scattered and mixed and incinerated. All manner of materials could be found strewn near the edge of the burn area and beyond, including wiring. Lewis and Batson scavenged the debris and found a useable length of it. A switch after all simply jumps the gap between two or more electrical terminals, connecting them to each other, and that's what the wire did. They connected it to serve as a makeshift switch, and the radio came to life.

In the months and years to come, many people who had been devastated by the tragedy would also be progressively endowed with a special, abiding growth in their humanity, becoming wiser and more compassionate through their terrible struggle to survive and carry on as feeling persons. Many people not crushed by the disaster would become more humane, in one small but significant measure or another, by the act of choosing to care about the people who lost their lives, or about the loved ones they left behind, or even about the lot of man in his powerlessness to control fate or evade it. But the first benefit to anyone was bestowed upon L. David Lewis and Raymond Batson in their ephemeral, purely practical, relatively trifling need to repair a radio. The horrendous tragedy that had befallen the victims had also provided the two rescuers with a piece of wire.

They draped a black and yellow reversible tarp over the edge of the cliff, yellow side out, at the eastern end of the promontory, securing it with stones. Like a flag, the tarp clearly indicated the position of the radio and its operator to the men at the base camp far below. The base camp was fairly easy to distinguish from high above, because of the volume of equipment and the numbers of men, but from below, no encampment would be visible above, any more than it would be if it were set up on the roof of a tall building. Only something positioned at the edge of the cliff or the edge of the roof would be discernible from below, and only then if it were big enough or colorful enough. The tarp was both, whereas the figure of a man, especially one dressed in drab hiking clothes, was neither.

Having established communications, Lewis and Batson began the work they had come to do. They began uncoiling about 2,000 feet of nylon rope, which they intended to cut into lengths of about 300 feet for use in climbing down into the lower reaches of the crash gully. To do this, they stretched the rope out, back and forth, across the small landing zone where the H-21 had alighted a short time before. When they finished unreeling it, over a third of a mile of rope lay zigzagged across an area of only about half an acre.

In the meantime, even though Allen Auten had arrived to take Lewis' place, the plan to scale the shoulder was called off, because it appeared that it would be possible to simply drop off all of the workers by helicopter. A landing had already been done twice. It was also beginning to look feasible to remove bodies and wreckage directly from the crest. The alternative was lowering them to the ledges, suspended from ropes, and from there to the talus slope. This would be an extremely difficult operation, largely because they would repeatedly drag and catch on the jagged surface of the cliff face. For a portion of its length near its middle elevation, the steepness of the gully actually increased beyond vertical, cutting inward under itself. Other than in that area, the gully was very steep over most of its length but not fully vertical, so anything lowered down it would slide down its face rather than dangle free, standing off from it. Airlifting the remains and the evidence from the crash area would be far superior if it could be done.

After cutting the lengths of rope and making hundred-yard coils of them, a bulk and weight that could be slung over a shoulder and carried easily enough, Lewis and Batson walked from the flattish landing area toward the narrower extremity of the crest to the east, and looked down the blackened gully. Everything in it was either charred or silver-colored, both of which were unnatural in almost any terrain, almost anywhere on earth, and this lent a bizarre cast to the whole scene. Everything that could burn had burned and turned black, and the ground was covered in a dense layer of black soot. Interrupting this ugly landscape were numerous shiny, silver formations, huge globs of melted aircraft aluminum. They had solidified as nodules, pools, and rivulets. In many areas the molten metal had run downhill, flowing like lava, and had coagulated and finally congealed as it spread and cooled. The simple geometries conceived by man had been dissolved and transformed into random shapes conforming to no regular schemes. Nowhere to be found was there a straight edge or a consistent curve or a uniform thickness or any symmetry, but only free-form expressions of metal cast outside of any mold. Moreover, the resolidified liquid metal had been purified by the fire, purged of all the flammable things that were attached to it, stripped of its paint, and cleansed as a refinery might have done. The formations of aluminum were in most cases spotlessly clean and shiny, as though they had been polished, completely at odds with the utter contamination that the violent mixing and burning of earth together with all manner of manmade materials had wrought. The purified metal that had burgeoned all over the place was as incongruous within the blackened wreckage area as the wreck itself was on the formerly pristine shoulder of Chuar Butte.

The two men slowly walked down into the gully, without the use of their ropes for the time being. They were in no significant danger near the top of the gully, because in that area it sloped downward at an angle of only about twenty degrees on average, not steep enough to make a person slide or tumble very far if he fell. One by one they discovered more bodies, but these had little resemblance to the one up on the crest. The bodies in the gully had been incinerated. None of them had any clothing, and all of them were encrusted over their entire surfaces in thick layers of charcoal. It was a horrific sight, and carried with it an instinctively recognizable, ghastly odor that saturated the surrounding air. Just as the presence of a cave in the forest is known first by an incongruous, damp, cold draft, it was not necessary to see the bodies in order to know that death was there.

Lewis and Batson had not included any body bags or protective sheeting in the minimal selection of vital equipment that they brought, so the remains could not be moved or even covered. For only two men to carry them up the rocky slope would be extremely laborious even with a stretcher; with only bags, it would be backbreaking, just barely possible, and definitely ill-advised. Without any hauling equipment whatsoever, the job would be so strenuous and awkward that it might as well be impossible. So they left them where they found them, to be moved later. All the two could do was memorize the locations.

During the early afternoon, the terrific heat surpassed 100° F. The stifling air and the blazingly hot, bright sun were so oppressive that the two men were forced to stop working. Lewis later recalled having submitted and said, "We hit a low point in morale that Thursday afternoon. As we sweltered in the hundred-degree heat on the butte, we watched the others below swimming in the river. We sat on the edge with our feet dangling toward the river, but two thousand feet is a long way down. It didn't help a bit." At river level, it was probably more like 110° F or 115° F, but the river was cool and refreshing. The men at the base camp suffered the more stifling heat, but they also had a way to escape it, whereas Lewis and Batson faced a less fiery oven but were captive in it. Both situations were miserable to such an extreme that there was little meaning in weighing which was worse, and if the men had been able to move back and forth between the crash site and the base camp, most of them would probably have changed their minds several times.

Later in the day, the temperature began to drop back toward a tolerable level. The stone walls of the canyon below were like firebrick inside a mythically huge kiln, whose power source was the sun's direct rays, but in the later afternoon the lower reaches of the gorge were in the shadow of Chuar Butte, and the stifling convection currents were subsiding. Moreover, the promontory on which Lewis and Batson sat was then in the shade of the top of the butte, which rose nearly another half mile skyward, toward the west of the wreckage area. They felt rejuvenated by the sensation of a little relief, meager as it was, and even though the air was still very hot, they resumed their work.

By the end of the day, they had found six bodies in the gully, all in the upper portion. Most of the wreckage was in the severely steep lower reaches of the gully, but they didn't venture there that day. Instead, they examined the lower gully from several vantage points on the crest, in an effort to discern a good route of descent. It was immediately apparent that the climb would be dangerous, due to the prevalence of loose debris. Though climbing down belayed would be essential because of the grade, the climb in itself was not any special challenge or hazard for mountaineers, and despite the debris, it did not even entail much risk of them losing their footing. Rather, the real danger was that rocks or fragments of wreckage might tumble down the steep slope and strike a climber below. The movements of his rope, wherever it was in contact with the terrain above him, might dislodge loose objects. An even greater risk was that if they both made the climb down, the following climber's boots might send debris crashing down the gully toward the leading climber below. In Lewis' own words, "A good part of the difficulty of this operation was getting the bodies out without killing each other with falling debris."

In humble observance of this ubiquitous danger, Lewis and Batson carefully planned how they would enter into the lower gully. They had already spent enough of the day that there simply was not ample time for the actual descent, and accordingly they planned it for Friday. Besides this, the men anticipated the arrival of their teammates early Friday morning, and possibly also a crack team of Swiss rescuers that were on their way to the United States from Zurich. (Unbeknownst to Lewis and Batson, the Swiss team had arrived in New York earlier in the day and was already en route for Denver.) The president of Swiss Air had telephoned Pat Patterson, the president of United Air Lines, via the transatlantic cable shortly after hearing the terrible news, to offer any help that he could and to suggest the Swiss mountaineers. Patterson had gratefully accepted, being a man of principles more than pride, because the United team was wrestling with extreme difficulties and at the time had not yet landed anyone up at the crash site. The plan was that Swiss Air would fly the men to New York, from where United Air Lines would take over transporting them to the scene, flying them to Denver's Stapleton Airfield, Flagstaff Municipal Airport, and Grand Canyon Airport in succession. The army would then fly them in helicopters across the last leg to the crash area.

In view of who was coming and who might be coming, it simply made more sense for Lewis and Batson to wait to hear the opinions of the other experts than to move ahead with a good, but only preliminary, assessment of the situation. For this reason, too, they refrained from attempting to climb farther down the gully Thursday. Instead, they began to set up their rudimentary camp for the night ahead.

* * *

Thursday was also the day of a somber, vital breakthrough. That morning, TWA overturned their avowal of Wednesday that no one would be identified and announced their first positive identification, that of Mrs. Virginia Elizabeth Goppert, of Kansas City, Missouri. They had identified her by her wedding ring. Mrs. Goppert was forty-six and left behind a husband, a son, a daughter, two brothers, two sisters, and two grandchildren. She had been the secretary treasurer for the Sunday school at her church, Swope Park Christian Church in Kansas City, for ten years, and for her service, a memorial fund was later set up in her name there. On July 12, the local memorial service for Mrs. Goppert was held, and four hundred people attended. Her niece and traveling companion, Sally Cressman, was never identified.

TWA also announced that the memorial grave at Flagstaff Citizens' Cemetery would be enlarged to seventy-two by twenty-four feet, triple its originally planned size. The recovered remains could have been accommodated by the smaller grave, but TWA officials, in consultation with the families, had made the decision to honor every one of the unidentified victims with a symbolic casket, and to include the remains of any identified victim whose family wished it. It appeared that several victims would be positively identified after all, and accordingly TWA anticipated that probably only sixty some caskets would be interred in the memorial plot, in view of the likelihood that the relatives of some of the identified victims would prefer private services and burials. Nevertheless, preparations were made to honor all seventy victims, not only in spirit but also in the actual interment of at least a representative casket, and in keeping with this the grave was enlarged enough to accommodate them all. The truth of course was that most of the caskets would be empty.

Late in the day, TWA announced to the press that they had made two more positive identifications, those of nineteen-year-old Stephen Robert Bishop and the infant, three-week-old Howard John Maag. Stephen Bishop lived in Kansas City, Missouri, where he worked as a file clerk for TWA, and he was returning there after a family reunion in his hometown of Medford, Oregon. He had taken the trip free of transportation charges, flying on an employee pass. Stephen Bishop left behind both of his parents, four sisters, and a brother.

Howard Maag's parents, Mr. John Otto Maag and his wife, Mrs. Claire M. Maag, were taking him to St. Louis to meet Mr. Maag's family. Instead of having a joyful family reunion and new uniting, members of the Maag family would fly to Arizona on Sunday, July 8, on a special TWA charter plane carrying mourners to the mass funeral service and burial. The family had already planned a memorial service for little Howard and his parents, to be held on the following day, Friday, July 6, at the St. Lucas Evangelical and Reformed Church in Sappington, Missouri, a suburb of St. Louis. In the early days after the accident, there had been room to doubt that Howard was on the plane, because his name was not on the passenger manifest. When TWA announced that they had positively identified him, any hopeful doubts were extinguished. Everyone attending the service the next day grieved all the more in the acute certainty that the baby they never even got to meet was gone.

Virginia Goppert, Stephen Bishop, and Howard Maag were ultimately buried four days later in the mass memorial grave in Flagstaff, at the wishes of surviving family members. Virginia Goppert stayed with her niece, and Stephen Bishop stayed with his friends from TWA. Being so new to the world, Howard Maag had not lived long enough to have any sort of life of his own outside the love and care of his parents. He was still in that magical, beautiful stage of life before identity, joined as one with them, and that pure and sacred union was to be revered. Howard's parents were never identified, and he stayed with them.

CHAPTER 17

AT TWO O'CLOCK in the morning, a United Air Lines Convair 340 took off from Stapleton Airfield with eight Swiss Alpinists aboard, heading southwest toward Flagstaff, five hundred miles away.

At about 5:00 a.m., the Convair 340 descended through a sky that was becoming suffused with light from beneath the eastern horizon, and it touched down at Flagstaff Municipal Airport, rolling down the lone cinder runway and coming to a stop. Along with a great deal of special climbing and rescue equipment, some of which was of their own design and unique in the world, the Swiss quickly transferred from the Convair 340 to a waiting United DC-3. The sun reached the surface while they worked, and the ethereal backlighting evaporated like a morning fog under its direct radiance. Soon the DC-3 took off and climbed away from the airport in the full brightness of sunrise. The same landscape below, which had been shrouded in the last shadows of night as they came in to land, was then gloriously vivified by the sun's brilliance, not only illuminated but enhanced in color and sharpness by the morning shadows that outlined the western edges of things. The travelers passed over this transformed wonderland as they headed northward toward Grand Canyon Airport, fifty miles away.

After about a half hour of flying, hardly enough time for their ears to pop and clear in the unpressurized DC-3, the Swiss team was on the ground at Grand Canyon Airport. The sun was hot as they unpacked their gear, and the air and the land still held the cool freshness of the night and the morning dew. They cast long shadows and felt the newness of the day as they transferred their equipment once more, this time to an army H-21 helicopter. It was Friday, July 6.

The sun gently and persuasively awakened Lewis and Batson with its bright light and its heat, and they arose with it. They marked the best landing spot, which was also the only reasonable landing spot, with the yellow tarp, to make its location clear to any new pilots that might be arriving and doubly clear to those who had already been there. The tarp had fulfilled its purpose of showing the men at the riverbed where the radio was stationed up high on the promontory, and it was no longer needed as a flag draped over the cliff.

The two men awaited the arrival of their fellow climbers, Charles Pavlik, Fred Welch, and Allen Auten. They also hoped to be joined by the Swiss climbers and Captain Carl Christenson. In addition to his involvement in the investigations of several other aircraft accidents, Christenson had distinguished himself in the field of safety in several areas, including research on the formation of ice on an airplane's wings in flight, and the development of exterior warning lights to make planes more conspicuous. Perhaps his most important work was in developing dim, red cockpit lighting for night flying. This eliminated the dangerous moments of blindness between looking at the instruments with a flashlight and looking at the dark sky outside, while still illuminating the instruments plenty well enough to be readable. His red lighting was eventually adopted by all the airlines and became an industry standard in both commercial and private aviation.

The three additional Colorado mountaineers were airlifted to the United crash site very early, along with a substantial complement of rations and equipment, including body bags. These gruesome devices were made of heavy canvas impregnated and coated with brown or olive drab rubber, and they were outfitted with handles at both ends. In their basic design they were very much like garment bags. A zipper ran the full length of the top surface down the center. Because the whole bag opened up rather than only an end, the remains could be spared the further indignity of being pushed in or having the bag shimmied up around them, as a pillowcase might be pulled side to side over a pillow. To use one, the rescuers would outstretch it next to a victim, unzip it lengthwise, lay the body in it as it might have been laid on a stretcher, and then pull the zipper closed.

Carl Christenson also arrived very early, accompanied by three other men from United Air Lines. With the bags, and with several men rather than only two, it became practical for Lewis and Batson to remove the bodies that they had found on Thursday. The men began the gruesome work of picking up the remains and encasing them, and one by one they carried the sacks up the slope of the gully and across the gentler grade up to the helicopter landing area. Once there, they opened the zippers just enough to permit pouring a bottle of formaldehyde into each bag, to retard further decay and to abate the stench. Before long they had prepared all seven for transport, and the men turned their attention to searching through the wreckage in the upper gully for more bodies.

As the Americans labored in the gully extricating remains from the wreckage, some of the Swiss mountaineers arrived on the scene. Rather than landing right away, they examined the situation from the air, hovering close by, in an effort to absorb it in its entirety and to ascertain how climbers might most safely enter the treacherous lower gully. At the same time, Coconino County Coroner Shelby McCauley was conducting the coroner's inquest into the TWA crash, which had convened at 9:00 a.m. in the Coconino County Courthouse. Some of the witnesses were Dr. Harold Dye, TWA's director of medical services, who had examined all of the remains; Robert E. Montgomery, regional vice president of sales of TWA, who presented the official list of those aboard the flight; and Captain Richard Mellor of Flagstaff, who accompanied the remains from the airport to the morgue and thus could vouch that no tampering had occurred. Without any complications, the six-man jury ruled all of the deaths accidental.

After finishing their aerial reconnoitering, three of the Swiss mountaineers landed at the crash site with some of their equipment; only these three would be brought there that day. They were Anton Spinas, the only full-time professional mountain climber and guide in the eight-man Swiss group; Ami Wisler, a railroad conductor by vocation; and Albert Bockhorn, a policeman. After friendly greetings and introductions, and a little briefing and discussion facilitated by the one man who could fluently speak both German and English, the Swiss got to work setting up a special rigging of rope and cable of their own design.

With the arrival of the Swiss mountaineers, there were a dozen men atop the promontory working on the disaster. By then the Americans had found several more bodies, concealed in the debris of the upper gully, and had carried them to the landing area. The remains were loaded onto two helicopters in succession and flown out of the canyon to Grand Canyon Airport, from where they would be flown to Flagstaff and taken to United's temporary morgue at the Coconino County Fairgrounds. The victims had vanished from life, and then as they departed from the place where they had died, they were taken away again. As they receded in the distance, they vanished for the second time and were moved to another way station, from where they would be moved several more times until they arrived at their final resting places. They had been denuded of absolutely everything and then denied even possession of the ground on which this had been done to them, displaced from their own deaths, and they would be displaced again.

After a time, the Swiss finished setting up their equipment and were ready to use it. The basic idea was that a steel cable with a handle on one end was used to lower a climber down a steep slope or over a cliff. This was ingeniously accomplished by wrapping the cable several turns around a braked rotating cylinder, positioned between the climber and a long storage spool of the cable. A man operating the braked cylinder would relieve enough of the brake friction that the cylinder would begin to rotate under the weight of the climber below. As the cylinder rotated, it unreeled more cable to the climber, enabling him to descend, and drew in more cable from the storage spool. A third man would gradually unroll the spool to supply the cylinder and the climber.

The braked cylinder was a two-piece device made of hardwood and looked much like a large pulley. It lay on the ground near the drop-off, held in position by ropes that opposed the climber's weight, which in turn were tied around boulders nearby. The man doing the braking merely had to step on the cylinder with varying pressure to control it. By doing this he produced enough binding friction inside of it to prevent it from rotating any faster than he wanted it to, effectively braking the descent of the climber. In principle the whole apparatus was like a rod and reel without the rod. The reel was there and the line was there, and the fish could be allowed to run into the depths under tension. In this case, however, the fish held on because he wanted to, and the braking tension in the line was designed to preserve his life, not to end it.

It took three people to make use of the equipment, a climber and two assistants, and this was the reason for which three of the Swiss Alpinists had been landed at the crash site. They made the first descent into the lower gully, with the idea in mind of testing the equipment and demonstrating it to their American colleagues, before allowing them to try it. The Americans had done what they could for the moment, so they stopped and sat down or stood nearby to watch the Swiss, partly out of curiosity, partly to learn, and partly out of respectful gratitude for their involvement.

Ami Wisler operated the braked cylinder, and Albert Bockhorn controlled the unreeling of cable from the storage spool. Wearing bold red pants to make him easy to distinguish from the rocky rubble of the butte even from a distance should he fall, and a black crash helmet to protect his head in the same event, Anton Spinas gradually dropped over the edge of the upper, shallowly sloped area, and backed down into the deeper gully. After a few minutes he reached the bottom. Here the grade returned from nearly vertical to only very gently sloped, and the gully fanned out in a widened apron before spilling over the cliff and down the cliff face. He was between 150 and 200 feet below the men above.

Wreckage was heavily concentrated at the inland end of the bottom and was scattered progressively less densely from there, down its moderate slope to the edge of the cliff. In the concentrated area it was severely burned and melted, and the ground was blackened with soot. Beyond this area the debris was only partially burned or only singed, and the natural ground was exposed. Evidently the deluge of fuel had not been able to flow any farther than the foot of the vertical grade, yet most of the debris beyond this, all the way to the edge of the cliff, had been in flames to one degree or another; it must have been soaked with fuel when the fuel tanks exploded, and had fallen carrying its own fire with it.

Among the mangled, unrecognizable pieces of the airplane were a few pieces that could at least be readily classed, even if it was not apparent where exactly they came from; most notable of these were several large sections of the wings and the fuselage. Their inner structures of parallel and perpendicular ribs and stringers were showing, painted as they were with olive drab or yellowish brown coatings to prevent corrosion. In grave, perplexing contrast to the mayhem of the scene, the utmost care was manifest in the construction of the airplane, even to the extent that the insides of the hollow wings and walls were painted, not just the outside surfaces. All of the investments made by engineers over a period of years and by hundreds of skilled workers over a period of weeks or months had been destroyed in the space of just a couple of minutes. The blatantly obvious clash between the intentions of everyone involved and the outcome was appalling and only made the magnitude of the loss clearer and the wrongfulness of it more atrocious.

At the extreme outer edge of the apron, right at the tops of the chimneys, was a section of fuselage wall about the size of a typical office desktop, from the area immediately behind the lounge windows. It was painted white and navy blue, and as if to declare to the world what had happened there, as if to speak for the fifty-eight human beings who had perished there and to identify them, it bore the letters "D AIR LIN."

Spinas walked amidst the debris to the edge of the precipice, out of the instinctive need to know if there was more, and maybe to test the boundaries of his domain by feeling them, as a leopard in a zoo paces the perimeter of its island world right at the edge of the moat.

Fifteen or twenty feet inland from where the ground dropped away and left only the open sky in its place, Spinas found two bodies, the ones that had tumbled the farthest without going over. He had to turn over a sizeable piece of crumpled sheet metal with red, white, and blue striping painted on it to free one of them.

The tentative plan was to use a rope, extending from the crest to the bottom of the gully, to haul out the remains. Spinas would encase a body in a body bag, which he would attach by its handles to a clip on the rope. Men on top would then drag the remains up the exceedingly steep slope of the gully. But in the particular situation at Chuar Butte, the slope was profusely covered with loose rock, and this was in turn overlaid and interspersed with numerous pieces of wreckage. It did not take long to prove that the technique was unreasonable. Even if a body could be dragged all of the way up without becoming snagged, it would dislodge one after another rock or piece of debris along the way, sending an ongoing barrage in Spinas' direction, and he had nowhere to go to get out of its way. He came back up, and the Swiss and the Americans discussed the situation. Without much debate, they decided to abandon the method. What they would try next, no one knew.

The day had grown hot, and a warm, heavy breeze swept over the men on the butte. Against the blackened gully filled with death as the physical background of their conference, they began brainstorming. They were alive, vibrant with insightfulness and creativity, while behind them the dead, whose wills had evaporated or fled, felt nothing and could no longer manifest even a breath, let alone a spark of awareness. The eventuality of life and the inevitability of death were profoundly juxtaposed, each clarifying the other by contrast beyond any ordinary measure. The human vestiges in the gully were incapable of movement, of thought, of feeling, of doing or knowing or being or becoming anything. The people they had once been were gone and had abandoned them as waste in a wasteland. The bodies were like ruins forsaken without a trace of the original owners, and with no claim left behind. The living men standing before the accidental memorial to loss were the antithesis of it in every respect. They were animate, they had wills, they incessantly moved and thought and felt in an unbroken stream of physiology and consciousness, and they were constantly learning and growing and achieving. As an artist vivifies the dull pile of rocks that was once a beautiful temple, by portraying it at its height of form and color, with citizens of the ancient community walking in its spaces, so did the rescuers, by the example of themselves, dramatically illumine what the dark things in the gully must once have been. The living made clear the immeasurable losses of the dead, and the dead made clear the fantastic bounty of the living.

The rescuers brilliantly solved the problem of how to remove the bodies from the gully. (See Appendix 8 for a diagram.) In exceedingly rough terms, the gully was like a huge, very wide toboggan chute, which over all of its length (except for the threshold area at the top and the terminal area at the bottom) was extremely steep, nearly vertical. In cross section the gully was very roughly semicircular like the chute, and so the top rim of the gully met the crest of the promontory in an irregularly crescent shaped edge. They strung a rope across the open air above the gully and anchored it to boulders near the crest that were located roughly at the ends of the crescent. In the perspective of facing the promontory from the south, say hovering in a helicopter and looking at the gully dead-on, the rope ran from left to right near the top of the gully, spanning the distance between its western and eastern edges. It might have marked, like a bricklayer's line, where the outer edge of the crest had once been, before nature gouged the cliff away to reveal the gully.

To rig it, a man simply had to walk the rope around the crescent under tension, from one side to the other, after tying it down on the starting side. He could have let the rope out loosely behind him as he walked along and then reeled it in from the far side and pulled it taut, but it certainly would have become caught on rocks or wreckage in the process. As the man took up the slack in it to transform its shape from that of a loose, uneven arc to that of a straight line, the rope would have slid sideways over the ground of the upper gully. By walking the rope around under tension instead, he kept it from sagging enough to touch the ground.

Once the rope was in place over the gully, the men had the beginnings of a way to hoist bodies straight up through the air from where they lay far below. Two small metal pulleys about the size of doughnuts, connected together in a metal frame one above the other, were installed on the rope, so that the upper pulley could roll along the rope and the lower pulley would hang the better part of a foot underneath. Through the lower pulley the men threaded a steel cable that could be uncoiled from a reel on the west side of the crest, the side nearer the landing zone. The free end of the cable was outfitted with a closed-loop swivel hook and in turn a spring clip.

The idea was to roll the pulleys out along the rope to a position above a body and then lower the steel cable to a man below waiting to receive it. He would attach the remains, inside a bag, to the spring clip, and they could then be hoisted away and up toward the level of the crest. Getting the pulley assembly out to the correct position was one of the tricky parts. A second rope originating on the far side of the gully was looped through an eyelet on the pulley frame and back, in a "V" configuration, with the point at the pulleys. To position the pulleys, men on the crest on opposite sides of the gully would have a controlled, cooperative tug of war. The men on the western end would pull lightly on their steel cable, with the swivel hook acting as a stop at the pulleys (because it was too large to pass through) while the men on the eastern end would pull lightly on their doubled-back rope. One side would yield just slightly to the other to allow the pulleys to be drawn to the other until the right position was achieved.

From there the problem became how to lower the steel cable; it could not simply be fed across space through the lower pulley and down. In answer to this problem, they fastened a rope to the spring clip, which dangled freely down to the bottom of the gully. A man stationed down there would pull the rope to himself hand over hand, drawing the steel cable with it. His action tended to push the pulleys back toward the side with the storage reel of cable, but anchoring the doubled-back "V" rope on the opposite side restrained the pulleys, counteracting that tendency.

Once the man working deep in the gully had drawn the steel cable down to his level, he would clip on one or two body bags that were ready for transport. The steel cable then became a hoisting cable, and the men above on the west side would reel it in, lifting the remains. To help them do this, they had special cable pulling handles that clamped onto the cable like pliers. The men would pull the cable across several feet and then release and reposition the handles to reel in more. Several men hoisted together because the loads were heavy, and because some of them had to hold the cable stationary while others moved their handles to draw in the next increment. Another man wound up the cable on its storage reel as the haulers brought it to him, to prevent it from becoming kinked. The cable would be weakened at any kink, and if even one strand broke and frayed, the whole cable might be unusable. Leaving the cable lying around haphazardly rather than coiling it neatly, posed the risk that it might become folded or tangled, either of which could kink it.

While the men on the west side hoisted, the "V" rope was still securely anchored on the east side and kept the pulleys from rolling westward under the force of the hoisting. The men on the east side had only to wait for the load to reach the top, at the main suspension rope that spanned the gully, but as the load ascended, the man down in the gully still had a job to do. His draw rope had become a tag line, with which he kept the load from swinging and from striking the sheer wall of the gully above him. Any contact could snag the load or knock wreckage or rocks down onto him. Because his freedom of movement was limited to the modest width of the apron, he could not get much of an angle between himself and the load when it was any appreciable distance above him, and so he had no choice but to pull primarily downward to deflect it. Most of his strength was wasted, opposing the men lifting the load in order to impress a small sideways force on it. It was hard work for him, and his efforts unavoidably made the hard work of the men above even harder. Fortunately, because of the location of the suspension rope, most of the transit was safely spaced away from the surface of the gully, so he was only intermittently required to manipulate the load in this way.

Finally the load would reach the top, with the swivel hook butting up against the pulley frame, and the last stage of the retrieval cycle would begin. The men on the east side would unfasten their "V" rope, while holding it taut and stationary, so that the load could be moved horizontally. Again the men on opposite sides had a tug of war, but this time both groups pulled strenuously—their exertions had to not only move the pulley, which took hardly any force at all, but also support the weight of the load, which took nearly all of the force that the men applied. The men on the west pulled slightly harder than the men on the east, so that the load could begin to move westward. It was a balancing act finely coordinated. The loads were drawn in short intervals, which inescapably made their overall movement somewhat jerky and in turn caused them to bounce up and down. The men kept this minimal by handling the rigging deftly. Were a load to have bounced dramatically, it would have been necessary for the men to stop and wait for this to subside before proceeding.

When the load reached the men on the west, everybody could ease up, allowing it to settle to the rocky ground. From there the bags were unfastened and carried to the helicopter landing zone nearby, the proximity of which was the reason for having the cable reel on the west and drawing the loads to that side.

It took the better part of Friday afternoon to complete this sophisticated aerial rigging, and because of this the men had little time to actually use it that day. The team had accomplished a great deal simply in figuring out how to remove the remains, devising the scheme of the equipment to do it, and setting it all up. They had cracked a brand-new problem through their ingenuity and long backgrounds of experience, essentially inventing new equipment. Passenger air travel was still a young and growing industry, and the tragedies that came with it were largely unforeseeable except in vague generalities. An accident like this one had never happened before, and so at the outset no one knew how to cope with it. The methods were even newer than the circumstances.

*   *   *

Late in the day Friday, to the astonishment of nearly everyone, TWA announced the identifications of more victims from their plane: Catherine Kennaley, Neal Alan Power, Mary Ellen Lytle, and Harry Harvey Allen.

Mrs. Kennaley was sixty-eight years old, and from the death of her husband in 1946 until she retired in 1953, she had owned and operated Kennaley's Barbeque and Tavern in Kansas City, Missouri. She had been visiting her son, a TWA employee in San Francisco, who arranged for her to fly free of charge roundtrip on a family member pass. Mrs. Kennaley's remains were sent home to Kansas City for private funeral services. She was one of only four TWA victims who were ultimately both identified and sent home, rather than being buried in the mass grave in Flagstaff.

Neal Power was a twenty-two-year-old college student who was returning to St. Louis from a two-week training cruise on the Pacific Ocean, as a member of the U.S. Naval Reserve. He was a sophomore at St. Louis University and left behind seven siblings and his parents in the same town. Mr. Power's remains were buried in the mass memorial plot in Flagstaff.

Mary Lytle was thirty-seven and lived in Long Beach, California, where she was a social worker. She was single and was on her way to Washington, Iowa, via Kansas City to visit her parents for a vacation. She had left the west coast a week earlier than planned in order to surprise them. Instead, only her remains were sent home. Like Mrs.

Kennaley, Miss Lytle was one of the four TWA victims who were returned to their families.

Harry Allen, the off-duty TWA flight engineer mentioned earlier in the book, was able to ride for free on the flight deck on his ACM status, which basically guaranteed his spot on the plane. A pass did not, because a paying passenger could bump a nonrevenue passenger and take his seat. This of course applied only to seats that were intended for passengers, and that's the point: Mr. Allen had no duties but sat up front with the acting flight crew. He used the flight deck jump seat for the takeoff and climb, and he may have remained there for the entire time that the *Star of the Seine* was airborne. This seat was not normally used and had been installed only in case the plane would ever cross the oceans, where a fourth crewmember, expert in radio and celestial navigation, would be required. The *Star of the Seine,* however, was never used for intercontinental flying, nor was any of its nine sisters. In practice the extra seat served only the purpose of carrying ACM "passengers" and, on occasion, check pilots and check engineers performing routine, periodic evaluations of their peers in flight. It is likely that Harry Allen stayed with his friends on the flight deck, even though he could have moved freely about the plane.

It is also likely that Mr. Allen *left* the flight deck and took a seat in the passenger cabin. His situation was one of the precious few about which anything special could even be meaningfully speculated. Considering him to have been a sort of honorary crewmember, which was just as accurate as calling him any kind of passenger, the seventy persons aboard the *Star of the Seine* consisted of six crewmembers and sixty-four passengers. There were only just sixty-four regular passenger seats in the passenger cabin, making it seem obvious that the plane was full, but one of those seats was probably unclaimed and empty. As already suggested, the Maags probably did not buy one for Howard; he was so little that there was no real need, and he likely stayed in his mother's lap or in a baby basket on the floor directly in front of her. This would have left one seat vacant for Harry Allen, unless Mrs.

Maag wanted to take advantage of the opportunity for Howard to have not only free passage but also a free seat. She would have been given priority, but chances are that the empty seat was not near her, certainly not right next to her, where presumably her husband sat.

If in fact one seat was never sold, meaning that the Maags didn't buy one for Howard, then in all likelihood it remained available for Harry Allen to take, and maybe he did. What he would not have done was take a seat in the lounge, even briefly. Company policy prohibited employees riding on passes or ACM from doing this, because it would be rude for anyone riding free of charge to effectively prevent a revenue customer, who had paid handsomely for first-class passage, from enjoying any of the luxuries, like the lounge.

Mr. Allen's wife decided to have his remains buried with those of his friends in the mass grave in Flagstaff. The rest of the crew, including the hostesses, were never identified. Neither were any of the other TWA employees, except for Stephen Bishop.

Four more people had passed into history. Their destinies were no longer open, but proved and closed. The stories of their lives had not just ended, as the first half of a book that has been torn in two ends where it stops, but had been concluded. The conclusions were abrupt and brutal, they made no sense, and they seemingly departed from the themes of the lives that they proposed finishing, but the positive identifications had made them concrete and in that respect had transformed the conclusions into destinies that upheld the victims' dignity. Destiny had not abandoned them to the everlasting insult of taking their lives without respecting them enough to even admit that it had taken them. What had happened was clear even if it was unjust.

And unjust it certainly was. To take them senselessly or ambiguously was wrongful, and destiny had taken them senselessly *and* ambiguously. Accidental death was senseless inasmuch as no purposeful motive lay behind it; it was meaningless. And being utterly unexpected, it contradicted its own senselessness: it was levied with an immediacy appropriate only to things of momentous purpose. As the final note in a meaningful life, the meaninglessness of accidental death conflicted with the theme of that life. And yet, accidental death was no less compatible with life's themes than the seemingly senseless fact that we are *all* cheated out of life by our own mortality. Mary Lytle, for example, had spent her life giving to others. For her to die without ever getting what she dreamed of for herself was consistent as a last expression of that theme of her life and in that regard made sense, yet because it was so tragic, so cruel, it made no sense at all. It made fate, as the power and motive intelligence behind destiny, seem demented, and it made destiny itself seem absurd, as though the universe was designed to stand in perpetual mockery of itself.

With the United victims identified earlier Friday and the two on Wednesday, and the three other TWA victims identified on Thursday, there had been over nine positive identifications. Many families across the country, from Medford to Philadelphia, knew for certain that they would never see their loved ones again. Even though they were separate, they shared one and the same utterly personal, unique grief. In them the suffering that all of the families felt had been sharpened, brought into clearer, more cuttingly painful focus. In them the hope, however tenuous, that had held back their grief had been vanquished and dissolved. With nothing to restrain it but their own refusal, most of these people were overwhelmed and seized by sadness so powerful that nothing could divert them from it. They were inconsolable. Few of them were able to choose when to stop crying. Their sadness itself released them and let their sobbing subside only when it had spent the greater part of itself for a time. It receded and gathered itself and resurged and overwhelmed them again and again.

Soon many more families would receive the same crushing news. As the day closed, all of the other families sat poised for being immolated. They were as vulnerable and helpless as Christians in the Colosseum. Most of them knew that there would be no reprieve, that the worst had come, and yet until the dreadful phone call it was not quite real; life was in a sense still intact.

Fate may have determined when and how the victims' lives would end, but on another level of reality and truth, it was the physical world that selected the families to have the special sufferings of knowing for sure. The laws of physics determined the complex and unalterable multitude of precisely ordered motions within the apparently chaotic deformations and disintegrations that composed the crashes. The dynamic order of the physical world, transfiguring all in a flash according to its unwavering nature, decided whose unique characteristics would all be obliterated and who would be left with at least one. Although its effect was cruel, it was not cruelty because it lacked the dementedness of malice; contrarily, the selecting was worse than cruelty and even more senseless, because it was devoid of awareness. Surely cruelty can be committed only by a human being—it requires harboring ill will and seeking to inflict harm for its own sake, which are exclusively human sentiments. In literal cruelty there is humanity, no matter how grotesque, and some impression of the victim's identity and worth, no matter how misguided. The victim matters in some perverse, tortured way to the abuser. But none of the victims, or their families, who were victims themselves, mattered in any way to the physical world. It was a judge with no soul or moral duty and it passed sentence without principle, as if by pure arbitrariness and caprice, though because it had no power of choice nor any responsibility, it could not truly act irresponsibly. The physical world was an inanimate thing, unconscious and mechanical, and as such it selected whose loved ones would be identified and whose would not, without reason. Its act could not be defined—it was not even an accident in the true sense of chance, because it unfolded in the only way it could.

In this sad truth, one major aspect of the whole tragedy was redoubled: namely, that it seemed to have happened without purpose. There was no intent behind it. The accident was the most tremendous sacrifice of human life, and yet it had no value because it was not predicated upon any need and because it accomplished nothing. An immeasurable price had been paid for nothing at all, or so it seemed.

Chapter 18

A week had passed since the accident. It was Saturday morning, July 7, and the dozen men who had camped overnight at the United crash site a quarter mile above the river arose and began their day. It was the second day for ten of them and the third for Lewis and Batson. Another day of heat and sweat and hard work lay ahead. Already they were grungy, unshaven, dirty, and, as Lewis later put it, fragrant. With their limited supply of water, none was allotted for bathing. Only the men at the base camp, who bathed in the river, enjoyed the pleasure and luxury of that. The men up high were at least able to use a little water for washing their hands and faces, but they reserved the vast majority for drinking first and cooking second. Each man drank about two gallons of water a day, an incredible amount by any standard, and yet most thirsted for more. It was hot. Jokingly, the men at the base camp ridiculed the men up high for being filthy, and the men up high shamed the ones at the base camp for feeling no guilt and flaunting their good fortune. They concocted the nicknames Ledge Lice and River Rats for each other.

About thirteen bags of remains had been airlifted out from the shoulder Friday morning, and then late Friday afternoon, well after all of the landing had stopped for the day, the team found more bodies and brought them in four or five bags to the landing area. The H-21 helicopters returned Saturday morning to drop off more workers and took these remains with them when they departed. Seven more men joined the crew on the shoulder, bringing the total to nineteen, eleven Americans and eight Swiss.

The work Saturday was almost exclusively far down in the gully, and all of it was dangerous. More than half of the men at a time worked together to operate the cable-pulley system. Two men deep in the gully extricated the bodies from the wreckage, while four to six men on the crest at the west side of the gully did the hauling. Two men on the crest at the east side of the gully were sufficient to counterbalance the exertions of the men on the west, despite being outnumbered, because they had the mechanical advantage inherent in their "V" rope being doubled back on itself: every foot that the pulley moved westward required two feet of the "V" to be let out.

Another man was positioned strategically on a large, flattish rock about the size of a kitchen table, which had slid fifty feet or so down the severely steep cliff face immediately west of the gully, probably ages before he stood there. From his precarious vantage point on the rock, he could see both the men above and the men down in the gully, whereas neither of those groups could see the other because of the contours of the terrain. The man standing on the rock was a signaler whose job it was to relay messages to pull or to wait or to stop, from the group below to the group on the crest. Although his job might have been the easiest, it was probably also the most perilous. One or two steps separated him from thin air, and from his small rock platform it was a sheer drop of about six hundred feet to the talus below.

Besides the danger of falling debris, the workers in the gully had to contend with the terrible odor and the monstrous sights, both of which were utterly nauseating. In the first minutes of the fire, the victims' clothing had entirely burned away, like the cover of a paperback book thrown into an incinerator, and the lack of it bizarrely accentuated the horror of their ends by blatantly revealing that there was nothing recognizable left to cover. It was a disgrace precisely because it could *not* be immodest. All of the bodies had been so severely burned that they were featureless.

The only saving grace was that there were no flies. It is instinctive to know that flies mean death. Among its ravages, death permits decay to supersede preservation and growth, and flies are the consigned accomplices of decay. Flies consume what life, in departing, forsakes. There is something primally horrifying about the idea of being consumed by flies. It is revolting in a way as reflexive as recoiling against a putrid taste and spitting out rotten food. It is in our genetics or our souls, from aeons of consistently awful experience, accreted through countless generations. The worst form of the untaught revulsion is that to the *progeny* of flies and the unspeakable horrors they wreak. The ghastly sight of them at work is unendurably sickening even without the odor.

The men at the United site were spared these most potent miseries. There were no flies. In fact, with only one exception, there appeared to be no creatures at all on the shoulder. Aside from the scrubby bushes and football shaped cacti scattered sparsely about the crest, the only native life the men observed up there was grayish-brown collared lizards, about eight inches long. (Insects are the prime constituents of their diet, so there must have been at least crawling insects like ants or beetles at the site.) It was very strange that there were no flies, which seem to be present everywhere on earth.

After hoisting only a few loads on Friday, the men had run out of time and had also concluded that the nylon support rope strung horizontally over the drop-off of the gully would have to be replaced by a steel cable. Under the strain of supporting the weight of a load, the support rope would bend sharply downward about the point where the hoisting pulley rested. Nylon rope is very stretchy, and it sagged a great deal, causing the load to bounce up and down significantly with each heave of the pullers, no matter how careful they were. Steel cable, on the other hand, stretched only about a half of one percent of its length under normal strain, one fortieth of the twenty percent increase in length that a normal load effected in nylon. Hoisting the remains would thus be much more precisely controllable with a steel support cable, and the men improved their rigging with it on Saturday. The setup was again largely an invention, something new to rescue teams, which they devised on the spot. It had never been tested, and the men worked out its problems by trial and error in actual use.

They worked until midday and then retreated to the shade of their makeshift shelter to escape the sun. They had set up a tarpaulin supported by stilts and secured with ropes in a natural two-sided enclosure in the rock. They had a roof and two walls, inside of which were all of their provisions. In addition to the typical camping things and the unusual rescue equipment, there were two remarkable items: a case of fresh oranges and a case of Schlitz beer. The perishable oranges were about as incongruous on that searing rocky griddle as a tray of ice cream cones would have been, and although the beer would keep, it would be hot by the time anyone drank any of it, despite the shade of the tarp.

The men sat amongst their unique collection of gear on the rock floor of the shelter and relaxed in the shade. They talked or read magazines or napped while they waited for the oppressive heat to subside. This was more of a wish than anything else; the air actually got hotter during the afternoon, but the long break made them feel cooler, and as the sun fell off to the west, its rays became less direct and imparted less heat to whatever they irradiated. The air might have been hotter, but the physical and psychological effects of turning down the furnace were still a relief.

After a long rest they resumed their work. They had not cooled off so much as sweltered less severely, but they were refreshed in spirit and had the encouraging notion that the worst part of the day had passed. It was midafternoon, and they could look forward to the sun dropping out of sight to the west by late afternoon. In a blessed precursor to sunset, the central peak of Chuar Butte would envelope them and the whole crash promontory in its shade.

In the overall lower gully operations, two positions were used for the support line of the aerial rigging. The whole improved setup using the steel support cable was dismantled and moved, just once. The impact shoulder was narrow and long in its thrust toward the Little Colorado

River. Its mean direction in extending from inland toward its extremity at its east end was just slightly south of east, nearly aligned parallel to a line of latitude. In both positions, the support line ran parallel to the approximate mean thrust of the shoulder, or nearly east and west, and was anchored to boulders in the upper gully, near the elevation of the crest of the shoulder rather than somewhere farther down the slope. In both positions the line stretched across the open space directly above the gully. In one it was above the nearly level apron at the bottom, and in the other it was roughly above the middle of the very steep main run of the gully. Between the two positions the entire lower gully was covered.

Because of the dangers entailed in it, the work at the crash site can only be characterized as daredevil exploits on a grand scale, disguised as methodical, modest goings-on. Had they been contrived to serve anyone's personal ambitions, rather than courageously conceived to fulfill a solemn duty, the operations and the thinking behind them would have been grandiose. As it was, they were an exercise of honor, a bizarre and powerful testament to the worth of human life and to the character of a small group of human beings. Two hundred feet doesn't sound like a lot or look like a lot horizontally, across level ground, but vertically it telescopes into awesome proportions. To lift a body through the open air from the bottom of the gully to the support cable at the height of the crest was like it would be to hoist one from the street to the top of a fifteen-story building.

The team found most of the bodies in the lower gully, and removed all of those with the special aerial rigging. The work was slow and exacting. The men down in the gully had to be careful not to start a cascade of debris by casting aside fragments of wreckage to search underneath them. Instead, the pieces had to be carefully laid to one side or slowly tipped over. Besides endangering the workers, a slide of debris could have carried crucial evidence or the remains of victims over the edge at the bottom of the gully and into the chimneys, from which they might as well have been impossible to retrieve. Possible or not, the men had decided to not even try climbing down into the depths of the chimneys to investigate what might be in them. They considered it to be entirely too dangerous. The scrap metal and rock strewn over the steep surface of the lower gully was an avalanche waiting for a vibration to set it off. It seemed incredible that anything had been able to come to rest on such a slope, so an avalanche appeared probable, and the men took it as a deadly serious threat. Because anything tumbling down the gully would as likely fall into the chimneys as sail over them and fall to the talus, there was a grave and immediate threat that debris would at some unpredictable moment rain down inside the chimneys. Anyone caught in there at that deadly time would be in as much peril as if he were trapped on a firing range during active use. It would simply have been madness for anyone to attempt the chimneys, and no one did.

What fell down them while the disintegrated Flight 718 was a multitude of fragmentary motions, each piece seeking a place to rest, may never be known, but if any victims lie there, then they are interred in a natural mausoleum of incomparable beauty and grandeur, far surpassing any manmade memorial. In the magnificence of the Grand Canyon, they are as close to God as they could have been laid anywhere on earth.

By the end of the day the nineteen men atop the crash promontory had brought about twenty more bags to the landing area, and they were convinced that they had found all of the appreciable remains that had lodged in the gully. They rested with the grim satisfaction of having finished, with the feeling of completeness, though it had not yet been officially decided for them to stop. It had been a very long day, and it felt rich to sit down in the shade of the top of Chuar Butte and relax, and have a bottle of beer while supper cooked. The sun was setting. Some of the men began to feel subtly elated, affirmed in their success by the sun itself, grandest of all phenomena in the experience and the domain of man, sympathetically enacting its own splendorous finale. From their position the sunset was perceptible as a glow cast on the rocks to the east across the Colorado River, in striking contrast to the shadows there. The beautiful light of the setting sun was as though reflected from the flash of a single great skyrocket exploding in gloriously slow motion, and as it gradually darkened and faded, it conveyed an agreement as rich as any could be that the work was done.

*　　*　　*

In Las Vegas, 200 miles to the west of the disaster area, nine congressmen who had flown in from Washington, D.C., on Friday were on their way to a late supper. They constituted a specially appointed subcommittee of the Committee on Interstate and Foreign Commerce, House of Representatives, and they had just finished conducting the first in a series of hearings that especially focused on the tragedy. (Other sessions would follow in Washington, D.C., later in July and then in September.) The hearings were conceived prior to the accident to assess how well or poorly the United States was using its airspace, in particular how safely or hazardously, and they would likely have been initiated within the year without such a terrible event prompting the committee, but the event had occurred and prompted they were. The Grand Canyon accident had made the need for this assessment immediately clear, and the hearings began without delay in response to it.

In the Gold Key Room of the Sands Hotel, the hearing had proceeded all day, except for a lunch recess, and had lasted into the evening. A public morning session from 10:30 to 12:45 took lengthy testimony from three officials: William K. Andrews, the director of the Bureau of Safety Investigation of the Civil Aeronautics Board; William S. MacNamara, an investigator in the same bureau; and John A. Garrison, the fourth regional chief of the Facilities Operations Branch of the Civil Aeronautics Administration. They were questioned extensively about the rules and procedures governing the conduct of commercial flight, and particularly about the movements of Flights 2 and 718 as far as they were known.

After lunch the hearing reconvened in executive session, and from 2:00 to 6:35 two men who had actually worked at the TWA and United crash sites gave testimony. The public was excluded because of the sensitive nature of the topics.

The public session reconvened at 6:35 and ran until adjournment, at 7:20. In the final segment, Oscar Bakke, the deputy director of the Bureau of Safety Regulation of the CAB, and Gerald White, an attorney of the Office of the General Counsel of the CAB, were the only witnesses. Mr. Bakke was queried extensively about air traffic control regulations and flight clearances, and he also made statements at his own initiative in an attempt to clarify some of what Mr. Andrews had said in the morning session. Mr. White requested the opportunity to speak and testified only briefly, merely to in turn clarify some of what Mr. Bakke had said.

Unfortunately, some reporters present in the morning session had grossly and damagingly misinterpreted some of Mr. Andrews' testimony. They hastily wrote stories that were printed in newspapers across the country that day and the next claiming that he blamed TWA for the tragedy. Andrews had neither stated nor implied any such thing, and that was what Bakke attempted to address. However, his attempt failed to correct any misunderstandings but for those in the minds of a few of the congressmen. The trouble was that Bakke was discreet. He stressed the correct interpretations of Andrews' statements without making it clear that his aim was to undo any misunderstandings of Andrews, and without even directly referring to Andrews. In short, he was attempting to clear the man's name without giving it. Perhaps even more of an error, Bakke did not delineate the particular misinterpretations that he sought to dispel, but only outlined the truth, reiterating in his own words the facts that he feared had been misconstrued. It would have been much more effective if he had used a format like that present in the sentence, "This morning some people thought they heard that two plus three is ten, but the truth is that two plus three is five, and that is what was meant." Instead he merely said, "Two plus three is five."

This is not to disparage Mr. Bakke, who made an honorable, sincere effort to avert a catastrophe of misunderstanding and wasted no time in getting to the job of it. In fact, it may very well be true that Mr. Bakke was the only person who made an effort, until it was too late to do any good.

For Bakke's testimony to have achieved its aim, the reporters would have to have made the connection themselves between Andrews' testimony and the specific points that Bakke amplified; they might then have realized that they goofed. But it never happened. They kept their fallacious stories intact and even wrote more of them. The blame for that of course lay much more on the reporters themselves than on Bakke or Andrews. In fact, their conduct was inexcusable.

It could be argued that the reporters did not know enough about aviation to recognize that Bakke was conveying meanings different from what they thought they had heard, but if they were not experienced, then where was their humble caution? They were responsible to honestly appraise their own competence to understand, and to trust or mistrust their impressions of the testimony accordingly. On the other hand, it might be suggested that simple human nature mitigated their mistakes, that in the passion of the moment they were captives of their own fervor. An official had seemingly condemned one of the two airlines, and that was a red-hot story. Surely, however, most reporters knew the pitfalls of their own trade, in particular the fact that their ambitions could very well deceive them. They were responsible to withhold their defamatory articles until their fervor subsided and they regained their balance and clarity, which they evidently did not do fully, if at all. The reporters who wrote the libelous stories at most had half of an excuse for their actions: namely, that they may not have returned to hear Bakke in the evening.

Irrespective of all of this, they were fundamentally responsible to make sure that their own articles were accurate, yet they pushed ahead and submitted their stories without even checking them out. No one asked Andrews if they had heard him correctly. Even worse, the editors involved in the terribly defamatory stories, who had a still greater responsibility to ensure the truthfulness of any articles in prospect for print, approved the articles without verifying them. They didn't ask Andrews if he had really meant what their reporters were claiming.

Heedless of the damage that they might inflict on TWA and on Captain Gandy's reputation, and heedless of the pain that they might inflict on his family, who were already suffering monumentally in grief, the perpetrating reporters and editors proceeded and served their own ends. It was hard to say which was worse, their inhumanity or their recklessness.

One of the most despicable phrasings to appear in the newspapers that day and the next was the heading, "CAB Expert Puts Blame on Pilot of TWA Craft," under which appeared the sentence, in reference to Andrews, "Earlier he testified that, 'TWA had full responsibility for maintaining separation,' of the two airliners after it had changed flight plans."

Andrews never said that, not even the fragment the article "quoted," and he certainly meant nothing of the kind. What he actually said at the point the article purported to quote was, verbatim, "TWA was flying under visual flight rules, and it was the responsibility of the TWA pilot to maintain his own separation under this type of clearance." What that meant was only that TWA was bound by the set of rules applying to visual flight (by virtue of their amended one thousand on top clearance) and would receive no help from Air Route Traffic Control in avoiding other aircraft, even while on the airways. In short, they had to look out for themselves at all times. That's all Andrews meant, period. This did not place the entire responsibility for preventing a collision on TWA. Obviously TWA had no way to keep United away, but only to keep themselves away from United. Moreover, the collision happened well off the airways in uncontrolled airspace, and in that vast area ARTC had no responsibility, even for United, so besides TWA having the entire obligation to see and avoid United, United had the entire obligation to see and avoid TWA. The responsibilities were identical and equally divided.

Once the newspapers were circulated, the damage had been done, and corrections or retractions could not have repaired it. It was cruel, and what was more, it was spurious rather than honest. It was a crime, and instead of subsiding it grew. The blaming spread in a backlash of its own kind: a great many pilots believed the newspaper stories that had so utterly garbled Andrews' statements. Representing the Air Line Pilots' Association on behalf of TWA pilots who were in protest, TWA's Master Executive Council wrote a letter to the chairman of the Civil Aeronautics Board, respectfully condemning Andrews' supposed prejudiced indictment of TWA 2, and urging that Andrews be instructed to publically retract his statements or deny that he had ever meant what he appeared to have meant. The Council was at least leaving open the possibility that Andrews had been misunderstood and misquoted, and it was not unequivocally demanding Andrews' action, but the tragic injustice of it all was still there: Andrews was being hounded to contend with the flood of mistrust and blame, as though it were his fault instead of the fault of the reporters and the editors!

CHAPTER 19

THROUGH THEIR SIMPLE DECENCY and courage, or more to the point, their nobility, the men at Chuar Butte had made it possible for United's team of forensics experts in Flagstaff to perform their own part in the work. On Wednesday two families had been notified, and then on Friday the recovery team's beneficence quickly spread and evolved into the immeasurable sorrow suffered by many other families, in the invaluable word that their loved ones had been positively identified. More identifications followed that day and the next, and with them more families' valiant struggle for hope came to a crushing end. One of them was mine. As with every phone call that came during the terrible week following the accident, everyone at Grandma and Grandpa's house was seized when the telephone rang. It was Saturday, and this time it was what they had all dreaded. United had positively identified Uncle Jack by his wedding band, which was inscribed around the inside with the unique, ineffably appropriate words, "Jack and Joyce Forever." Aunt Joyce went completely to pieces, wailing, "It's so final! It's so final!" Grandpa had known in his heart that his son was gone and had already accepted it with every part of himself but his mind. For him the news was more of a relief than a final blow. He could stop fighting and trust what he had already known, with all of his being. He surrendered and he wept. Everyone did.

At four o'clock on Sunday, July 8, the Chicago memorial service for Uncle Jack was held at Normal Park Methodist Church, at 71st Street and Union, on Chicago's South Side. It was the church in which Uncle Jack had grown up, in the neighborhood where he and my mom had grown up, and where Grandma and Grandpa still lived, in the original home. The big city didn't change very fast back then and was really like a small town, just one that curiously seemed to have no city limits in sight from most locations within it.

The church was filled beyond capacity with many people standing even in the balcony. All of the relatives from Chicago and Indiana, the two principal territories of the family, were there. Many, many of Uncle Jack's friends from high school and from college and beyond were there. Many of my mom's friends from high school and from college and beyond were there. Many of Grandma and Grandpa's friends were there, and many of Grandpa's friends from work. Many of Aunt Joyce's friends were there. Her family was there and her family's friends were there, and practically the entire congregation of the church. They, too, loved Jack and knew him well. Many of them had known him all his life. Most of them had been a part of that community since before he was born.

The Reverend Lester Springer gave a wonderful, heartfelt sermon—he was talking about someone he knew and admired. Hymns were sung, but my mom, who had a beautiful voice and had long been a member of the choir, first at this church and then at her own, could not bring forth any expression but crying every time she tried to sing. Many others could not sing either, much as they wanted to give that tribute to Jack.

All across the country other memorial services took place that day. Several had been held in the previous few days, and many more would follow. Numerous victims remained to be honored, and many of them, including Uncle Jack, would be honored with more than one service, often in parts of the country far removed from each other.

*   *   *

Earlier in the day the last remains to be found at the United site were flown out of the Grand Canyon and ultimately to Flagstaff. One last victim was discovered that morning and was removed along with over twenty bags that had been collected on Saturday. Five of the nine congressmen who had conducted the special hearing at Las Vegas on Saturday were brought to the United site Sunday morning by helicopter, to inspect the scene and to talk with the rescuers.

Among others, they conferred with David Lewis and Fred Welch. The short meeting on the crest of the promontory, in sight of the blackened gully, may have helped the congressmen to become convinced of the need to improve air safety by showing them firsthand the horrendous consequences of the inadequate system, but it was far from helpful to the men directly contending with those consequences. To quote Lewis, "Rescuers actively engaged in an operation don't like to talk to nonrescuers." It broke their focus and made it difficult to resume and finish the job. Talking with outsiders reconnected a rescuer with the rest of humanity, reminding him of the rest of his own humanity, the parts of himself he had temporarily suppressed in order to face his grave task. Although the last bodies to be removed had already been removed, the job of searching for more had not yet been officially suspended, and Lewis was not pleased to be interviewed. Nevertheless, he politely submitted.

Because the work of retrieving bodies appeared to be finished, the group was reduced later Sunday morning, after the congressmen left. Seven of the nineteen men who had worked at the United crash site Saturday and had camped overnight there were airlifted from the promontory and flown out of the area. Their work was done, but twelve of their comrades stayed behind and would work for yet another day, until Monday. Two of the seven who had finished were David Lewis and Raymond Batson. They had been up there for a day longer than anyone else and two days longer than many, and they were exhausted.

Before the group divided into those who would stay and those who would leave, the men signed an official register of the Colorado Mountain Club declaring that they had been there. The signatures, each but Wisler's followed by the date, July 8, 1956, read as follows:

Allen Auten, CMC, Denver, Colo.

David Lewis, RMR, Boulder, Colo.

Ray Batson, RMR, Boulder, Colo.

Harold Zürcher, Switzerland, Burgdorf

Fred Welch, CMC, Denver, Colo.

Chuck Pavlik, CMC, Denver, Colo.

Dale Medland, United Air Lines, Denver, Colo.

Bob Graham, United Air Lines, Denver, Colo.

Vuilleumier, Andre, Switzerland, Bienne

Frank Clark, United Air Lines, Denver, Colo.

Robert J. Whatley, W/O United States Army, Columbus, Ga.

Carl Christenson, United Air Lines, Denver, Colo.

Günther Erzinger, Basel, Switzerland

Toni Spinas, St. Moritz, Switzerland

E. Weiss, United Air Lines, Denver, Colo.

H. Hunzicker, Schaffhausen, Switzerland

Max Stampfli, Kloten, Switzerland

Wisler, Ami, Lausanne, Switzerland

Albert Bockhorn, the eighth member of the Swiss team, did not sign the register. David Lewis and Ray Batson indicated their group with only the three letters, RMR for short. Whatley wrote, "W/O," which stood for warrant officer.

The register was enclosed in a special weatherproof box, which in turn was secured in a cairn, a crude mound of piled stones that would keep the winds from blowing the box away. They left the shrine there on the promontory for posterity, though unfortunately it would be removed some years in the future by a cleanup crew intent upon restoring the site to its original state, untouched by man.

Seventeen of the nineteen men who had worked at the site posed for a group photograph to commemorate their comradeship and their achievement, while one of the two others took the photo and the last observed. The five Colorado mountain climbers, Lewis, Batson, Pavlik,

Welch, and Auten also posed for a more exclusive picture. The men said their good-byes with strong feelings of mutual respect and gratitude and kinship, and the group of seven left, heading for Grand Canyon Airport, their first stop.

Though he retained lucid memories of a multitude of details of his experience, Lewis could not recall the trip from the crash site to Flagstaff, not even landing at Grand Canyon Airport, getting off the H-21, and walking over to a conventional airplane to transfer to it for the flight to Flagstaff. He definitely "wasn't there" on the helicopter or the plane; maybe his mind was still back in the canyon.

In Flagstaff, Batson and Lewis, and doubtless the others, were given the use of rooms at a motel to clean up. There they each had the sublime pleasure of a shower. Lewis and Batson had labored for over three days, sweating in the dirt and the heat and the sun, without having been able to wash. The experience was at least as rejuvenating spiritually as it was bodily, and had they not been so tired they would have been transported into ecstasy or even crazed jubilation.

One could imagine them laughing like madmen alone in their showers, alarming the employees or the other guests at the motel, but that did not happen.

A merchant who ran a department store in Flagstaff came to the motel and measured Batson and Lewis for clothing sizes. Their clothing was ineradicably permeated with the odor of death and had to be thrown away or incinerated; they saved only their very expensive professional mountain climbing boots, which were relatively impervious. Being Sunday, all of the town's businesses were normally closed, including the department store, but the man opened it up especially for the rescue workers.

*   *   *

In Kansas City later that afternoon, a special charter bound for Winslow departed from Gate 4 at Kansas City Municipal Airport.

On board as passengers were seventy-seven mourners and two TWA officials, destined for the mass funeral service for TWA victims to be held the following morning in Flagstaff. The flight crew was Captain N. G. Carper, First Officer Jack Prouty, and Flight Engineer Joseph Tunder. Captain Carper was a mere five spots above Captain Gandy in the Kansas City Domicile Seniority List, and First Officer Prouty was only two spots above First Officer Ritner in the same list. Prouty and Ritner had been in the same copilot class and were hired on the same day by TWA. Carper was probably hired sooner than Gandy, but not by much. They probably knew each other, and certainly Prouty and Ritner did.

The plane was a Constellation of an early model called an L-049. It was configured for all tourist class seating, with room for eighty passengers, in contrast to the more roomy arrangement of sixty-four passenger seats on the *Star of the Seine*. The 049's first fifteen rows of seats were five seats each, separated into groups of two on the left and three on the right by an off-center aisle. The sixteenth and seventeenth rows were three and two seats on the right, respectively, and none on the left. In all, from the back wall of the flight deck to the lavatories at the extreme rear, there were simply, monotonously, row after row of seats. No galley interrupted their succession, and there was no lounge. Despite the cabin being no wider than a 1049's, there was one more seat per row than there was on a 1049. It was cramped. Moreover, there were only two lavatories for eighty passengers rather than three for sixty-four. That was double the passengers per lavatory. In these very awkward circumstances the cabin crew of three hostesses—Gloria Davies, Loretta Brook, and Edna Martz—managed to bring small comforts to a full planeload of uncomfortable, severely pained people.

Thirteen of them had flown into Kansas City from St. Louis on a regularly scheduled trip called Flight 103, which originated at Pittsburgh and terminated at San Francisco, making intermediate stops at St. Louis, Kansas City, and Los Angeles. TWA Flight 103 was always conducted with a 1049 Constellation, an exact twin of the *Star of the*

Seine. In fact, the *Star of the Seine* itself had probably been used many times for Flight 103.

Some of the people in the St. Louis group must have noticed the parallel. Some of them must have imagined their loved ones in the same surroundings, perhaps enjoying themselves in the time before the collision while everything was still perfectly normal, or perhaps in the terrible final moments. It takes only a little imagination to picture one of the mourners boarding Flight 103 in St. Louis, walking to his seat and sitting down, acutely aware of his every perception and movement as if it were his lost loved one's perceptions and movements of only eight days before, boarding Flight 2. In anguish he might have talked to his loved one in his thoughts or out loud, saying, "So this was the place. Why didn't you get up and get out, as I could now!"

Flight 103 was scheduled to arrive in Kansas City at 2:15 p.m. CST, but it was very late. This in turn delayed the special 049 Constellation charter flight, which finally took off for the West at 4:22 p.m. Some of the TWA employees at Kansas City responsible for its departure were embarrassed, and others were mortified that the airline should foul up taking the mourners to the funeral. Some of the employees were too frustrated or angry to feel ashamed, and a few were just plain sad that the mourners had been further burdened.

But most of the passengers hardly noticed. As they ascended and saw Kansas City sweeping underneath them, it was the last time that those who lived there would ever see their familiar town, or see their town as familiar. When they took off, a part of their lives ended forever. The last semblance of the life they had known was gone, which the funeral would make absolutely clear. Their loved ones were gone, and when they would again set foot in Kansas City, it would be a different town, a different home, a different world for each of them. It would be starkly, inescapably obvious that someone vital was missing, and would be forever. Some were oblivious to the symbolism and the implications, oblivious to what really was going on, and they submitted and followed like little children, while others had a glimpse or a clear and persuasive view of the turning point they had reached in their lives. Either way, to them there could not have been much meaning in leaving late.

Besides the Constellation charter from Kansas City, another TWA charter flight carrying friends and family made the journey to northern Arizona on Sunday. Another group of bewildered people, drawn together by the tragedy and having nothing more than that in common with each other, were shuffled from the places where their trauma had begun to a remote place that held no meaning for them, in order to face an incomprehensible reality as intimately momentous to them as any had ever been. Like their counterparts on the Constellation charter they were completely unprepared for what had come about, and they were overcome.

And like their counterparts on the Constellation, some of them felt broken, some of them felt crazy, and some of them felt nothing at all. A few of them had begun to purely grieve, to feel, without restraining or depreciating their feelings with disbelief. They had somehow come to believe the terrible reality. But the majority was in one way or another, to one degree or another disbelieving still, and that was draining them of their sanity and their humanity. They were in an unnatural and inhuman, tortured state, or they were in the unreality of unfeeling, and had lost their clarity, lost the legitimacy of their own minds and hearts, lost a measure of *themselves*. Only honoring the truth with their whole being could restore them. Their plight was terrible. They could not bring themselves to believe, and they would never be able to see with their own eyes that their loved ones were gone. There would be no wake with its inestimable benefit of enabling the living to look as many times as they needed in order to become convinced. One look could not be enough to accept as true something so horrible and sudden—even a hundred looks might not suffice, but for those poor souls there would not even be the one. For them there could only be faith, which they did not know how to summon. The beliefs of others, the sheer size and power of the mass funeral service to come, and the indisputable sorrow of those who did not doubt, would be their salvation. Through others they would find their own resources as persons and finally gather the strength, the courage, and the clarity to believe what had happened.

But on this day most were stunned, lost in disbelief and stultified by it, unable to really feel their own sorrow even while they were overwhelmed with it. Instead they were only heavy with its burden and with the burden of suppressing it, and they were incapable of authentically interacting with others. They lifelessly enacted the rituals, unable to invest the simple feeling that would have made their actions genuine, unable to invest their own true personhood. They were no longer in their own lives.

The few who had fully surrendered to believing the terrible reality that they were facing, and who were actively living the tumult of their own rising and subsiding grief, through wave after wave, were fully in their own lives. They were present, not absent, and as sensitive and genuine and human as human beings could ever be. Between the waves, when they could see other people and not only their own grief, they interacted with others with fully the gentleness and respectfulness and kindness of saints, cleansed as they were from the impurities of mind and heart that great sadness washes away. However it was that they had managed to become wide open and to see—whether they were by nature more vulnerable or receptive or passionate, whether chance had given them be told in the right way at the most opportune moment by the right person, whether they had had deeper direct knowing, more intuitive certainty or something else, perhaps more magical, possibly even divine—they believed, and they had become exemplary human beings, as good as all of us should aspire to be and few of us ever become. For the time at least, they had no drive to be elsewhere and all the time in the world to be where they were, and there was no self-imposed limit to how much they could give.

Their magnificent choice to believe their sadness and to feel it had elevated them in itself to a higher sphere of humanity; and their profound sadness had exalted them in turn by baring their innate goodness. For those moments they were whole.

The group had met at the airport in Phoenix, having come there from various places in the West, and had boarded a TWA DC-3 that the company still maintained for its own internal use. In this plane they traveled northward, piloted by Captain Larry De Celles. Whether their destination airport was the one in Winslow as with the Kansas City group, or the one in Flagstaff to be much more direct, has possibly been lost to history; it could have been either one because Flagstaff's airport was adequate for a DC-3 even though it was not adequate for a Constellation.

Captain De Celles was a figure who should have had a more prominent place in aviation history than he was given. He was a legendary fellow who sadly was never honored with much legend even though he deserved it. Unfortunately, people are usually remembered more for their successes than for their efforts, more for what they created than for how much they cared about creating.

About two months before the Grand Canyon accident, Larry De Celles was appointed to assist in efforts of the Air Line Pilots' Association (ALPA) to reopen an accident case in which the CAB had blamed the pilot. On February 19, 1955, TWA Captain Ivan Spong, First Officer James Creason, hostess Sharon Schoening, and all thirteen of their passengers, lost their lives in the crash of a TWA Martin 404 at Sandia Mountain, near Albuquerque, New Mexico. On October 12 of the same year, the CAB issued their official accident report on the tragedy. They had done one worse than to call it pilot error—they had actually concluded that Captain Spong intentionally flew off course and directly toward the mountain, at an altitude lower than its peak, and that he did not deviate from this deadly path even though, supposedly, he could see the mountain in front of him. Obviously this was an implied indictment of suicide and murder, and Captain Spong's peers, especially at TWA, were outraged. They organized an effort to clear him, and six months into its mission De Celles joined the team.

That was in April of 1956, but what led to his appointment, what qualified him to be involved, began concretely over two years earlier in

January of 1954. He was then a TWA copilot, in training to become a captain. On a particular flight on a Martin 404, the same type of plane in which Spong perished, the captain instructing De Celles decided to demonstrate a problem that could occur in what was called the flux gate compass. This was a modern instrument superior in some ways to a traditional magnetic compass, but it had a fatal flaw: the gyroscopic mechanism that made it more accurate could stick at a given relative tilt, as during the banking of the airplane in a turn, and create false directional readings as a consequence.

De Celles rolled out of a turn and was shocked to discover that the airport that should have been in front of him was considerably off to one side. The captain tripped a switch and the compass swung around to a different reading, the one that corresponded with what lay in front rather than with the mislaid airport. The captain had caged the gyro, correcting its tilt. Whether he had somehow deliberately induced the error or the gyro had opportunely become stuck just by chance, the lesson that the flux gate compass was fickle was dramatic, and De Celles was alarmed. There had been no warning that the compass was off, and had he been flying at night or in clouds, he would not have realized that anything was wrong.

Later that year De Celles was weaving his way through summer storm clouds in another Martin 404 and got the strange feeling that things were not what they seemed. He had passed through the huge storm area too quickly and instinctively sensed that he ought to have been on the dark backside of the storm rather than on the sunlit side. He remembered his pointed experience with the flux gate compass the previous January and flipped the switch to cage the gyro. Sure enough, the compass rotated fully 180 degrees, revealing the largest error it could have had—he had been flying in completely the opposite of the direction that his instruments had told him.

This was enough to convince De Celles to dedicate himself to resolving the flux gate problem, which was unusual in itself—most people would at best have become resigned to mistrusting the system and to frequently checking up on it—but his solution was truly exceptional. Larry De Celles was not an engineer, but he had decided to solve the flux gate problem himself rather than to persistently push someone else to do it. He began studying the electrical wiring of the system in his free time.

Soon he was promoted to captain, and from that position of credibility greater than a copilot's, he wrote a letter to his superiors at TWA detailing the hazards of the compass. In it he also suggested how the system could be improved. As with all airliners, the instrument panel on the Martin 404 was provided with duplicate instruments arrayed in front of the captain's and copilot's seats, so that the plane could be flown equally well from either position. The two flux gate compass indicators were wired to a single gyro located in one of the wingtips, but they could be switched to instead receive their signals from a second, standby gyro in the other wingtip. De Celles pointed out that an error in the running gyro would always be duplicated on the two dashboard indicators. He suggested that both gyros be used all of the time and that each indicator be wired to its own respective gyro. This would cause the indicators to disagree whenever one gyro became stuck, giving a clear warning of the problem.

The company took him seriously and had one of their staff engineers interview him in January of 1955. The engineer was convinced and recommended that TWA investigate the problem and determine how best to solve it. Tragically, Captain Spong flew his Martin 404 straight into Sandia Mountain in the clouds the following month, way off course. There had been too little time for TWA to rewire the fleet, and some pilots, probably none more than Larry De Celles, began to suspect that the flux gate problem had deceived Captain Spong. This possibility, combined with his already established concern and knowledge about the compass system, was what precipitated De Celles being selected and asked to join the ALPA investigative team.

In April of 1957 De Celles became TWA's Central Air Safety chairman, and he submitted to the CAB a summary that he had written of ALPA's objections to their findings in the Spong case. In August of the same year, the CAB issued an amended accident investigation report in which they omitted their indictment that Spong had intentionally flown off course. But the new report still held that Spong must have known he was off course unless he wasn't paying attention, in essence saying that the accident was his fault and implying that he was at least incompetent.

De Celles was very disappointed but undaunted. The CAB's inconsiderable, almost imperceptible reaction to his efforts made it astoundingly, disconcertingly clear that it would be a long and difficult fight. He retreated and got to work preparing what would be a formidable argument. De Celles worked with TWA's engineering department to compile a comprehensive scientific study of the various ways in which flux gate problems could be expected to occur. Over the better part of the next year, this project and others supporting Spong's innocence were fruitful, and the foundation of a strong case took form.

De Celles studied the entire transcript of the CAB's accident investigation hearing, and all of the documents that had been submitted as exhibits to support the testimony. His foremost goal was to find evidence that would undo the CAB's contention that Spong could see the mountain in front of him—it was their most damning criticism of him. As the hours and the days passed in his research, De Celles became astounded by gradual degrees to find an abundance of the evidence he needed. It was all there, right in the testimony. One witness after another observed the weather at Sandia Mountain at the time of the accident and stated or implied that most of the mountain was obscured by clouds. The most competent among them was an air force colonel, upon whose misquoted and misleadingly excerpted testimony the CAB's claim of good visibility was largely based. He said that the upper third of the mountain was obscured, but separately he contrarily indicated that the base of the cloud layer was at an altitude at which it would have hidden about the upper eighty-six percent of the mountain. Furthermore, those opinions were gauged from the ground. From the air even more of the mountain must have been obscured.

The CAB's conclusion that Captain Spong had good visibility was invalid, as the emerging evidence amply showed. Even more, the same evidence proved that the visibility was poor or even nonexistent. Whether anyone intended it or not, this grave example was a fresh proof of the axiom that almost anything can be shown by manipulating a given set of facts from the right bias.

That of course goes both ways. De Celles' bias probably tended to undermine the fidelity of his own conclusions, but bias or no bias, it can safely be said that he found a good deal of evidence that Spong intended to follow his planned course, rather than deviate from it toward the area of Sandia Mountain. For instance, the radio was found in the wreckage, and an analysis of it revealed it to have been set up for communicating on the frequency used by a station along the planned route, pretty difficult to explain if anyone in the cockpit knew they wouldn't be going that way. But far and away the most sensational piece of evidence was a report on the analysis of one of the flux gate compass indicators from the instrument panel. The CAB had measured the plane's final heading on the basis of the wreckage distribution and damage to the terrain, but the instrument was seized at a reading that differed from their measurement by fully forty-seven degrees. The magnitude of the disparity strongly suggested a flux gate compass error and was furthermore almost exactly right to explain why Spong had flown northeast to the mountain rather than north to bypass it, yet none of this had been mentioned in the official, published accident investigation report.

By this time De Celles had TWA's complete backing, and he felt ready to take on the CAB again. He wrote a seventeen-page argument in which he disputed or refuted point after point in the CAB's evidence and in their interpretations of the evidence, countering with his own conclusions. ALPA submitted De Celles' report to the CAB in midsummer of 1958. In August of 1958, the president of ALPA appealed personally to the CAB to hear De Celles' argument, writing a letter and attaching a multitude of exhibits prepared by De Celles. The CAB agreed to hold a conference with all the concerned parties, to be held on October 10, 1958. At that informal hearing De Celles made a seven-hour-long presentation of the evidence and of his and ALPA's interpretations of it. He employed the elaborate visual exhibits that he had prepared at the expense of TWA to demonstrate some of his points, but the most impressive thing was the man himself, with his seemingly endless reserves of dignity and self-confidence, from which he drew all day long. The CAB members present were initially skeptical or even antagonistic, because it was their own beliefs and their own work that De Celles was criticizing, and because he was not an accident investigator by profession. But De Celles' presentation was brilliant and his logic outstanding, and no one could fail to be sympathetically inspired by his conviction. As the day progressed, the CAB members hearing him out became undeniably moved.

More than anything else the CAB was dedicated to finding the truth, and soon afterward they reopened the case, ordering their Bureau of Safety to start a new investigation.

As a part of their own effort, the Bureau of Safety decided to send a man back to the crash site up in the mountains to remeasure the heading of Captain Spong's plane at the moment of impact. At the time of the original examination of the scene, this final heading had been measured using an ordinary magnetic compass, which was susceptible to errors induced by iron ore. This time the instrument would be a sun compass, which was invulnerable to distortions in the local magnetic field. The same investigator who took the original reading was the one who returned to the site. In November of 1958 he climbed Sandia Mountain, accompanied by Larry De Celles.

The sun compass disagreed with the ruined flux gate indicator from the wrecked airplane, but by only eleven degrees, not forty-seven. The mountain itself had turned the needle to a false direction in the magnetic compass used over three years earlier. De Celles' most spectacular piece of evidence, the one that essentially proved a flux gate error, had just dissolved, and he was severely disappointed. This was not to say, however, that he had been wrong, and he knew that. The scientific research studies done by TWA's engineering department had also shown that flux gate errors were generally self-correcting. A deadly error in Captain Spong's instruments could have vanished at the last moment before the crash. It appeared that this incredibly frustrating case would never give up all of its ambiguities.

Nevertheless, De Celles remained dedicated and continued to devote nearly all of his spare time to the case. He was exhausting himself and his health was deteriorating, but he was sure that Spong was not to blame. For the sake of the truth and for Spong's widow and young son, he persisted.

On January 15 and 16, 1959, the CAB held a new hearing for the purpose of officially taking into evidence their own bureau's new findings and De Celles' findings. De Celles' presentation predominated, taking up fully a day and a half of the two-day proceedings. A number of expert witnesses testified on behalf of his and ALPA's side of the case, and De Celles presented even more detailed arguments than he had in 1958, using even more sophisticated demonstrations.

When the hearing ended, De Celles was done. He knew he had done all he could, and he returned to simply being a pilot. On June 15, 1960, the CAB released the unprecedented third version of their official accident investigation report. In it they stated that Spong's deviation from his planned course could not have been intentional or even known to him, and they admitted the possibility of a flux gate error. They listed the probable cause as unknown.

Captain De Celles had worked on the case for nearly three years, and when all was finished his satisfaction was hollow. He had failed to fully prove that a flux gate compass error killed Captain Spong and his crew and passengers, at least in the minds of the CAB. Instead he had only convinced the CAB that they didn't know what happened. De Celles had substantially cleared Spong but not completely, as a statement from the CAB that the probable cause was a mechanical failure would have done. There was nowhere else for De Celles to take his case. He had applied all of his ingenuity to all of the evidence unrelentingly year after year, and he had run out of ideas. He had exhausted even his own phenomenal creativity and he never returned for another round.

If the measure of a person is the values he holds in his heart and the effort he makes in standing for what he believes, then Larry De Celles was an exceptional person. By 1960 this would become obvious to anyone who really looked at him and his life.

But on July 8, 1956, he was just a relatively undistinguished young airline captain with TWA, who happened to have more than a usual interest in safety.

After a trip of only about an hour, Captain De Celles landed the DC-3. As he taxied his plane up to the ramp, the ramp crew were standing there at attention, and they saluted to honor the mourners. Suddenly he knew the gravity of what he was doing, and he was moved to tears.

CHAPTER 20

THE CHARTER CONSTELLATION flight from Kansas City landed in Winslow at about 7:30 p.m., just before sunset. The group of about eighty people transferred from the plane to buses. No one was in a hurry; for them time held no meaning. They had long since surrendered their wills to the tragedy they could not overturn, and they meekly, passively went along with however those in charge wanted to transport them. Eventually all the luggage was transferred, and the buses pulled away westward into the glow that the sun had left behind. The drive from Winslow to Flagstaff on Route 66 was about a fifty-mile trip and would take about an hour. They rolled hypnotically over the road, and as they sank into the deepening twilight, the balmy evening air wafted them amicably through the open windows. It felt as though the air and the growing darkness were gently carrying them along, like a stream, and the road beneath them had become as insubstantial as the sky. In the dark Sunday night, the buses arrived in Flagstaff, and a United plane carrying L. David Lewis and Raymond Batson home from Flagstaff landed at Stapleton Field in Denver.

For Lewis and Batson, the risk had passed and the mission had ended. For the grieving souls in Flagstaff, only the traveling had ended, and that was the safest part. It was the lull in which they were between trials, neither at home where the tragedy had devastated them and made its terrible, permanent impact, nor in the place where they would know their loss as if it were happening anew. Lewis and Batson could let go of their concerns and sleep soundly, but the mourners were still facing one of the hardest things they would ever face. Many of them suffered greatly through the night, getting only oppressive, fitful sleep like that of a condemned man the night before his end. Likewise, the coming of daybreak brought no relief. As night gave way to day, the nightmares passed, but they did so in giving way to reality.

Monday, July 9, began as a day of confusion or a day of clarity, and the queer twilight that dissolved the difference between the two. Many awoke disoriented, disturbed, or startled by their strange surroundings, confused about where they were and why. Others awoke startled, too, but by the unquestionable realization of where they were and why. Some took deep breaths to brace themselves, sitting on the edges of their beds, before taking the first footstep into the day and into what they knew they were facing. Some prayed for strength. Some turned desperately to their companions for support or to give up and be carried emotionally. A few had the temperament to try to control the situation by composing themselves in routines and began their morning rituals as a person lost in the wilderness might again light the signal fire, long after all hope of being rescued has gone. Others had no illusions of control or composure and clung to their routines in a struggle merely to survive, as a flood victim might cling to a piece of floating debris too small to support him.

For all their variety of approaches, they were alike in grief. Each of them was trying to cope with the situation and do what he had come to do. Each of them had come to stand for the one he loved, to advocate by his presence and by the courage with which he publicly faced his own overwhelming sorrow, the worth and virtue of the person he had lost. Each had come to honor his loved one as a public demonstration, for all to see.

Almost everyone, that is. A few forlorn individuals had come more to tackle the dramatic change in their own lives or to fulfill customs than to honor the person they had lost. It is probably more lamentable and more terrible for the one who perishes than for those he leaves behind, to come to the end of life not being cherished by anyone at all. Some of the victims had this most tragic, most lonely destiny and passed from this world without being missed by the very people to whom they should have mattered the most. Those of them who were nevertheless represented in the funeral party were actually denounced more than dignified by the presence of whoever had come in their name, because these few attendees were not in grief. In effect they publicly defamed the victims they represented by showing, through their lack of sorrow, the low regard they had for them. The only pain these misplaced persons felt was sympathy for the others or the bitterness of having been cheated: the final hurt of losing someone who should have mattered and did not.

And then there were also a few who felt cheated in a wholly different vein. For them the cheat was not dry and bitter but absolutely rending, and they suffered terribly. They had come to mourn the immeasurable loss to themselves represented in the death of someone who mattered greatly but never gave of himself, and now for certain never would—the father who was never there, the mother who was there but was unloving, and so on. These people grieved as powerfully as anyone, but for what they never had rather than for what they lost. To an observer they appeared to honor the deceased in the extreme in the depth of their sorrow, but the truth was that they honored who the deceased should have been, and they honored themselves in their own true need for the relationship that never was.

*   *   *

By midmorning a magnificent display had been assembled at Flagstaff Citizens' Cemetery. It was a scene that was at once exceedingly beautiful and painful to behold. Flowers were everywhere in such profusion and diversity that the memorial plot seemed as much a garden as a grave. Sixty-seven caskets had been arranged in three columns extending northward in the midst of this "garden," in front of a temporarily erected pavilion. In the left-hand column, on the west, were twenty-two; in the center column there were twenty-three, five of which, in a group near the middle, were the smaller caskets of children; and in the column on the right, to the east, were twenty-two, the last of which, farthest from the pavilion toward the north, was the tiny casket of Howard Maag. (See Appendix 9 for a drawing of the entire arrangement.)

The caskets glistened in the sunshine in their various metallic finishes—bronze, copper, gunmetal blue, and silver—and they exemplified several design aesthetics. Some were unembellished and others were ornamented. Some were angular and had sharp corners, and others were more curvaceous and had smoother corners and edges. Their manifold appearances were surprisingly beautiful and suggested the variety of unique persons who had lost their lives together.

As was customary, the caskets were suspended directly over the open grave, but in this instance their numbers were so great, and the grave was so huge, that scaffolding had to be built down in it to support them all. The scaffolding was covered by plywood flooring, which in turn was carpeted with artificial grass, and it was on top of this platform that the caskets rested.

Four of them were draped with large, forty-eight-star American flags to honor servicemen who had perished in the disaster. These were located at the very front of the center column and the next to last places of all three columns. The remaining sixty-three were all decorated with large, wreath-like floral sprays. These were arrangements of fern fronds that radiated from a common center in a circular pattern, adorned with wide satin ribbons and many carnations. In the center column the carnations and ribbons were white, and in all but two of the sprays in the outer columns, the carnations and ribbons were red. Each of the outer columns was divided into three series of red sprays by single white sprays located six or seven places from the front and rear.

Between this whole array and the pavilion was a railing that ran side to side, made of simple lumber painted dark blue. Behind the railing, as viewed from the pavilion, was a lectern facing into the pavilion, outfitted with a gracefully carved wooden book easel and a brass reading lamp, and equipped with two microphones. A small partition, covered completely by about four hundred flower blooms, stood on the ground directly in front of the lectern. In its floral artwork were represented the Christian cross, formed of white carnations, and the Star of David, made of daisies that had been dyed blue, with white carnations for interior highlights. Both religious symbols were inlaid on a background of red carnations, and the whole perimeter of the panel was outlined in palm leaves. The combined effects of the railing, the lectern, and the floral façade constituted a simple, beautiful outdoor altar.

To embellish what was already exquisite, the narrow aisles between the three long columns were lined full length with many types and colors of flowers, arranged in series of bouquets. Framing the entire immense display on all four sides, including alongside the altar, were numerous, very large, free-standing floral arrangements, some symbolic as in the shape of a ship's anchor, and some simply collections of nature's designs.

In the background, about ten miles to the north, was San Francisco Mountain, rising over a mile higher than the elevation of Flagstaff. It had an ethereal bluish cast because of the distance, giving the impression of being reposed in a world apart. The columns of caskets guided the eye in a panoramic, sweeping motion that crossed over them in extending succession and ended at the distant mountain, creating the sensation of travel, of movement, as though in empathy with the souls whose funeral it was. It was as though seeing and feeling where the deceased were going, in a mystic revelation of the other side and of what was drawing them. And it was especially right that Howard Maag's casket was placed all the way at the back, nearest to this image of heaven, "touching" the base of the mountain in line of sight at the horizon. He was so new that he had not been able to stray very far from God in life, and he had surely been the nearest to his Creator of any victim.

In sympathy with the impression that the mountain was of the afterlife, the perfumes of the myriad flowers mingled together to make a scent as glorious as if the angels had blended it. Divinity itself suffused the air. The full effect of this visual and olfactory splendor was spiritually uplifting, and in another setting it would have been spiritually intoxicating. It was more than apt as a rendering of man's conception of the doorway to heaven, with the light and scent of purity and joy filtering through from the other side.

*   *   *

The pavilion was simply a very large canvas tent with no sides, a canopy supported by poles that were lashed to stakes in the ground. Its primary purpose was to shade the congregation from the midsummer Arizona sun, but just in case, it was there secondarily to keep them dry in the event of rain. Under the canopy were a great many metal folding chairs, with padded seats covered in brown Naugahyde. The seats were set up in rows of about sixteen with an aisle running down the center from the back to the front, analogous to the pews of a church. In all, seating had been prepared for a congregation of about 250 people.

The businesses of Flagstaff closed at 10:30 that morning in honor of the funeral. It was a very small town, only about seven thousand residents, and the funeral procession was to move along its main street, passing in front of many of the stores. Nearly everyone in town felt involved and cared to show humble concern. Most of them wanted to participate and accordingly freed themselves of anything detracting, including business.

The private citizens, businesspeople, and civic organizations of Flagstaff contributed the loan of dozens of automobiles for the funeral procession. Added to these were some from out of state, making a long file of over fifty vehicles. Just after 10:30 the procession began to move, like the cars of a train lurching into plodding motion one at a time. The cars moved slowly from downtown to the cemetery, as though carried along by the meek and weary current of a stream of discouragement. People lined the street and prayed or solemnly watched as though someone very near to them, like a civic leader from their own town, had died.

Shortly before 11:00 a.m. the last car in the procession pulled into the cemetery and stopped. Everyone had arrived. The dreadful ride had ended, and they were in the place where they would say good-bye, and where great periods of their lives would end. They stood at the juncture between the past and the future and felt the change coming deep within themselves, like the subtle tremors that precede an earthquake. All of them were scared, though some were too numb or disoriented to feel it, and a few began to weep.

The lane on which the cars parked bordered the huge burial plot, and from it the mourners could see the multitude of coffins and flowers. There were no intervening bushes or other obstructions, so that as each car found its place and the passengers got out, they were suddenly and boldly faced with the enormousness of the ceremony they had come to join. Some of them gasped while others softly exclaimed, "Dear Lord," or, "Oh, my God," or other appeals for strength or courage or for the simple ability to believe what they saw. Few were prepared for the sight of sixty-seven caskets. Few had truly grasped the situation, and now many cried.

An organist was playing hymns on a Hammond electric organ. The members of the funeral party walked slowly across the grass with the unaffected gentleness of complete humility, and a few at a time took their seats in the pavilion. About 350 had come, embodying only a select few family members and friends on behalf of each victim, and yet still far exceeding the number that were anticipated. Soon every one of the chairs was filled by someone; and nearly a hundred people had to stand.

The American Red Cross had set up a temporary hospital tent outfitted with cots off to the side, in case anyone would succumb to the emotional strain and need medical attention. One of their white supply trucks with the large red crosses painted on it was parked near the tent. Their expression of compassion was one of the most tangible, human, and genuine in the entire proceedings. They were there to literally touch people and to immediately, directly, personally care for anyone who needed it.

A military guard of honor consisting of members of the navy, the marines, and the army stood at attention facing the congregation from the far end. Among those who represented the army were Major Jerome B. Feldt, who had commanded the army's Grand Canyon operations and had flown the first bodies of TWA victims from Grand Canyon Airport to Flagstaff Municipal Airport, and Captain Walter E. Spriggs, who had made the first landing atop the United crash promontory at Chuar Butte, dropping off David Lewis.

In reverence for the bereaved friends and family members of the victims, Arizona State Senator Robert Prochnow, of Flagstaff, and the Honorable Ernest McFarland, Governor of Arizona, sat amongst them and joined their congregation. Several TWA officials were present out of a humble sense of duty, but there was something more: in their various capacities they had each promoted air travel, whether by directly attempting to influence the public, or by working behind the scenes to help the airline thrive as an entity that was attractive to people. Either way, they had encouraged travelers to entrust the airline with transporting them and ultimately with their lives, and a group who had given their trust had died. Stirring within their souls the TWA officials felt an undercurrent of remorse. They knew it was not their fault in the usual sense of blame, where there is a direct, determining connection, but there was nevertheless a connection: influence. In the face of such a terrible loss of life, no one could deny that we all take a hand in what happens to others. No man of conscience could entirely dismiss the truth of this, and no matter how tenuous or indirect a connection they had, and no matter how vaguely they sensed it, the TWA officials were compelled to wrestle with their consciences and could not help but feel great sorrow.

All told, many thousands of people attended the numerous private services held throughout the country. A large proportion of them would have been in Flagstaff, had it been appropriate. Their multitudes were nevertheless shadowed in the far background at the cemetery, where the better part of two thousand people, mostly residents of Flagstaff, stood in reverent observance.

At 11:00 the service began. A few thin, gray clouds had formed to the north and floated between the cemetery and San Francisco Mountain, but at the gravesite the sky was clear. The sun's brilliance and heat poured forth, saturating the scene and enclosing all of the people in it; even the shaded space under the canopy was very warm and suffused with light. Four clergymen representing the Mormon, Jewish, Protestant, and Catholic faiths conducted the service. In the order in which they spoke, they were: Elder Delbert Stapley, Church of Jesus Christ of Latter Day Saints, in Salt Lake City; Cantor Maurice Chesler, Temple Beth Israel in Phoenix; Pastor Wyburn Skidmore of the Flagstaff Federated Community Church in Flagstaff; and Father Anthony Vorst of the Catholic Church of the Nativity, also in Flagstaff.

It is difficult to imagine how hopeless and desperate it must feel to attempt giving comfort to 350 grieving people, from the same stage that bears the caskets of 67 of their loved ones. It is difficult to imagine the struggles that each church leader encountered within himself to find meaningful words, without feeling so much empathy as to dissolve in heartache and be unable to speak. Surely no number of typical funerals honoring one or even a few deceased persons at a time could have prepared them, and though they did not fail, they faltered.

In the face of overwhelming feelings it is sadly natural, perhaps not nature's natural but man's accustomed second nature, to take refuge in intellectualizing. In much of what they said, the clergymen resorted to well meant but ineffectual palliatives, concepts rather than heartfelt, directly personal truth. Talking about everyone's desolation and anguish could have helped them release their hold on themselves, so that they could fully *feel* their own pain. It could have helped them to face their loss. Instead, the clergymen's predominant approach was to try making the pain a little less difficult to bear by mitigating it. They expressed the faithful beliefs that no one had died in vain, and everyone had gone to a better place, and God was not to blame, and so on.

It is hard to see of what use consolation was in a situation so dire. The wife still had no mate, no partner in raising her children and no husband to support them, even if Air Traffic Control stood to be improved out of the tragedy prompting greater safety, and even if others who might have been destined to perish had been saved. It is hard to fathom how thinking of others could be of any use to anyone who had just lost his loved ones. For once it was absolutely appropriate for those people to focus on themselves. This was the greatest trial in most of their lives, and thinking of others grievously missed the point. The husband and father still had to face a world in which he was no longer a husband or a father, and the horrifying emptiness of a life that for him no longer had any purpose, even if his wife and children had gone to heaven. And it is inconceivable that abstract ideas could have nurtured the orphaned children—they were frightened and would still have to trust for today that whoever was taking care of them would not abandon them, too; they would still have to grow up without their parents' love and guidance, and with terrible voids in their identities, even if God could not be faulted for permitting the tragedy.

These were the relevant, concrete realities, and no one was helped to face them by any references to abstractions, or to realities that they might experience after this life; it was *this* life that they had to endure and resolve. Of course it was comforting to feel a moment's pride that in his death the loved one accomplished a noble purpose, or a moment's gratitude and loving relief in the belief that he had gone to a far better place and had achieved beatitude in the life hereafter. These were wonderful ideas, but they could not help the grief-stricken people at the service to face the fact that their own lives had become infinitely worse, and the children just needed to be overwhelmingly loved.

Each in his own way, the clergymen knew this. To one degree or another each one did invest his own humanity in his sermon and spoke personally to the people whom he was privileged to help. The dignity with which they all sat there and listened could not have failed to inspire admiration, humility, compassion, and intimacy even in a person resolutely determined to remain at some distance, even if his purpose were unselfish and honorable, and the clergymen were not trying to remain distant or dispassionate so much as composed. They had spent their lives caring about people, serving God by serving their fellow man, and they could not help feeling love for the people in front of them time after time during their sermons. Perhaps nowhere else in the entire service did love engender a more supportive, human, relevant statement, reflecting the magnitude of the tragedy, than the moment when Pastor Skidmore said simply, "Millions of prayers have been raised for all of you here. All America prays."

That was real help, real support, direct and pertinent to the mourners themselves. The sheer scope of that notion overwhelmed many with encouragement, dissolving their entrapment for a time, no matter how powerful and resistive their despondency was. The first response of many to that liberation was to let themselves have their pain and cry; it was as though they could breathe freely again after long being short of breath. And in letting themselves live again as feeling persons, even if only for a moment, they had begun to reclaim their will to live, their will to carry on, their will to face their grief and the struggles that their changed lives would require of them.

Near the end of the service, members of the armed forces removed and folded the American flags and presented them to the families of the honored servicemen. In place of the flags, floral sprays were laid, so that all sixty-seven caskets were adorned alike. The distinctiveness of the four flag-bearing ones had vanished, in agreement with the relinquishment in death of worldly roles and the resulting equality among persons. Members of the navy fired a salute with rifles, as much commemorating this surrender and liberation as honoring the service that the deceased gave in life.

Taps was played in staggered meter by two buglers, positioned off to either side at the far end of the plot, creating the timeless sensation of each being the echo of the other, of the past eerily, preternaturally resounding there in the present and yet being elsewhere at the same time, and the present not being confined to just a single moment. The sky had become overcast, though not so heavily as to make things appear dark. The sun's light still shone through, illuminating things brightly but dampened enough that colors seemed richer and contrasts greater, while shadows were relatively lightened and had become indistinct. It was a dreamlike lighting effect, and combined with the sensation that time itself had expanded beyond the narrow present, it was scintillatingly spiritual. On the background of the light, Taps was the flawless focus of everyone's awareness. It pierced their souls and resounded within them. It at once heightened their awareness of being alive in the present moment and signified that something great had ended and become the past. The sublime purity of that utterly simple melody, given extraordinary dimension by the apparent echoing, was so transcendent and powerful that it stopped everyone present. All were stripped of their complexities, of everything that could shield them from the profound simplicity of their own hearts. All were rendered defenseless and began to cry, even the most hard-bitten military men.

The time had arrived for saying good-bye. Accompanied by organ music, one row at a time in the congregation stood up and walked forward, filing past the caskets slowly, each person trying both to set free his loved one and to hold on. One after another broke down. Many cried out in woe, and all of them sobbed or wept. The emotion was too much for some to bear. Eight persons were overcome and collapsed, and four of them were carried to the Red Cross tent on stretchers.

Many members of the congregation were so taken by the power of that event, of feeling all of that passion and pain through so many hearts at once, that their individuality had been largely washed away. They were adrift as persons, in a sea of raw emotion. They were detached, dissociated from the comparatively meaningless details of their surroundings, and they followed in a daze wherever they were led. They were utterly disoriented and had no will to get a grip on themselves, so lost were they in their ordeal of grief. And there was another side to it: they were single-mindedly focused in their grief, actively working through it by going straight into it and abiding there. They were deep within their own hearts. What they were going through was not physical, it was spiritual, and they ignored most of the externals, the actions and circumstances like getting into a car, closing its door, being aware of riding as a passenger, and so on. The physical world was all nothing, as vague and impalpable as fog in the face of how real and substantial their spirits had become.

After submissive, outwardly absent meanderings that would be difficult or impossible to recall later, and guided by others who still had the presence of mind to organize events and take responsibility for them, they rediscovered themselves at their hotels, preparing to leave Flagstaff. Others among the mourners could contrarily remember clearly much of what they saw and did between the service and their packing, yet they could not relate these events to themselves any more than the ones who had passed through a fugue. The mind could not grasp such a momentous, rending experience, and so it either could not identify the experience as real, or it could not verify it as something in which the person had actually participated. It was a wholly new kind of personhood, and no one could define it. Many had been through a trauma, and nearly everyone had been singularly moved. Such power could only be felt, and in its wake a person could only witness, not judge.

Somewhere in the middle of the afternoon, the group that had flown to Winslow from Kansas City boarded their buses for the ride back to Winslow. To most of these people, Arizona was as remote as Africa, and with its pine forests and deserts and canyons and cacti, it was just as strange and unfamiliar. It felt as though it lay in another world, and for most, the distance separating their homes from Flagstaff would make it impractical to return. As the buses rolled eastward along Route 66, it was as though the bereaved were abandoning those lost in the disaster. Most of them would be able to come back only once in several years or even in a lifetime, and some would sadly never return. A profound loneliness and isolation enveloped the group as the last perceptible traces of their loved ones vanished with Flagstaff in the distance behind them. Some knew they would not be back, and many felt real guilt or sorrow for leaving their loved ones in a place so far removed from their homes.

Yet it had to be. Of the seventy persons aboard the *Star of the Seine,* only ten had been positively identified. Fully sixty of the sixty-seven caskets at the mass funeral represented unidentified victims, and it was of course impossible to send them home.

Three who were identified had been sent home for private burials prior to the mass service, and they had not been part of the display at Flagstaff Citizens' Cemetery. They were:

Mrs. Catherine Kennaley
Miss Mary Ellen Lytle
Mr. Robert B. Nelson

Of the seven identified victims at the mass gravesite, one more was returned home after the service:

Mrs. Almeda Evans

Sixty-six caskets remained at the TWA memorial. Sixty of these either held unidentified remains or were purely symbolic. The other six contained the remains of identified victims whose families wanted for them to be buried with the rest. They were:

Mr. Harry Harvey Allen
Mr. Stephen Robert Bishop
Mr. Donald Lloyd Flentie
Mrs. Virginia Elizabeth Goppert
Master Howard John Maag

Mr. Neal Alan Power

The plane from Winslow landed in the dark at Kansas City Municipal Airport, at about 10:10 p.m. CST. Soon afterward the passengers had collected their luggage and vanished into the night. To some of the employees at the terminal watching them walk out through the doors, it was like watching the last vestiges of the tragedy eerily dissolve and disappear, the final subsiding of the tumult. They knew that most of those people would never return, having no connection with the airline and no interest in flying except for the accident. It seemed somehow too simple, too easy, that the bereaved had been brutally robbed of what they held most dear and now humbly walked away, not even expressing indignation, much less torment or rage. They simply, quietly left, with no demonstration at all.

The worst for some was arriving home. For some who had lost a member of their immediate family, the house that had represented love and togetherness and security now blatantly, dreadfully symbolized terrible wrong. It was now heartbreaking instead of heartwarming, and threatening instead of welcoming. It was no longer a home, but only a building that menacingly stood in cruel mockery of what a home should be. It had become a horrible travesty.

For others home was salvation, the only refuge. Going back home enabled them tangibly to feel the presence of their loved one, giving them deep comfort. Home rescued them from losing their minds. For them, the house personified the legacy of the missing family member in all that he had done there and created there. The absent person's caring and efforts and intimate investments could be found everywhere, in the smallest things and the largest, and this was a great consolation. His consciousness and life force were still there, quiet yet vibrant, hidden inside the stillness, perceptible like the subtle throbbing in the ears when sound suddenly and unexpectedly gave way to silence.

CHAPTER 21

ON TUESDAY, JULY 10, the families of the TWA victims woke up to their new lives. They fought no more and ran no more. They began their new day as they had begun the first morning of their lives, purely aware. The storm had subsided and moved on, and their focus had returned. In it they had returned to themselves, and their minds were unfettered and tranquil. No will stirred at first within them, no reaction to their perception. They were undivided, as an infant does not differentiate between itself and its surroundings. And then they *recognized* that they were alive. They became aware that they were aware, and doubled themselves as with a mirror. The difference between the knower and the known returned, and then the difference between themselves and their lives. The exclusive nature of identity came back to them, and they saw what they and their lives were, and were not. In clarity for the first time, they knew that the people they had lost were *not* alive, and were gone.

*   *   *

For the officials involved directly in the aftermath of the disaster, July 10 was a day that lacked the concrete emotional validity of the previous days. It was a day of disbanding, of dissolution and business, not of noble and clearly necessary action. There were no more victims' remains to retrieve from the indignity in which they had lain, and plenty of telltale wreckage had been removed from the sites to prove that there was a collision, and hopefully to demonstrate in what manner the planes had collided. There was no one to be served by further work there.

The men who had remained on top of the crash promontory at Chuar Butte Sunday had been flown out on Monday, and on Tuesday those of them that were still in the area dispersed. The eight-man team of mountaineers from Switzerland left Flagstaff that day bound for Los Angeles. The last of the twin-rotor army helicopters left the Grand Canyon area to return to Fort Huachuca in southern Arizona. Mr. John McLaughlin, the superintendent of Grand Canyon National Park, announced to the press that all recovery operations in the canyon had ceased. It was an ending, and the most real part of the official response to the accident had passed.

Some of the workers were simply done and had been released from further obligation. They were no longer involved. Others were transferring their work to elsewhere, many of them to their offices, and its whole character was changing from humanitarian to rationally dutiful. For both, the underlying compassion and clarity in dedicatedly helping other human beings, deceased or living, had subsided and been replaced by comparative dullness. The Grand Canyon operations had been stirring and singular, changing almost everyone who took part in them, but now they could all largely resume their ordinary lives and become reacquainted with themselves as the familiar persons they were before the tragedy, even most of the ones who continued to work on the accident, because contending with aircraft accidents was a major part of their normal lives.

At 9:00 a.m. on this day, the coroner's inquest into the United Air Lines crash began. Like the TWA inquest, it was held in Coconino County Courthouse in Flagstaff, with County Coroner Shelby McCauley presiding. Again the hearing was straightforward, and the jury's verdict expressed the most fundamental, overwhelmingly obvious fact of the tragedy: fifty-eight persons had been killed by accident.

Following the inquest, Dr. George Kidera of Chicago, the medical director of United Air Lines, announced to the press that a total of twenty-nine positive identifications had been made and that it would be impossible to identify the other twenty-nine. He also said that all of the identified remains had been sent home to the families for burial. United's President William "Pat" Patterson also made a statement to the press, which was prepared in advance. In part, he said, "With the invaluable aid of many individuals and agencies United Air Lines has been able to identify twenty-nine of the fifty-eight persons who were aboard the company's aircraft when it met with an accident over the Grand Canyon. It is with regret that the company must report it is unable to identify the balance of the victims. For their vital assistance United is indebted to the United States Army, United States Air Force, the identification division of the FBI, Rocky Mountain Rescue Group, a Swiss mountain climbing team, and many others. When the accident occurred we were told that it would be physically impossible to remove anything from the scene. Due to the inspired courage of many groups, we have removed the recoverable remains from the scene and have made twenty-nine positive identifications. The vital assistance rendered by the military cannot be overemphasized. Without their great effort, we could never have accomplished what we did."

Exactly half, that many and that few, had been recognized and sent home. In that one respect their lives had been completed—they had come around to where they started, returned to their families and their homes. The other victims left and kept on going, never to return in any sense. Half had vanished, had been hidden somewhere in the Grand Canyon. Their lives would remain unfinished because they had desisted more than concluded. No semblance of most of these could have been among the unidentifiable remains, which were so meager a proportion of all that had been found as to represent possibly as few as four persons. Possibly as many as twenty-five persons were literally missing, and it could not even be deduced where they were. The body of any particular one of them could have been the origin of some of the nameless remains, but even ruling that out, it did not follow that a particular victim's body must still have lain somewhere on Chuar Butte, because it might no longer exist.

The other side of this tragic reality was that fully half of the United victims had been identified, which was exceptional. It was also considerably better than TWA's results of one in seven. Of course on face value, it was only to be expected that more United victims than TWA victims would be identified. The rude fact that United recovered forty-three bags of remains for fifty-eight persons, while TWA recovered only twenty-six bags for seventy persons, foretold the outcome, although it did not explain it. Rather, in a sense it merely rephrased it: the United victims' remains had come through better.

One reason for the disparity was that all of the TWA victims were concentrated at the center of the fire, whereas the United victims were scattered throughout the fire area, coming to rest not just at the center but also at the less ferocious edges. Four had even escaped the fire entirely. Still, the malevolence of the inferno at Chuar Butte was terrible, and the United forensics team did what could only be called a remarkable job, considering what they had to work with. Of this grim reality L. David Lewis later said, "How they were able to make any identifications at all is beyond me." On the scale of Lewis' eyewitness impressions at the United site, the TWA team's performance would much more aptly be considered miraculous than inferior.

On Thursday, July 12, United Air Lines held a very small, unostentatious interment service for the unidentified victims. United had arranged for the remains to be buried in a permanent memorial plot in Grand Canyon National Park Cemetery, in Grand Canyon Village. The somber ceremony began at 10:00 a.m. and was performed by a modest group of ten officials. They were: Pastor Hilka Green of Grand Canyon Community Church, Grand Canyon Village; Father John Faustina of St. Joseph's Catholic Church, Williams, Arizona; Cantor Maurice Chesler of Temple Beth Israel, Phoenix, who had performed the Jewish rites at TWA's funeral in Flagstaff; J. M. Klapp, Assistant to the President of United Air Lines, Chicago; Jim Kennedy,

Public Relations Officer for United, Denver; John S. McLaughlin, Superintendent of Grand Canyon National Park; Lynn Coffin, Chief Ranger of Grand Canyon National Park; Vernon Rausch, a ranger of Grand Canyon National Park; Glenn Compton, Mortician from Flagstaff; and Charles Whitney, Mortician from Phoenix.

Three clergymen, two United Air Lines representatives, three officers of Grand Canyon National Park, and two morticians enacted the solemn duty.

There were only four caskets. Four were sufficient to contain all of the unidentified remains. United Air Lines had consulted the families of the unidentified victims and, with their acceptance, had decided on the undisguised practical course of providing only these necessary coffins, rather than adding twenty-five more to their number for symbolic purposes. It was in keeping with United's corporate character that they had chosen the direct, dignified, rational course, just as it was true to the nature of TWA at the time that they had followed the passionate, dramatic, heartfelt course, in presenting one coffin for each unidentified victim even though most of them were empty.

Besides it being sensible and candid, United could not have obtained a plot large enough for twenty-nine caskets at Grand Canyon National Park Cemetery, which was quite small, like a rural cemetery, and had a policy of being for residents only; the park had made a compassionate exception for the essential burials.

United's president Pat Patterson was a banker before entering the airline industry, and the flamboyant Hollywood producer and playboy Howard Hughes, a visionary with a fortune to make his dreams become realities, basically ran TWA. Well-ordered reason guided United, while a spirit more akin to artistic creativity was expressed in TWA. Logic and feeling, equally valuable and highly dissimilar, had become the two airlines, exemplified and promoted by their leaders, and these themes abided in the sad and difficult decisions about the two funerals.

Many victims on each flight were simply never found, and that was the real reason for which they were not identified. Each airline had to decide how to respond to this deplorable reality in their funeral arrangements, and the two had come to superficially opposite solutions, even though their fundamental compassionate intentions to honor the dead and the bereaved were much the same. What is at first difficult to accept is that United also decided to have no family members or friends present at the interment. The ten officials who conducted the service also constituted the entire funeral party. With the consent of the families, a separate memorial service had been planned for later.

One of the reasons behind this ostensibly peculiar arrangement was that by July 12, the people who would have come had been through nearly two weeks of continual hell, and most of them were emotionally and mentally strained to their limits. It would have been cruel to compel them to attend. The delays in reaching the United crash site had delayed the removal of the remains; this in turn had delayed the identification process, which ultimately delayed the coroner's inquest, and the final result was that too much time had passed.

It had also been hard enough already for the families to be informed, even over the telephone, that their loved ones could not be identified. Even forewarned, it would have been devastatingly painful to them to actually see in the display of a mere four coffins, that twenty-five victims were just plain missing, and to realize that this most likely included their own loved ones. It was much kinder to bury the four caskets before any family members arrived.

In United's sensible way, however, the primary reason for which they decided to dissuade the families from attending was probably the practical fact that the gravestone was not yet in place. It had not been finished and was still to be shipped from Chicago. It simply would have been unacceptable to offer the families nothing concrete representing their loved ones.

After a brief service in which Protestant, Catholic, and Jewish rites were performed, the somber group of ten left the cemetery. For a moment only the birds in the branches of the surrounding Ponderosa pines, attracted by the sunlight gleaming on the four caskets, watched over the unidentified victims. For a moment the interest of man had ceased, and the remains stood alone in the fullness of nature, undisturbed by humankind, reposed in a pristine serenity that was by nature unknowable and would vanish under man's gaze. And then the crew of cemetery workers arrived and it was gone.

By the end of the second week in July, there was very little left to be done in Grand Canyon Village or in Flagstaff by the officials from out of state, and nearly all of them had disbanded and left. As they progressively dispersed over the course of the week, both towns reverted to a semblance of normalcy, yet it was a normalcy that was not only familiar but also contrarily strange. For the whole month of July up until then, overshadowing even Independence Day, both towns had been inundated with strangers conducting grave and bizarre business pertaining to one of the worst transportation disasters that had ever occurred, and all of that was already disappearing. It was difficult to believe that such a momentous thing had happened and had subsided so soon. It was difficult for the townspeople to comprehend, and they were disoriented. Already there were occurring times in which no impression and no sign of the tragedy could be found, and that was odd. The premature normalcy felt almost artificial or fraudulent. It seemed like a betrayal of the victims or an insult to them, a denial of their trauma and their loss. It was too abrupt and made no sense, and some of the more sensitive townspeople felt guilty about it, as though they were taking part in a travesty.

As the days passed and the normalcy was daily repeated, however, it gradually took on its former genuine feel, its comfort and dependability, and it ceased to cause anyone any guilt or confusion. Confusion gave way to simple affirmations that things had really returned to normal, and guilt transformed into the humble gratitude to have been spared the terrible fate of the victims. The people of both towns were beginning to feel confident and secure, and glad to be alive.

The peace in Grand Canyon Village was short-lived. In the last days of July, officials of United Air Lines returned to Grand Canyon

Village to make the final preparations for the United memorial service, scheduled to take place a few days later on Thursday, August 2. A month had passed since the accident. Most people were deep in the spell of the midsummer heat, entranced by its oppressiveness and its vibrancy. These were the summer doldrums, and a self-contradictory intense apathy prevailed. There was little relief because few people had air-conditioning in their homes. The sentiment or lack of sentiment in their boredom was solidified by its persistence. Throughout the nation most people had already forgotten the tragedy, or thought of it only occasionally or with only mild resignation rather than any real feeling. They were operating more on dull instinct than out of values and free choice, having been rendered less empathetic and contemplative by the heat. It drove them like it drove a horse to find water and shade. They would have forgotten anyway, but perhaps not so soon. Possibly if it had been winter, the crisp clarity of the cold, clean air would have prolonged or inspired or permitted a similar clarity in people's minds.

Even some of the family and friends of the victims were beginning to have lapses in their remembrance. All of the individual memorial services held in their hometowns had come and gone. It was time to begin taking up some of the routines of life again, and time to begin new ones, and in absorbing themselves in small and large actions, they were beginning to find much-needed moments of forgetfulness.

But for those of them whose loved ones were among United's twenty-nine unidentified, there was one more service to face. By the night of Wednesday, August 1, United Air Lines had brought 104 of them to Winslow via three chartered flights, and from there three buses had taken them to lodgings in Grand Canyon Village. Others had come in their own cars or by train, bringing their numbers to about 130. Along with the numerous officials and other workers who would conduct and support the services, some directly and some behind the scenes, a total of nearly 200 persons had congregated.

United set up a special reception room where family members could go for assistance or information, or for the consolation of meeting with members of other families, and here there was something being done, something unobtrusive happening late into the night. But most of the mourners merely settled into their rooms, and in keeping with this the night was heavy and somber and outwardly uneventful, even though its character was momentous. Something important and very painful had been set to occur the following morning, and the power of it could be felt in the air, like the electric presence that precedes a thunderstorm.

*   *   *

On the other side of the country that evening, inquisitors and witnesses alike were discussing over dinner or cocktails what had for them been a very trying day. The Civil Aeronautics Board had begun their public accident investigation hearing in the Department of Commerce Auditorium in Washington, D.C., and had finished conducting the first of what would be four long days of difficult questioning and testifying. It was not that the questioning had been particularly intense or confrontational; rather, it was the subtle atmosphere of guilt that was so hard. An inexpressibly terrible thing had happened, and anyone with half a soul was moved at least unconsciously by a strong urge to do something to set it right, to say something helpful, to be of use in preventing such a thing from ever happening again, not only because it was so clearly imperative, but also because he had not done as much as he could have in the past to prevent the disaster that *had* occurred. Most of the participants were also humbly, earnestly resolved to make sure that they did not do any additional harm, as by inadvertently focusing any blame on anyone, and so besides the urgency they felt in doing what was right, many were in some degree of guilt-ridden conflict within themselves over trying to *weigh* what was right, trying to balance fearlessly searching for the truth with being careful. Moreover, the public scrutiny of the hearing amplified everyone's introspection and circumspection. In all of these ways, the hearing had strained nearly everyone and had been very trying for many.

It was the Civil Aeronautics Board's job to determine, as far as possible, what had caused the accident, and one of the efforts they made in every serious civil aviation accident was to hold formal hearings. These were strictly fact-finding sessions, and by law no testimony given in them could be used later in lawsuits. This stipulation of course was meant to remove any compunction that the witnesses might feel to avoid being fully open, and so it tended to make the hearings more productive and valuable. But more important, the aim was to preserve the Board's independence and impartiality, by ensuring that no person or organization would directly gain or lose anything as a consequence of the Board's findings. The idea was that no member of the CAB should have a conflict of interests in pursuing the truth, and the rule did reduce the potential for that. However, information developed in the hearings could very well guide litigants in building their cases; all they had to do once they knew a particular truth was to "discover" it by their own means, and this was facilitated greatly by their knowing what truths to pursue. This was obvious to nearly everyone, and so the moral absolving afforded by the rule was only on about the order of that obtained by a landowner who permits others to hunt on his land. He himself kills none of the animals, but he is still to blame because he enables the hunters to kill them through giving his permission. Somehow this indirect responsibility seems less of a crime, and that of course is its appeal, even though it is at least equal.

The hearings had been nobly conceived to encourage truthfulness by being in themselves benign, but the moral dilemmas they were meant to avoid were nonetheless inescapable. People could be hurt, perhaps many people, by truths told imprecisely or elicited out of context by poorly placed questions, and knowing this put the more alert, caring participants in the position of having to be restrained rather than purely free and open. They had to evaluate and choose their words carefully, and this seemed somehow contrary to honesty. Whether they asked the questions or answered them, it had been difficult.

The hearing lasted for three more days, concluding on August 4. A great amount of information was collected in testimony and in the form of documents submitted in evidence. No conclusions were made—doing so would have been recklessly premature, and it was extraneous to the hearing's purpose, which was to assemble the groundwork upon which conclusions might hopefully be formulated later, after careful, incisive study.

In the months that followed, the Civil Aeronautics Board thoroughly analyzed the collision evidence, the weather, the cockpit visibility limitations of both planes, and many other things, and they produced an extensive, detailed report. They outlined a representative selection of the physical and documentary evidence along with their interpretations of it, and then summarized their findings with an overall conclusion about what had caused the accident, which they called the probable cause. This was the format of the conclusion in all of their reports, no matter how well the cause was established, but in this case it was also literally forthright because they simply did not know. On April 17, 1957, the CAB released this report, making it available to any and all interested organizations and persons.

For lack of evidence, the Board was unable to prove how the accident happened. The rude fact that the planes collided was proved with exceeding clarity in the physical evidence, but why they collided was not demonstrated. The first line of their summation was, "The Board determines that the probable cause of this mid-air collision was that the pilots did not see each other in time to avoid the collision." And that's as far as they took it.

This was almost like no answer at all, because it stated only just what anyone would presume. Everyone knew that in most accidents, the people involved didn't see what was coming until it was too late, and so without even knowing any of the facts or circumstances, anyone could soundly propose the same probable cause. The Board's view was of course an actual conclusion, based on examining all of the evidence and on finding no indication of any other cause. This seemed more substantial and was certainly more responsible than presuming the same view, even though it was fortified only by default. But because the Board's finding was not a logical consequence of any evidence, it was actually no more concrete than presumption.

A better answer would have treated the unproved supposition that they didn't see each other until it was too late as given, and then sought to explain it. Instead, in the second sentence of their summation, the Board flatly pronounced, "It is not possible to determine why the pilots did not see each other…" This sentence went on for another ninety-eight words and finished the report, solely enumerating the most plausible possibilities, but it favored none of them over the others. The excerpt quoted here constitutes the only conclusion in the sentence and presents the entirety of it, every word.

The statement that it was impossible to determine why the pilots did not see each other involves several fallacies. In it, the Board proffered as *fact* the assertion that the pilots did not see each other, conflicting with their claim in the previous sentence that the pilots *probably* did not see each other. Furthermore, the Board's contention that it was impossible to determine *why* the pilots did not see each other (*if* in fact they didn't), and the Board's concomitant omitting of an educated guess, requires that this question be characteristically more difficult to answer than why they *collided,* to which the Board gave an answer that they thought probable. But there was a good deal of evidence pertaining to what might have prevented the crews from seeing each other, while the inference that the planes collided because the crews failed to see each other could not be demonstrated. Finally, the Board used the word "determine" with a meaning at odds with that which they gave it in the previous sentence, connoting certainty rather than reasonable assurance. The only thing that was not possible to determine was the incontrovertibly proved explanation. On the other hand, if the second sentence is taken to be correct, then the first one should read, "It is not possible to determine the probable cause of this accident."

No explanation was provable, but only supportable, and it is inconsistent that on these grounds the CAB didn't commit themselves further. That very condition applied exactly to their stated probable cause, yet they worked until they had formulated that belief and had adopted it as more credible than the alternatives, and then they published it. They could have done the same with the "probable cause of the probable cause." It was not only legitimate but also entirely feasible.

This book takes such a stand and the Board did not. The people who lost a loved one in that disaster desperately needed to know what happened. They needed to know how or why the planes collided, so that they could gain yet another small foothold on the precipice they were trying to scale between hell and sanity. It would have helped them a great deal for someone trustworthy to tell them, in the best of his judgment, what probably happened. That was the CAB's responsibility.

When the public demands information, the officials with the authority to give it are usually careful to avoid speculation, in the view that to mislead people who have a stake in knowing the truth is irresponsible, even if it is done unintentionally. That is an honorable ethic and I agree with it. I disagree that speculation is irresponsible and that incorrect speculation is misleading. Speculation in many instances is the best that can be offered, and it is consoling to know what others believe, even if they aren't certain. Doing what *can* be done is hardly irresponsible; in fact, the contrary is the truth: *not* doing what can be done is irresponsible. And speculation that turns out to be incorrect is not misleading—failing to clarify at the outset that it is in fact speculation, is misleading.

Everyone hates being patronized, protected from himself by parental officials. Most of us would say, "Give me the information, tell me you're not certain of it, tell me how probable you think it is, and let me decide for myself what to do with it." The CAB could have given the public more, a lot more. The families needed more than the obvious notion that probably the planes collided because the crews didn't see each other in time. They needed at least the answer to the next question, Probably *why* didn't they see each other in time?

CHAPTER 22

EARLY ON THE morning of Thursday, August 2, a limestone monolith about the size of a refrigerator door stood at the small plot in Grand Canyon National Park Cemetery. It had been roughly hewn, and its face had been ground flat and highly polished so that it was very smooth. Near the top, the face was engraved in six lines with the inscription:

In memory
of these persons
who lost their lives
in the aircraft accident
at Grand Canyon, Arizona
June 30, 1956

Below this heading, and separated from it by scrollwork, the names of thirty-one victims were engraved in a single column. All twenty-nine who were not identified were named, and also two that were: Jeffrey Crider and Albert Vogt. Master Crider and Mr. Vogt had been sent home for burial early in July, along with all of the other identified victims; their names on the tombstone did not signify that they were buried there, but rather that they had perished with a family member who was not identified and who might be buried there. The unsurpassed intimacy shared between family members who lost their lives together deserved to be revered and preserved. In respect for the pairs of family members who had that bond, and for the sanctity of their union, Mrs. Elizabeth Crider's name was accompanied by that of her son, Master

Jeffrey Crider, and Miss Carol Jean Church's name was accompanied by that of her grandfather, Mr. Albert Vogt.

In their entirety, the names engraved on the headstone were:

John A. Barry, Lt. Col., C. E., A.U.S.
Phyllis G. Berman
Frank C. Caple
M. Barry Carlton
Carol Jean Church
Frank H. Clark
L. David Cook, Jr.
Elizabeth Crider
Jeffrey Crider
Elizabeth Frances Doering
Girardo Fiore
Lillian Ruth Hahn
Robert W. Harms
Russell Charles Huber
Francis Robert Johlie II
Nancy Lou Kemnitz
Dee D. Kovack
Sally Lou Laughlin
Joseph M. Levis, Jr., Lt. U.S.M.C.
Theodore Henry Lyman
John J. Muldoon
Gerald Murchison
Floyd A. Nixon
John George Reba
Carl J. Snyder
Thomas J. Sulpizio
Albert Vogt
Stanley Jerome Weiss
Albert E. Widdifield

Roberta E. Wilde
Donald L. Winings

The ground was carpeted with pine needles, and on this soft bedding were beautiful bouquets of flowers that had been laid in front of the stone marker. Square partitions measuring about four feet tall, outlined in palm leaves and covered with carnations, flanked the headstone on each side. Each one carried 1,200-1,300 blooms in various colors, arranged so as to depict simple, natural landscapes. Near the tops of these floral walls were spelled out some of the words of the 23rd Psalm, chosen so as to constitute an abridged encapsulation of both its meaning and phrase. The left-hand panel bore the first and best-known verse, "The Lord is my shepherd," and next to it, a fragment of a middle verse, "He restoreth my soul." The right-hand panel carried the last verse, "I shall dwell in the house of the Lord forever." Alongside the panels, several large, freestanding floral arrangements framed and completed the memorial.

In front of this stood a lectern, and out in front of that was a canvas pavilion much like the one that had been raised at the TWA funeral, though smaller. Again the structure was a simple canopy supported on poles and held taut in position by guy lines tied to stakes in the ground. Under the canopy were many metal folding chairs arranged in rows like the pews in a church. To the right of the lectern, as viewed from the pavilion, were three folding chairs for the clergy. Beyond these, two more rows of chairs were arranged in curving lines for the choir, in such a way that each chair was approximately facing the lectern. (See Appendix 9 for a drawing of the entire arrangement.)

Before the guests arrived, this scene lay vibrant with tranquility, situated among the pine trees, and the insects and birds flying and singing in summer's vitality, as though as wild and natural as those living things were. The duties that the scene compelled and the grief it signified and honored were elsewhere. Chairs, a gravestone, and a pulpit stood as inanimate as boulders and for a moment as uncontrived, as though they had lost their overlay of man's designs and were again simply forms of earth; and yet some trace lingered. For a moment all of it stood resonating in a virgin reality of its own, hanging between man's and nature's realities. It was a setting in which, to anyone who might have paused to apprehend it, humanity felt long past, a setting that was somehow as far removed from mankind as the abandoned artifacts in a long disused camp far out in the wilds. There was a profound simplicity and serenity about it, which spoke of man only in a whispered reverberation of him, long gone. Soon those qualities vanished as people dominated the scene. Everyone was arriving.

It was a gorgeous morning. The weather was absolutely perfect in every respect. The temperature and humidity were moderate, the sky was clear and bright and vivid blue, and the air moved in a gentle breeze. The scent of pine trees and the perfume of flowers suffused the area, as though in joyous affirmation of the weather. In this glorious atmosphere the tragic people whose pain all but obscured the beauty around them took refuge, as a way stop between two periods of dismal hardship. Their lives had become little more than a protracted exodus, every day walking again farther from the lives they had known, and ultimately to where they did not know. Tentatively they stepped to their places, so unassumingly that it seemed a mild wind could have carried them away. They gave the impression of frailty, and yet they moved with the steadiness of determination. They appeared weak, but this was more appearance than fact, more circumstance than character, and it belied their underlying wherewithal as persons. They had survived over a month of anguish, much of it beyond measure of description in its severity, and they had not been ground under. They were not so much weak as weary.

At 10:00 a.m. local time, the memorial service for United's twenty-nine unidentified victims began. If there is any meaning in the idea of preparing for such an emotional occasion, then it could be said that those in mourning were better prepared than their counterparts at the TWA funeral had been. Thirty-three days had passed since the accident—a small amount of time in which to cope with such tremendous grief, yet enough time for many to have begun finding a stable emotional stance and resigning themselves to essential beliefs about the realities that the tragedy had wrought and about the realities that it had destroyed. They had begun to sort it out and to embrace meaningful views, like that the accident was destiny, or meaningful but somewhat depressed views like that the whole of life was as much an accident as a purposeful thing. If the accident were destiny, then it deserved respect and awe—there was a grand scheme after all, a plan and an Intelligence behind all creation. On the other hand, if life itself were an endless natural cycle that alternated sporadically from aberration to order and back again, then human beings were as helpless as they were capable, and surrendering to reality was as appropriate as fighting it. Either view led directly to accepting what had happened, at least by confirming it and believing it.

Thirty-three days had given the bereaved a chance to begin coming to terms with their loss, whereas most of the mourners at the TWA funeral, only nine days after the accident, were still in utter shock or bewilderment and had hardly begun to accept what had happened. Many of them at the earlier funeral did not even truly believe that they were at their loved one's funeral. As though in a strange dream, some of them still expected for their missing loved ones to come home. But the people at the United service had nearly all by then accepted it as reality that their loved ones were gone, and they were in the next stage of adapting to that terrible change in their lives.

The congregation sat solemnly under the canopy while a military guard of honor stood at attention off to the side. Three clergymen in turn performed the services, and a twenty-voice choir sang several hymns. The same three men who had given the interment rites over that ground three weeks earlier officiated, offering Jewish, Protestant, and Catholic services in that order. None of the mourners collapsed or cried out, though many quietly wept.

Pastor Hilka Green of Grand Canyon Community Church called everybody's attention to the natural splendor surrounding them. After a month of almost continual anguish, they needed not only to feel the sadness in their hearts but also to remember the joy. While the breeze lightly rustled the upper branches of the pine trees, he said, "Our small world may be shattered many times, but God's world goes on. Where can we be made more conscious of this than in this national park where, through aeons of time, God's hand has etched out of stone unmatched wonder and beauty?" Pastor Green's pure-hearted, sincere, gentle suggestion that everyone attune himself just then to the limitless beauty and bounty of nature all around touched everyone's hearts, giving them a moment's remembrance and a glimpse of the hope that they might again feel simple joy and admiration in God's creation. It was such a relief to again have hope and to again appreciate the goodness in life, regardless of how faintly, and it was such a blessing to feel this in the context of their long month of seemingly never-ending sorrow, that they nearly all cried. It felt like salvation.

It lasted only briefly, and then each in his own moment remembered his loved one. The monumental sorrow they carried swept over them, and then they cried again for that reason, too. They were more composed than their fellow group in Flagstaff had been, but underneath that they were in truth inconsolable. Who could lessen their pain with words or deeds? And though many of them had begun to conceive of the tragedy in a way that they could accept, still, how could anyone truly decide what to believe about something so terrible?

This pitiful circumstance could not have been put more clearly, more fully, more tenderly, and more powerfully than it was by Mr. Santolo Fiore, the father of the flight engineer, Girardo Fiore. In his simple, broken English, Mr. Fiore expressed his own struggle with devastation and bewilderment as eloquently and unequivocally as anyone who had ever vocalized the meaning of tragedy. He and Mrs. Marge Harms, widow of the first officer, Robert Harms, spoke to each other after the service. Mr. Fiore looked up toward the heavens, shaking his head and opening his arms to portray the boundless sweep of the sky, with its limitless room for maneuvering and avoiding another plane, and its emptiness of answers, and he implored simply, "How this happen?"

THE END

Appendix 1

TWA 2 Cabin Configuration

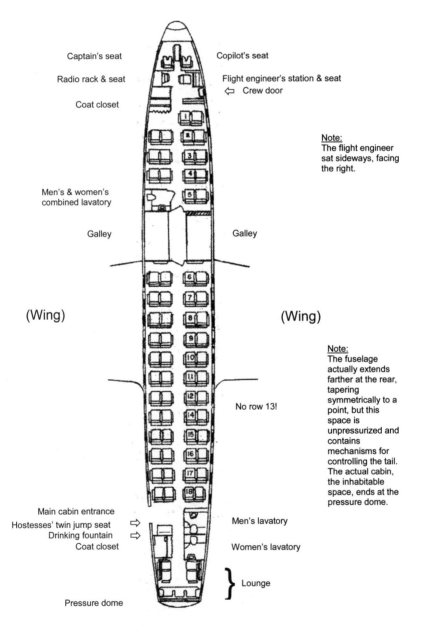

Captain's seat

Radio rack & seat

Coat closet

Copilot's seat

Flight engineer's station & seat
⇦ Crew door

Men's & women's
combined lavatory

Galley

Galley

Note:
The flight engineer
sat sideways, facing
the right.

(Wing)

(Wing)

No row 13!

Note:
The fuselage
actually extends
farther at the rear,
tapering
symmetrically to a
point, but this
space is
unpressurized and
contains
mechanisms for
controlling the tail.
The actual cabin,
the inhabitable
space, ends at the
pressure dome.

Main cabin entrance
Hostesses' twin jump seat ⇨
Drinking fountain ⇨
Coat closet

Men's lavatory

Women's lavatory

} Lounge

Pressure dome

United 718 Cabin Configuration

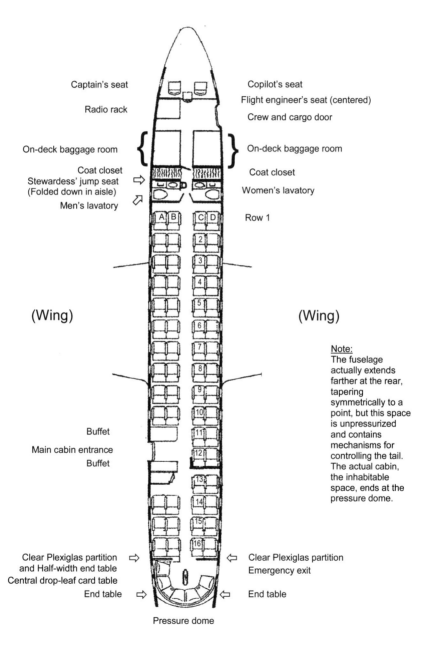

Captain's seat

Radio rack

On-deck baggage room

Coat closet
Stewardess' jump seat
(Folded down in aisle)
Men's lavatory

Copilot's seat

Flight engineer's seat (centered)

Crew and cargo door

On-deck baggage room

Coat closet

Women's lavatory

Row 1

(Wing)

(Wing)

Note:
The fuselage
actually extends
farther at the rear,
tapering
symmetrically to a
point, but this space
is unpressurized
and contains
mechanisms for
controlling the tail.
The actual cabin,
the inhabitable
space, ends at the
pressure dome.

Buffet

Main cabin entrance

Buffet

Clear Plexiglas partition
and Half-width end table
Central drop-leaf card table
End table

Clear Plexiglas partition

Emergency exit

End table

Pressure dome

Appendix 2

Los Angeles International Airport, 1956

~~~~~~~~~~ Pacific Ocean ~~~~~~~~~~

Usual direction of takeoff

Magnetic compass West

True directions

[Parking lot]

Ramps

TWA

United

Adjoining
TWA and United
Air Lines terminals

Control tower

25 L

25 R

Run-up pad

Appendix 3

Route Map for Both Flights

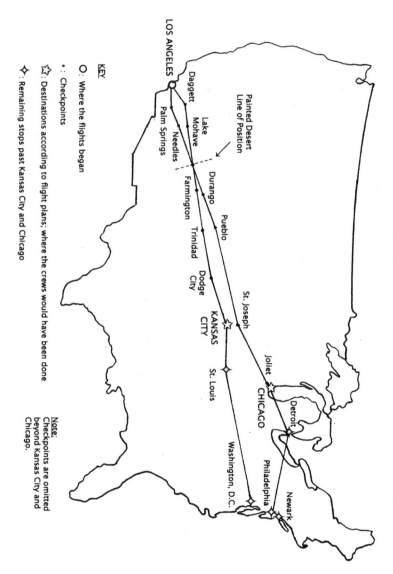

KEY

O: Where the flights began

•: Checkpoints

☆: Destinations according to flight plans; where the crews would have been done

✧: Remaining stops past Kansas City and Chicago

LOS ANGELES

Daggett

Palm Springs

Lake Mohave

Needles

Painted Desert
Line of Position

Durango

Farmington

Trinidad

Pueblo

Dodge
City

St. Joseph

KANSAS
CITY

St. Louis

Joliet

CHICAGO

Detroit

Washington, D.C.

Philadelphia

Newark

Note: TWA 2's route was north of United 718's from Los Angeles to the Painted Desert Line of Position, where the two routes were to have crossed, placing United 718 to the north of TWA 2 for the remainder of the trip.

Note: Checkpoints are omitted beyond Kansas City and Chicago.

Appendix 4

Probable paths that TWA 2 and United 718 followed into Grand Canyon airspace, when they detoured from their proposed courses.

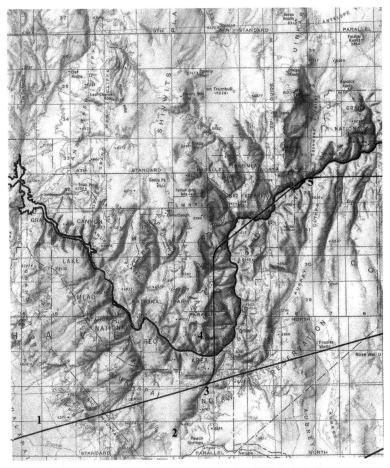

Typical square is about six miles on a side.   Courtesy of U.S. Geological Survey.

1. TWA 2's proposed course
2. Peach Springs Canyon
3. Location where TWA 2 may have turned for sightseeing
4. Lower Granite Gorge
5. Location and latitude where TWA 2 may have turned east

6. United 718's proposed course
7. Location where TWA 2 had to turn if the giant cumulonimbus cloud was in their way
8. Grand Canyon Village
9. Location of Grand Canyon Airport in 1956; locally known then as Red Butte Airfield
10. Location where United 718 probably turned after passing the giant cloud

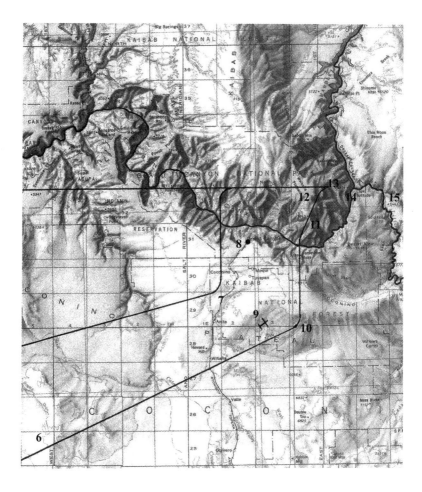

11. Slanted path taken by United to avoid the smaller, second cumulonimbus cloud
12. The Walhalla Plateau
13. The approximate place in the sky where TWA 2 and United 718 collided
14. Confluence of the Colorado and Little Colorado rivers; the area of the two crash sites
15. The Little Colorado River

Appendix 5

The first diagram shows that for a smaller cloud to lie northeast of the big one, it need not extend any farther northward and could be right behind it to the east. The second diagram illustrates how the big cloud obstructs the flights' view of each other; the final diagram shows that in circumnavigating also a small, second cloud, the flights are much nearer to each other, and they have much less time to react when they first come into each other's view.

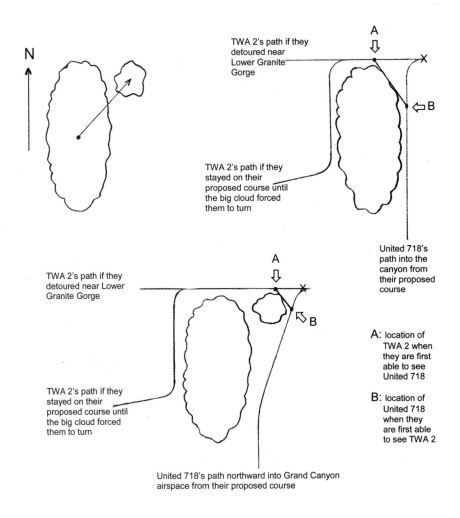

Appendix 6

The Crash Sites.   Squares are about 0.6 statute miles on a side.

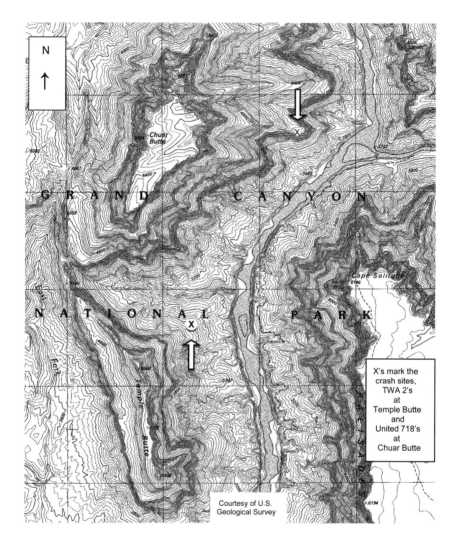

X's mark the
crash sites,
TWA 2's
at
Temple Butte
and
United 718's
at
Chuar Butte

Courtesy of U.S.
Geological Survey

Appendix 7

The Collision.

This diagram depicts United 718 in a dive and not turning, pitched about 10°, and TWA 2 in a left turn, banked about 20° left wing down (right wing up).

It could be that instead, United 718 was diving and turning to the right at the same time, and that correspondingly, they were banked about 10° right wing down, and TWA 2 was banked only about 10° left wing down.

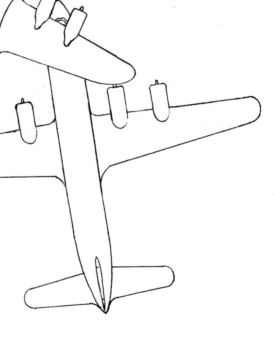

TWA 2

United 718

Appendix 8

Schematic view of the United crash gully and aerial rigging at Chuar Butte. Pulleys and take-up reel are extremely oversized for clarity. Inset is for fuller scale perspective.

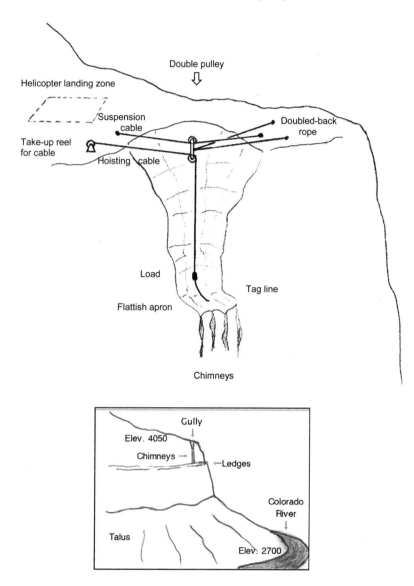

Appendix 9

The collective funeral service for TWA victims, held in Flagstaff Citizens' Cemetery, Flagstaff, Arizona, on Monday, July 9, 1956.

Infant Howard Maag's casket

Five children's caskets in center

Organ and seat

Altar railing

Lectern

Pavilion

United 718 Memorial Service, held August 2, 1956 at Grand Canyon
National Park Cemetery, in Grand Canyon Village, Arizona.

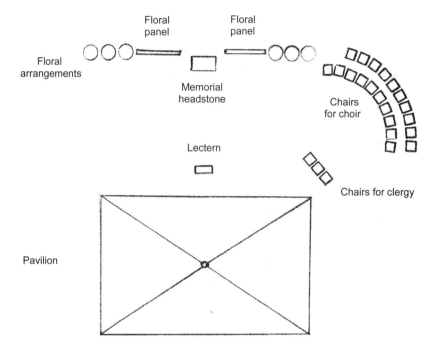

Los Angeles International Airport, as it was in 1956. The apparent horizon is actually the beach, and the apparent sky is the Pacific Ocean. In the lower right, the ramps can be seen, with several airliners parked at them. The terminal buildings are immediately right of that, and then in turn the parking lot, full of cars. (City of Los Angeles Department of Airports)

The fronts of United Air Lines' and TWA's terminal buildings at Los Angeles International Airport, as they were in 1956, taken from the parking lot, looking about southeast. (City of Los Angeles Department of Airports)

The ramp shared by United Air Lines and TWA at Los Angeles International Airport. Two United DC-7s are parked on the left, and three TWA Constellations on the right. Note the underground walkway, and the fence beyond which visitors were not permitted. Likely taken late 1956, based on the United paint scheme, which was dramatically changed in 1957, and the sharply pointed, cone-shaped propeller hub spinners, which were absent in early 1956 and before. View is looking south, toward the airfield. (City of Los Angeles Department of Airports)

A United Air Lines DC-7 painted exactly as the *City of Vancouver* was on the day of the accident. Note the absence of propeller hub spinners. They were retrofitted in late 1956; the *City of Vancouver* didn't have them either. (Kase Dekker)

A United Air Lines DC-7 in flight, painted exactly as the *City of Vancouver* was except for the vertical tail fin, which is shown here in the very first version of the paint scheme. It was soon changed to the design in photos #3 and #4. (United Press Photo)

The *Star of the Seine*, painted exactly as it was on the day of the tragedy. Note the unusual, graceful curvature of the fuselage. (Lockheed)

The disaster scene. Chuar Butte takes up the entire lower right half of the photo, as divided diagonally from the lower left corner to the upper right corner. The shoulder on which the United DC-7 crashed is prominent just below the photo's center, and is seen from the backside. The Colorado River is flowing southwestward from foreground to background on the left. The TWA crash site on the lower part of Temple Butte is the small, tilted dark line with a hump in the middle, directly left of the photo's center, about halfway to the left edge. (Morel Guyot)

Chuar Butte, from top to bottom, with the crash promontory in the very center of the picture. Taken looking west-northwest, at about 1:00 p.m., in late summer. Note the Colorado River, flowing from right to left, and the Little Colorado River, at the bottom right corner, flowing toward it from foreground to background. (The author)

The United Air Lines crash promontory, in the very center of the photograph. Taken at about 1:00 p.m. in late summer, from the side that the plane hit, looking about north. Over half a century of rain has washed away all trace of the black soot left behind by the fire. The Colorado River is flowing from background to foreground at the right, and the giant sandbar at the confluence of the two rivers can be partially seen at the bottom right. (The author)

The United Air Lines crash promontory, taken from the shoreline very shortly after the accident, looking roughly northward. The dark vertical smear at the crest is the blackened fire area. Note the ledge system running horizontally across the photo's middle, separating the talus slope and lower sheer band from the top half of the promontory. The boulder just below the photo's center and the one directly to its right are bigger than most two-story houses. (Margaret Eiseman)

The TWA memorial gravesite marker, at the mass plot in Flagstaff Citizens' Cemetery. It bears the names of sixty-six of the seventy persons aboard: all sixty that were not identified, and six that were. The four missing names are those of victims who were both identified and buried elsewhere, privately. (The author)

In memory
of these persons
who lost their lives
in the aircraft accident
at Grand Canyon Arizona
June 30, 1956

JOHN A. BARRY, LT. COL., C.E., A.U.S.
PHYLLIS G. BERMAN
FRANK C. CAPLE
M. BARRY CARLTON
CAROL JEAN CHURCH
FRANK H. CLARK
L. DAVID COOK, JR.
ELIZABETH CRIDER
JEFFREY CRIDER
ELIZABETH FRANCES DOERING
GIRARDO FIORE
LILLIAN RUTH HAHN
ROBERT W. HARMS
RUSSELL CHARLES HUBER
FRANCIS ROBERT JOWLIE II
NANCY LOU KEMNITZ
DEE D. KOVACK
SALLY LOU LAUGHLIN
JOSEPH M. LEVIS, JR., LT. U.S.M.C.
THEODORE HENRY LYMAN
JOHN J. MULDOON
GERALD MURCHISON
FLOYD A. NIXON
JOHN GEORGE REAR
CARL J. SNYDER
THOMAS J. SULPIZIO
ALBERT VOGT
STANLEY JEROME WEISS
ALBERT C. WIDDIFIELD
ROBERTA C. WILDE
DONALD L. WILLINGS

50

The United Air Lines memorial gravesite marker, at the plot in Pioneer Cemetery (formerly Grand Canyon National Park Cemetery), in Grand Canyon Village. The plaque with the number "50" on it commemorates the fiftieth anniversary of the tragedy. The stone bears thirty-one names, those of all twenty-nine unidentified victims, along with those of two that were identified, though the latter were not buried there. (The author)

TABLE OF RESOURCES

THE FOLLOWING LIST of resources is indexed by topics in the order in which they are introduced in the text, chapter by chapter. It is not meant to be anything like a complete catalog of resources used in the preparation of this book, but rather, a faithfully representative, abridged cross-section of them.

Many points came most valuably and persuasively from interviews I conducted with persons who were involved with the airlines or air traffic control at the time, or who contended with the aftermath of the tragedy itself. In respect for them and their privacy, I have not named any of them that were not already named in the text.

Chapter 1

1. **Land area and lengths of runways at Los Angeles International Airport:** *A Brief History of Los Angeles International Airport*, published by the City of Los Angeles Department of Airports, 1995.

2. **Outlay of the airport:** ground and aerial photographs from the City of Los Angeles Department of Airports, taken in 1955 and 1956.

3. **750 flights daily:** *1956 Annual Report for the Fiscal Year Ended June 30, 1956*, published by the City of Los Angeles Department of Airports, 1956.

4. **Interior arrangements of United and TWA terminal buildings:**
    photographs from the City of Los Angeles Department of Airports,
    taken in 1955 and 1956.

5. **Arrangements of observation patio and facilities on ramp:** same
    resource as in number 4.

6. **Eighty-five-hour legal limit on flying time per month:** *Corporate
    and Legal History of United Air Lines, Inc., 1946-1955,* published by
    United Air Lines, Inc., 1965, Chapter XV, Subdivision B, Section
    4; *High Horizons* by Frank J. Taylor, published by McGraw-Hill
    Book Company, Inc., 1951, page 168.

7. **Flight numbers and departure times for various other TWA
    and United Air Lines flights:** TWA timetable effective June 1,
    1956; United Air Lines timetable effective July 1, 1956.

8. **TWA hostesses tagged coats and jackets on board:** *Life* Magazine,
    July 16, 1956, photo of tagged coat on page 24; interviews with
    hostesses from the era.

9. **Dress codes for stewardesses and hostesses:** *Legacy of the Friendly
    Skies* by Gwen Mahler, published by Gwen Mahler, 1991; *Wings of
    Pride* by Gwen Mahler, published by TWA, 1985.

10. **Styles of uniforms for stewardesses and hostesses:** same two
    books as in number 9.

Chapter 2

1. **Routes, and departure and arrival times of TWA 2 and United
    718:** TWA timetable effective June 1, 1956; United Air Lines
    timetables effective March 1 and July 1, 1956; *Civil Aeronautics*

Board Accident Investigation Report SA-320, released April 17, 1957, pages 1 and 3.

2. **Composition of TWA's Constellation fleet:** *TWA* by George Cearley, Jr., published by George Cearley, Jr., 1988, pages 58 and 72.

3. **United Air Lines bought a total of 57 DC-7s; and had 27 at time of accident:** *United Air Lines Aircraft Identification Record*, internal United Air Lines, July 28, 1956; *Lifespan of Retired Aircraft*, internal United Air Lines, 1966; *The DC-6 and DC-7 Series*, published by Air Britain, 1971.

4. **United's exact paint scheme on June 30, 1956:** blueprint for United DC-7s from Douglas Aircraft Company, Inc. current through January 8, 1957; author's personal examination of a propeller blade from the *City of Vancouver*; author's examination of numerous photos of other United DC-7s, many taken on known dates.

5. **Dimensions and weight limits of L-1049:** *The Lockheed Constellation*, by M.J. Hardy, published by David & Charles Limited, 1973.

6. **Dimensions and weight limits of DC-7:** *Douglas Service: DC-7 Study Guide*, published by Douglas Aircraft Company, Inc., 1954.

7. **Weights of both planes at takeoff on June 30, 1956:** *CAB Accident Investigation Report SA-320*, released April 17, 1957, pages 2 and 4.

8. **Takeoff and cruising horsepower for TWA 2:** *TWA Constellation Flight Crew Operating Manual*, internal Trans World Airlines, issued page-by-page in running updating, 1950s.

9. **Takeoff and cruising horsepower for United 718:** *United Air Lines Combined DC-6 and DC-7 Flight Manual,* internal United Air Lines, issued page-by-page in running updating, 1950s and early 1960s.

10. **Engine types for the two planes:** *CAB Accident Investigation Report SA-320,* released April 17, 1957, pages iv and v.

11. **Engine specifics for TWA 2 and United 718:** *CAA Aircraft Specification Sheet E-270-4,* March 10, 1953; *FAA Type Certificate Data Sheet No. E-272,* April 15, 1966, taken directly from its earlier CAA counterpart.

12. **Configuration and floor plan of TWA 2:** *TWA Flight Service Manual,* internal TWA, issued page-by-page in running updating, 1950s, diagram on page 03.45.01, as it stood May 20, 1956.

13. **Interior color scheme on TWA 2:** from a scene in the movie *How to Marry a Millionaire,* 1953. The plane in which Marilyn Monroe and David Wayne flew together was a TWA L-1049, exactly like the *Star of the Seine.*

14. **United's use of the term "buffet":** *Douglas Service: DC-7 Study Guide,* published by Douglas Aircraft Company, Inc., 1954; *Legacy of the Friendly Skies* by Gwen Mahler, published by Gwen Mahler, 1991, page 124.

15. **Configuration and floor plan of United 718:** *United Air Lines Combined DC-6 and DC-7 Flight Manual,* internal United Air Lines, issued page-by-page in running updating, 1950s and 1960s, diagram on page 24.5.

16. **Cigar and pipe smoking in the lounge:** *Legacy of the Friendly Skies* by Gwen Mahler, published by Gwen Mahler, 1991, page 122; interviews with Gwen Mahler.

17. **Configuration of DC-7 lounge:** *Douglas Service: DC-7 Study Guide,* published by Douglas Aircraft Company, Inc., 1954.

Chapter 3

1. **Three landing gear locking pins:** *TWA Constellation Flight Crew Operating Manual,* internal TWA, issued page-by-page in running updating, 1950s.

2. **TWA's prestarting checklists:** same resource as in number 1.

3. **TWA's counting blades aloud:** same resource as in number 1.

4. **United's counting blades aloud:** *United Air Lines Combined DC-6 and DC-7 Flight Manual,* internal United Air Lines, issued page-by-page in running updating, 1950s and early 1960s.

5. **Engine starting order 3-4-2-1:** same resource as in number 4.

6. **The scheme of outbound flights' passing from ground control, to local control, to departure radar control, to ARTC:** *Air Traffic Control: The Uncrowded Sky* by Glen A. Gilbert, published by the Smithsonian Institution, 1973, Chapter 1.

7. **Dialogue between the tower and TWA 2 and United 718 at Los Angeles International Airport:** transcript of tape recorded radio communications between the flights and the tower, prepared by Robert Buckles, Acting Chief Airport Traffic Controller, Los Angeles Tower, July 1, 1956.

8. **Runway nomenclature:** *Aviation Fundamentals,* compiled and published by Jeppesen Sanderson, Inc., 1986, Chapter 3.

9. **Nose gear steering wheel only by captain's seat:** *Douglas Service: DC-7 Study Guide,* published by Douglas Aircraft Company, Inc., 1954; L-1049 cockpit photo, Lockheed Aircraft Corporation.

Chapter 4

1. **The flights were handed off to departure radar control:** *CAB Accident Investigation Report SA-320,* released April 17, 1957, page 2; transcript of tape recorded radio communications between the flights and the tower at Los Angeles International Airport, forwarded by Robert Buckles, Acting Chief Airport Traffic Controller, July 1, 1956.

2. **Radarscope in tower:** *Baughman's Aviation Dictionary,* Aero Publishers, 1951, photo of interior of Los Angeles Tower, on page 351.

3. **Twenty-six ARTC centers:** *Takeoff at Mid-Century* by Stuart Rochester, published in 1976 by the U.S. Department of Transportation/FAA, page 150.

4. **Centers were linked to each other by telephone and Teletype:** *Guide to Air Traffic Control* by Robert T. Smith, Sports Car Press, 1963, Chapter 2.

5. **ARTC had long-range radar only in the East:** *The Federal Airways System,* edited by William E. Jackson, published by the Institute of Electrical and Electronics Engineers, Inc., 1970.

6. **ARTC used flight progress strips on grid boards:** *Lawsuit* by Stuart M. Speiser, published by Horizon Press, 1980, page 233.

7. **Both flights' plans cleared by ARTC en route:** transcript of tape recorded radio communications between Los Angeles ARTC and both flights, prepared by Clyde V. Van Horne, Chief Controller at Los Angeles ARTC, date omitted but certainly between June 30, 1956 and July 9, 1956.

8. **Airways ran between navigational radio stations:** *Baughman's Aviation Dictionary*, Aero Publishers, 1951.

9. **Airway nomenclature:** *Guide to Air Traffic Control* by Robert T. Smith, Sports Car Press, 1963.

10. **TWA 2 requested routing change almost right away:** *CAB Accident Investigation Report SA-320*, released April 17, 1957, page 2.

11. **Definitions of VFR and IFR:** *CAB Accident Investigation Report SA-320*, released April 17, 1957, pages 16-19; *Civil Air Regulations Manual*, April 1, 1957, parts 60.30, 60.40, and 60.60.

12. **TWA 2's request for 1000 on top:** *CAB Accident Investigation Report SA-320*, released April 17, 1957, pages 17-19; transcript of tape recorded communications between Los Angeles TWA radio, Los Angeles ARTC and Salt Lake City ARTC, prepared by Clyde V. Van Horne, Chief Controller at Los Angeles ARTC, date omitted but certainly between June 30 and July 9, 1956.

13. **Definition of 1000 on top:** *CAB Accident Investigation Report SA-320*, released April 17, 1957, pages 17-19; CAB internal memorandum from Robert J. Ables, International and Rules Division, to Ross Newmann, Chief of the International and Rules Division, July 11, 1956.

14. **Traffic advisory relayed to Los Angeles TWA radio:** transcript of tape recorded telephone conversations between Los Angeles ARTC and each of Salt Lake City ARTC and Los Angeles TWA radio, prepared by Clyde V. Van Horne, Chief Controller at Los Angeles ARTC, date omitted but certainly between June 30 and July 9, 1956.

15. **Captain Gandy repeated clearance verbatim but acknowledged traffic advisory only by saying, "Traffic received":** *CAB Accident Investigation Report SA-320*, released April 17, 1957, pages 15-16.

16. **ARTC tape recorded all radio and telephone communications:** *CAB Accident Investigation Report SA-320,* released April 17, 1957, page 15.

17. **TWA company radio used a manual typewriter to "record" what was said to them, not a tape recorder, and did not type their own words:** interviews with radio and Teletype operators who worked for TWA at the time.

18. **Definition of Quadrantal Rule:** *Civil Air Regulations Manual,* April 1, 1957, parts 60.32 and 60.44; CAB internal memorandum from Ross Newmann, Chief of the International and Rules Division, to the General Counsel, John Wanner, July 12, 1956.

19. **Definition of service ceiling:** *Baughman's Aviation Dictionary,* Aero Publishing, 1951.

20. **The L-1049's specific service ceiling:** power charts from the *TWA Constellation Flight Crew Operating Manual,* internal TWA, issued page-by-page in running updating, 1950s; *Lockheed Constellation and Super Constellation* by Scott E. Germain, published by Specialty Press, 1998, page 61.

21. **Captain Gandy ruled out 23,000 feet for his altitude:** CAB internal memorandum from Robert J. Ables, International and Rules Division, to Ross Newmann, Chief of the International and Rules Division, July 11, 1956.

22. **TWA 2 attained 19,000 feet only a couple minutes before reaching Daggett:** simple deduction based on the fact that they attained 20,000 feet right at Daggett, which is in turn from transcript of tape recorded telephone communications between Las Vegas TWA radio and Salt Lake City ARTC, compiled by Harold C. Howard, Chief Air Route Traffic Controller at Salt Lake City ARTC, June 30, 1956.

23. **Weather conditions along TWA 2's route from Los Angeles to eastern end of Grand Canyon:**

   A. Forecasts for June 30, from:
      a) Los Angeles Flight Advisory Weather Service
      b) Salt Lake City Flight Advisory Weather Service
      c) Albuquerque Flight Advisory Weather Service

   B. Observations taken on June 30, by:
      a) Prescott U.S. Weather Bureau Surface Observation Station
      b) Flagstaff U.S. Weather Bureau Surface Observation Station
      c) Grand Canyon National Park Headquarters Station at Grand Canyon Village
      d) Inner Canyon Station
      e) Bright Angel Ranger Station
      f) aviators that flew in the area that morning and afternoon

24. **Airspeed increases with altitude for a fixed power setting:** *Trans World Airlines Power Chart Manual*, internal TWA, issued in page-by-page running updating, 1950s, charts for 1049 Constant Power Cruise.

Chapter 5

1. **TWA 2 reached Daggett at 10:34, at 20,000 feet:** transcript of tape recorded telephone communications between Las Vegas TWA radio and Salt Lake City ARTC, prepared by Harold C. Howard, Chief Air Route Traffic Controller at Salt Lake City ARTC, June 30, 1956.

2. **TWA 2 reached 21,000 feet at about 10:39:** simple calculation based in part on previous note.

3. **Names of victims and exact spellings:** the United memorial gravestone at Pioneer Cemetery (formerly Grand Canyon National Park Cemetery), Grand Canyon Village; the TWA memorial gravestone at Flagstaff Citizens' Cemetery, Flagstaff, Arizona; consensus of numerous newspapers nationwide.

4. **Personal information on passengers of both flights:** interviews with family; consensus of numerous newspapers nationwide.

5. **Personal information on TWA crew and other TWA employees on board:** TWA's employee newspaper, *Skyliner*, July 5, 1956 edition.

6. **Personal information on both crews:** *CAB Accident Investigation Report SA-320*, released April 17, 1957, pages ii-iv, 2 and 3; interviews with coworkers.

7. **United 718 reported Riverside at 10:24 at 12,000 feet, and Palm Springs at 10:37 at 18,000 feet:** *Air Line Pilots' Association Accident Investigation Report*, adopted December 17, 1956, page 2.

8. **United 718 reached 21,000 feet at about 10:50:** simple calculation based in part on previous note.

Chapter 6

1. **It was ARTC's duty to separate only those IFR flights from each other that had specific altitude clearances, i.e. not 1000 on top clearances:** internal CAB memorandum from Robert J. Ables, International and Rules Division, to Ross Newmann, Chief of the International and Rules Division, July 11, 1956, in which Ables variously quotes the *ANC Manual* of air traffic controllers' responsibilities; *CAB Accident Investigation Report SA-320*, released April 17, 1957, pages 17 and 18.

2. **A flight could remain IFR and obtain an amended thousand on top clearance:** *CAB Accident Investigation Report SA-320*, released April 17, 1957, pages 17 and 18.

3. **While on a thousand on top clearance, an IFR flight had full responsibility for itself in collision avoidance, even in control areas:** same resource as in number 2.

4. **It was ARTC's duty to refuse TWA 2's request for 21,000 feet as the only way to ensure they would not collide with United 718 on Red 15:** *CAB Accident Investigation Report SA-320*, released April 17, 1957, pages 16 and 17; interviews with air traffic controllers form the era.

5. **The false story blaming the Salt Lake City controller for the disaster:** various newspapers across the country, among them the *Deseret News Salt Lake Telegram*, Aug. 4, 1956.

6. **The effort to undo the false story blaming the Salt Lake controller for the disaster:** various newspapers across the country, including the *Deseret News Salt Lake Telegram*, Aug. 7, 1956.

7. **The children of the Salt Lake City ARTC controller who handled the two flights were ridiculed by other children for his supposed error:** *Lawsuit* by Stuart M. Speiser, published by Horizon Press, 1980, page 198.

Chapter 7

1. **TWA 2 was at Lake Mohave at 10:55 and reported this at 10:59:** transcript of tape recorded communications between Las Vegas TWA radio and Salt Lake City ARTC, prepared by Harold C. Howard, Chief Air Route Traffic Controller at Salt Lake City ARTC, June 30, 1956; *CAB Accident Investigation Report SA-320*, released April 17, 1957, page 3.

2. **Definition of Painted Desert Line of Position:** *CAB Accident Investigation Report SA-320*, released April 17, 1957, pages 20 and 21.

3. **United 718 was at Needles at 10:58:** transcript of tape recorded communications between Needles INSACS and Albuquerque ARTC, prepared by Chief Controller at Albuquerque ARTC (signature illegible), date omitted but had to be between June 30 and July 11, 1956; written statement of Herbert Dennis, communicator on watch at Needles INSACS to whom United 718 reported, submitted July 1, 1956.

4. **The controller at Salt Lake City ARTC who received both flights' estimates of Painted Desert LOP at 11:31 was the same one who disapproved TWA 2's ascent:** *CAB Accident Investigation Report SA-320*, released April 17, 1957, page 20; transcript of tape

recorded communications between Salt Lake City ARTC and each of Las Vegas TWA radio and Needles INSACS, prepared by Harold C. Howard, Chief Air Route Traffic Controller at Salt Lake City ARTC, June 30, 1956.

5. **Particulars of Captain Stephan's flight and observations:** transcript of Congressional hearings entitled *Airspace Use Study, Hearings before a Subcommittee of the Committee on Interstate and Foreign Commerce, House of Representatives, Eighty-Fourth Congress, Second Session, on Use of Airspace,* second of three hearings, held July 18, 1956, pages 78-92; *CAB Accident Investigation Report SA-320,* released April 17, 1957, pages 31, 32, 35, and 36; interviews with Captain Stephan.

6. **United 718 did not have weather radar equipment:** *Corporate and Legal History of United Air Lines, Inc., 1946-1955,* published by United Air Lines, 1965, page 648.

7. **TWA 2 did not have weather radar equipment:** photos of the *Star of the Seine,* and of TWA's other nine L-1049s taken both before and after the accident, showing that none of these planes ever had radar—they lacked the characteristic "radome" nose.

8. **The CAB's use of the term "towering cumulus" was a misnomer—Captain Stephan never called it anything but "cumulonimbus" or "buildup":** transcript of Congressional hearings entitled *Airspace Use Study, Hearings before a Subcommittee of the Committee on Interstate and Foreign Commerce, House of Representatives, Eighty-Fourth Congress, Second Session, on Use of Airspace,* second of three hearings, held July 18, 1956, pages 78-92.

9. **High altitude winds toward east at 23 mph in collision area:** transcript of Congressional hearings entitled *Airspace Use Study,*

Hearings before a Subcommittee of the Committee on Interstate and Foreign Commerce, House of Representatives, Eighty-Fourth Congress, Second Session, on use of Airspace, third of three hearings, held September 11-13, 1956, pages 135-144.

Chapter 8

1. **Harms sent the mayday message:** *CAB Accident Investigation Report SA-320*, released April 17, 1957, page 24; friends of his that listened to the tape made by ARINC identified the principal speaker's voice as that of Harms.

2. **The second voice on the recording of the mayday message was Flight Engineer Fiore's:** interviews with an accident investigator who was involved in playing the tape to a selection of United flight crewmembers, who knew the crew of Flight 718 and identified Fiore's voice.

3. **The long standing conflict between pilots and flight engineers:** *Corporate and Legal History of United Air Lines, Inc., 1946-1955*, pages 1072, 1073, and 1079-1086; interviews with United pilots and flight engineers from that era.

Chapter 9

1. **There were other cumulonimbus clouds northeast of Grand Canyon Village, within canyon airspace:** transcript of Congressional hearings entitled *Airspace Use Study, Hearings before a Subcommittee of the Committee on Interstate and Foreign Commerce, House of Representatives, Eighty-Fourth Congress, Second Session, on Use of Airspace*, second of three hearings, July 18, 1956, testimony of Captain Lionel Stephan, pages 78-92.

2. **Location of western boundary of Albuquerque ADIZ:** *Prescott Airways Sectional Chart*, published by U.S. Coast and Geodetic Survey, March 13, 1956.

3. **Seven ADIZ's at the time; their locations:** same resource as in number 2.

4. **Rule stipulating lateral separation of at least 2000 feet from clouds:** same resource as in number 2; *Civil Air Regulations Manual*, published March 15, 1957, section 60.

5. **About a ten-degree difference in pitch at impact:** *CAB Accident Investigation Report SA-320*, released April 17, 1957, finding No. 15, page 52.

6. **Illusion of same altitude can be caused by sloping cloud deck:** *Civil Aeronautics Board Accident Investigation Report SA-389*, regarding midair collision on December 4, 1965, near Carmel, New York, between TWA Flight 42, a Boeing 707, and Eastern Air Lines Flight 853, a Lockheed 1049-C, released December 20, 1966.

Chapter 10

1. **The No. 1 engine's propeller inflicted the cuts, not some other:** simple deduction based on the planes' orientations in relation to each other when they collided, which in turn was from the *CAB Accident Investigation Report SA-320*, released April 17, 1957, page 34.

2. **Light materials from TWA 2 drifted eastward:** *Civil Aeronautics Board Bureau of Safety Investigation Structural Investigation Report*, July 24, 1956, page 12.

3. **The DC-7 lost its No. 1 main fuel tank, and not its No. 1 alternate:** *Douglas Service: DC-7 Study Guide,* published by Douglas Aircraft Company, Inc., 1954, fuel tank diagram, page 182; *CAB Accident Investigation Report SA-320,* released April 17, 1957, page 8, delineating how much of the left wing was lost.

4. **United 718 was running on alternate tanks when collision occurred:** *United Air Lines Combined DC-6 and DC-7 Operating Manual,* internal United Air Lines, issued page-by-page in running updating, 1950s and early 1960s, Chapter 7, fuel distribution and consumption schedules; Chapter 14, climb power; Chapter 22, cruise performance.

5. **Elevations of river and top of talus on Chuar Butte:** topographical map, 1:24,000 scale, Cape Solitude Quadrangle, U.S. Geological Survey, 1988.

6. **4,050 foot elevation of United 718's point of ground impact:** *CAB Accident Investigation Report SA-320,* released April 17, 1957, page 7; *CAB Bureau of Safety Investigation Structural Investigation Report,* July 24, 1956, pages 3-4.

7. **Pitch and roll of United 718 at ground impact:** *CAB Bureau of Safety Investigation Structural Investigation Report,* July 24, 1956, page 3.

8. **United 718's forty-five degree magnetic heading at moment of ground impact:** same resource as in number 7.

9. **United 718's elevators and horizontal stabilizers tore off just before ground impact:** *CAB Bureau of Safety Investigation Structural Investigation Report,* July 24, 1956, page 8.

10. **United 718's elevators gouged their center hinge A-frames, and therefore must have been wildly oscillating:** same resource as in number 9.

Chapter 11

1. **TWA 2 and United 718 entered Salt Lake City ARTC advisory area at about 10:49 and 11:08:** *CAB Accident Investigation Report SA-320,* released April 17, 1957, map in Attachment 1; calculation of positions based on Lake Mohave and Needles position reports.

2. **The flight progress strips for both flights were on Lynn McCreary's board:** *Lawsuit* by Stuart M. Speiser,   published by Horizon Press, 1980, page 234; transcript of tape recorded telephone conversation between Salt Lake City ARTC and Albuquerque ARTC, with controller "LM" relaying progress of TWA 2 and receiving progress of United 718, prepared by Harold C. Howard, Chief Air Route Traffic Controller, Salt Lake City ARTC, June 30, 1956; transcript of tape recorded telephone conversation between Albuquerque ARTC and Salt Lake City ARTC, again with controller "LM" relaying progress of TWA 2, prepared by the Chief Controller at Albuquerque ARTC (signature illegible), date omitted but had to be between June 30 and July 9, 1956; interview with coworker of Lynn McCreary.

3. **Details of Stuart Halsey's activities:** interviews with Stuart Halsey.

4. **Albuquerque TWA radio called Albuquerque ARTC to ask if they had heard from TWA 2:** transcript of tape recorded telephone conversation between Albuquerque TWA radio and Albuquerque ARTC, prepared by the Chief Controller at Albuquerque ARTC (signature illegible), date omitted but had to be between June 30 and July 9, 1956.

5. **United 718 had upcoming checkpoints at Durango and Pueblo; TWA 2 had upcoming checkpoints at Farmington and Trinidad:** *CAB Accident Investigation Report SA-320*, released April 17, 1957, pages 1 and 3.

6. **Stuart Halsey began trying to contact the flights at 11:40:** *Salt Lake City ARTC Incident Report SLC-ARTC-244*, written by Harold C. Howard, Chief Air Route Traffic Controller at Salt Lake City ARTC, July 1, 1956; interviews with Stuart Halsey.

7. **Halsey held a joint conference with Los Angeles, Albuquerque and Denver ARTC centers:** same two resources as in number 6.

8. **Halsey held a joint telephone conference with United Dispatch, TWA Dispatch and the U.S. Air Force:** same two resources as in number 6.

9. **Both airlines prepared for the worst while awaiting the official declaration of the Missing Aircraft Alert:** interviews with airline personnel who were involved.

10. **The Missing Aircraft Alert was issued at 12:51:** *CAB Accident Investigation Report SA-320*, released April 17, 1957, page 5; interviews with Stuart Halsey.

11. **Air Rescue Service regions, bases and squadrons:** *Civil Air Patrol Manual*, published August 1, 1949, map of Air Rescue Service areas of responsibility, page 6-4; *History of the 4th Air Rescue Group, January 1-June 30, 1956*, section on redesignating Flight A and Flight B in November, 1952, as the 41st Air Rescue Squadron, at Hamilton Air Force Base, and the 42nd ARS, at March AFB.

12. **The 42nd Air Rescue Squadron, stationed at March Air Force Base, directed the Air Search and Rescue mission:** *History of the 4th Air Rescue Group, January 1-June 30, 1956,* section on operations.

13. **Winslow's modern facilities:** *Prescott Airways Sectional Chart,* U.S. Geological Survey, issued March 13, 1956.

14. **The 41st Air Rescue Squadron, stationed at Hamilton Air Force Base, and Transport and Medical Squadrons from Luke Air Force Base, assisted the 42nd ARS:** same resource as in number 12.

15. **The Civil Air Patrol was a legally chartered auxiliary of the U.S. Air Force:** *Civil Air Patrol Manual,* published August 1, 1949, page 1-1.

16. **Details of Palen Hudgin's activities:** statements of Palen Hudgin, printed in a special article about him and the tragedy, the *Arizona Republic,* June 27, 1971.

17. **Facilities at Red Butte Airfield, also called Grand Canyon Airport:** *Prescott Airways Sectional Chart,* U.S. Geological Survey, issued March 13, 1956.

18. **Involvement of Francis Shamrell and Flagstaff Municipal Airport with United:** interviews with Francis Shamrell; interviews with an executive of United Air Lines who was involved.

19. **Details of the scenes at the various airports at which the flights were to have stopped:** consensus of numerous newspapers nationwide; interviews with family members.

20. **Scheduled arrival and departure times for both flights at various airports:** United Air Lines timetable effective July 1, 1956, and TWA timetable effective June 1, 1956.

21. **Details of private events among victims' families:** interviews with family members.

Chapter 12

1. **Details of Palen Hudgin's activities:** statements of Palen Hudgin printed in a special article about him and the tragedy, the *Arizona Republic*, June 27, 1971.

2. **Capt. Lewis and Sgt. Hessel made the official identifications of the planes:** consensus of newspapers nationwide.

3. **Location of DC-7's vertical tail fin:** *CAB Bureau of Safety Investigation Structural Investigation Report*, July 24, 1956, page 8.

4. **Capt. Ryan's quoted statement:** many newspapers nationwide, including the *Detroit Times*, July 2, 1956.

5. **Lt. Prince's quoted statement:** newspapers nationwide, including the *Los Angeles Times*, July 2, 1956.

Chapter 13

1. **Description of H-21:** *United States Civil and Military Aircraft for 1958*, compiled, edited, and published by Robert R. Longo Company, Inc., 1958; interviews with one of the investigators that rode in it.

2. **The various official activities:** consensus of newspapers nationwide; *Life* Magazine, July 16, 1956; interviews with TWA Captain Jasper Solomon, an investigator who worked at the TWA site.

3. **The climate of the Grand Canyon:** *Grand Canyon: A Visitor's Guide* by George Wuerthner, published by Stackpole Books, 1998, pages 12 and 14.

4. **The team stayed overnight in the canyon by plan, not by being stranded:** interviews with several of the investigators involved.

5. **Details of the U-1A:** *United States Civil and Military Aircraft for 1958,* compiled, edited, and published by Robert R. Longo Company, Inc., 1958.

6. **Major Feldt flew out the first remains to Flagstaff:** consensus of numerous newspapers nationwide.

Chapter 14

1. **Overall official activities:** consensus of numerous newspapers nationwide.

2. **Landing on sandbar:** photos in *Life* Magazine, July 16, 1956.

3. **Details of sandbar:** interviews with United team members; 1:24,000 scale map of Cape Solitude quadrangle, U.S. Geological Survey, 1988; photos in *Life* Magazine, July 16, 1956.

4. **United team's equipment:** photographs taken by a member of the team.

5. **Activities of investigators from Medicine Bow Peak accident:** interview with Captain John Lovett.

6. **Transport of remains:** TWA's employee newspaper, *Skyliner*, July 5, 1956; interviews with TWA employees from the era; interviews with Francis Shamrell, manager of Flagstaff Municipal Airport at the time.

7. **Details of RMRG, their involvement, and their communications with Earl Isaacson at United Air Lines:** interviews with Dave Lewis; Boulder RMRG log of telephone calls from Sunday, July 1, through Tuesday, July 3, 1956.

8. **The anecdote about how RMRG and United Air Lines became acquainted at Medicine Bow Peak:** interviews with Dave Lewis.

9. **Personal information on Lewis and Batson, and their activities Tuesday, July 3, and at dawn Wednesday, July 4:** interviews with Dave Lewis.

Chapter 15

1. **Most details of official activities:** consensus of numerous newspapers nationwide; interviews with Dave Lewis; photographs taken on the ledge system by one of the climbers.

2. **Details of accident investigation at the site at Temple Butte:** consensus of numerous newspapers nationwide; interviews with investigators who worked at the site; *CAB Accident Investigation Report SA-320*, released April 17, 1957, pages 10-12; *CAB Bureau of Safety Investigation Structural Investigation Report*, July 24, 1956, pages 4-7 and 9-11.

Chapter 16

1. **Details of David Lewis' landing on top of Chuar Butte:** consensus of numerous newspapers nationwide; interviews with Dave Lewis.

2. **Details of Lewis and Batson's activities on top of Chuar Butte:** same resources as in number 1.

3. **A DC-7 had 90,000 feet of electrical wire:** *Douglas DC-6 and DC-7* by Harry Gann, published by Specialty Press, 1999, page 96.

4. **Condition of the United wreckage:** color photographs taken by a member of the team.

5. **TWA's announcements of identifications:** consensus of numerous newspapers nationwide.

Chapter 17

1. **Details of Swiss team's traveling and arrival on the scene:** consensus of numerous newspapers nationwide; newspaper photos.

2. **Information on Christenson, especially his work on safety:** *Corporate and Legal History of United Air Lines, Inc., 1946-1955,* published by United Air Lines, 1965, pages 649 and 650.

3. **Details of activities on top of Chuar Butte before the Swiss were landed:** consensus of numerous newspapers nationwide; interviews with Dave Lewis.

4. **TWA Coroner's Inquest:** consensus of numerous newspapers nationwide.

5. **Joint activities of Swiss and Americans on top of Chuar Butte:** interviews with Dave Lewis; color photographs taken by a member of the team.

6. **Activities of Anton Spinas; wreckage; piece with "D AIR LIN" on it; bodies on apron:** color photographs taken by a member of the team.

7. **Description of aerial rigging devised on-site:** interviews with Dave Lewis.

8. **Announcements of more identifications, and personal information about those identified:** consensus of numerous newspapers nationwide.

9. **Details of Harry Allen's possible activities; one seat not sold:** consensus of numerous newspapers nationwide; TWA's employee newspaper, *Skyliner*, July 5, 1956 edition; interviews with TWA captains, flight engineers and hostesses from the era; TWA timetable, effective June 1, 1956, information on policies.

Chapter 18

1. **Details of conditions, activities, personnel and equipment on top of Chuar Butte:** interviews with Dave Lewis; color photographs taken by a member of the team.

2. **Hearing at Las Vegas:** consensus of numerous newspapers nationwide; transcript of Congressional hearings entitled *Airspace Use Study, Hearings Before a Subcommittee of the Committee on Interstate and Foreign Commerce, House of Representatives, Eighty-Fourth Congress, Second Session, on Use of Airspace*, hearing of July 7, 1956; interviews with one of the witnesses.

3. **The false stories about Andrews' testimony:** numerous newspapers nationwide, including *The Salt Lake Tribune*, July 8, 1956.

4. **Andrews' testimony was garbled:** comparison of the obviously distorted, sensationalized newspaper stories about it with his actual testimony, taken from the same transcript cited in number 2.

5. **Bakke's ineffective attempt to clear Andrews:** Bakke's testimony taken from the same transcript cited in number 2.

6. **ALPA's condemnatory letter about Andrews' testimony:** letter from W. F. Merrigan, Chairman of TWA's Master Executive Council, representing ALPA on behalf of TWA, to James R. Durfee, Chairman of the Civil Aeronautics Board, July 16, 1956.

Chapter 19

1. **The signatures on the register:** photocopy of the register, which the cleanup crew returned when they restored the site.

2. **Descriptions of the group photos:** examination of prints.

3. **The likelihood that Carper, Prouty and Tunder knew the crew of TWA 2:** captain, copilot, and flight engineer seniority rosters for the Kansas City domicile, internal TWA, current at the time of the accident.

4. **Charter plane from Kansas City was an L-049:** photo in *Kansas City Times*, July 9, 1956.

5. **Details of configuration and facilities on the charter plane:** floor plan diagram from *TWA Constellation Flight Crew Operating Manual*, internal TWA, issued page-by-page in running updating, 1950s.

6. **Schedule and airplane type for TWA Flight 103:** TWA timetable effective June 1, 1956.

7. **Second charter, piloted by Captain Larry De Celles:** consensus of numerous newspapers nationwide; interviews with Larry De Celles.

8. **Biography of De Celles' work on the Spong case:** *The Probable Cause* by Robert J. Serling, published by Doubleday and Company, Inc., 1960, Chapter 5; *Howard Hughes' Airline* by Robert J. Serling, published by St. Martin's/Marek, 1983, pages 188-194; interviews with Larry De Celles.

9. **The ground crew's salute and De Celles' reaction:** interviews with Larry De Celles.

Chapter 20

1. **Details of the display and facilities at TWA memorial service:** excellent newspaper article by Justin Bowersock, aviation editor of *The Kansas City Star*, July 9, 1956, appearing in many newspapers July 10, 1956, and reprinted in TWA's employee newspaper, *Skyliner*, July 12, 1956; full-page color photo in *Life* Magazine, July 30, 1956; photo in *The Kansas City Times*, July 10, 1956.

2. **Taps was played in staggered meter:** interviews with an attendee, and with a friend of an attendee.

3. **The profound effect that Taps had on everyone present:** article by Bowersock, cited in number 1; interviews with an attendee, and with a friend of an attendee.

4. **Names of the ten identified TWA victims:** correlated consensus of partial listings from numerous newspapers nationwide.

5. **Names of the three identified TWA victims sent home before the service:** consensus of newspapers nationwide.

6. **Name of the one identified TWA victim sent home after the service:** TWA employee newspaper, *Skyliner*, July 12, 1956.

7. **Names of the six identified victims buried in the TWA memorial plot:** combined effect of number 4 and the fact that six of their names are engraved on the memorial stone, whereas the four names in numbers 5 and 6 are not.

Chapter 21

1. **Details of official activities, disbanding, announcements, etc.:** consensus of numerous newspapers nationwide.

2. **Patterson's statement to the press:** consensus of numerous newspapers nationwide, including the *Arizona Daily Sun*, July 10, 1956.

3. **Details of United interment service:** consensus of numerous newspapers nationwide; interviews with a participant; interviews with park employees.

4. **Reasons for no family members being at the interment:** interviews with a United Air Lines executive involved in contending with the tragedy.

5. **Arrangements and arrival of family members for the memorial service for United's unidentified victims:** consensus of numerous newspapers nationwide.

6. **Nature and purpose of the public CAB hearing:** official transcript of opening statements of CAB Chairman James R. Durfee, August 1, 1956.

Chapter 22

1. **Inscription and names on the marker:** photo in the *Arizona Daily Sun*, August 3, 1956; photos taken by the author.

2. **Details of the display and facilities at the memorial service:** photo in the *Arizona Daily Sun*, August 3, 1956.

3. **The beautiful weather at the service:** interviews with a participant, Jim Kennedy, then in United Air Lines Public Relations, Denver.

4. **Description of the service:** the *Arizona Daily Sun*, August 2, 1956; interviews with a participant, Jim Kennedy, then in United Air Lines Public Relations, Denver.

5. **Story about Mrs. Harms and Mr. Fiore:** interviews with Marge (Harms) Gibson, widow of Robert Harms.

GLOSSARY OF TERMS

THE FOLLOWING DEFINITIONS are given as they apply to the circumstances of the accident, or to aviation, or to the 1950s. In many instances the full definition of a term is broader or involves multiple meanings.

Also, the definitions are phrased with the aim of conveying the crucial facts or concepts or principles in straightforward terms, without sacrificing any relevant aspect of the meaning. The idea was to make them concise without being simplistic.

A

above ground level: altitude as measured from the ground directly below.

ACM: a qualified flight crewmember riding free of charge and free of duties, in the extra seat on the flight deck. ACM stood for additional crewmember.

Additional crewmember: see ACM.

ADIZ: one of several huge territories within which the U.S. Air Force used long-range radar to monitor all flights, for the sake of national defense. Airlines notified each ADIZ along their routes of where and when to expect their flights. Upon arrival in the ADIZ airspace, if an aircraft could not be identified nor contacted by radio, fighter jets were sent up to intercept it and identify it, with the authority to force it to land. ADIZ stood for Air Defense Identification Zone.

Aeronautical Radio, Incorporated: a company providing contract radio service to airlines as a direct link to their flights in progress, through a nationwide network of facilities.

aft: in or toward the rear.

aileron: one of two hinged, movable flaps at the rear edges of the wings, used for banking the plane as part of a turn. The ailerons worked in unison but oppositely, one tilting upward as the other tilted downward, tending both to lower the one wing and raise the other.

Air Defense Identification Zone: see ADIZ.

Air Line Pilots' Association: a fellowship of airline pilots that worked to further the interests of all airline pilots. Some of their pursuits were greater safety and accurate, fair accident investigating, and reporting.

Air Rescue Service: a branch of the U.S. Air Force composed of highly trained squadrons stationed at various air force bases across the country. The ARS served both to search for downed aircraft and to rescue survivors.

Air Route Traffic Control: the body of persons who staffed the Air Route Traffic Control Centers.

Air Route Traffic Control Centers: facilities located regionally throughout the country, from which the control of IFR flights was administered.

airways: imaginary, though well-defined, three-dimensional aerial channels along which ARTC monitored and controlled IFR flights.

Albuquerque ADIZ: the ADIZ centered at Albuquerque, New Mexico.

ALPA: see Air Line Pilots' Association.

alternate airport: an airport selected in advance of a flight to serve as an alternate destination should some unforeseen circumstance prevent landing at the intended airport, or make it imprudent or impractical.

alternate tank: the secondary fuel tank normally used for a given engine to supplement using fuel from that engine's main tank.

altimeter: an instrument used for gauging a plane's altitude by measuring the ambient air pressure in comparison with the current air pressure at a known altitude.

ARINC: see Aeronautical Radio, Incorporated.

arrival: the completion of a plane's landing, by it being taxied all the way to the passenger gate and parked there. Technically, a plane hadn't arrived until its parking brake had been set, and wheel chocks had been placed under its wheels.

ARS: see Air Rescue Service.

ARTC: see Air Route Traffic Control.

ARTC Flight Plan: a flight plan presented by a crew as a proposal for ARTC's approval.

attitude: the orientation of an airplane in terms of the inclinations of its axes or its major parts, in any given frame of reference, usually in relation to the ground. For example, a laterally level attitude, a nose down attitude, a right wing down attitude, and so on.

B

before takeoff checklist: the final list of items to be checked in preparation for a flight, usually performed out at the runway, and always just before takeoff.

belay: a mountaineering term meaning, "to secure, as with a rope," as in tethering a climber to rocks above.

boarding ramp: a sturdy portable staircase with safety railings (usually full-panel sides) rolled into position at the entryway of an aircraft, to enable passengers to enter or exit.

buffet: United Air Lines' term for the galley onboard their airplanes, where the flight attendants prepared beverages and where food was stored, heated, and arranged for the passengers.

butte: a mountain-shaped formation of rock sculpted in relief by erosion over aeons.

C

CAA: the federal body in charge of operating airport control towers, Air Route Traffic Control Centers, and Interstate Airways Communications Stations, as well as certificating aircraft and aircraft components in airworthiness, and enforcing aviation regulations. CAA stood for Civil Aeronautics Administration.

CAB: the federal body in charge of aircraft accident investigations, including conducting formal hearings. The CAB also formulated aviation regulations. CAB meant Civil Aeronautics Board.

cab: the boxlike enclosure atop a control tower, in which controllers worked. The cab housed their equipment and had windows all around.

CAP: a volunteer group of civilians dedicated to preserving or aiding in national defense by air in wartime, and to assisting in aerial search and rescue missions both in wartime and peacetime. CAP stood for Civil Air Patrol.

center of gravity: in rough but useful terms, the balance point of an aircraft; the theoretical point at which the entire weight of the airplane is considered to be concentrated.

centers: informal for Air Route Traffic Control Centers.

center spar: the main brace that supports and strengthens the wings of an airplane and runs down the lengths of the wings span-wise inside them.

checkpoint: a location on the ground that is used to define the whereabouts of a plane overflying it, and referenced in the position reports given to check in with ground personnel.

chimneys: mountaineering jargon meaning a natural vertical cleft or channel in a cliff face.

Chuar Butte: the butte where United 718 crashed; the plane hit the promontory that projected directly toward the Little Colorado River.

City of Vancouver: the fleet name of the United DC-7 involved in the Grand Canyon accident.

Civil Aeronautics Administration: see CAA.

Civil Aeronautics Board: see CAB.

Civil Air Patrol: see CAP.

clear: a reference to aircraft statuses or movements on the ground or in the air, meaning, "clear of obstructions or prohibitions."

clearance: the express approval of a flight's movement or status in the air or on the ground.

closure rate: the speed at which the gap between two planes on collision paths closes as they near the spot where they will collide.

CMC: a mountaineer's group based in Colorado designed to promote mountain climbing and to preserve the mountain wilderness. CMC stood for Colorado Mountain Club.

cockpit: the small, forward-most area in the interior of an airplane in which the pilots sit, outfitted with all of the necessary controls and instruments needed to conduct a flight. It is the front half of the flight deck.

collision courses: courses that cross each other at the same time, so that the planes on them pass through a common vertical line simultaneously. Actually a misnomer because they may very well not be at the same altitude and therefore will not collide.

collision paths: the actual tracks in three dimensions that two planes follow in colliding with each other.

Colorado Mountain Club: see CMC.

company flight plan: an airline flight plan delineating the same proposal given in the corresponding ARTC Flight Plan, and which is also a record of a flight's progress, filled out en route, for comparison to its proposed plan and other analysis by the company dispatch department.

control tower: the structure from which control of aircraft at and near an airport is exercised, built as a tower to afford controllers a better perspective view of the airport than could be had from the ground.

converging courses: courses that cross each other, in the special case where the airplanes flying them will arrive at the vertical line through the intersection point simultaneously.

course: a line representing a plane's movement in flight, which can be drawn on a map because it excludes any considerations of altitude. The track a plane's shadow would follow on the ground if the sun were exactly overhead during its whole flight.

crossing courses: courses that crisscross each other, with no implication of the planes arriving at the vertical line through the intersection point simultaneously, much less at the same altitude.

cruise power: the horsepower needed to maintain steady, level flight at a given speed and a given altitude.

cruising: flying at a steady speed and altitude.

cumulonimbus clouds: massive rain clouds that usually produce thunder storms.

D

de Havilland Beaver: a stout, heavy-duty, single-engine plane with its wings mounted on top of the fuselage, used in rugged country. The U.S. Air Force designated theirs as type L-20.

de Havilland Otter: same description as for the Beaver, except that this model was larger and could carry twelve people. The army designated theirs as type U1-A.

departure: leaving the passenger gate and beginning to taxi out toward the runway at the beginning of a flight. Technically, a plane hadn't departed until it began to move, and once it began to move, it had departed, even if it halted temporarily nearby.

departure radar: a service provided by air traffic controllers, using radar, to assist flights in leaving the area of the sky near an airport, where competing traffic was often a problem.

direct: a reference to flying a straight-line course between two points rather than a longer, multi-segmented course.

dispatch release: a document stipulating that a particular plane, set up under specified conditions preparatory to a flight—most important how much fuel had been loaded—is given over into the care of a particular captain, for the express purpose of his conducting a particular flight. By signing it, he accepts the offer and takes responsibility.

E

elevators: the hinged flaps at the rear edges of an airplane's horizontal tail planes, for use in pitching the airplane to descend or ascend. These operated in unison and in the same sense, either both up or both down.

Etoile de la Seine: the adjunct French equivalent of the fleet name given the L-1049 Constellation in the accident. Painted on the sides of the fuselage near the nose, right under the English version, *Star of the Seine.*

explosive decompression: extremely rapid loss of air pressure in the cabin of a plane, akin to popping the cork on a champagne bottle.

F

flight deck: the forward-most compartment of an airliner, in which the pilots and the flight engineer sit and run the plane; includes the cockpit area and the flight engineer's station immediately behind it in a single "room," whereas the term "cockpit" is more restrictive and excludes the flight engineer's station.

flight engineer's seat: the seat used by the flight engineer for his part in conducting a flight, situated where the controls and instruments he uses are located. Installed right behind the central console of the cockpit in the DC-7, forming a triangle with the pilot's seats; and farther behind the copilot's seat on the 1049, forming a capital "L" with the pilot's seats. The DC-7's engineer faced forward, and the 1049's faced sideways, toward the starboard. Both of their seats were lower than those of the pilots'.

flight engineer's station: the area on a flight deck designed for the use of the flight engineer, having the gauges and controls he needed to oversee the operation of the engines and a place for him to sit to do that, and sometimes also a diminutive desk on which he could write.

flight kitchen: a ground-based kitchen designed expressly for the purpose of preparing meals to be put aboard flights that offered meal service.

flight progress strip: a strip of paper bearing information on a flight's identity and plans; was placed strategically in a grid board that schematically represented the territory under a particular ARTC center's control.

flying direct: flying a straight-line course between two objective points on a route, usually long-distance, rather than following airways from one point to an other, which often was relatively circuitous and took longer.

G

galley: the kitchen facility on a ship or an airplane. On airplanes, it was more of a holding or reheating and arranging station; food was not cooked there.

gate: literally a gate in the fencing bordering a ramp, where passengers' tickets were checked, and through which they passed out to their plane.

gate agent: the airline official who checked tickets at the gate and permitted or, in rare instances, barred passengers from passing out to the awaiting airplane.

ground controller: a traffic controller authorized and responsible for overseeing the operations of a plane while on the ground, such as taxiing and crossing runways.

ground power: electrical power fed into an airplane while it was on the ground with its engines not running and thus not generating its own electricity.

groundspeed: the rate at which an aircraft in flight progresses overland. If a plane flies directly from one airport to another, its average ground speed is simply the straight-line distance between the two airports divided by the time it takes to get from the one to the other.

gully: a downhill, groove-like channel worn in rock or in the ground through which rain water passes, often carrying debris.

H

H-19: an air force transport helicopter with a single rotor, used on Temple Butte in the first landing at either site, to determine if there were survivors.

H-21: an army transport helicopter with twin rotors, used on Temple Butte and Chuar Butte to recover remains and telltale wreckage. Nicknamed the flying banana.

Havasau Canyon: the approximate area of the Grand Canyon that marked the western boundary of the best sights from the air in the opinion of many airline captains in the 1950s. The boundary was at roughly 112 degrees 40 minutes W longitude.

holding pad: a paved space behind the threshold of a runway where a flight would be held pending a controller clearing it to enter the runway. One and the same piece of pavement as the run up pad.

horizontal stabilizers: the fixed horizontal tail planes to which the elevators are attached. These help maintain the balance of the plane by exerting a small downward "lift" force, so that it can reliably fly horizontally.

hostess: TWA's title for their stewardesses.

I

IFR: the collection of rules regulating the conduct of flights that were under ARTC's care. Among many other things, these rules stipulated that a flight maintain its cleared altitude while within any controlled airspaces, except in its initial climb-out and its descent to land. IFR flights were permitted to fly blind if need be. IFR stood for Instrument Flight Rules.

IFR flight plan: a flight plan requesting ARTC's supervision and aid.

ill-defined separation: unknown or indeterminate spacing between two aircraft.

INSACS: one of many federal radio installations set up to communicate with flights that might otherwise be too far from their typical stations to be able to make contact. INSACS stood for Interstate Airways Communications Station.

Instrument Flight Rules: see IFR.

Interstate Airways Communications Station: see INSACS.

J

jump seat: a small folding seat for a crewmember that took up little space when folded. In some instances, it provided auxiliary accommodation for a crewmember not usually present.

K

kinetic energy: the energy due to the motion of a mass. It is equal to one-half the mass times the velocity squared.

knot: a nautical mile per hour, equal to about 1.15 statute miles per hour; a statute mile is simply an ordinary mile, like what is used to measure the distance along a road.

L

L-1049: a Lockheed model 1049 Constellation.

L-20: a de Havilland Beaver, as commissioned for army use.

Lake Mohave Intersection: an intersection of airways near Lake Mohave, on the state line between Nevada and Arizona.

lavatory: term used in aviation for a bathroom aboard an aircraft. The lavatory consisted of a sink, a mirror, a waste bin, and a toilet. An electric outlet was provided for appliances that needed to be plugged in—electric razors or hairdryers, for example.

loadmaster: the crewmember on a military helicopter in charge of unloading and loading cargo and passengers.

local controller: the air traffic controller at an airport who supervised and aided flights on the active runways and in the air near the airport.

lounge: the area in an airliner, usually at the rear, where passengers could go as an alternative to their regular seats, and be more comfortable.

Lower Granite Gorge: the southernmost extension of the Grand Canyon, located in the western third of the canyon.

M

magnetic heading: the heading measured by a magnetic compass. In 1956, this was fifteen degrees less than a true map heading in the Grand Canyon area. The disparity varies with location and also varies as time passes and the earth's magnetic north pole moves.

magneto: a small, electric generator that supplied the spark plugs of an engine with the energy to fire the cylinders, and was driven by the engine itself.

main landing gear: the set of wheels that provides the principal support of an aircraft's weight while on the ground, usually located under the wings; the main landing wheels, and associated mechanisms and structures.

maximum cruise power: the highest power output that can safely be maintained by an engine over the duration of the cruising phase of a flight, usually a fairly long time (several hours).

mean sea level: the midpoint between the mean of high tides and the mean of low tides. Water is self-leveling; if the oceans of the world all leveled themselves out once and for all, the surface of the sea would be at mean sea level everywhere on earth from then on.

Missing Aircraft Alert: the official notice alerting all responsible agencies that a flight has disappeared and is presumably in serious enough trouble to be in need of rescue.

N

nautical mile: about 1.15 ordinary, statute miles, or about 6,076 feet.

nonrevenue passenger: a passenger flying free of charge, typically an airline employee or a family member of an airline employee, who is utilizing the employee benefit of flying at no cost.

nose gear: the front wheel or wheels and associated mechanisms and support structures of an airplane located in the forward fuselage, near the nose. Used for a small proportion of support of the airplane, and for steering.

O

off airways: an approximate reference to flying in uncontrolled airspace, typically on a direct course.

one thousand on top: a type of altitude clearance requiring a flight to avoid all clouds, and most pertinent, to remain at least one thousand feet above any and all clouds that it flew over. Given this, the pilot could choose any altitude he wanted within the provisions of the Quandrantal Rule.

P

Painted Desert Line of Position: an imaginary reference line connecting navigational radio stations at Bryce Canyon, Utah, and Winslow, Arizona, to each other. It ran approximately from north-northwest to south-southeast and served as a rough navigational locator for flights passing through the Painted Desert.

Painted Desert LOP: same as above; LOP stood for Line of Position.

passenger agent: a ground crewmember who filled in as needed, performing the various tasks involved in boarding passengers and loading their luggage. He was dressed in a suit or a uniform and greeted passengers at the boarding ramp as they approached the airplane for their flight. He then turned them over to the care of the cabin crew. He also usually gave the crew the final weight tally sheet, and when everyone was aboard, he locked the main cabin entry door from the outside. Finally, he officially saw the flight off.

path: the line in three dimensions that a plane follows as distinguished from its two-dimensional map course or track; the plane's actual trajectory through the air.

Peach Springs Canyon: the small side canyon at the south edge of Lower Granite Gorge, and over which TWA 2's proposed course crossed. Located roughly 113 degrees 20 minutes W longitude.

pitch: in reference to attitude, the tilt of the fuselage, usually relative to the earth, whether with the nose higher than the tail, as in ascending, or with the nose lower than the tail as in descending, or with the nose and tail at the same level, as in cruising.

pitch: in reference to propellers, the extent to which the propeller blades are twisted about their longitudinal axes. This was adjustable in flight, and like the twist at the ends of a lawnmower blade, it determined how big a bite the propeller blades would take out of the air.

port: the side of an aircraft that is on the left when one is facing forward. The main cabin entrance is on this side.

position report: a crew's report to a ground radio station as to their location, usually over a preplanned checkpoint and at a forecasted time.

power recovery turbines: devices installed in the exhaust system of the engines on United's DC-7s, but not on TWA's 1049 Constellations, that captured some of the waste energy in the exhaust gasses and transferred it to the crankshaft via a coupling, thereby increasing efficiency and power.

pressure dome: the hemispherical aft wall of the passenger compartment on a pressurized plane. This shape was stronger under pressure than a flat wall.

pressurization: the active pumping of compressed air into an aircraft cabin when flying at high altitude, to maintain a safe and comfortable air pressure, rather than allowing the thin outside air to determine the inside pressure as it would otherwise do.

promontory: a high ridge that overlooks lower lying land or a body of water.

Q

Quadrantal Rule: a rule that specified permissible cruising altitudes off airways according to in which quadrant of the compass a flight's course lay. Flights on magnetic compass courses from 0-89° could cruise at any odd thousand foot altitude; flights on magnetic courses from 90-179° were allowed the series of odd thousands plus five hundred feet; on magnetic courses from 180-269°, the options were even thousands; and from 270-359°, even thousands plus five hundred.

R

ramp: a covered walkway analogous to a marine pier, out along which passengers walked from the terminal building to their flights for boarding.

ramp office: the office on or near the airfield where flight crewmembers signed in, filled out flight plans, and received dispatch releases and weather information preparatory to a flight.

rappel: a mountaineering term meaning to descend a cliff face on a rope in short controlled drops.

reserve fuel: fuel beyond the minimum required to reach the destination. A reserve was always included in a flight's fuel load so that it could divert to an alternate airport if need be, and even circle for up to an hour once there.

RMRG: a volunteer group of mountaineers founded for the purpose of rescuing injured climbers. The group also aided in mountain accidents of any other sort, where mountaineering expertise was needed. RMRG stood for Rocky Mountain Rescue Group.

Rocky Mountain Rescue Group: see RMRG.

roll: the extent to which an airplane is tilted side to side, with one of its wings lowered and the other correspondingly raised.

rudder: a movable flap hinged to the rear edge of the vertical tail plane that is used for turning. Used in conjunction with the action of banking, the rudder helps make turns well coordinated, smooth, and precise, keeping the nose pointing in the changing direction of the airplane as a whole. This keeps the plane from "fishtailing."

run up pad: a large temporary parking area for aircraft, at or near the threshold of a runway, where the crew would run up the engines to very high power as a last check in preparation for takeoff. One and the same piece of pavement as the holding pad.

S

SCD: an acronym standing for "subject to captain's discretion."

service ceiling: the height above sea level (under standard atmospheric conditions) up to which a given type of airplane can efficiently climb. The meaning of "efficient" is standardized as a minimum climbing rate.

shoulder: a narrow, three-sided projecting ridge on a butte, which drops off in steep cliff faces on all three sides.

skin: the outside sheet metal covering of an airplane's structure.

standard temperature: the global yearly mean temperature.

starboard: the side of an aircraft that is on the right when one is facing forward.

Star of the Seine: the fleet name of the TWA 1049 Constellation used for Flight 2 on June 30, 1956.

statute mile: an ordinary mile, 5,280 feet.

supercharger: a device that forced outside air into a piston aircraft engine under pressure to help it maintain good power output, even in the thin air at high altitudes.

T

tag line: a rope that dangled from the spring-clip end of the hoisting cable in the aerial rigging at the United crash promontory, and that was used by a man down in the gully to steady the load as it was lifted, keeping it from swinging. Conventionally, a tag line is a cable that is part of a hoisting crane and complements the main hoisting cable. The tag line is attached to a bucket or other implement and is used to steady it while it is being lifted.

takeoff power: the extremely high power output to which engines were pushed for taking off, and which could not safely be maintained more than briefly.

talus: the sloping fan of accumulated rubble surrounding the base of a butte.

taxi: to move an aircraft on the ground under its own power for the sake of getting from one place to another on the ground, as distinguished from accelerating it on the runway with the aim of taking off, and decelerating it on the runway in a landing.

Temple Butte: the butte where TWA 2 crashed. The plane hit a spot on this butte about 1,000 feet west of the west bank of the Colorado River at a location about 1.3 miles south of its confluence with the Little Colorado River.

tourist service: economy passage on TWA flights.

transportation agent: TWA's term for their passenger agents.

true airspeed: the speed of the airplane, along its flight path, with respect to the air mass through which it is moving. This can be quite different from ground speed. For example, in the days of biplanes, a pilot took off into a 60 mph headwind. His plane left the ground, but just hovered over one spot, giving him a ground speed of zero. Even though his true airspeed was 60 mph, he never got out of the airport.

true course: the direction a plane is moving in relation to lines of longitude and latitude, based on the geometric earth, irrespective of where the slowly wandering magnetic north pole might be.

tug: a small low profile tractor used for towing airplanes from the hangar to the ramp and vice versa, analogous to a tugboat towing ships to and from the dock.

TWA Constellation Flight Crew Operating Manual: an internal TWA manual covering various step by step operating procedures for each of the Constellation models owned by the company. It also included many charts of performance specifications relating two or more quantities to each other: engine rpm, horsepower, fuel usage rate, true airspeed, and altitude. The manual was intended for pilots and flight engineers.

TWA Flight Service Manual: a manual conceived to provide TWA's hostesses with most information they would ever need in order to perform their duties during flight. Among other things, it included highly detailed floor plans of all of TWA's types of aircraft, showing exactly where all of the equipment was located. These floor plans included emergency exits, fire extinguishers, emergency egress ladders and ropes, first aid kits, and fire axes, in addition to the obvious things like the lavatories, the galley, and the water cooler.

twin row radial: a type of aircraft engine having two circular rows of radially arranged piston cylinders. Schematically the setup was like two wooden-spoked wagon wheels fitted onto the same end of an axle, with the spokes representing the cylinders.

type specification sheet: an official document that was actually multiple pages, describing in detail the specifications of a given type of aircraft or aircraft engine. The CAA published these documents as precise descriptions of the engines or planes that they certificated as airworthy.

U

U-1A: the designation of an air force de Havilland Otter.

V

VFR: a system of rules governing the operating of flights that were on their own even on the airways, looking out for themselves. Most literally a VFR flight was conducted by visual means—the pilots were required to see where they were going at all times. VFR stood for Visual Flight Rules.

VFR flight plan: a proposal to operate a flight under visual flight rules.

victor airways: airways that ran between VHF navigational radio stations and were delineated by beacons from those stations, which could be picked up by a flight.

Visual Flight Rules: see VFR.

W

Walhalla Plateau: a flattish peninsular feature of about thirty square miles near the eastern end of the Grand Canyon, cut off by gorges from the ground surrounding the Grand Canyon around nearly all of its circumference, making it almost island-like. Because it is contiguous with the primary land mass north of the canyon, it is part of the North Rim. The plateau is forested like the rest of the North Rim, and slopes downward from north to south, extending from the elevation of the main land mass to about that of the South Rim. It is roughly centered northeast of Grand Canyon Village, and west of the crash sites and the confluence of the Colorado and Little Colorado rivers.

wings: an ornament awarded to newly qualified hostesses and stewardesses signifying their achievement and competence, analogous to a graduation pin or a medal of rank.

X

(no entries)

Y

yoke: a dual control column in an aircraft, used by the cockpit crew to control the pitch and roll of the plane. Rotating either control wheel moves the ailerons and banks the plane. Fore and aft movement of the control column moves the elevators and pitches the airplane downward or upward.

Z

(no entries)

About the Author

MIKE NELSON has been a writer for more than forty years, primarily focusing on psychology, philosophy, and sociology.

Having lost his uncle in the accident described in this book, Mike spent more than a decade studying aviation and aeronautics, researching, interviewing, and analyzing to better understand the incident and his family's loss. In 2014, he gave a speech at the ceremony dedicating the crash sites as a National Historic Landmark. Subsequently, he became one of the founders and directors of a group for people who lost a loved one at that now-protected place. The group has recently opened itself to families of other, similar disasters.

Mike relishes steeping himself in the solitude of nature—especially on sunny spring, summer, and fall days—where he does his best thinking. Mike lives with his wife on a five-acre country homestead in northeast Iowa. They have a thousand trees, native tall-grass prairie, four house cats, transient great horned owls, a welcome population of opossums and raccoons, and an unwelcome population of skunks and woodchucks.

You can visit Mike Nelson at www.wearegoingin.com.